Preserving Public Lands for the Future

American Governance and Public Policy

A SERIES EDITED BY

Barry Rabe and John Tierney

This series examines a broad range of public policy issues and their relationship to all levels of government in the United States. The editors welcome serious scholarly studies and seek to publish books that appeal to both academic and professional audiences. The series showcases studies that illuminate the successes, as well as the problems, of policy formulation and implementation.

Preserving Public Lands for the Future

The Politics of Intergenerational Goods

William R. Lowry

GEORGETOWN UNIVERSITY PRESS / WASHINGTON, D.C.

Georgetown University Press, Washington, D.C.
© 1998 by Georgetown University Press. All rights reserved.
Printed in the United States of America

10 9 8 7 6 5 4 3 2 1   1998

THIS VOLUME IS PRINTED ON ACID-FREE OFFSET BOOK PAPER

Library of Congress Cataloging-in-Publication Data

Lowry, William R.
    Preserving public lands for the future : the politics of
intergenerational goods / William R. Lowry.
        p.   cm. — (American governance and public policy)
    Includes index.
    1. National parks and reserves—Management—Case studies.
    2. National parks and reserves—Government policy—Case studies.
    3. Nature conservation—Case studies.   4. Nature conservation—
Government policy—Case studies.   I. Title.   II. Series.
    SB421.L72   1998
    333.78′3—DC21   98-13259
    ISBN 0-87840-701-4 (cloth).
    ISBN 0-87840-702-2 (pbk.)

For my hiking and camping partners

"Here about the beach I wander'd, nourishing a youth sublime
With the fairy tales of science, and the long result of Time;

When the centuries behind me like a fruitful land reposed;
When I clung to all the present for the promise that it closed:

When I dipt into the future far as human eye could see;
Saw the Vision of the world, and all the wonder that would be."

Alfred Lord Tennyson, 1853, "Locksley Hall," in *The Works of Tennyson,*
ed. by Hallam, Lord Tennyson (New York: The Macmillan Company, 1918), p. 95.

Contents

List of Illustrations   xi

List of Tables   xiii

Acknowledgments   xv

1   **Meeting the Needs of Future Societies   1**
PUBLIC PROVISION OF INTERGENERATIONAL GOODS 3,   THE CONTEXT OF
PRESERVING PUBLIC LANDS 13,   OUTLINE OF THE BOOK 18

2   **Creations of the Political Process   21**
EVOLUTION OF THE PRESERVATION IDEA 21,   VARIATION IN DELIVERY 26,
CONCLUSIONS 43

3   **United States: Political Reality vs. Scientific Desire   44**
BACKGROUND 44,   SYSTEM EXPANSION 56,   ENHANCEMENT OF
INDIVIDUAL UNITS 77,   CONCLUSIONS 99

4   **Australia: Late in the Day   101**
BACKGROUND 102,   NATIONAL PARK SYSTEM EXPANSION 120,
ENHANCEMENT OF INDIVIDUAL UNITS 130,   CONCLUSIONS   145

5   **Canada: A Lot of Negotiating   148**
BACKGROUND 148,   NATIONAL PARK SYSTEM EXPANSION 158,
ENHANCEMENTS OF INDIVIDUAL UNITS 169,   CONCLUSIONS 187

6 **Costa Rica: Making the Transition?**   **188**
BACKGROUND 188,   SYSTEM EXPANSION 199,   ENHANCEMENTS OF
INDIVIDUAL UNITS 204,   CONCLUSIONS 213

7 **Free-Riding on the Future?**   **214**
THE ARGUMENT AND THE EVIDENCE 214,   THEORETICAL
EXTENSIONS 220,   EMPIRICAL EXTENSIONS 225,   CONCLUSIONS 231

Notes   **233**

Bibliography   **255**

Index   **285**

Illustrations

Figure 3-1   Development in the Greater Yellowstone
            Ecosystem   86
Figure 4-1   Management Zones at Kakadu   134
Figure 4-2   Wet Tropics Management Authority Structure   140
Figure 4-3   Wet Tropics Area   142
Figure 4-4   Fraser Island Management Structure   145
Figure 4-5   Fraser Island   146
Figure 5-1   Plan for Completing the Canadian Parks System   162
Figure 5-2   The Planning Process for the 1988 Banff National Park
            Management Plan   177
Figure 6-1   Land Area of the ACG.   208
Figure 6-2   Organization Structure for Regional Conservation
            Units   209

Tables

1-1   A Broad Classification of Goods   6
1-2   Institutional Tensions Affecting Intergenerational
      Behavior   13
1-3   Institutional Tensions Affecting Systematic Preservation   17
2-1   Variables Related to Preserved Lands   17
2-2   Descriptive Statistics of Key Variables   28
2-3   Nations Protecting Natural Areas   35
2-4   Protected Lands in World, 1993   36
2-5   Preserved Lands as Percent of Total Area   37
2-6   Analyses for Different Levels of Affluence   39
2-7   Analyses for Nations in Different Political Systems   40
3-1   Recreation Visits to National Park Service Sites   46
3-2   Membership in Relevant Interest Groups   47
3-3   Land and Water Conservation Funds   51
3-4   Expansion of National Park System   58
3-5   Historic Themes Identified in 1972 Plan   61
3-6   Adequacy of Natural Region Representation   63
3-7   Adequacy of Natural History Theme Representation   64
3-8   National Park System Units As of 1995   76
3-9   Park Threats by Category   78
3-10 Annual Appropriations to the NPS   79
3-11 NPS Line-Item Construction Funding   79
3-12 Yellowstone Priority List   88
3-13 Yosemite Transportation Alternatives   98
4-1   Australian Conservation Foundation Membership and Federal
      Grants   104
4-2   Survey Responses on National Parks   107
4-3   World Heritage Areas in Australia   111
4-4   Postwar Australian Prime Ministers   112
4-5   Early Australian Nature Conservation Areas   122

4-6   Growth in National Park Systems   123
4-7   Appropriations to AHC and AHC Expenses   124
4-8   Tourist Expenditures at Australian Parks   136
5-1   Public Priorities for British Columbia Park Programs   151
5-2   Recent Governments of Canada   151
5-3   Provincial and Territorial Protected Areas   161
5-4   WWF Grades for Park System Expansion   165
5-5   Total Value of Building Permits 1984-89   175
5-6   Banff-Bow Valley Study Recommendations   184
5-7   Land Jurisdiction in Central Rockies Ecosystem   185
6-1   Costa Rican Governments   193
6-2   Federal Protected Areas in Costa Rica   203
6-3   National Parks of Costa Rica   204
7-1   Characteristics of Studied Nations   217

Acknowledgments

Author Ed Abbey once praised efforts to save wilderness areas but then reminded those of us involved in such a pursuit to "Save the other half of yourselves and your lives for pleasure and adventure." Like many things Abbey wrote, the wisdom in this comment is worth remembering. Thus, my acknowledgements are in several parts. First, I want to acknowledge those who attempt to preserve natural places for future generations. Second, I'll thank those who helped me in writing about those preservation efforts. Third, I want to mention some of those who have helped me enjoy such places.

First, this book is about preservation efforts in various settings. Recently, we took a class of 30 Washington University freshmen on a spring field research trip to several national parks in the southwest. When we visited Hovenweep National Monument, Superintendent Art Hutchinson spoke with the students at some length. Afterwards, he mentioned to me that he had some picnic tables that needed moving in the campground. Knowing that Hovenweep is a small park that does not have extra staff, I wanted to volunteer our students but did not think I should order them to participate. So I simply explained the situation to them. I have rarely been more proud than I was to see them race each other to the tables and start carting them throughout the entire campground. Several told me later that helping the park staff was the most rewarding thing they did on the trip. Having visited several parks by then, the students understood that these places need our help. I am grateful to all who are engaged in preservation efforts in different nations, but I particularly want to thank those who shared with me their thoughts and insights. Though I can't name all of them here, one or two in each country I studied warrant special mention. Thanks to Denis Galvin in Washington and Mike Finley at Yellowstone, Mark Gough in Queensland, Dan Janzen in Costa Rica, Judy Otton at Banff and Bob Page in Calgary. I wish you and your colleagues success in your endeavors.

Second, in writing about those preservation efforts, I received assistance from the following. The analysis in Chapter 2 was shaped by Mike Goetz, Tim Johnson, Scott Comparato, Larry Handlin, John

Sprague, Ken Meier, and several anonymous referees at the *American Journal of Political Science*. Other parts of the book were improved by comments from Lisa Baldez, John Carey, Maria Hunter, Barry Rabe, John Samples, Glenn Stone, and the anonymous referees at Georgetown University Press. I thank my department chair, Lee Epstein, and my colleagues and students at Wash U for keeping me employed so that I can do this kind of research.

Third, I also thank those who, over the years, have helped me remember why natural areas are worth saving. Abbey also wrote, "So get out there and hunt and fish and mess around with your friends, ramble out yonder and explore the forests, encounter the grizz, climb the mountains, bag the peaks, run the rivers, breathe deep of that yet sweet and lucid air, sit quietly for awhile and contemplate the precious stillness, that lovely mysterious and awesome space." I can't name all who have joined me in doing those things, but I will single out a few. Thanks to my brother who was as excited as I have ever seen him when we had a bear ramble through our camp at Yosemite, to my father who never found a log that was too wet for a fire, to John Bruni who never saw a river he didn't want to raft, to Bill Caler who never tried an uphill climb he couldn't take, to Bob Griffin who never met a hostess he couldn't make laugh. Finally, I thank my friend Lynn for so much, not the least being the reminder that state parks, like their national counterparts, can also be great places to hike and camp. Who knows, L.A., next time we go hiking maybe we can find some picnic tables that need moving.

Preserving Public Lands for the Future

1

Meeting the Needs of Future Societies

More recently there has been increasing recognition of the range of the value of protected areas and of their contribution to meet the needs of society by conserving the world's natural and physical resources. These values range from protection of representative samples of natural regions and the preservation of biological diversity to the maintenance of environmental stability in surrounding country.—P. H. C. Lucas, 1991

A park is an artificial unit, not an independent biological unit with natural boundaries.—George Wright, 1933

If current American plans are implemented, future generations will travel to Yosemite and Grand Canyon National Parks without their automobiles. If promises by Australian officials are realized, future travelers will see the pristine beaches of Cape Tribulation and Cape York in their natural condition. If Canadian planners achieve their goals, someday ecosystems as diverse as Banff and Grasslands will be restored. If Costa Rican policymakers are successful in their ongoing efforts, natural areas such as those at Guanacaste and the Osa Peninsula will be large enough to sustain migratory routes for a remarkable number of species. The "ifs" in these statements are immense, however.

The opening quotes from the chairman of the International Commission on National Parks and from a pioneering scientist suggest a fundamental question regarding the role for national parks and equivalent reserves. Many hope, as Lucas suggests, that these places preserve biological diversity and representative ecosystems for this and future generations even while realizing, as Wright did decades ago, that they are artificial creations. Can national governments effectively provide such goods for future generations? Will the goals described in the first paragraph be realized?

1

Preservation efforts regarding national parks and equivalent reserves reflect upon broad issues. Preserved lands are an intergenerational impure public good. Impure public goods comprise the vast array of goods and services that are neither pure private goods, divisible through the market for individual consumption, nor pure public goods, indivisible in that consumption by one does not affect availability to others. Though both the private market sector and the public government sector enjoy support from vocal advocates, neither sector is immune to questions regarding their ability to deliver impure public goods. Those questions are even more compelling for one subset of impure public goods, those that are intergenerational in character, intended for provision to future generations. The questions regarding market delivery of intergenerational goods are obvious. Is the market too focused on the short term? Can future demand be measured? Do incentives exist for firms to deliver intergenerational goods? Thus, the public sector is often called upon to provide such goods, leading to an important question: How effective are governments at providing impure public goods for future generations?

The answer to that question is not immediately obvious. Much conventional wisdom, the short-term incentives motivating politicians, and a long list of failed policies suggest skepticism. Yet, policymakers are constantly called upon to provide results that will benefit citizens decades hence. Virtually every day, we can hear politicians claim that some policy outcome, ranging from retirement pensions to space exploration to balancing the budget, is essential for our children's children. In dealing with these issues, governments throughout the world pursuing similar policy goals display considerable variance in their ability to achieve long-range provision of goods. Thus, we are motivated to explain this variation and to be explicit about the conditions under which delivery of intergenerational goods are more effective.

In this project, I analyze the effect of institutional structure on the public delivery of intergenerational goods. I argue that basic tensions involving present consumption and future provision of certain goods, such as national parks, exist between different institutional players in government. Specifically, the efforts of public agencies with responsibility for establishment and delivery of intergenerational goods are substantially affected by political actors at the same level of government as the agency, notably elected officials, and by subnational governments at different levels. Tensions between these players contribute to the variance between governments in efficacy of intergenerational provision and make delivery difficult even under otherwise favorable circumstances.

This project applies that theoretical argument in a specific context. In few other policy areas is long-term provision as essential and as challenging as in the preservation of public lands. Commitment to the future is essential because public lands are faced with severe present threats like pollution and development that can alter their fundamental character. Future commitment is difficult because strong material incentives exist to use these lands for short-term purposes such as extraction of natural resources. Yet, policymakers in many governments, at some point in the last thirty years, have formally initiated or renewed public sector attention to the preservation of some lands, usually as national parks, in relatively natural condition for future generations. National parks and equivalent reserves constitute those public lands designated for extremely high levels of long-term protection. This project seeks to explain the variation among nations in the delivery of preserved lands.

This chapter is organized as follows. The first section builds a theoretical framework using various literatures related to the provision of intergenerational impure public goods by national governments. The second section poses the theoretical issues in the context of preservation of certain public lands. The third section outlines the general plan of the work.

PUBLIC PROVISION OF INTERGENERATIONAL GOODS

A variety of perspectives in different literatures reflect upon the question of provision of intergenerational goods by national governments. Most of those perspectives are consistent with a conventional wisdom that governments are largely ineffective at long-term planning and implementation. Still, these perspectives provide insights into how delivery of intergenerational goods might be more likely should certain factors vary. This section describes intergenerational goods, suggests why delivery is difficult, and then poses certain variables as necessary but not sufficient and certain variables as constraining on ultimate behavior.

Provision of Intergenerational Impure Public Goods

Some goods and services are not easily categorized. Typologies are further complicated when those goods and services are to be provided for future generations.

Broadly Defined

The economic literature identifies three broad categories of goods and services.[1] Pure private goods are divisible in that they can be divided up and parcelled out for consumption. Examples include virtually everything, from guns to butter, sold on the free market. Markets are the obvious mechanism for provision of pure private goods. Pure public goods are indivisible in that consumption by one does not diminish the quality or quantity available to other consumers, and they are nonexcludable in that once provided, other consumers can't be excluded from enjoying their benefits. The most cited examples of pure public goods are national defense and lighthouses, although defining even these as purely public is subject to some debate.[2] The public sector has traditionally been relied upon for provision of pure public goods. Defining the third category of goods and services is somewhat more involved.

Many goods and services are neither purely public nor purely private, but are better classified as what James Buchanan called "impure public goods" and others have termed "mixed goods."[3] Goods such as canals or public spaces are collectively owned and thus not pure private goods, but they are also not pure public goods for at least two reasons. First, due to congestion or crowding, use of such a good by many consumers can affect the quantity or quality still available. Thus, these goods cannot be accurately described as purely indivisible. Second, these goods may be subject to exclusion costs whereby consumers must pay for received benefits, such as a fee to use a canal. The optimal means of delivery for these impure goods is open to question. Even noted economist Buchanan admits that his chapter entitled "Which Goods Should Be Public?" does "little more than introduce some of the complexities" involved in this decision.[4]

Delivery of one subset of impure public goods is particularly challenging. Intergenerational goods are those to be provided for future generations. As political economists point out, "Intergenerational public goods are even more difficult to provide, since indivisibility and nonappropriability concern both present and future generations."[5] Demand cannot be measured. Future citizens cannot directly pay for them, although they may pay indirectly through debts and the consequences of deficit spending. Yet, citizens do express the desire for delivery of goods to future generations.

The intergenerational nature of this subset of goods leads away from reliance on markets and toward demands on public sectors. Nobel laureate economist Robert Solow explains quite succinctly the low faith in the marketplace for providing intergenerational goods: "The future is not adequately represented in the market, at least not the far future."[6] Future benefits tempt little market-oriented behavior because "no entrepreneur could readily convert benefits of this kind into profits."[7] The short-term focus of the marketplace has been described by economists ranging from Adam Smith to John Maynard Keynes to Mancur Olson. The oft-cited Keynes line about how "In the long run, we're all dead anyway" is illustrative.[8] Political economists have found occasional instances of long-term oriented market institutions but admit that the circumstances fostering such arrangements are "relatively rare."[9] Thus, demands are focused on governments to provide intergenerational impure public goods.

A Specific Example

A classic example of an intergenerational impure public good, and the empirical focus of this project, is public land preserved in relatively natural condition. I define preservation as long-term protection of public lands from destruction, development, or impairment of natural conditions. This definition is used in the legislative mandates for two of the oldest national park systems in the world, statutory language in the United States and Canada calling for managing parkland to leave it "unimpaired" for future generations. Further, this definition is consistent with that of the International Union for the Conservation of Nature (IUCN) which defined national parks at the 2nd World Conference on National Parks in 1972 as "not materially altered by human exploitation and occupation." Even this definition is obviously open to controversy and various interpretations.[10] Operationally, however, preserved land is to be kept in, or if necessary restored to, pristine condition, as it existed before extensive human alterations, in perpetuity.

Historically, governments have been relied upon to provide this good for future generations. Advocacy of public protection of natural places dates back over two thousand years to Greek societies.[11] Even the most renown advocates of the free market have emphasized the role of the public sector. In 1776 Adam Smith wrote: "Lands for the purpose of pleasure and magnificence—parks, gardens, public walks, etc., possessions which are everywhere considered as causes of expense, not as sources of revenue—seem to be the only lands which, in a great and civilised monarchy, ought to belong to the crown."[12] Governments have traditionally, at least in rhetoric, assumed the role of provider of these and other intergenerational goods.

Differentiation from Common-Pool Resources

Categorizing preserved lands more precisely than as an intergenerational impure public good is difficult. A recent growing literature that often focuses on natural resource questions offers a typology that further differentiates the impure public goods category. This literature has been produced by scholars from anthropology, economics, political science, and other fields who study common-pool resources and the related development of property rights.[13] Common-pool resources are conceivably intergenerational in character, consisting of "natural or human-made facilities or stocks that generate flows of usable resource units over time."[14] Oft-studied common-pool resources include

TABLE 1-1
A Broad Classification of Goods

		Degree of Subtractability	
		Low	High
	Difficult	Public Goods	Common-Pool Resources
Degree of Exclusion:			
	Easy	Toll Goods	Private Goods

Sources: Ostrom and Ostrom 1977: 12; Ostrom, Gardner, and Walker 1994: 7.

fisheries or acquifers of ground water. As table 1-1 shows, these common-pool resources are differentiated according to two dimensions from other goods that are neither public nor private. First, common-pool resources are highly subtractable in that one person's use diminishes availability of the use of the good by others. Second, exclusion from usage is much more difficult with common-pool resources than with toll goods.[15]

Of the categories presented in table 1-1, the closest fit for preserved lands may well be toll goods. Many preserved lands are managed as national parks or reserves with controlled access, entrance fees, joint usage, and a low degree of subtractability. Usually, however, toll goods are thought of as private roads, theaters, cable TV, or often other services that are purchased on an immediate basis.[16] Preserved lands may be used for immediate gratification, but the stated goals for the lands are much more long term.

The literature on other impure public goods such as common-pool resources provides valuable insights to this project, particularly in that many of these studies have identified conditions that are conducive to sustainability over long periods of time. Theoretical extensions to consider such goods will also be made in the last chapter, but for purposes of this analysis, preserved lands are best thought of simply as intergenerational impure public goods.

Why Public Provision of Intergenerational Goods Is Difficult

Much conventional wisdom and many classic pieces of literature suggest skepticism toward long-term delivery of intergenerational goods. This skepticism is directed at both the demand and the supply side of the policy-making process.

Demand for Intergenerational Goods

Demand for intergenerational goods is, at best, unpredictable. The most obvious means for citizens to express demands in democracies is through voting. The voting literature suggests that voters, however, are an unpredictable source of effective demand for long-term commitment. First, the impact of public opinion on provision of intergenerational goods is limited by inconsistent behavior over time, the lack of salient concern over intergenerational affairs, and the fact that many citizens are conflicted on specific issues.[17] Second, voters are at least as likely to use retroactive judgments as they are to use proactive speculation to make ballot decisions.[18] Third, even if citizens have stable underlying attitudes towards some intergenerational goods, providing consistent assessments over time may be difficult due to measurement error.[19]

Even given complications regarding voting, can one not find a tradition of support within a society for certain intergenerational goods? The context of preserved lands invites such consideration. The roots of support for protection of some lands as wilderness are deep in many countries, often voiced in spiritual terms by devotees such as Thoreau and in political spheres by advocates such as Theodore Roosevelt.[20] Even the most ardent voices in such a tradition recognize, however, that tradition without consistent and significant access and influence on political systems will have little impact. Intergenerational goods may be revered over generations, but such reverence does not guarantee provision over the long term.

Because they are institutionalized as long-standing entities, political parties could provide an effective source of demands for provision of future public goods. Certain ideological positions associated with parties may seem more or less conducive to an emphasis on the long term. Again, however, the demands of parties are shaped by the next electoral cycle and their behavior directed to short-term success.[21] Indeed, even after the elections, the opposition party will likely do whatever it can to ensure that the majority party does not produce successful long-term outcomes so as to make its own services more desirable in the future.

Interest groups could also provide a source of demands for intergenerational goods. The literature notes, however, that the most powerful interest groups have generally been more concerned with short-term gains and have been able to shape political behavior accordingly.[22] Some interest groups, environmental organizations for example, state as a mission the pursuit of provision of intergenerational goods. For many, that goal may be quite sincere and at least some of their efforts are directed at the long term. In the context of preserved lands, for example, groups such as the Nature Conservancy have created a market for purchasing some lands to be protected over the long term. At least two factors limit such efforts, however. First, all such groups have limited resources and thus their accomplishments cannot replace those of the broader public sector. Second, even if the interest a group is pursuing involves some future state of affairs, the group itself must devote considerable attention to short-term concerns such as attracting and keeping its membership.[23]

One final source of potential demand is increasingly visible. Demands from the global community on the actions of individual nations are becoming more common in policy issues ranging from trade to deforestation. International demands can stimulate or increase pressure on national behavior.[24] As with domestic demands, international demands for provision of future public goods are limited. In particular, international bodies making demands often lack effective monitoring and enforcement mechanisms. Even if they have signed on to international agreements, governments often ignore subsequent demands.

Elected Suppliers of Intergenerational Goods

On the supply side, the incentives facing elected legislators are rarely directed at the long term. Legislators must necessarily focus on their reelection chances before they can attend to other concerns such as making public policy.[25] Their planning timeframe can thus rarely afford to extend beyond the next electoral cycle, let alone subsequent generations. As one study notes, "Government officials, both elected and appointed, also focus primarily on immediate political gains."[26] While this phenomenon may be most magnified in the U.S. Congress, similar incentives mandate comparable legislative behavior in other democracies.[27]

Because they have national constituencies, presidents and prime ministers may be expected to attend to wider concerns such as cross-generational policy outcomes. Chief executives are, however, also constrained by electoral realities and the strategic requirements of their parties. Their long-term intentions may also be hampered by a relative lack of formal tools.[28] Chief executives are not often likely to want to use precious resources of persuasion on long-term projects that bear little short-term fruit. Thus, elected officials face considerable incentives to supply impure public goods for current purposes but few to ensure long-term provision.

Necessary Conditions for Intergenerational Concern

Under what conditions is provision of intergenerational goods more likely? Unfortunately, few comparative public policy studies exist that attempt to compare such behavior across national lines. Most character-izations of public provision of intergenerational goods, if they go be-yond untested theoretical generalities, are empirically grounded in analysis of a specific country.[29] The literature provides some important ideas regarding provision of impure public goods for future gen-erations but no synthesis with which to conduct cross-national comparisons.

Still, various lines of research suggest certain variables as at least logically important to intergenerational responsiveness. For example, some comparative policy literature posits the importance of various factors for short-term responsive behavior by governments that may well be applicable to long-term concerns as well. The literature on common-pool resources also suggests certain conditions that are condu-cive to sustaining usable levels of goods over long periods of time.

Consistent Public Support

The simplest potential motivator for responsive behavior by gov-ernments is public demand. Extending this logic to provision of inter-generational goods is straightforward. Demand must exist for future provision of some good. The literature on common-pool resources is consistent with the notion of demand as crucial, often concluding that sustainability of such resources is much more likely if those concerned with the resource are motivated enough to communicate their interest and to coordinate to effectuate delivery.[30]

As mentioned above, public opinion is often not consistent nor easily identified. Variance among different societies is thus often ap-proached by comparison of the potential for support for certain goods. Proxies are commonly used that are based on demographic characteris-tics that are available for many nations. These include measures of population, urbanization, unemployment, relative affluence, and edu-cation levels.[31] Measurement becomes even more problematic when attempting to assess support over long periods of time. The simplest hypothesis is to posit consistent public support, as measured in at least potential terms, as essential to public provision of intergenerational goods.

Political Stability

The comparative literature also describes considerable variance among nations in terms of long-term stability for political systems. Systems that experience frequent upheaval or conflict are less likely to sustain the focus and effort necessary to provide long-term responsive behavior. Further, stable systems are more likely to foster consistent public support for intergenerational missions. The importance of political stability to sustainability is also asserted by analysts of common-pool resources. Studies have found that systems that could produce long-term outcomes "may collapse if their legitimacy is challenged, or if large exogenous economic or physical shocks occur."[32] Measuring political stability is not easy, but comparative analyses utilize factors such as active political cultures, easy access of interest groups, and partisan competition.[33]

Incorporating the importance of political stability produces a more refined version of the previous hypothesis. Public demand for intergenerational goods is more effective if channeled through stable and available means such as parties and interest groups.

Official Commitment

Official commitment to the provision of intergenerational goods occurs when elected policymakers explicitly authorize efforts to deliver some good to future generations. Such commitment is easily dismissed as merely rhetorical, but it does provide other actors with a license to prioritize long-term effects. Again, the literature on common-pool resources also finds this condition important, arguing that sustainability is at least somewhat dependent upon the presence of "credible commitments."[34]

How can government officials provide credible commitments? The most apparent mechanism generally takes the form of explicit delegation of responsibility for pursuing long-term goals to some public agency. Explicit authorization can be essential for agencies to avoid having their own goals replaced by those of others. Indeed, the lack of precise commitment from officials can facilitate agencies being responsive to other short-term pressures and not to any long-term goals.[35] Explicit commitment to long-term responsiveness can provide a counter to dominance of short-term concerns.

One line of literature suggests that, once delegation has been made, nonelected bureaucrats will be more receptive to intergenerational missions than elected policymakers. Numerous studies have compared politicians (and their appointees) with career civil servants to contrast the short-term focus of the former with the long-term concerns of the latter.[36] Further, bureaucrats in a relevant public agency can affect both demand for and supply of intergenerational goods. In terms of demand, they can provide the education necessary to stimulate public interest and they can act in an advocacy role within the government. Though the comparative literature on public administration is not extensive, studies do posit an important role for bureaucrats in cross-national analyses.[37]

Bureaucrats are motivated to think long term for several reasons. First, the obvious, though not totally compelling, reason is coercive.

They are assigned the responsibility to find and utilize the resources necessary to facilitate long-term provision. A second reason is self-selection. Many employees work for the particular agency precisely because they consider the relevant intergenerational good to be important. The third reason is survival. They want to maintain the existence of the good they are assigned to monitor. Such a desire is sustained across generations for logical reasons similar to those found by anthropologists in tribal structures and in families.[38] As generations overlap (in this case, bureaucratic employees), they pass along to each other a preference for intergenerational attention. Thus, institutional attention to intergenerational goods can last longer than members.

Agencies do not inevitably pursue intergenerational goods. The ability of civil servants to pursue long-term goals depends upon their professional skills as well as their willingness and ability to use them.[39] Empirical analyses have shown that agencies can provide a long-term commitment to policy goals, particularly if they are at least somewhat insulated from short-term political fluctuations.[40] To hypothesize, provision of intergenerational goods is significantly affected by the presence and form of official commitments.

Summary

The provision of intergenerational goods is not easily achieved. Promises of significant delivery of goods such as renewable energy sources and balanced budgets await fulfillment. Many factors work against real delivery of intergenerational goods. Still, certain conditions—public demand, political stability, and official commitment—are essential to long-term efforts. Yet these factors are all limited in impact. Demand is ephemeral and inconsistent. Stability does not ensure any behavior. Commitment is often only rhetorical. Agency capability depends, as discussed below, on other factors. These conditions are thus termed as necessary but not sufficient to guarantee delivery of intergenerational goods.

Constraining Conditions on Long-Term Responsiveness

I argue that even with relatively substantial demand, political stability, and official commitment to provision of intergenerational goods, establishment and delivery of those goods by a public agency is affected by tensions resulting from the short-term perspective of other institutional actors. These actors can pose serious constraints on agency efforts. The constraints are most easily conceptualized as vertical or horizontal, depending on whether the potentially constraining institutional actor is located at different levels of government or at the same level as the agency.

Vertical

The first set of constraints are conceptually vertical, arising from sources located hierarchically below the agency in the same political system or outside the system entirely. A persuasive literature has focused on the complications created when implementation of national programs, particularly in federal systems, requires coordination of different levels of government.[41] Such an arrangement most often involves material resources. For example, one level of government is responsible for raising resources and another is responsible for spending them. Or, a subnational level controls a resource the national level needs to deliver intergenerational goods.

Tensions are created with such interlevel arrangements. Institutional actors at different levels of government, such as state or provincial legislatures, face different incentives and timeframes than the national agency with responsibility for the intergenerational good. Stated most simply, national intentions can be confused, delayed, even sabotaged by interactions between levels of government. Delivery of intergenerational goods that depends upon the actions of state, provincial, local, or other levels of government is potentially significantly constrained.

Intergenerational efforts can also be affected by institutional actors located outside of the system. Such actors are usually manifest as international commissions or conventions. Their impact is debatable, but, theoretically at least, they can offer or withhold advice, resources, and information.[42]

Horizontal

A second set of constraints is horizontal in nature, reflecting the actions of political actors at the same level of government as the relevant public agency. In short, are the relationships between different actors, even at the same level of government, cooperative or conflictive?

A broad literature posits the importance of the autonomy of the relevant public agency in carrying out delegated tasks. If one task is pursuing long-range objectives, the discretion available to agency professionals is a crucial factor. As stated earlier, short-term incentives shape the motivations of politicians to be quite different than those of bureaucrats, even after the agency is established. The ability of the latter to pursue intergenerational goals is dependent upon their professional skills and the autonomy from short-term political intervention to utilize those skills.[43] One example of how bureaucratic capability to pursue long-term goals can affect provision of intergenerational goods is provided by a literature in economics asserting that the more capable and independent a central banking authority, the more stable the macroeconomic policy.[44]

Hypothetical Framework

Thus, even under otherwise favorable circumstances, the ability of national governments to provide intergenerational goods will vary according to the relationship between national and nonnational entities as well as the interaction between the relevant public agency and other institutional actors operating at the same level. That variance is depicted as a two-by-two in table 1-2. The axes should be thought of as scales representing the relative tensions between institutional actors, not yes-no categories. The operationalization of those scales is more apparent in a specific context, as described below.

TABLE 1-2
Institutional Tensions Affecting Intergenerational Behavior

		Conflictive Relations with Other National Actors	
		Low	High
Tensions with Nonnational Actors	Low		
	High		

If public support, political stability, and official commitment are termed as necessary but not sufficient factors, can these institutional relations be thought of in terms of sufficient conditions? I argue that the closer the situation is to one of cooperative institutional relations across levels and between national actors, the more likely the government will be capable of pursuing intergenerational goals.

THE CONTEXT OF PRESERVING PUBLIC LANDS

In what empirical context can the preceding theoretical argument be assessed? As mentioned earlier, the preservation of public lands for future generations provides an important challenge to national governments. The questions that opened this chapter suggest some implications for some of the most revered places on earth. I use the term "systematic preservation" to describe two major emphases of recent national efforts: representation of diverse ecosystems in park systems and restoration/protection of entire ecosystems at individual units. Many national governments have responded to recent domestic and international demands for these preservation emphases with promises of intergenerational attention. Yet, delivery remains a daunting task.

Systematic Preservation

How can intergenerational efforts in individual nations be systematically assessed in this context? The quote from Lucas at the top of the chapter reflects emphasis on two very different aspects of preservation that necessitate analysis in systemwide terms as well as at the level of individual units.

At the system level, systematic preservation involves attempts to implement long-term plans that emphasize expansion into ecosystems that were previously unrepresented among existing protected areas. This goal focuses on the desire to preserve biodiversity so that future generations will see all kinds of ecological entities, not just the few that are popular for whatever nonscientific reasons. Scientists have increasingly utilized such techniques as Geographic Information Systems (GIS) and GAP (Gap Analysis Program) analysis to identify different natural ecoregions based on such factors as plant cover, vegetation, and species.[45] The operational goal for governments then is to represent each diverse ecoregion within the nation's system of protected areas.

At the level of individual units, systematic preservation involves restoration and retention of natural conditions within specific protected units through such means as reintroduction of species and alteration of boundaries to contain whole ecosystems. Though precise definitions of ecosystems remain elusive, scientists and planners have increasingly called for protected areas to be large enough to facilitate migration, reproduction, evolution, and other ecological processes for native species.[46]

These goals of preservation through representation and restoration have been increasingly prominent in recent decades to the point of becoming quite common, stated explicitly by international commissions (discussed in chapter 2) and within national plans (discussed for each nation). They are not so much drastic new goals for protected lands as they are the result of a refocusing (described in chapter 2) of traditional goals of preservation. Yet, the question of goal attainment remains.

Lack of Existing Answers

The extant literature provides few answers to this question. The comparative environmental literature offers insights into cross-national differences that will be useful in this study, but substantive attention has been focused on issues such as property rights, environmental movements, and pollution regulation rather than on long-term preservation of public lands.[47] Indeed, in his review of the environmental literature, David Vogel states, "Substantively, the issue least well represented in the comparative literature is that of resource management."[48] The literature that is more focused on public lands provides rich empirical detail and some compelling arguments, but it is limited in several important respects.

Lack of a Comparative Context

First, most analysts focus on preservation efforts within a single nation.[49] The comparative work that has been done on this subject has been mainly confined to world conferences on parks and statistical summaries by the IUCN. The two have yet to be combined in a systematic theoretical argument. The former have produced informative histories but no rigorous analysis.[50] The latter are mostly sheets of raw data.

Lack of Emphasis on the Future

Second, empirical examination is largely limited to past and current behavior with little attention to commitment to the future. Most studies are explicitly historical in nature.[51] Some of the single-nation studies include consideration of long-range plans, but these discussions are only small parts of larger studies and they lack comparative context.[52] A few recent efforts are comparative in nature but do not offer a focused argument on long-term commitment. Machlis and Tichnell discuss threats to parks throughout the world but provide only minimal attention to long-term system planning and implementation. Allin's edited volume provides valuable historical accounts of park formation but no rigorous comparative analysis nor systematic conclusions about how nations pursued long-range plans in preserving public lands. Lowry's comparison of American and Canadian national park systems concentrates on management in recent years rather than on capability for intergenerational provision.[53]

Demand-Based Explanations in Single Countries

Third, when analysts have discussed long-range efforts, their explanations have focused on the timing and stated goals of official intentions that resulted from demands by interest groups, economic sectors, and politicians with little consideration to future supply.[54] Once long-term goals have been stated, have governments really followed through? For instance, one of the few arguments to focus on supply of public lands posits the "worthless lands" thesis stating that lands have been set aside to be protected only when no other use industry wants them.[55] This thesis has yet to be given comparative examination. Are some national agencies more likely to be able to overcome this tendency, given that many recent long-term national plans call for more "precious" lands to be protected?

Cross-National Analysis of Systematic Preservation

This project analyzes cross-national variation in the systematic preservation of public lands to future generations. The theoretical argument to explain variation in this context is based on the earlier discussion, at that point stated in generic terms, of delivery of intergenerational goods.

Necessary But Not Sufficient Conditions

Several conditions are posited as necessary for systematic preservation efforts. These include meaningful demands, stable democratic processes to hear those demands, and some degree of official commitment to intergenerational delivery. For each nation studied in depth later, each condition is described as evident but not sufficient for the provision of intergenerational goods.

Constraining Conditions

Given the presence of the conditions stated above, responsibility for provision of preserved lands as intergenerational goods is inevitably assigned to a public agency. These agencies can then stimulate public demand, author long-range plans, and coordinate actions necessary to enhance natural conditons. However, the behavior of that agency is significantly affected by certain institutional tensions. As suggested earlier, these can be conceptualized as vertical and horizontal. Vertical constraints are created when the resources necessary for systematic preservation are shared between levels of governments. Horizontal constraints are manifest when relations between political actors at the highest level of government are not supportive of systematic preservation.

The empirical analysis of this part of the overall argument is necessarily limited to a few nations. Only so many nations can be realistically studied in enough depth to provide meaningful analysis. In addition to logistical necessity, the selection of a few cases is theoretically justified if the cases are determined by the relevant independent variables. Thus, nations are selected to represent each of the cells in table 1-2.

Cases

The cases studied in depth were selected on the following grounds. The four nations studied in depth have several important factors in common regarding land issues. The conditions posited as necessary for preservation are evident. All four nations to be studied enjoy political stability and relatively consistent public support for preservation emphases. They also have central agencies in place, motivated employees, and mission statements emphasizing long-term preservation. However, they vary in terms of the vertical and horizontal constraints on bureaucratic behavior described above.

Variance among these nations in long-term responsive behavior will be hypothetically affected by institutional constraints on the relevant public agency. Table 1-3 reconstructs table 1-2 with the selected cases. Nations are described as high or low on vertical constraints based on the degree of interaction with subnational governments necessary for national agencies to implement long-term plans. Nations are described as high or low on horizontal constraints based on the level of autonomy enjoyed by the relevant public agency at the top level of government. These characterizations are more apparent in the following justifications for placement of the four selected cases.

The United States is categorized as low on vertical constraints and high on horizontal. Although a federal system, federalism has little impact on long-term behavior by the National Park Service. Rather, each state has its own state park system and national parks are relatively free, with some exceptions, from state influence. Horizontal constraints are immense, however. The autonomy of bureaucrats, in other policy areas as well as parks, to pursue implementation of long-term plans is severely constrained by political intervention.[56] I hypothesize that intergenerational behavior regarding American parks will be sacrificed to short-term political concerns.

Australia is characterized as relatively high on both vertical and horizontal constraints. Federalism is a dominant institution in Australia, particularly in policies affecting public lands where power is retained, except in several prominent recent cases, at the state level.[57] Horizontal constraints on national agencies are also relatively high as politicians often talk of delegation but retain and use the capacity to intervene in agency affairs.[58] I hypothesize that Australian efforts at

---

TABLE 1-3
Institutional Tensions Affecting Systematic Preservation

		Conflictive Relations with Other National Actors	
		Low	*High*
Tensions with Subnational Actors	*Low*	Costa Rica	United States
	High	Canada	Australia

preservation through representation and restoration will be significantly slowed by dependence upon other institutions, notably state governments.

Canada is categorized as moderately high on the vertical dimension and relatively low on horizontal constraints. Canada is a federal system in which the provinces retain considerable power, particularly in the policy area of natural resources.[59] Indeed, the national government must acquire lands from provincial governments to designate them as national parks. Horizontal constraints are relatively low, however, in that Canada's public agencies are professional and increasingly autonomous in recent years.[60] Indeed, the most recent parliamentary efforts call for increasing agency autonomy from fiscal dependence by making the parks more self-sufficient. I hypothesize that Canadian officials will be moving toward implementation of long-term plans, but that their efforts will be slowed by negotiations with provincial governments and, perhaps ironically, by the transition to greater fiscal independence.

Costa Rica is described as low on both horizontal and vertical constraints. Horizontal constraints are so low and Costa Rican public agencies have attained such levels of discretion that they are often referred to as "the autonomous institutions."[61] The "low" vertical measure is actually changing. Power in Costa Rica has been historically centralized, although this is currently changing in land management to allow greater local participation. I hypothesize that systematic preservation efforts in Costa Rica will have been relatively effective, though the current changes pose more complex issues.

One obvious question regarding this case selection involves the comparison of Costa Rica to the other nations. Indeed, Costa Rica is much less affluent, its institutions less experienced, and its park system much younger than the other nations. Rather than a detriment to the study, however, I argue that these differences actually enhance the importance of the dimensions studied. In other words, in spite of a lack of some factors many would expect to be crucial to pursue systematic preservation, Costa Rica has made great strides largely because of the relative lack of institutional tensions that have troubled other systems. I do not pose Costa Rica as representative of all developing nations. Rather, preservation efforts in Costa Rica are interesting to study because of the conditions affecting behavior there that can be compared to other nations, whether those other nations are developed or not.

OUTLINE OF THE BOOK

This first chapter has posed the following question: How effectively, and under what conditions, can governments provide intergenerational, impure public goods? My argument is that efforts to provide intergenerational goods, such as systematically preserved lands, are enhanced by certain conditions such as demand and commitment but also constrained by the institutional tensions created by relations between relevant public agencies and other political actors. Intergenerational provision will vary according to these conditions.

Chapter 2 provides a broad historical and quantitative overview of preservation efforts throughout the world. The historical record describes increasing demands for and commitments to preserved lands as well as the growing focus on representation and restoration. The quantitative analysis in this chapter uses the widest possible comparative lens to examine preservation, assessing data on park systems from over one hundred nations. The data are drawn from a variety of sources including IUCN documents, studies from the World Resources Institute, almanacs, and others. The data are current and, for the most part, systematic enough to be comparable. This analysis enables a general and historic perspective on national park systems in terms of how much land has been set aside, how much land is in preserved condition, the existence of central agencies and national plans, and how different variables are related to preservation. The quantitative analysis supports the argument that the conditions cited above as necessary are indeed correlated to preservation efforts.

Chapters 3 through 6 are devoted to the case studies of individual national efforts at systematic preservation. The case studies utilize research information from each nation, examination of official documents, and interviews with principal policymakers to assess progress on both system-level and individual unit plans and decisions. Most of the interviews were with planners, either those within the agencies or those attempting to influence park decisions from outside. I did some interviews with legislators and legislative aides, but for the most part, I let their actions speak louder than their words.

Each study provides background information on necessary conditions, discussion of the posited constraints on agency behavior, and then assessments of system-level expansion and restoration of natural conditions at individual units. The emphasis in these discussions is on actions currently underway and those taken since systematic preservation goals were adopted in each country, roughly within the last two or three decades.

Within each national study, examination of all individual parks is obviously impractical. I used a straightforward technique of site selection, using international designation through such bodies as the World Heritage Convention when possible, to examine the most important units in the nation. Two reasons underlie this selection mechanism.

First, given that the overall goal for the project is to assess provision of intergenerational goods, the studied units constitute those preserved lands considered most crucial by the public and by international organizations to be delivered to future societies. Second, if systematic preservation is not occurring in these sites, expectations must be low for other less prestigious units. I don't automatically conclude that problems experienced at these units will also be evident at less prestigious, possibly more remote, units, but rather that the political dynamics can be important anywhere.

Conclusions are presented in chapter 7. This chapter combines the general analysis with the case study evidence to offer specific conclusions about systematic preservation of lands and broad conclusions about the ability of governments to deliver intergenerational goods. The answers to the questions that opened this chapter are obviously important to national parks, the most precious lands in the world. The answers are also important in the broader context. If, on the one hand, public sectors are universally ineffective at long-term responsive behavior, then debates over privatization and decentralization of delivery of intergenerational goods are further intensified. If, on the other hand, long-term responsiveness is more effective under certain conditions, then understanding of those conditions can benefit future efforts.

2

Creations of the Political Process

Parks are a creation of the political process.—Harold Eidsvik, chair
of IUCN Commission on National Parks, 1985

The theoretical argument of chapter 1 fosters several questions regarding national parks. First, where does the idea of systematic preservation come from? Second, have nations actually differentiated between levels of protection for public spaces? Third, are the political variables hypothesized in chapter 1 as important really evident in statistical comparisons of national efforts? I use brief historical and broad quantitative analyses in this chapter to answer these questions. At the core of these answers is a simple fact. National parks do not just appear, nor do they automatically receive protection as designated land. Rather, as the above quote suggests, parks are created by people through political processes. This fact has significantly influenced the evolution of the preservation idea as well as national efforts at putting that idea into practice.

EVOLUTION OF THE PRESERVATION IDEA

The idea of preserving natural areas existed long before the 1872 designation of Yellowstone as a national park. Over two thousand years ago, Plato encouraged protection of the hills of Greece from the loss of forest cover. Preserves and hunting grounds have been recognized and used for centuries. Some preserves were even considered worthy of national protection. Only in the late nineteenth century, however, did a national government commit to the preservation of public land in relatively natural condition for future generations. When establishing Yellowstone National Park, the U.S. Congress called for "the preservation, from injury or spoliation, of all timber, mineral deposits, natural curiosities, or wonders . . . and their retention in their natural condition."[1] The long gestation was over, the idea of national commitment to preservation had been born.

Early Efforts

The idea of national preservation entered a period of youthful growth. National efforts at preservation occurred in a variety of forms in a variety of places. During this youth, little consensus was reached on the precise goals of preservation. Explicit debates over the exact goals date at least to the early twentieth-century battles between conservationists advocating controlled use of natural resources and preservationists like John Muir encouraging setting land aside to be unaltered by humans.[2]

Different versions of the idea of preserving natural areas for perpetuity spread quickly outside of the United States. Indeed, other national governments took what British ambassador Lord Bryce praised as "the best idea you [Americans] ever had" and established their own systems of protected lands, usually as national parks. Australians claim the first land officially designated as a "national park" at what is now called Royal National Park (in New South Wales) in 1879. The Canadians designated Banff (in Alberta) in 1887 and created the first version of a national park service with the Dominion Parks Branch, the forerunner to the Canadian Parks Service, in 1911. The U.S. National Park Service (NPS) was established in 1916. Other nations followed these examples and established their own protected areas.

Enough nations had systems of protected areas by the middle of the century to foster interest in international coordination of the preservation idea. Coordination efforts grew slowly. Following World War II, numerous individuals and organizations suggested various forms of international institutions. The International Union for the Conservation of Nature (IUCN) grew out of a conference held in France in 1948 with representatives from eighteen governments and numerous associations as an organization committed to, as its constitution states, "the preservation of the entire world biotic community."[3] The IUCN's Commission on National Parks and Protected Areas was established in 1961 to provide a more specific focus.

By the 1960s, systems of protected areas were spread sufficiently throughout the world to motivate calls for systematic information. The first World Conference on National Parks convened in Seattle in 1962. Delegates agreed on the need for a comprehensive listing of national parks and equivalent reserves and solicited the help of the United Nations to commence the process. In 1969, at the tenth General Assembly of the IUCN, criteria for national parks were made explicit. To be recognized, national parks were to contain large areas where 1) ecosystems had not been materially altered, 2) the highest authorities had "taken steps" toward protection, and 3) visitors were allowed to enter. In the official list, ninety-five nations listed over one thousand national parks or equivalent reserves.[4]

Though many protected areas had been established in the hundred years following Yellowstone, little consistency existed between them. At the second World Conference on National Parks in 1972, delegates expressed pride at a century of achievement but some dismay at the lack of scientific and systematic growth. As historian E. M. Nicholson stated, "To this day, piecemeal and opportunist aims have remained uppermost."[5] Because parks are creations of the political process, they often lacked elements that allowed restoration or maintenance of natural conditions. Further, what these places were to accomplish varied from one country to the next and from one site to the next within individual countries.

Maturation of the Idea

By the time of the Yellowstone Centennial Celebration in 1972, interest in national park systems was ubiquitous. The 1972 conference finished with a call for more parks, more biogeographic representation of diverse areas, greater protection of existing parks through better management and more attention to ecosystem needs. These demands were formally echoed and joined by concerns for historic preservation in a prominent international convention later that same year. The national preservation idea had entered a period of maturation.

This maturation was shaped by the political process. Renewed attention to preserved areas was part of a larger shift of public focus that occured in the late 1960s and early 1970s. In nations throughout the world, citizen awareness of environmental issues, including the lack of systematic ecological focus in national parks, increased dramatically. Correspondingly, their demands on government behavior intensified. In the United States, for example, the newly created Council on Environmental Quality termed 1970 a "turning point" in public emphasis on environmental issues.[6] This shifting emphasis occurred in similar, if not explicitly emulated, ways and in roughly the same time period in nations all over the globe. The commonality of increased environmental awareness resulted in the seminal U.N. Conference on the Human Environment in Stockholm in 1972.[7]

A variety of factors contributed to this increased attention. Empirically, many environmental problems became increasingly pervasive and noticeable during this time. At least as important was the publicizing of environmental concerns in such internationally renown books as Rachel Carson's Silent Spring (1962) and Paul Ehrlich's The Population Bomb (1968). Futher, events like civil rights marches and the Vietnam

War made more people willing to question the commitment of govern-ments to address societal ills. Finally, the presence of nuclear weapons may have contributed to a change in perceptions about the fragility of the world and the chance to preserve some precious parts within it.

Increased attention to preserved areas was also occasioned by sev-eral international conventions created in the early 1970s. The first, International Biosphere Reserves (IBR), constitutes an attempt to pro-vide for more ecosystem-oriented management of park units. These areas are designated by the Man and the Biosphere (MAB) program, established in 1970, of the United Nations Educational, Scientific, and Cultural Organization (UNESCO). The MAB program calls for inter-governmental cooperation to focus research and education on under-standing relations between humans and specific biosphere reserves.[8] The MAB program designates four essential criteria for selection of reserves: representativeness of biomes, diversity of ecosystems pro-tected, naturalness (being relatively unmodified), and effectiveness of an area in terms of size, shape, and location.[9] When the reserve centers around a national park, the park unit serves as a core of a protected area while lands around the park are managed to be compatible with park purposes. Experts term this program the "closest existing concept" to natural-oriented boundaries.[10] The IBR planners called for designa-tion of at least one area in each of the world's major ecosystems. As of 1988, twenty-five units of the U.S. park system were designated as MAB Reserves.

The World Heritage Convention (WHC), formally termed the United Nations Convention Concerning the Protection of the World Cultural and Natural Heritage, constitutes a second international pro-gram that can focus global attention on preserved areas. The WHC was first established in 1972 and has since grown into the world's most ratified international conservation agreement. The Convention explicitly calls for increased recognition of cultural and natural heritage by preservation of sites with "outstanding universal value from the point of view of history, art, or science."[11] The Selection Committee for the World Heritage Convention meets once per year to review nominations of sites by member nations. Sites can represent cultural or natural heritage, but are to possess "outstanding universal value."[12] No guarantee for greater protection of approved sites is offered, but member nations agree to cooperate on joint efforts and to provide some limited funding. As of 1992, 358 sites were listed, including 96 of "natural" heritage.[13]

A third international event affecting preserved areas occurred in 1987. The United Nations World Commission on Environment and Development published a document titled *Our Common Future* but more often referred to as the Brundtland Report after the Commission's chair, Norwegian prime minister Gro Harlem Brundtland. The document formally endorsed the concept of sustainable development as an international goal. The concept was defined in long-range terms as "development which meets the needs of the present without endangering the ability of future generations to meet their own needs." Further, the Commission established several more specific goals related to public lands, including a recommendation that all nations strive to set aside at least 12% of their land as protected areas. Several of these recommendations have been formally incorporated into various treaties and agreements.

To summarize this maturation period, preservation efforts received considerable attention and debate. Some observers contend that the environmental fervor of the 1960s and 1970s left an emphasis that called for locking people out of preserved areas and leaving those areas to their own self-regulating devices.[14] Such an emphasis contributed to problems when ecosystems that had already been altered by humans were then left on their own to somehow restore their natural balance. Many preservation advocates, however, learned from such mistakes and adjusted their goals to allow human involvement in restorative programs. In many areas, park planners and policymakers moved toward a new emphasis on sustainability, one that called for human management of diverse ecosystems.

Focus on Systematic Preservation

The preservation idea has arguably entered a period of adulthood. The idea has evolved into an emphasis on systematic expansion and scientific restoration of natural conditions.

One major goal of this new emphasis is representation of diverse ecosystems in collections of protected areas. Policymakers in many systems now use sophisticated techniques of mapping and GAP analysis to identify biological regions in need of protection. Conferences recommend not just that certain percentages of land be in protected status but also that those percentages include diverse ecosystems.[15]

A second major goal of the new emphasis is to restore and then maintain conditions in park units that approximate the natural state of the park before significant alteration by humans, particularly by Euro-Americans.[16] Thus, for example, wolves were reintroduced into Yellowstone in 1995 to restore the presence of natural predators. Such efforts receive international verification as entities such as the IUCN use categories to define the level of protection given individual units.

The focus on systematic preservation for future generations has stimulated official commitments at both the national and international levels. One of the earliest calls for representation of diverse ecosystems occurred in the United States in 1972. In his official proclamation opening the Centennial Year for Yellowstone, for example, President Nixon called for care and embellishment of a national park system containing "the most magnificent examples of America's natural and historical heritage."[17] As an example of international attention, Article 4 of the World Heritage Convention calls for "the identification, protection, conservation, presentation, and transmission to future generations" of heritage sites by each nation. The establishment and delivery of this intergenerational good had presumably entered a new era.

VARIATION IN DELIVERY

Verbal commitments are one thing, actions are another. Without question, the idea of national parks and preserved areas has received considerable attention, particularly in the past twenty-five years. Has that idea been translated into action? Have governments really acted to preserve lands, or are protected areas still receiving little systematic attention? What explains the variation in national efforts? Are certain factors consistent with greater delivery of intergenerational goods?

Data

A considerable amount of data is available to begin to answer these questions. The IUCN has developed fairly thorough and systematic monitoring of national efforts at conservation. Other organizations, such as the World Resources Institute, also produce extensive amounts of cross-national data. Table 2-1 lists a number of variables derived from these and other sources that are used in the following analyses.

Dependent Variables

How can provision of intergenerational goods be measured systematically? One way is to quantify the amount of national land set aside for some degree of safeguarding for future generations. This measure provides at least an estimate of the initial step of creating such goods. As discussed later, such a measure does not fully capture all important aspects of preserving lands. For instance, this measure does not reflect any assessment of diversity of ecosystems represented. However, officially designating lands as protected does offer an indication of commitment to future generations. This measure is more realistic if it can be differentiated by degree of protection offered various land units.

The measures analyzed below utilize IUCN categories designating different levels of protection for land. The IUCN uses ten categories, but this analysis will concentrate on lands receiving enough protection to qualify for Categories I through V. Category I includes scientific and

TABLE 2-1
Variables Related to Preserved Lands

Name	*Description*
Preserved Land Variables	
Protected area	% of land in Categories I–V in 1992 (1)
Pristine area	% of land in Categories I–III in 1992 (1)
Advocacy Coalition Variables	
Population	Total population in 1995 (1)
Urban population	% of population in urban areas (1995) (1)
Literacy	Adult female literacy (% in 1990) (1)
WHC years	Years in World Heritage Conv. (1992) (5)
Free systems	Systems of free and open elections (3)
Agriculture	% of GDP from agriculture sector (1)
Extractive uses	% of GDP from mfg. and mining (1)
Tourism	% of GDP from tourism (7)
Other Variables	
Total area	Nation's total area in hectares (1)
Agency	Federal, national conservation agency (2)
Agency years	Years since federal parks agency est. (2)
GNP per capita	Gross national product per capita (1)
GNP growth	Avg. annual GNP growth rate (1980–91) (1)
RGDPC	Real gross domestic prod. per capita (6)
Plan	Presence of systematic expansion plan (2)
Montreal Protocol	Signatory to ozone control agreement (1)

Sources
(1) World Resources Institute, *World Resources 1994–95*
(2) World Conservation Monitoring, *Protected Areas of World*
(3) Freedom House, *Freedom in the World 1995–96*
(4) IUCN, *1994 UN List of National Parks*
(5) World Resources Institute, *World Resources 1992–93*
(6) Alan Heston and Robert Summers, *Penn World Tables 1997*
(7) United Nations, *Statistical Yearbook 1995*

Note: All data and the documentation necessary to replicate this analysis can be obtained from the author.

strict nature reserves where public access is strictly limited. Category II includes national and provincial parks. Category III includes natural landmarks and monuments. Lands in these three categories are considered preserved areas that are maintained in a natural state and closed to extraction. Categories IV and V include areas allowing some extractive uses. Category IV includes nature or wildlife reserves. Category V includes landscapes and seascapes. For purposes of this analysis, "protected area" refers to land contained in all five categories as of

TABLE 2-2
Descriptive Statistics of Key Variables

Variable	Minimum	Maximum	Mean	Stnd. Dev.
% Protected (1992)	0	40	5.87	6.59
% Pristine (1992)	0	17.5	2.66	3.63
Domestic env.	.1	55	11.7	14.3
WHC years	0	18	6.9	6.2
Agriculture %	.3	64	20.6	15.3
Tourism %	.1	27	2.8	3.8
Agency years	0	80	11.5	14.4
Total area	61	1,699,580	86,233	209,618
Real GDP per cap.	368	17,186	4,675	4,382
Agency	0(91)	1(58)	.39	.49
Free	1	3	1.97	.80
Urban population	.10	100	16.1	17.3
Literacy	.7	99	56.6	29.2

1992, whereas "pristine area" refers to that in the first three. Land variables also include measures of land totals in 1970 and calculations of increases in both sets of land groups (protected and preserved) since 1970.[18] Table 2-2 provides descriptive statistics for the land categories and several other key variables.

The theoretical framework outlined in chapter 1 suggests several conditions that may be conducive to long-term responsiveness. These conditions include domestic demand, international demand, stability of political processes, official commitment, and agency capability. Other conditions also need to be assessed such as relative affluence and the presence of economic sectors affected by land designations. How can these variables be made operational to assess their impact?

Demand Variables

Cross-national variation may well be related to demand from both domestic and international sources. Demand levels for protection of lands in many nations are not directly measured and thus difficult to quantify. One recent model provides a theoretical foundation upon which to build demand conditions for intergenerational goods. The Advocacy Coalition Framework (ACF) does not focus explicitly on intergenerational goods, but it does specifically examine long-term policy.[19] The ACF posits that policy changes over long periods of time (more than a decade) will result from the interaction of competing advocacy coalitions within a policy subsystem, changes to the system from external conditions such as economic shocks, and the stability provided by certain system parameters such as constitutional rules. Advocacy coalitions are not simply interest groups but rather consist of all the various actors pursuing a policy position within a subsystem. For example, the "commodity coalition" pursuing timber production in national forests in one analysis consists of timber companies, mill workers, ranchers, many Forest Service employees, and sympathetic members of Congress.[20]

Using the ACF provides several benefits. One is that the use of advocacy coalitions simplifies modeling the involvement of hundreds of actors. Rather than assessing the impact of each interest group or each sympathetic politician, a challenging task even regarding current goods, the ACF posits the impact of coalitions of actors working together to further their policy position. Second and related, advocacy coalitions include actors that can participate on both sides of demand and supply models, thus avoiding the problem of forcing such actors into exclusively demand or supply roles. Third, the focus on the entire coalition diminishes complications resulting from the attention any individual group must pay to retaining its members, an important benefit particularly regarding long-term group behavior. Fourth, the hypothesized impact of these coalitions has received empirical verification in a variety of settings.[21]

Applying the ACF to a comparative analysis of many nations requires care in extending the model. Access to the political process for advocacy coalitions will vary in different political systems. The comparative policy literature agrees, citing the impact of interest groups and entrepreneurs on policy outcomes but emphasizing that their input will depend upon their ability to access the system.[22] Specifically, as chapter 1 discussed, analyses stress the importance of stable processes such as free, regular elections and party competition.[23] The ACF recognizes cross-national differences on these grounds with its attention to constitutional rules.

The variance between nations in accessibility is particularly important for certain advocacy coalitions. For example, while the presence of some coalitions within systems will be readily apparent through their economic clout, the impact of others, such as environmental advocates, will depend upon free channels of expression through which to demand intergenerational goods. Thus, measures of the potential impact of some advocacy coalitions must necessarily include assessment of their ability to access and influence the system.

A second extension of the ACF for purposes of comparative analysis of intergenerational goods is to simply acknowledge that advocacy coalitions may cross national lines. International demand for some intergenerational goods is increasingly apparent, particularly on environmental issues such as global warming where international coalitions call for more reliance on renewable sources of energy. International demands, often presented through conventions, can alter national agendas and foster more comprehensive concerns for future outcomes.[24] Some analysts posit substantive impacts on the delivery of intergenerational goods.[25]

The impact of international advocacy coalitions is subject to debate, however. International conventions are notoriously lacking in resources and enforcement powers. Even the most cited example of an effective international convention to protect an environmental good for future generations, the Montreal Protocol regarding the ozone layer, has been evaluated as "not sufficient" to ensure desired behavior.[26] Still, other international agreements, particulary when backed by strong environmental nongovernmental organizations (NGOs) have made impacts on issues such as a global ban on ivory trading.[27] Thus, the presence of international coalitions warrants examination.

The role of advocacy coalitions in provision of intergenerational goods can be summarized in a simple hypothesis. Provision will be greater in nations where supportive advocacy coalitions have access over time and antagonistic coalitions are less evident. How are these coalitions measured?

The "domestic environmental" coalition includes people within individual nations supporting greater quantities of preserved lands. The coalition approach is useful as direct measures of environmental interest groups and supportive public opinion are not systematically available for comparative purposes. I created a simple proxy. Public opinion studies consistently reveal two common demographic measures as being highly correlated to support for environmental issues: literacy and urbanization.[28] Counter to much conventional thought, environmentalism is not highly correlated to income levels. While the logic for the literacy correlation is fairly straightforward (awareness leads to concern), two reasons for an urban correlation are proposed. First, the more urban dwellers, the smaller the rural population that might want land for other purposes. Second, the more concentrated the urban areas, the more city dwellers may demand natural areas to which they can "escape." Thus, a proxy for domestic demand for preserved lands is simply the product of literacy rates and percentage of urban population. One might argue that such a proxy represents potential demand more than actual demand, but given the discussion of latent demand for intergenerational goods offered earlier, measuring potential rather than actual levels of demand is a plus.

I also applied the extension to the ACF suggested earlier to facilitate comparative analysis. As mentioned, some advocacy coalitions will have little impact if not applied to stable political processes that will recognize citizen concerns. To address this issue, I used the Freedom House data that categorizes countries according to whether or not they have basic political rights and free and open elections. This data set is upgraded every year and is quite comprehensive. Later in the analysis, I use the categories to assess relationships in separate groups of nations. For the basic model, however, the domestic demand variable is an interaction term, the product of the proxy described above and the Freedom House rankings.[29]

A second advocacy coalition is "international demand." As described earlier, demand for many intergenerational goods crosses national boundaries. International bodies like the IUCN, world conferences on parks, seminal meetings as at Stockholm in 1972 and Rio de Janeiro in 1992, and various conventions provide means for commonality and coordination of goals. International demand is most readily measured by participation in global treaties or conventions. One recent paper, for example, posited a relationship between participation in GATT and protected lands.[30]

This analysis uses a measure that is specifically appropriate to land protection decisions. The World Heritage Convention (WHC) is the world's most widely ratified conservation agreement that calls for participating nations to nominate and then protect lands according to the highest international standards. The WHC variable is measured in years prior to 1992 that a nation had been a signatory member, the idea being that the higher the number, the longer the time that the international coalition could encourage provision of preserved lands. The WHC has had a significant impact in some nations, notably Australia; but like other international conventions, its effect may be limited.[31] Thus, I expect a positive, but not large, correlation with quantity of preserved lands.

A third advocacy coalition is expected to have a negative impact on provision of this intergenerational good. The "alternative use" coalition includes members of a society who would prefer to see land used for purposes other than preservation, such as agriculture. The measurement and hypothesized impact of such coalitions is straightforward. At least two measures are possible. One is the percentage of a country's economy (in gross domestic product) dependent on agriculture. A second is percentage of GDP dependent on extractive industries like mining. Most of this analysis uses the former as it is more appropriate for developing as well as for developed nations. Hypothetically, the more dependent the economy on alternative uses, the lower the provision of preserved lands.

The impact of a fourth advocacy coalition is more difficult to predict. For many nations, particularly those such as Costa Rica that now emphasize ecotourism, preserved areas can be useful in attracting tourism and visitors.[32] One might thus expect that the more important the tourism industry is to a nation's economy, the more likely preserved lands will be provided. The relationship, however, is not that clear. The tourism industry often prefers commercial developments such as resorts in natural areas. Preserved lands, as measured in this analysis, are generally expected to be somewhat insulated from such development.[33] Thus, a variable measuring percentage of GDP from tourism is included in the equation, but without the ability to differentiate commercial tourism from ecotourism, its impact is ambiguous.

Public Agencies

As chapter 1 described, the role of public agencies can be crucial to the provision of intergenerational goods. Indeed, I argue that non-elected bureaucrats are more likely to foster and stimulate long-term concerns than are elected politicians. To summarize, although some recent work suggests that politicians may occasionally develop policies that respond to potential publics, such as future generations, most political behavior is directed at short-term electoral cycles.[34] Career civil servants, on the contrary, often have the motivation and resources to pursue more long-term goals, often in spite of short-term political fluctuations.[35]

How can bureaucratic capacity be operationalized so as to hypothesize its impact on provision of intergenerational goods? Public agencies are more capable of acting in a strong supportive role if located at the highest levels of government.[36] Public agencies are also likely to have more prestige and clout if they have proven to be durable authorities.[37] One admittedly crude measure of durability is longevity, at least an indicator that the agency is astute enough or supported enough to last. Thus, one simple means of assessing variance in bureaucratic capacity to pursue intergenerational goods across a large number of nations is the amount of time an agency with responsibility for the good in question has been able to pursue provision. Thus, I hypothesize that provision of an intergenerational good is more likely the longer a relevant agency has been operative at the highest level of government. How is agency presence measured?

One measure is a dummy variable, coded 1 if conditions conducive to the agency having a strong advocacy role in government are evident. The agency must be centrally located, the sole recognized authority for protected lands, relatively independent in stature, and in existence since before the late 1980s. Several countries, such as Austria and Germany, are thus coded as 0 because their federal systems preclude central agencies. Others, such as Ireland (1991) are coded as 0 because their agencies were created after the 1980s. As table 2-2 shows, of the

149 nations in the total data set, 58 had such an agency.[38] Such a measure is worth testing but has limitations. For instance, the internal validity of the measure is questionable given that prominent examples of countries known for preservation do not easily meet these criteria. In the United States, for example, depending on how one measures protected lands, the NPS is not the sole authority.

A second and somewhat more refined measure is the amount of time a relevant public agency, generally some form of national park service, has been responsible for a major portion of the nation's preserved lands. As examples, the United States established the NPS in 1916 and the Canadians their comparable agency in 1911. While this does not provide sophisticated measures of bureaucratic capability, a task that would be difficult for the 149 nations in the data set, it does give an indication of how long an agency has been in place at the highest level of government to provide support for supply of this intergenerational good. A positive relationship between length of time an agency has existed and quantity of preserved lands is also not inevitable. Switzerland has had a parks agency for twenty-five years but has no land area in Categories I–III. South Africa has had an agency for sixty-five years but has only 6% of its land protected. Costa Rica, on the other hand, has had a parks agency for only twenty-two years but already has 12% of its land protected and 10% in pristine status. Panama's agency dates back only twenty-three years, but 17.5% of the nation is in pristine categories.[39]

The use of park service agencies is particularly appropriate given the analysis of lands with high levels of protection. Using the United States as an example, several other agencies also manage public lands. However, much of the land managed by agencies other than the NPS, such as the Bureau of Land Management, is in IUCN Category VIII wherein multiple uses, such as grazing, are allowed. On the contrary, nearly all NPS land is in Categories I–V. Further, while agencies like the NPS may have some internal conflicts over specific projects, the overall thrust of the agency, particularly compared to other land agencies, has generally been to pursue preservation.[40] Surveys of agency personnel also show that the majority of employees feel preservation is the "major purpose" of the agency.[41]

Other Factors

Many other factors affect the provision of intergenerational goods in each nation. Examining all in one equation is not practical, but at least two other variables should be included in broad comparative analyses. Like advocacy coalitions and public agencies, these variables affect both demand and supply conditions.

One factor regards relative availability of the good in question. In other words, some nations may already have more of some goods that they can then "save" for future generations. A country attempting to pass on certain species to future generations may be more capable of doing so if they currently have more of those species. Availability may also make citizens more willing to set aside some of the good for future generations.

The measure for availability is straightforward, though its impact is not. The measure is simply total land area from which preserved lands can be created. Higher amounts of land obviously create more potential for lands to be designated for protection, but it also means that percentages based on preservation within total area may be statistically lower. I expect that total area will correlate positively with amount of preserved lands in raw numbers but negatively with preserved lands as a percentage of total lands.

Another factor, as mentioned in chapter 1, is some measure of relative affluence of the country. Affluence can affect provision of many goods, an impact that has been noted in state-level analyses as well as in comparative analyses.[42] The inclusion of such a variable is also consistent with the ACF in its recognition of the impact of broad macroeconomic conditions on policy outcomes. Comparing GNP or GDP numbers across countries is notoriously problematic for various reasons. However, Heston and Summers' Penn World Tables provide a purchasing power parity corrected measure of GDP per capita which provides a more accurate reflection of the real economic position of average citizens in each nation.

Even with as accurate a measure as possible, predicting the impact of this variable is difficult. Many might expect a positive correlation between affluence and preserved land. However, because of the way GNP and GDP are calculated, preserving lands does not necessarily increase and may in fact decrease most measures of wealth. These measures reflect material goods and services. Preserved lands may bring in some revenues from activities such as hunting and recreation, but these fees are traditionally quite low. In contrast, once preserved (according to the IUCN categories) most of this land is not available for agricultural and mining activities that would actually increase GDP. As Herman Daly says, "The problem with GNP is that it counts consumption (not preservation) of geological capital as current income."[43] This statistical relationship is a fact that has inspired numerous proposals for revised measures of national affluence.[44] The hypothesized statistical relationship of GDP per capita with amounts of preserved lands is negative.

Even with these variables included, the simple model suggested here will inevitably be underspecified and will thus not produce definitive answers regarding societal behavior. Nevertheless, it does allow cross-national comparison of conditions that foster provision of inter-generational goods.

National Participation

Most nations contain at least some public lands. By 1993, as table 2-3 demonstrates, over 140 nations contained protected areas. Criteria for inclusion on this list are: 1) significant size; 2) management objectives including protection; 3) some degree of attention by appropriate levels of government. Of these nations, 128 nominally preserve land in the natural conditions described by Categories I–III. Over 110 nations are now contracting parties to the WHC and 80 are parties to the "Man and the Biosphere" program sponsored by the United Nations.

TABLE 2-3
Nations Protecting Natural Areas

Timeframe	Nations with Protected Areas	Nations with Preserved Areas	WHC Nations	MAB Nations
Early 1970s	93	0	20	50
Early 1990s	141	128	111	80

The data also reflect an increase in designated areas since the early 1970s. Care must be taken in this interpretation. The 1993 UN list includes areas managed by state authorities in federal systems whereas previous lists did not include such areas. This inflates the number of areas protected, but not the number of countries with protected areas. These figures may still be inflated simply by countries reporting in 1993 that had not done so in 1971.[45] Nevertheless, data in the other columns of the table support the conclusion that more nations are paying attention to protected areas. Both international conventions have gained substantially more signatory nations since 1975.

The number of protected areas throughout the world has increased even more dramatically than numbers reflecting national participation. In the decade following the 1972 World Conference on National Parks, for example, the number of national parks and equivalent reserves in the world increased by 47%, from 1,823 to 2,671. The total area covered expanded by 82%, from 536 to 979 million acres.[46] By 1993, as shown in table 2-4, the list of total protected areas throughout the world numbered 9,832 covering 926 million hectares (2,288 million acres), or roughly 6% of the earth's land area.[47] Again, this number includes all

TABLE 2-4
Protected Lands in World, 1993

Category	Number of Units	Total Area (hectares)
I	1,460	86,473,325
II	2,041	376,784,187
III	250	13,686,191
IV	3,808	308,314,011
V	2,273	141,091,932
Total	9,832	926,349,646

Source: IUCN, 1994, *UN List of National Parks:* 246.

IUCN categories. But even using just totally protected Categories I–III, areas worldwide number 3,751 covering 477 million hectares (1,179 million acres).

This growth is important in itself, but it also serves a theoretical purpose. The periods of greatest growth occurred under conditions of relative political stability (at least lack of world wars) and when domestic demands and international support were highest. Further, these years of tremendous growth occurred in the period of maturation for the preservation idea. Thus, the potential existed for many nations to take substantial steps toward more systematic preservation of natural areas.

Variance in Preserving Lands

Considerable variance exists among nations in the provision of preserved lands. The following analyses use Ordinary Least Squares (OLS) multiple regression. The basic model described uses the following form: Quantity of preserved lands as % of total area = constant + domestic environment coalition + WHC years – alternative use coalition +/– tourism coalition + agency years – total area – real GDP per capita.[48]

All Nations

Table 2-5 displays the results of testing the model for all nations in the data set. Due to missing data, the number of nations analyzed is eighty. The equations are quite strong, with five of the seven independent variables significant at the .05 level and an impressive amount of the overall variance explained considering the wide differences on so many dimensions of the nations in the data set.

TABLE 2-5
Preserved Lands as Percent of Total Area

	Protected Areas	Pristine Areas
Constant	7.63	5.51
	(2.42)	(1.34)
Domestic env.	.167***	.092***
	(.063)	(.035)
Intl. env.	.055	−.051
	(.114)	(.063)
Alternative use	−.106*	−.085**
	(.065)	(.036)
Tourism	−.382**	−.173*
	(.177)	(.098)
Agency years	.231***	.184***
	(.049)	(.027)
Total area	−.001**	−.001**
	(.000)	(.000)
Real GDP per cap.	−.001***	−.001***
	(.000)	(.000)
N	80	80
R^2	.32	.45
Adj. R^2	.25	.39
Standard error of equation	5.83	3.23

Figures are unstandardized coefficients.
Standard errors in parentheses. *p<.10, **p<.05, ***p<.01.

The hypothesized relationships are evident. In terms of advocacy coalitions, the domestic environmental coalition is strongly correlated to protected and pristine lands. Consistent with the discussion regarding international conventions earlier, the international demand coalition has little impact on provision of this good. The alternative use coalition is negative in both equations. The measure reported here is for the agriculture coalition.[49] It has a higher level of significance in the equation for pristine lands, logically consistent with the idea that these lands preclude extraction whereas protected lands allow some. Only the behavior of the measure for tourism as a percentage of GDP is difficult to interpret. Again, however, the negative sign is likely a result of the fact that current measures of the contribution of tourism to an economy emphasize commercial activities more than ecological forms of tourism.

Regarding other conditions, the agency variable is the most consistently powerful, both in coefficient and significance, in the equations.

The table reports the variable using agency years, but the results were the same when using the cruder dummy variable described earlier. The sign for the impact of the total land area variable is negative, surely reflecting the statistical artifact that nations with great size may still end up with low percentages of preserved land even if they have provided considerable amounts. This interpretation is supported by the fact that a straight correlation between total area and preserved lands (in raw total amounts) is strong.[50]

The relationship between relative affluence and amount of preserved lands is statistically significant and negative for both protected and pristine lands. Little wonder that economists such as Solow have called for measures of national wealth that can reflect intergenerational concerns.

Disaggregation by Wealth

Obviously, the nations examined vary widely on many dimensions. The simplest dimension is economic wealth. One major concern with such variance focuses specifically on the hypothesized impact of public agencies on intergenerational goods. Public agencies in many poor nations are often described as ineffective if not corrupt. Is bureaucratic capability still related to provision of such goods in poor nations? I disaggregate the data set to examine nations with RGDP per capita either more than $1,500 or less than $3,000.[51] Table 2-6 displays the results of testing on just pristine lands.[52]

Several aspects of this analysis are worth noting. First, the variables for bureaucratic capability and domestic demand continue to be strongly correlated to preserved lands in both sets of nations. Second, the signs for the other variables remain consistent although some of the relationships, particularly in the equation for less wealthy nations, are no longer significant. Third, the equation overall remains quite robust, explaining roughly half of the variance among nations. The R-square term is slightly higher than in the pristine lands equation for the whole data set, a logical result in that each disaggregated set contains less variance that has to be explained.

Disaggregation by Political System

A second way to disaggregate the data set is according to the categories of political systems. One might expect that the hypothesized relationships apply only in systems with free and open elections. Thus, I separated the data set to run one analysis with nations that are at least somewhat repressive (Freedom House Categories 2 and 3) and one analysis with nations that are at least partially free (Freedom House Categories 1 and 2). Obviously, the two sets of nations overlap. This

TABLE 2-6
Analyses for Different Levels of Affluence (dept. var. = % pristine lands)

	Nations w/ GDPPC>1500	Nations w/ GDPPC<3000
Constant	7.14	2.98
	(2.34)	(2.39)
Domestic env.	.093**	.166***
	(.039)	(.066)
Intl. env.	−.005	−.087
	(.086)	(.075)
Alternative use	−.177*	−.040
	(.098)	(.046)
Tourism	−.198*	−.133
	(.118)	(.109)
Agency years	.228***	.186***
	(.042)	(.033)
Total area	−.001**	−.000
	(.000)	(.000)
Real GDP per cap.	−.001***	−.000
	(.000)	(.000)
N	50	49
R^2	.50	.55
Adj. R^2	.42	.47
Standard error of equation	3.52	2.87

Figures are unstandardized coefficients.
Standard errors in parentheses. *p<.10, **p<.05, ***p<.01.

is essential since Categories 1 and 3 each contain just less than one-third of the nations in the overall data set, too small a number of cases to run meaningful OLS equations. Table 2-7 displays the results.

Again, the results are generally consistent with the analysis for all nations. The variables representing agency capability and domestic environmental advocacy remain significantly positive. The other relationships are consistent in sign if somewhat variant in levels of significance. Nevertheless, the robustness of the agency and demand variables across different types of political systems is impressive.

Discussion

What do the empirical results of the second chapter say about the theoretical questions posed in the first chapter? Under what conditions

TABLE 2-7
Analyses for Nations in Different Political Systems (dept. var. = % pristine lands)

	Less Free	*More Free*
Constant	4.38	5.35
	(1.55)	(1.49)
Domestic env.	.172***	.095***
	(.055)	(.037)
Intl. env.	−.059	−.000
	(.067)	(.082)
Alternative use	−.050	−.102**
	(.036)	(.042)
Tourism	−.352**	−.166
	(.146)	(.108)
Agency years	.165***	.198***
	(.033)	(.034)
Total area	−.000	−.001**
	(.000)	(.000)
Real GDP per cap.	−.001**	−.001***
	(.000)	(.000)
N	55	61
R^2	.49	.48
Adj. R^2	.41	.41
Standard error of equation	2.84	3.34

Figures are unstandardized coefficients.
Standard errors in parentheses. *p<.10, **p<.05, ***p<.01.

are nations likely to provide greater amounts of intergenerational goods?

Dependent Variable

The variance among nations in provision of intergenerational goods is substantial. This analysis uses only very simple measures of preserved lands, percentage of total area designated in certain categories. These calculations give some sense of national efforts at preservation, but one can easily imagine more sophisticated measures. For example, are entire ecosystems preserved? Do the preserved areas include a wide range of ecosystems? To address these questions will require more indepth analyses of specific cases that are presented in the following chapters.

Nevertheless, even the simplest measures of intergenerational goods show wide variance among nations in terms of provision. Percentage of protected land, for instance, ranges from 0 in a few nations to 40 in Ecuador.[53] Pristine lands range from 0 to 17.5 in Panama.

Limitations to the Model

This econometric model is limited in several ways. First, the model is admittedly underspecified. Certainly, other factors affect preservation decisions within individual nations. For example, one variable that might be compelling would provide some measure of scientific consensus in each nation regarding the intergenerational good in question. While potentially intriguing, such a variable is obviously difficult to measure.[54] Nevertheless, even this parsimonious model produces impressive results and support for the hypothesized relationships.

Second, while the dependent variable represents a buildup of preserved lands over time, several of the independent variables are cross-sectional. Measures of three of the advocacy coalitions are simply for one year in time. This is not that great a problem for two reasons. First, most of the accumulation of preserved lands in the world has occurred in the last twenty-five years or so. Between 1972 and 1982 alone, the total area of protected land increased by 82% (see chap. 2, n. 46). Second and related, during that time period, measures for variables such as agricultural percentage of GDP have not changed that dramatically. To check this, I ran the model using data from different years and got very similar results.

Third, the model does not guarantee that the relevant public agency preceded the designation of much of the preserved land. Thus, one can question the claim that park service type agencies act as advocates for expansion. Both quantitative and qualitative evidence supports this assertion, however. Quantitatively, as the preceding paragraph suggests, more than half of the preserved land in the world has been designated since 1972. Correspondingly, whereas the mean number of agency years for the data set is 11.5 (table 2-2), this mean is diminished by nations without park agencies. The mean number of agency years for nations with at least 2.5% preserved land is 23 (N=50, s.d.=18). Thus, at least on average, a parks agency existed before most expansion took place. Qualitatively, the evidence presented in subsequent chapters is consistent. Briefly, park service agencies in the United States (especially during the years when George Hartzog was director), Canada (systematic expansion plan in place since early 1970s), Costa Rica (parks department created in 1970 to manage expansion), and elsewhere have provided strong advocacy positions for expansion.[55]

Fourth, more refined measures of the independent variables might produce more compelling results. In particular, the measurement for bureaucratic capacity is somewhat crude. Numerous analyses reflecting variable impact by bureaucracies on policy outcomes suggest ways of differentiating public agencies according to such factors as skills, discretion, and relative autonomy.[56] Assessing those factors for this many nations is a formidable task. An approximation of those factors was the dummy variable discussed earlier that reflected the presence of a "capable" (as described by the IUCN) agency at the central level of government. Again, this dummy variable produced virtually identical results as did the measure used in the displayed analysis.

Relationships

In spite of these limitations, the results of the analysis are consistent with the theoretical arguments put forth in the first chapter. The presence of certain variables are necessary conditions for the establishment of lands to be preserved for future generations.

The variance among nations in provision of preserved lands is correlated to the presence of domestic demand for such goods. Domestic environmental advocates have a positive impact on provision whereas alternative use coalitions such as agriculture have a negative impact. International demand has little impact on delivery of intergenerational goods, a finding counter to some recent analyses but consistent with characterizations of such pressure as generally inconsistent or ineffective. The ACF is a promising tool for explaining the variance among nations in provision of intergenerational goods. The impact of domestic demand is enhanced by official commitments and by political stability over time.

Variance is also explained by the presence of relevant public agencies. Even crude measures of bureaucratic capacity perform as expected, a result consistent with arguments that nonelected bureaucrats are important actors in the provision of intergenerational goods. This finding is robust, evident when analyzing the entire data set or categories based on wealth or political system. In this context, bureaucratic presence is usually manifest as some sort of national parks agency. In other policy areas as well, efforts at intergenerational responsiveness can be enhanced by the energy and long-term focus that, ironically enough, only nonelected officials often provide.

The stated importance of the impact of a public agency is not a trivial theoretical point. Rather, it is both a counter to public expectations and an analytical extension to theoretical models of responsive public sector behavior. Public demands for intergenerational goods are nearly always focused on elected officials. Yet, as this analysis shows, politicians' official responses may not be as consequential as is the role of pertinent nonelected officials. Similarly, theoretical models of responsive behavior have also typically understated the importance of public agencies largely because the models focus on short-term outputs. However, as shown here, even the mere presence of a relevant agency is a powerful predictor of the variance among nations in long-term efforts.

Having asserted the role of these variables as necessary conditions for meaningful preservation of lands, however, how sufficient are they? As mentioned above, the simple establishment of preserved lands does not guarantee representation of diverse lands or protection of entire ecosystems. In pursuing such goals, even the presence of powerful public demands and motivated agencies may not be enough to ensure delivery. The pursuit of such goals is hypothetically constrained by systemic factors that are not easily measured in econometric models.

CONCLUSIONS

The conclusions reached in this chapter should not be overstated. The theoretical argument poses interesting hypothetical relationships more than it offers definitive answers. Nevertheless, some conclusions are compelling. Public sectors can deliver, at least nominally, intergenerational goods. Nations vary considerably in quantity of provision. A considerable portion of that variance can be explained by cross-national differences in demand and supply as represented by citizen demands and the presence of relevant public agencies.

How effective is that provision, however? Is the establishment of preserved lands a major step toward protection and representation of diverse ecosystems? Answers to these questions depend upon indepth empirical examination of behavior in specific cases.

3

United States: Political Reality vs. Scientific Desire

There's a real clash between political reality and scientific desire.
—Duncan Morrow, NPS spokesman

I woke up before dawn, packed up my campsite at Phantom Ranch, and began the climb up out of the Grand Canyon while the skies were lit only by a thousand stars and a full moon. As I hiked along the Colorado River, the first light of the sun appeared behind the cliffs to my back while the moon rested on the rim of the canyon in front of me. In addition to the low roar of the Colorado's rapids, the only sounds I could hear were the birds awakening. I savored the moment, free from the noise and intensity of life that so many of us face every day. This was what national parks could be. To achieve such conditions, Americans have called for systematic and science-based preservation of natural areas. However, as the opening quote suggests, these desires face significant political realities. Moments like mine are unfortunately not that easily found.

This chapter describes the record of system expansion and unit enhancement in the United States. The first section provides some historical background by describing the presence of certain conditions essential for systematic preservation and the existence of institutional factors, most notably political control of the bureaucracy, that constrain long-term oriented behavior. The second and third sections present the empirical record in both system expansion and enhancement of prominent units for future generations.

BACKGROUND

NPS director of planning Denis Galvin was easy to find. He was one of the few "essential" personnel still in the Interior Building during the shutdown of the federal government in December 1995. The setting

44

was ironically appropriate for a discussion of congressional impact on NPS behavior. Galvin and I discussed several units of the system and several projects for existing units that had been approved by Congress in spite of agency objections that they were not scientifically justified. I asked him, "What about standards of national significance for inclusion of new units?" "As one member told me," Galvin answered, "you just have to expand your definition of national significance."[1]

Necessary Conditions

National parks have always been to the United States what castles and cathedrals are to Europe. Thus, they receive significant public support. Politicians have been aware of that support at least since the start of this century and have accordingly made official commitments to preservation efforts. These factors are necessary but not sufficient conditions to ensure systematic representation and restoration of park units.

Strong but Not Always Salient Public Support

In the mid-1990s, scholars at Colorado State University conducted several public opinion surveys regarding national parks. They found that a vast majority of Americans see preservation as the primary goal for national parks management. In fact, "providing an important experience for future generations" was the most important value to respondents with over 87% citing it as very important.[2] This widespread public support is the culmination of a century-long love affair between Americans and their parks and several recent decades of growing environmental concern.

Tracking public opinion through the decades is difficult, but one proxy is possible in that public support for the parks is strongly related to their popularity. Table 3-1 displays increasing visitation to national parks during the twentieth century. The table shows a steady increase in visitation at least until the mid-1990s.

Popularity does not necessarily reflect demands for preservation, however. These demands have been slower to grow. One of the earliest scientific recommendations came from biologist George Wright in the 1930s. Wright was one of the first and few research specialists to work for the NPS in the early decades. In 1930 he and two others began a systemwide survey that became the study titled *Fauna of the National Parks of the United States*. Wright's team argued that the health of wildlife within the parks depended upon the provision of sufficient habitat through natural, not artificial, boundaries of the park units. They recommended, "In order that our parks may be able to adequately protect

TABLE 3-1
Recreation Visits to National Park Service Sites (in thousands)

Year	Visits	Year	Visits
1910	199	1980	220,000
1920	1,058	1981	200,000*
1930	3,260	1982	205,000
1940	16,755	1983	206,000
1950	33,253	1984	208,000
1960	72,288	1985	216,000
1971	154,000	1986	237,000
1972	166,000	1987	246,000
1973	169,000	1988	250,000
1974	171,000	1989	256,000
1975	190,000	1990	263,000
1976	217,000	1991	268,000
1977	211,000	1992	273,000
1978	222,000	1993	281,000
1979	205,000		

*NPS changed counting procedures in 1980.
Sources: U.S. NPS *Statistical Abstracts*, 1940, 1954, 1964, 1980, 1990;
U.S. D.O.I. *Budget Justifications FY 1995*: NPS–16.

and preserve their wildlife as part of our national heritage, it is essential that they be formed principally of natural boundaries, and not arbitrary boundaries."[3] Many in the NPS were receptive to Wright's ideas, including Director Albright who created a Division of Research and Education. Wright recruited foresters, biologists, and other scientists for the division, but plans for action were ended dramatically. Wright and a colleague were killed in an automobile accident in New Mexico in 1936. Many new ideas for the park system died in that accident.

Wright's recommendations resurfaced in scientific reports published in the early 1960s. The government-sponsored Leopold Report of 1963 called for preserving, or if necessary recreating, parks "as nearly as possible in the condition that prevailed when the area was first visited by the white man."[4] Also in 1963, a National Academy of Sciences committee recommended much greater attention to research by the NPS, particularly in regard to the effects of activities on lands adjacent to park units.[5] These reports were certainly noticed by NPS personnel if not exactly received with open arms. Many NPS personnel retained traditional views of the highest priority being to manage parks so as to accommodate the visitors. Scientific resource management took a back seat to the development of roads and tourist facilities.[6]

Allowance of certain activities and uses of the parks in the years between World War II and 1970 fostered increasing questions. Dramatically increased visitation following World War II prompted a 1953 article questioning easy access to natural areas.[7] The logging industry demanded access to forests such as those holding the great redwoods. The Bureau of Reclamation, actively pursuing dam construction, saw rivers in several parks as prime opportunities. All of these activities were questioned. Logging in the Northwest stimulated various public protests. Dam building inspired intense concern. One of the largest fights was over a proposed dam in Dinosaur National Monument's Echo Park. After a five-year fight in Congress, the plan was stopped in 1956. Two proposals for dams in the Grand Canyon fostered tremendous uproar in the 1960s.

Organized demands for ecological attention grew rapidly. Table 3-2 displays the growth in membership of three interest groups that often focus on national parks policy. As the table shows, all three groups experienced dramatic growth in membership between the early 1960s and 1975. The Grand Canyon fight stimulated much of the growth in these groups. The Sierra Club membership, for example, jumped from thirty-nine thousand in 1966 to sixty-seven thousand two years later.[8] Sierra Club members became so politically involved in the fight over the dams that the club lost tax-exempt status.

Prodevelopment programs such as Mission 66, encouraging more roads and vehicles into parks, brought questions from across the politi-

TABLE 3-2
Membership in Relevant Interest Groups (in thousands)

Year	National Parks and Conservation Association	Sierra Club	Wilderness Society
1962	25	22	21
1966	35	35	30
1968	41	80	50
1970	55	135	70
1973	55	140	80
1975	55	162	90
1977	45	183	70
1979	35	183	55
1981	33	225	50
1984	45	350	110
1987	65	416	190
1989	100	500	315
1990	200	565	390

Source: *Encyclopedia of Associations,* various editions. The year depicted is two years before the date of the volume to allow for compilation and publication time.

cal spectrum. The conservative *Wall Street Journal* joined environmental groups in criticizing the Mission 66 program by decrying the effects in Yosemite. The *Journal*'s editors wrote, "But the program's planners failed to anticipate the full extent of the tourist explosion. Indeed, this spectacularly beautiful park is wrestling with problems that would give any fair-sized city cause for alarm."[9] Such questions were consistent with the growth of broader concern in American society on many environmental issues. Environmental legislation passed by wide, bipartisan margins in Congress.

Many in the NPS were also questioning their own direction. Some recognized the potential downside to too much emphasis on making parks usable. One indication of such a perception came with an admission from the previously use-oriented Director George Hertzog in 1971: "We've simply got to do something besides build roads in these parks if we're going to have any parks left."[10] Planners in the agency also recognized that they had not added many new natural areas since World War II. The new nontraditional units were fine in some ways, but new natural parks were increasingly difficult to establish. Of the roughly twenty-four million acres in natural areas as of 1971, 96% existed in parks that predated World War II.[11] The agency needed a new strategy to pursue additional natural areas.

Public demand for environmental preservation has remained high since the environmental awakening of the early 1970s, as shown by the Colorado State poll, but one fact about that support must be remembered. Public opinion on environmental issues in the United States is considered strong but not salient. Only in the early 1970s have environmental issues been at or near the top of concerns voiced by Americans. Since then, issues such as controlling pollution are described as one of the issues in immediate need of attention by only a relatively small percentage of Americans.[12]

The same phenomenon is true for the idea of preservation of natural conditions in national parks. When asked, people support the goals of scientific expansion and restoration of natural processes. Again referring to the Colorado State University surveys, they found that 75% of respondents considered their representative's record on national parks important when they voted.[13] However, these people were reminded of the parks in the question itself. Voicing of preferences for systematic preservation often requires some stimulus. Public demand is not salient enough on its own to motivate systematic preservation.

Stable but Entreprenurial Political Environment

Public demands for ecological attention to national parks can find receptive ears. The United States has one of the most stable and enduring political democracies in the world. Further, the system is, at least theoretically, remarkably accessible.

To review, the U.S. system is one of separated powers whereby the president and members of Congress are chosen by separate elections. The Congress is further divided into a Senate with two members from each state and a House of Representatives containing members from 435 single-member districts spread throughout the country according to population. Entreprenurial behavior by individual members of Congress as well as by the president is not only allowed but, by most accounts, has been increasing in recent years. One reason is that political parties are notoriously weak. Party discipline is evident on some highly visible occasions, such as the government shutdown in 1995, but is much less noticeable on less salient issues such as national parks. In addition, power is decentralized to numerous committees and subcommittees. Since the early 1970s, that decentralization has actually increased.

Such a political environment ensures accessibility. Demands on national parks can be heard. The strength of the voice, however, depends upon numbers or on material resources such as campaign contributions. Further, these voices are heard by individual players. Thus, demands for systematic preservation are likely to be heard, but concerted political responses are not to be counted upon.

Official Commitments to National Parks

The history of national parks in the United States over the first century of their existence reflects a stated emphasis on attention to preservation principles but variable degrees of real commitment.

Primary examples are evident in the first parks. Yellowstone was established in 1872 as "a pleasuring ground" but also as an area wherein Congress mandated "preservation from injury or spoliation" of natural resources. Nevertheless, in the early years, Yellowstone managers received little official attention and even fewer material resources to do their job. By the time the NPS was created in 1916, a dozen national parks and numerous monuments existed in what cofounder Horace Albright termed "no system at all."[14]

Though the NPS was created in part to attempt more systematic attention, several characteristics of the new agency diminished the likelihood of such behavior. First, due to opposition from the Forest Service, the NPS was created as a service, not a full-fledged bureau or department. Thus, the NPS had less institutional clout to achieve its goals. Second, the NPS was placed within the Department of the Interior with sister agencies that encouraged extractive uses of lands, such as mining and grazing. Boundaries for protected areas were therefore

often in dispute. Third, the new agency was assigned a mandate that would lead to significant tensions, if not confusion, in later years. The NPS is to "conserve the scenery and the natural and historic objects and the wildlife therein and to provide for the enjoyment of the same in such manner and by such means as will leave them unimpaired for the enjoyment of future generations."[15] The agency is to preserve natural conditions even while allowing for unspecified means of use and enjoyment. This rather paradoxical mandate allows for criticism and legal challenges from all sides in policy disputes.[16]

Fifty years after creation of the agency, the emphasis was clearly on use rather than preservation. The centerpiece of this emphasis was the program entitled Mission 66. Mission 66 was a ten-year project begun in 1956 to, as Director (1951–1964) Conrad Wirth said, "restore to the American people a national park system adequate to their needs."[17] Resource needs of the parks were secondary to those of the users. For example, Mission 66 built 1,197 new road miles, three times as many as trail miles, and reconstructed 1,570 more to make parks more accessible to automobiles. Over 1,500 new parking areas were constructed with capacity for 50,000 cars. Over one hundred new, spacious visitor centers were developed.

By the late 1960s, however, official emphasis was swinging back toward preservation. The seeds of this shift were sown in the early 1960s. President Kennedy often touted the virtues of preserving relatively undeveloped conditions.[18] Congress created notable means to pursue such emphasis with passage of the Wilderness Act in 1964 and the creation of the Land and Water Conservation Fund (LWCF) in that same year. The former called for setting aside land in totally undeveloped condition. The LWCF was designed to funnel revenue from sales of federal properties, some user fees, and offshore oil leases to purchase state and federal parklands. The federal portion of LWCF funds appropriated over subsequent years is shown in table 3-3. By the late 1960s, President Johnson could announce that "History will say that in the 1960s the Nation began to take action so long delayed . . . to (preserve) nature's bounty."

In the decades following, highly visible attempts to reverse official commitment to preservation were short-lived. In the early 1980s, the Reagan administration, particularly Secretary of the Interior James Watt, were quite explicit that preservation was not a high priority. Two months after taking office, Watt admitted in an interview, "If I err, I'm going to be erring on the people side." The flow of LWCF funds, so prominent in the 1960s and 1970s, was virtually shut off in the early 1980s. The political fallout was intense. Watt's actions led to his forced resignation and to the dramatic growth of environmental groups. Again in 1995, after taking over Congress for the first time in

TABLE 3-3
Land and Water Conservation Funds (Federal Portion)
(in thousands of dollars)

Year	Current Dollars	Constant 1982 $
1965	5,555	16,435
1966	39,183	111,951
1967	41,737	116,259
1968	51,416	136,382
1969	116,725	293,278
1970	65,900	156,905
1971	167,841	378,020
1972	101,669	218,643
1973	112,957	228,196
1974	5,000	9,259
1975	121,092	204,202
1976	165,433	262,176
1977	355,597	528,375
1978	490,166	678,901
1979	359,988	457,999
1980	201,801	235,474
1981	107,282	114,130
1982	167,386	167,386
1983	212,593	204,959
1984	213,113	197,877
1985	206,245	183,819
1986	116,883	101,549
1987	153,126	132,007
1988	144,040	120,835
1989	179,992	144,576

Source: U.S. DOI, 1989, *LWCF Report to Congress 1988:* Table 1.

decades, Republican calls for reversal of many park policies were cut short when other Republicans realized the extent of the political backlash.

For most of the period to be considered in later sections, then, at least a rhetorical commitment to preservation has existed at the highest levels of government. This, along with at least latent public demand and a stable democracy provide conditions necessary, though not sufficient, for systematic preservation to occur.

Constraining Conditions

American national parks are established and maintained in a political environment. Unlike some other countries, the accumulation and dissemination of financial resources for the parks all occurs at the federal level. Thus, vertical constraints on long-term responsiveness are low. However, the institutional relations between political actors at the federal level dominate NPS efforts to provide intergenerational goods.

Low Vertical Constraints

Vertical constraints on provision of intergenerational goods in this context is termed low. Systematic preservation is affected by the U.S. federal system, mainly in that increased centralization provides further means for federal political actors to affect the NPS. For instance, unlike other systems studied here, the financial resources used to fund and to manage the national parks is raised and spent by the same level of government.

The lack of subnational involvement in national parks is furthered by the fact that between the period of the New Deal in the 1930s and the Reagan Revolution of the 1980s, the central government grew to a position of dominance in the American federal system. Centralization was stimulated by many factors such as the revenue available to the federal government through income taxes, greater recognition of externalities such as air pollution crossing state lines, and the increasing mobility of the national population. Perhaps most important, national politicians increasingly utilized federal actions to further their own interests. This was especially apparent in the proliferation of categorical grants for various programs. Between 1929 and 1980, federal domestic spending jumped from the lowest of the three levels of government to more than twice as much as the other two levels combined.[19] Political analysts and politicians alike have described the increasing national presence "in all areas of social and economic endeavor."[20]

The recent apparent rejuvenation of state governments and the decentralization rhetoric of many politicians in the 1980s and 1990s may have shaken federal dominance, but the federal presence remained intact in many policy areas, including national parks.[21] Even the Republican takeover of the Congress in 1994, with promises of decentralization and delegation, could not overcome certain factors that have maintained a strong national presence. These include the Washington-centered influence of interest groups, a federal hierarchy of intergovernmental bureaucrats, and the desires of national politicians to be able to mold and shape policies at the state and national levels. NPS leaders attempted, partly in response to demands to "downsize" Washington, to restructure the agency in 1994 and 1995 to decentralize the administration and move more personnel away from Washington and out to the field.[22] These efforts did not include, however, a corresponding turnover of powers to state or local governments regarding national parks.

Possible vertical changes in the political system have potential impacts on systematic preservation in obvious and not-so-obvious ways. First, the continuation of centralized power contributes to the influence of political actors at the federal level who can intervene in agency affairs. Second and less apparently, the backlash to centralization may make expansion of federal lands even more difficult in the future. Centralization has fostered significant resentment to federal involvement in public lands, particularly in the western states where so many parks are found. Some state legislatures are considering "takings" legislation on issues involving personal property rights that may have an effect on public lands in the near future.[23]

One might expect significant impact on the national park system from the presence of state park systems. Each state has its own system of parks. Together, they total roughly twelve million acres and serve almost twice as many visitors as do the national parks. In fact, surprisingly little interaction occurs between the national and state park systems. Though managers in both kinds of systems pursue some goals in common, the state systems are generally more oriented toward revenue generation.[24] Indeed, some state park systems are mandated to be self-sufficient. State parks can come into play, as discussed in the section below on the Grand Canyon, when state officials criticize federal management of national parks and suggest turning over control of the lands to state governments.

High Horizontal Constraints

Horizontal constraints on provision of intergenerational goods is termed high because of the extent to which politicians control federal bureaucracies. Individual members in the fragmented, specialized U.S. Congress have always taken advantage of opportunities to affect the behavior of agencies such as the NPS. Because of the entreprenurial nature of the American system and the ability of individual constituents to make demands, individual members have historically used goods provided by public agencies for political reasons. The willingness and the ability of all members to do so has actually increased in recent years. Inspired largely by the excesses of the Nixon administration, members of Congress reasserted institutional power during the 1970s. At the same time, they looked internally to reform their own procedures by diffusing and decentralizing power to individual members.[25] The new arrangements facilitated entreprenurial behavior by members and enhanced their ability to intervene in the affairs of individual bureaucratic agencies.[26] Because individual members do have influence, agency employees and political appointees must respond to their demands. This theoretical point is supported by comparative surveys of legislators in different nations.[27]

Parks tempt congressional involvement for various reasons. First, land-use decisions are always contentious, thereby allowing members the opportunity to act as ombudsmen for various interests. They can, in response to various advocates, affect boundaries and allow certain uses since each park is created by an act of Congress. Second, park events are highly visible, thereby allowing members the means for position-taking and ceremonial activities. Third, parks are also tempting for their potential pork-barrel value of added jobs and capital spending, especially when other similar opportunities, such as those with the Corps of Engineers, have diminished.[28]

Occasionally, congressional intervention can push parks policy toward a long-term focus. For example, in the 1960s and early 1970s, individual members were cognizant of the public opinion shifts and interest group behavior described above and were eager to appeal to preservation advocates. Thus, legislation such as the Wilderness Act and the LWCF were possible. Individual members have been and, in some cases, continue to be supportive of preservation. One recalls how Senator Paul Douglas (D–IL) admitted that his legislative goals shifted over time from saving the world to saving the Indiana Dunes.[29] More recently, Representative Bruce Vento (D–MN) has offered several pieces of legislation consistent with goals of systematic preservation.[30]

More commonly, however, the intervention of individual members makes implementation of long-term plans difficult. The frequent promises of congressional members to increase emphasis on long-term planning is quickly subsumed by political realities. Members of Congress generally have relatively short timeframes based on electoral cycles, two years for representatives and six years for senators. Further, members have to respond to powerful constituents who have demands on parks or on park boundaries that are not consistent with the protection of ecosystems. Both these realities have been at least reinforced in recent decades by the professionalization of Congress and by the degree of attention paid by members to reelection. Finally, appropriating funds for implementation of long-term restoration plans has never had the same appeal to members as work projects and capital spending that provide more immediate benefits.

Congressional involvement in public agency behavior has also increased in recent years in response to the aggressive efforts of the executive branch. The Johnson and Nixon administrations are often termed the "Imperial Presidents" for their efforts to centralize control. Later, the Reagan administration (1981–1988) centralized and politicized the bureaucracy arguably more than any other modern presidency.[31] In the Reagan, Bush, and Clinton administrations, political appointees greatly expanded their control over public agencies. The congressional response to these various presidential attempts at control led to an upward spiral of political involvement in agency affairs. By the late 1990s, observers characterized the NPS as more a "responsive" than an "expert-centered" agency.[32]

The fact that members of Congress can dominate agency behavior is evident virtually every budget cycle. For a recent example, the FY96 budget process for the NPS displayed the impact of several members. Though total spending was down, the House agreed to $1 million for an administration building on the Blue Ridge Parkway in the district of Representative Charles Taylor (R–NC), a member of the subcommittee writing the bill, and $2 million for the Saratoga Monument in the district of Representative Gerald Solomon (R–NY), chairman of the Rules Committee. The NPS had recommended neither expenditure. The Senate included $6 million for construction on the Natchez Trace Parkway in Mississippi, home state of Senator Thad Cochran (R–MS), as well as nearly $1 million for the New River Gorge National River in Senator Robert Byrd's (D–WV) home state. Both senators were members of the subcommittee that wrote the bill.[33] For a more general assessment, consider the following: Between 1994 and 1997, no money was authorized for construction projects in Yellowstone, Grand Teton, or the Great Smokies. During the same time period, Senate Majority Leader Trent Lott (R–MS) delivered over $16 million to the Natchez Trace site and powerful Senator Robert Byrd brought home over $8 million for the New River Gorge.[34]

In part, congressional micromanagement is also facilitated by the actions of members of the NPS themselves. For decades, NPS personnel were only partially committed to the preservation goal, often welcoming congressionally inspired developments that brought additional funding into their parks.[35] Even with a shifting emphasis among employees to be more critical of development ideas, NPS personnel are not expert at resisting political demands. Legislative aides told me in interviews that most NPS employees are relatively naive regarding political actions, particularly early in their careers. Further, their own behavior is still often shaped by the needs of their own parks. Thus, an NPS manager may seek extra funding for his unit even if it means that other areas in the park system may suffer. NPS employees acknowledge such limitations, expressing concern in the 1992 Vail Symposium document that the agency may be "at the mercy of policy participants which are better prepared and armed with persuasive arguments and information."[36]

Theoretical Expectations

The potential impact of the described theoretical factors on systematic preservation is important. NPS efforts are strongly influenced by political preferences, particularly those of members of Congress. I argue that expansion of the American system is individualized and entreprenurial, determined on a case-by-case basis of political calculations rather than according to any systematic plan focused on natural resources. I expect that enhancement of individual units according to long-term plans will also be determined by political circumstances.

SYSTEM EXPANSION

The contrast between Steamtown National Historic Site (in Scranton, Pennsylvania) and the Tallgrass Prairie National Preserve (in eastern Kansas) could not be more stark nor more illustrative of the impact of politics on U.S. national park system expansion. The former was created by a political maneuver, an amendment to an appropriations bill by a high-ranking representative from Pennsylvania. The latter received congressional approval only after decades of seemingly futile efforts to get a strong endorsement from the Kansas delegation. Steamtown has received nearly $80 million in federal money since the 1986 amendment.[37] The Tallgrass Prairie Preserve has received very little money. The site is marked on roads leading into the preserve only by local protest signs urging "No Government Acquisition." The Steamtown site is noisy and congested, bustling with construction activity. Often the only sound heard in the Flint Hills of Kansas is the wind. Steamtown was neither recommended nor desired by the NPS. Rather, as a Smithsonian transportation curator said, "Its determination as a historical site was simply a political trick."[38] The tallgrass prairie is a major ecosystem that the NPS has tried for decades to have represented in the system. Why was expansion so easy at Steamtown and so difficult at Tallgrass? In more general terms, is system expansion determined by political or resource issues?

Historical Expansion

In 1972 the NPS offered a comprehensive plan for system expansion. The idea of the plan was to define a complete representative system and identify existing "gaps."[39] Further, many in the agency felt that such a plan would enable the pursuit of additional natural areas that had been largely dormant since before World War II. Ironically, what actually happened to this plan did anything but increase agency independence in pursuing natural areas. Looking back on it twenty-three years later, director of planning Galvin summarized, "The 1972 plan is great as intellectual exercise, but it's not the way the system is built, the system is built by individual acts of Congress."[40]

Historically, members of Congress and occasionally the president, not agency planners, have determined system expansion. Congress creates national parks and monuments through individual pieces of legislation. The president, under powers granted in the Antiquities Act of 1906, can declare areas as national monuments. Selection of sites and specifications for boundaries of parks and uses therein were rarely based on ecological concerns. Indeed, boundaries were generally drawn to include only relatively "worthless" lands that contained no extractive values.[41]

Occasionally, land was selected for inclusion in the system on the basis of representation of a certain ecosystem. For examples, Shenandoah and the Great Smoky Mountains were established after these areas were selected by a commission appointed by the Secretary of the Interior in 1924 to survey the eastern mountains. Even then, the final boundaries of the parks were determined by the availability of land donated or purchased from private owners. One park established for its natural resources rather than its scenery was the Everglades. The park was created in 1934 to be "permanently preserved as wilderness" largely because it is home to hundreds of species of birds and other wildlife and despite the claims of opponents that it was a "worthless swamp."[42]

More often, sites were pushed by specific individuals. In the year the NPS was created, for instance, members of Congress introduced bills to add sixteen new parks to the system.[43] The fathers of the NPS were particularly influential. Stephen Mather's (director from 1916 to 1929) Save the Redwoods League was responsible for setting aside several areas of redwood forests as state parks that later became Redwoods National Park. Horace Albright (director from 1929 to 1933) enlisted the financial help of John Rockefeller Jr. to purchase enough Jackson Hole Valley lands to create Grand Teton National Park. Congress signed onto these additions but, even after understanding the need to protect more than just pretty scenery, legislators refused to protect anything like whole ecosystems when land surrounding scenic wonders contained valuable material resources.[44]

During the 1920s and 1930s, the park system became a popular target for political manipulation. Members and delegations from individual states fostered proposals to add units of questionable significance. This occurred often enough to inspire the National Parks Association, forerunner to the National Parks and Conservation Association, to begin emphasizing strict standards for inclusion and to adopt a contrary position to the establishment of several units. NPA officials such as Sterling Yard were critical of "the fatal belief that different standards can be maintained in the same system without the destruction of all standards."[45] After Mammoth Cave was designated following substantial advocacy by the Kentucky delegation, Yard fumed that "Politics controlled the situation."[46]

The national park system expanded significantly during the New Deal. Albright and President Franklin Roosevelt reorganized the NPS to include jurisdiction over historic areas such as Civil War battlefields. Whereas the NPS managed thirty-three national monuments, historical, and recreation areas in 1933, a year later the agency was responsible for sixty-one such sites. Congress reinforced new responsibilities for the agency with passage of the Historic Sites Act in 1935. Under this act, the NPS is to identify and list nationally significant sites as National Historic Landmarks. Although some argued that such expanded responsibilities might dilute the attention of the NPS to the national parks, agency leaders welcomed the new units and their relevant constituencies. This warm reception was inspired, to some extent, by the increased budgets for the agency that came with the New Deal and its various work programs.

Expansion of the national park system stopped during World War II but then resumed speed in the postwar years. By 1954 the national park system contained 181 units. The numbers within different categories are shown in the 1954 column in table 3-4. Between 1954 and 1960, the system gained twenty-eight new units, but only two of them were parks. In the 1960s, the system gained seventy-two units but only five of them were parks. The system grew in this decade through the creation of different kinds of units, such as four new historical parks, nine new recreation areas, six national seashores, and four new national battlefields. For expansion advocates both within the agency and within Congress, nontraditional units offered a ready tool to create new units.

The emphasis on utility in the 1950s and 1960s carried over to expansion of the system. Several new units were added during this

---

TABLE 3-4
Expansion of National Park System

Type of Units	1954	1960	1970	1980	1990
National Parks	28	30	35	40	50
National Monuments	83	80	85	91	78
National Historic Sites	11	28	52	60	69
Other	59	71	109	130	160
Total Units	181	209	281	321	357

Source: NPS Statistical Abstracts, various years.

period. Many units were chosen for their economic promise. In the postwar period, many organized economic interests saw the parks as holding great opportunities for development. The growing tourism sector proposed more parks, more roads, and more developments within parks. Rarely did the new units come with a commitment to ecosystem protection. Top NPS officials were receptive to such an emphasis. For example, Director Wirth proposed such modest recommendations for Olympic National Park, based on what he thought would be acceptable to Congress, that even Senator Henry Jackson (D–WA) expressed concern about the lack of ecological attention.[47]

Director Hartzog's team energetically pursued expansion of the park system, but they used expansion for political purposes. Between 1960 and 1970, as shown in table 3-4, the number of units in the system jumped from 209 to 281. These new units were strategically placed, not to represent diverse ecosystems but rather to solidify congressional support for the agency. In his memoirs, Hartzog boasts that before he left office, the NPS had designated some landmark "in every one of the then existing 435 congressional districts." Not all these places were under NPS jurisdiction, but of the more than seventy new units added during Hartzog's term, nearly two-thirds were placed in congressional districts that previously lacked NPS presence. "Never again," Hartzog asserted, would a member of Congress not be interested in the NPS.[48] Because the goal of expansion was strategic placement, natural conditions of new units were often compromised.

For example, Redwood National Park was established only after decades of political struggle. Proposals to create a national park to preserve the remaining giant redwood trees on the California coast pitted conservationists on one side and the timber industry on the other.[49] The Sierra Club argued for an ecosystem approach including groves, drainage areas, and buffer zones in ninety thousand acres. However, the shape of the park contained in the 1968 establishing legislation reflected the compromises of the battle that preceded its passage. The 1968 boundaries contained only fifty-eight thousand acres. Most of these acres (thirty thousand) were land purchased as corridors to link existing state parks. Thus, neither the desired Mill Creek nor Redwood Creek watersheds were designated in their entirety. Secretary of the Interior Udall called this alternative "the art of the possible" and admitted that he wanted to "pick a park, not a fight."[50] As a result, many of the most vital areas were only narrowly surrounded by parkland. Director Hartzog admitted that "The park was too small, we had lost some of the most valuable stands, we had accepted areas that could not be protected from floods, etc."[51] Indeed, the buffer zone around the park was generally less than eight hundred feet across.[52]

The result of such compromises often carries into the future. The original compromises in Redwood National Park necessitated changes in 1978. By then the inadequacy of the original boundaries to protect even the most valuable areas, such as Redwood Grove, was apparent. Logging and pollution from timber operations on areas left out of the original legislation were damaging conditions within the park.[53] Congress added forty-eight thousand acres to the park. Of course, by then, not only had the natural condition of these acres been significantly altered with many of the greatest trees cut, but the purchase price had gone up, timber companies realizing the opportunity to sell the lands at huge profits. Ultimately, Redwood's price tag was roughly $1 billion, the most expensive park to that date.[54]

As another example, during congressional deliberation concerning the boundaries of the proposed Canyonlands park, members explicitly excluded certain areas that had been recommended by the NPS because they contained potentially valuable oil reserves. Rather than designating these lands as national parks, members added certain areas to the proposed Glen Canyon National Recreation Area where mineral extraction is much more readily allowed. Senator Frank Moss of Utah stated, "I left them (areas) off deliberately because they have tar-sands deposits and the state geological and mineralogical survey was quite concerned that these sections be available for exploration, and I have included them, therefore, in the National Recreation Area. . . ."[55] Analyst John Freemuth studied this area extensively and concluded, "It is obvious that both the political process and chance played a much larger role in this issue than rational land-use planning."[56]

Along with the willingness to accept compromises, an obvious means for expansion was to encourage nontraditional units. The precedent established by creation of the Cape Cod National Seashore in 1961 enabled eight other national seashore designations by the end of the 1970s. Creation of the Ozark National Scenic Riverways in 1964 provided a forerunner to the Wild and Scenic Rivers system. The first national lakeshore, Pictured Rocks in Michigan, was authorized in 1966. Expansion of historic sites was facilitated by the Historic Preservation Act of 1966. Congress also established a National Trails System in 1968. In addition, Hartzog's team laid the groundwork for the urban parks to come in the 1970s.

The Plan

In 1972 the NPS offered its proposal to change the way expansion of the system occurred. The plan was comprehensive, explicit, and at least rhetorically supported.

Part 1 of the 1972 *National Park System Plan* calls for expansion of historic sites. The plan categorized American history into nine major themes (such as the original inhabitants or westward expansion) which then contained forty-two subthemes, many with their own specific niches. Table 3-5 lists the various facets to be represented. Agency personnel attempted to fit existing units within these niches to determine what lacked representation. The right-hand column in table 3-5 shows the percentage of subthemes represented within each facet. At the time of publication, the NPS counted 163 historical areas, but those areas represented only 85 of the 281 total facets.[57]

TABLE 3-5
Historic Themes Identified in 1972 Plan

	% Niches Represented
1. Original Inhabitants	
a. earliest Americans	25
b. native villages and communities	33
c. Indian meets European	0
d. living remnant	29
e. native cultures of the Pacific	17
f. aboriginal technology	25
2. European Exploration and Settlement	
a. Spanish	80
b. French	50
c. English	50
d. other	67
3. Development of the English Colonies, 1700–1775	43
4. Major American Wars	
a. American Revolution	80
b. War of 1812	50
c. Mexican War	0
d. Civil War	80
e. Spanish-American War	0
f. World War I	0
g. World War II	0
5. Political and Military Affairs	
a. 1783–1830	17
b. 1830–1860	20
c. 1865–1914	25
d. after 1914	25
e. American presidency	41

Continued

TABLE 3-5
Continued

	% Niches Represented
6. Westward Expansion, 1763–1898	
a. great explorers of the West	25
b. fur trade	83
c. military-Indian conflicts	83
d. western trails and travelers	33
e. mining frontier	0
f. farmers' frontier	20
g. cattlemen's empire	14
7. America at Work	
a. agriculture	0
b. commerce and industry	40
c. science and invention	38
d. transportation and communication	33
e. architecture	11
f. engineering	17
8. The Contemplative Society	
a. literature, drama, and music	10
b. painting and sculpture	22
c. education and intellectual currents	0
9. Society and Social Conscience	
a. American ways of life	60
b. social and humanitarian movements	15
c. environmental conservation	40
d. recreation in the United States	0

Source: U.S. *National Park System Plan*, 1972, Part 1: 83–84.

Part 2 of the plan focuses on natural representation. Similar to the historic plan described above, agency personnel identified different themes to categorize "essentially all the natural phenomena of the country."[58] Those themes included such natural conditions as tundra or boreal forest. The agency also identified different relatively homogeneous natural regions based on physiographic and biologic features, such as the Colorado Plateau or the Great Plains. Using both listings as a matrix, the agency then categorized existing units as representing different themes in different regions. The idea was that different themes display different characteristics when found in different regions. These calculations were used to achieve the levels of adequacy for representation shown in tables 3-6 and 3-7.

TABLE 3-6
Adequacy of Natural Region Representation

	% Represented		% Represented
North Pacific Border	70	New England-Adirondacks	29
South Pacific Border	25	Atlantic Coastal Plain	21
Cascade Range	95	Gulf Coastal Plain	16
Sierra Nevada	88	Florida Peninsula	63
Columbia Plateau	12	Island of Hawaii	54
Great Basin	10	Maui Island Group	53
Mohave-Sonoran Desert	85	Oahu	0
Chihuahuan Desert	90	Kauai, Niihau	0
Mexican Highland	0	Leeward Islands	0
Colorado Plateau	78	Pacific Mountain System, AK	56
Northern Rocky Mountains	85	Interior and Western AK	0
Middle Rocky Mountains	83	Brooks Range	0
Wyoming Basin	0	Arctic Lowland	0
Southern Rocky Mountains	70	Virgin Islands	100
Great Plains	35	Puerto Rico	0
Central Lowlands	16	Guam	0
Superior Upland	71	Mariana Islands	0
Interior Highlands	45	Samoa	0
Interior Low Plateaus	72	Caroline Islands	0
Appalachian Plateaus	0	Marshall Islands	0
Appalachian Ranges	55		
Piedmont	0		

Source: U.S. *National Park System Plan,* 1972, Part 2: 14.

Not surprisingly, the motivation for this plan has been questioned as well as the techniques. Some of the techniques are, perhaps because alternatives don't exist, arbitrary. For example, the different cells within the matrix are assigned scores reflecting no, some, or prime significance. The NPS admitted some degree of judgment calls but asserted that these efforts were "fundamental in producing a realistic plan of what the National Park System should contain."[59] In his critical study, Foresta argues that expansion had slowed since "most of the appropriate areas had already been included in the System" and that this plan enabled further expansion in a seemingly scientific way.[60] Both the NPS and Foresta appraisals have some merit. Coming up with a comprehensive plan inevitably involves some strategic aspects, but certainly some areas of the country were overrepresented and some natural regions were conspicuously lacking.

TABLE 3-7
Adequacy of Natural History Theme Representation

	% *Represented*		% *Represented*
Plains, plateaus, mesas	25	Paleocene-Eocene	32
Cuestas and hogbacks	30	Oligocene-Recent	15
Mountain systems	44	Tundra	40
Works of volcanism	58	Boreal forest	60
Hot water phenomena	75	Pacific forest	80
Sculpture of the land	46	Dry coniferous forest	45
Eolian landforms	42	Eastern deciduous forest	26
River systems and lakes	42	Grassland	30
Works of glaciers	50	Chaparral	66
Seashores, lakeshores, islands	42	Desert	55
Coral islands, reefs, atolls	18	Tropical ecosystems	31
caves and springs	55	Marine environments	25
Precambrian	78	Estuaries	25
Cambrian-early Silurian	21	Underground ecosystems	20
Late Silurian-Devonian	0	Lakes and ponds	38
Mississippian-Triassic	44	Streams	36
Permian-Cretaceous	34		

Source: U.S. *National Park System Plan*, 1972, Part 2: 15.

Continued Growth

The system continued to grow during the 1970s at rapid rates. Growth was supposed to occur as follows. The Division of Park Planning, usually through the New Area Studies Office, determines the qualifications for a proposed new unit. Several criteria are used for the evaluation, including representation of a particular type of resource as well as recreational opportunities and relatively unspoiled condition. Following a two-year review, the NPS determines the proposal's merit and then considers alternative designations such as state park systems before making a recommendation to the Department of the Interior and Congress.

The *National Park System Plan* did provide justification for some of the natural areas established after 1972. For example, one argument for creating Guadalupe Mountains National Park was that it combined "natural features of exceptional scientific importance" such as verdant plateaus of conifer forests and the Permian marine limestone reef.[61] The John Day Fossil Beds represented several geologic periods that had previously been "gaps" in the system. Many of the Alaska lands designated in 1980 were characterized by the NPS as important for filling slots that were previously unrepresented in the 1972 plan.[62]

However, much growth resulted more from political considerations, the 1972 plan serving more as justification than as motivation. Looking back on the plan after twenty-five years, Charlie Clapper, head of the Planning Center in Denver and a thirty-year veteran of the NPS, says at best the plan can serve as a tool, "as a way of heading off some proposals" when members of Congress attempt to contravene the process.[63] Congressional involvement took several forms during the 1970s.

The Park Barrel

The 1978 National Parks and Recreation Act provided so many new projects that it came to be known as the Park Barrel Bill.[64] This one piece of legislation alone authorized $1.2 billion for twenty-one new units and one hundred different projects, such as boundary adjustments and wilderness designations, in forty-four states. The money was available in part because of the huge amount of LWCF funds appropriated, by far the largest yearly amount, as shown in table 3-3.

This legislation was shepherded by Representative Phil Burton (D–CA). Burton became chairman of the House Subcommittee on National Parks and Insular Affairs in 1977 and immediately pushed for dramatic expansion. Burton instituted procedures to ensure an active flow of proposals for new park units and was more interested in quantity than quality of expansion. Further, he paid little attention to the desires or the opinions of members of the NPS. Agency planning official Clapper attributed "very little consideration" to the 1972 plan in formulation of this bill.[65] Rather, this single piece of legislation, according to Representative Burton, offered positive financial impacts for more than two hundred congressional districts.[66]

This bill was hardly the only one of its kind. Rather, it offered a model to be emulated in subsequent years, albeit on a smaller scale, by other members of Congress.

Urban Parks

One tempting means of expanding the system and reaching many constituents immediately involved urban parks. Official approval of urban parks as part of the national park system was hatched in the heat of the 1972 presidential race. Although some had pushed the idea of national park units within easy access of densely populated urban communities for years, the idea became politically popular in the fall of 1972. Proposals for National Recreation Areas surrounding the New York and San Francisco harbors were too tempting for presidential candidate George McGovern and his opponent, President Richard Nixon, to pass up. After all, the two states with these proposed park areas contained the first and third most electoral votes in the country. In September, at a rally in Queens where his support was reportedly growing, McGovern criticized Nixon for having removed several hundred acres from the Gateway NRA proposal.[67] The president had the final say on the matter, signing both Gateway and Golden Gate NRA into the national park system on October 28, just weeks before the election.[68]

The urban park idea has merits. Gateway and Golden Gate offer sixty thousand acres of relatively natural land within easy access of more than twenty million people. Within years, urban parks had also been established near Cleveland (Cuyahoga), Atlanta (Chattahoochee), Boston (Lowell), New Orleans (Jean Lafitte), Los Angeles (Santa Monica), and Philadelphia (Pinelands). Many of the nearby people had enjoyed little opportunity to visit the more traditional western parks. As one advocate said, these parks enabled the NPS to get involved "into the gut, controversial issues—racial harmony, jobs, etc." that trouble American society.[69] These places offered recreation for city dwellers, particularly appealing following the urban riots of the 1960s. In a more political vein, some of the leadership of the NPS welcomed the opportunity to appeal to a new, and potentially supportive, constituency of urban dwellers.[70] In addition, these new units did contain some valuable areas. As the Conservation Foundation survey concluded, these parks often contained "significant cultural and natural resources ... threatened by suburban growth."[71] Further, the units often utilized land that was already publicly owned, such as abandoned military bases.

Still, the place of urban parks in the national park system is questionable. None of them are in the relatively pristine condition of more remote areas. Further, the explicit goal for managers of these places is to provide recreational outlets, a goal quite different from that of preserving natural or historical conditions in other units. Perhaps most problematic to the NPS is that these parks are expensive. Even if initial establishment costs are not that much, Gateway originally cost $92.8 million, for example, maintenance and operating costs are high. The costs at Presidio, added in the 1990s, included $100 million to update road, water, and electrical systems and then at least $45 million per year for maintaining grounds and buildings.[72] Nor do these parks bring in much revenue since they are so accessible that even if the NPS wanted to charge fees, they would have a difficult time setting up entrance gates.

Unfortunately for the agency, the total operating budget for the NPS has not gone up correspondingly with the addition of the urban units. Thus, the money to operate Gateway and the others has to come from the funds for other parks that seem more consistent with the agency mission. Little wonder that NPS employees offered mixed reactions to the new units. In addition to diluting the budget, some argued that the role of the agency was not to conduct social policy.[73] Ultimately, many view the urban parks as an "experiment" including some successes but at very high prices.[74]

Alaska

The debate over expansion in Alaska actually started in 1971. In that year, Congress passed the Alaska Native Claims Settlement Act that included among other things Section 17(d)(2) designating eighty million acres of land to be studied for possible establishment as national parks, wildlife refuges, scenic rivers, or forests. The so-called "d-2" lands contained some magnificent territory that was also rich in oil, minerals, and timber. Secretary of the Interior Morton was given two years to make a recommendation regarding these lands, and in 1973 he called for 83.5 million acres to be set aside, including 32.2 million in nine national parks. Congress had until 1978 to respond to this recommendation and actually did little until 1977. At that point, President Carter's Interior Secretary Andrus submitted a new recommendation that increased the park portion to 41.8 million acres.

The subsequent debate was intense. Proponents, including the fifty-two conservation organizations that had joined together to form the Alaska Coalition, supported a House of Representatives bill (H.R. 39) championed by Representative Mo Udall (D–AZ) that actually increased the protection offered in the Andrus proposal. Some of the proposed areas were, as NPS historian Everhart said, "so enormous that entire ecosystems could be preserved."[75] The fact that the agency historian would remark about this suggests just what a new concept it was for park system expansion. As Alaska Coalition official Edgar Wayburn said, "In Alaska we have the opportunity to learn from our past mistakes." Wayburn even cited the Redwoods and several other "mistakes."[76]

Though Udall's bill passed in the House, this version met strong opposition in the Senate. Opponents included many state residents who wanted these lands available for economic development. They argued that federal designation of over one hundred million acres not only locked up valuable resources but violated state's rights. Among the opponents were many Alaska residents including Governor Jay

Hammond who criticized federal designation as "a de facto repeal of statehood." Senator Mike Gravel (R–AK), supported by Senator Ted Stevens (R–AK) and Representative Don Young (R–AK), managed to stop passage of a compromise bill in the Senate before the 1978 deadline could be reached. Gravel's alternative would have protected only twenty-five million total acres. The congressional session ended without protection of the d-2 lands.

Ultimately, the fate of the d-2 lands was determined by Congress and two different presidents. Before 1978 ended, President Carter rescued the failed efforts in the Senate. Under the authority of the 1906 Antiquities Act, Carter and his Interior secretary provided federal protection for over one hundred million acres, declaring roughly half as national monuments. This delaying action enabled Congress to resume deliberation on what Carter called his "number-one environment priority." Again, the acrimonious debate slowed progress on the legislation until the election of 1980. Faced with the coming arrival of newly elected President Reagan and his antiexpansion administration, proponents were forced to accept a much different version of H.R. 39 than they wanted. As Udall said, "Political realities dictate that we act promptly on the Senate-passed bill. . . . We must accept the fact that Reagan is here for four years."[77]

Not surprisingly then, the Alaska Lands Act was full of political compromises. The legislation did create roughly one hundred million acres as protected federal lands, including 43.6 million in new or expanded (as at Denali) parklands. More than half of the lands were also to receive wilderness designation so as to remain virtually unchanged by human hands. However, the legislation also exempted a vast area of Gates of the Arctic from wilderness designation to enable the continuation of copper mining. A substantial area of Misty Fjords National Monument was taken out of the plan so that U.S. Borax could continue mining. The coastal plain of the Arctic National Wildlife Refuge was exempted from wilderness status and thus subject to future controversy regarding energy exploration. The bill, in a last-minute concession to Senator Stevens, continued federal funding of timber-cutting in much of southeastern Alaska. Roughly twenty million acres were set aside as national preserves rather than national parks, the former designation allowing considerably more discretion in terms of use than the latter. Perhaps most problematic for preservation of natural conditions was that few guarantees for implementation and subsequent decisons on these vast lands, even the parks, were written into the law. Many issues were to be settled by subsequent administrations and congresses after all.[78]

Growth at Political Convenience

System expansion continued in the 1980s and 1990s when convenient for political actors. The NPS had little control over the decisions regarding expansion that were made.

The Reagan Years

In 1981 Secretary of the Interior James Watt signalled a new era when he announced, "We must be stewards of what we have before we reach out for more."[79] Watt actually had little interest in stewardship, but he was determined to avoid reaching out for more parklands. Immediately upon entering office, Watt slapped a moratorium on parkland acquisition. Funds to be available from the LWCF were withheld from the NPS. This included roughly $800 million to purchase inholdings within existing parks that had already been identified by the agency. Watt even refused to accept a gift of Army surplus land for Gateway NRA only to be forced otherwise by court action.[80] Permission for conducting land transactions was removed from NPS field professionals so that only the administration had final say. Most field requests were rejected. The Office of New Area Studies was also dismantled through budget cuts during this time. System expansion continued but it was at the mercy of congressional whims.

Congress filled the void left by executive abdication. James Ridenour, NPS director in the late 1980s, testified in 1995 that "The Executive branch basically stepped away from the responsibility of running the NPS and it essentially became a captive of the Congress during these years."[81] Congress defended its authority by eventually rejecting some of Secretary Watt's proposals, for example appropriating some funds for acquisition in 1982 and 1983 even after Watt had requested none.[82] Watt and others, especially Budget Director Stockman, also wanted to deauthorize several of the urban parks but met stiff congressional resistance.[83] According to Ridenour, between 1983 and 1993, the NPS received $1.4 billion more than it had requested for construction and acquisition. However, most of the money was designated for congressional projects, as Ridenour testified, "not high on the priority list of the NPS, if they appeared on the list at all."[84]

The establishment of Great Basin, the only national park added during the Reagan years, resulted from political considerations. As shown in table 3-6, the Great Basin area has been severely unrepresented. The NPS advocated a national park there and was supported by at least one member of the Nevada delegation for over twenty different sessions of Congress. Advocates of a park there had been stymied for years by Nevada mining and ranching interests. The logjam was broken only when Senator Paul Laxalt (R–NV), a staunch Reagan ally, retired and the president wanted to honor him. According to NPS planner Galvin, the administration reversed its opposition based on mining only when Laxalt said he wanted the park.[85] Even then, cattle grazing was allowed to continue within the park, a compromise justified by designating cows as part of the natural ecosystem.[86] Further, one of the country's largest copper mines continues to operate just west of the park.

By the end of the Reagan years, as a result of political impacts, many areas remained unrepresented, underrepresented, or represented by significantly compromised units. In 1988 the National Parks and Conservation Association (NPCA) listed forty-six areas as still needing protection in order to fill gaps in the natural regions and natural history themes. The NPCA also identified over forty historic sites that needed to be added to the system. These included Civil War sites, places of significance for American Indians, and other historic landmarks.[87] Though some have since been achieved, such as the War in the Pacific NHP, most remain undesignated.[88] Efforts to establish units commemorating important but controversial periods in American history, such as the pre–Civil War underground railroad and the World War II internment center at Manzanar await funding. Ultimately, the NPCA called on the NPS to revise and update its 1972 plan.[89] Scientific assessments of system expansion agree that most of the recommendations in the plan were "largely ignored."[90]

Congressional Dominance

Congressional dominance of the expansion process continued through the years of the Bush and Clinton presidencies. Director of planning Galvin recalled that the NPS, during the Bush years, did revitalize new areas planning using systematic criteria and priority lists submitted by personnel. These procedures continued under President Clinton. However, the impact of the office was diminished. As Galvin said, "Our lists didn't move as fast as they might because our studies were being displaced by lists from Congress."[91]

Indeed, while the system did not expand dramatically, the actions that were taken carried a distinct flavor of pork. In retrospective hearings in 1995, several noted experts testified as to the impact of congressional intervention. One agency official said, "The approach in recent years has become increasingly political with standards for national significance which were envisioned by the Congress in 1916 being subverted by the need, it appears to us, to have some type of area with the term 'national' in its title in every congressional district."[92] Historian

Robin Winks added, "Many of the inappropriate units (in the system) were produced through political clout by Congress."[93]

Questionable sites such as Fire Island National Wilderness Area, Roger Williams National Historic Site, and Allegheny Portage National Historic Site were offered by their relevant congressional representatives as filling niches within the overall plan. Ron Foresta's fascinating account of some of this expansion concludes, "The net result of congressional interest in historical parks was that the Service's determinations of national significance, carefully laid out in the 1972 plan, usually counted for less than whatever impromptu notions of significance were advanced by congressmen."[94]

The most egregious example of congressional manipulation involved the previously mentioned Steamtown National Historic Site. Steamtown became an NPS unit in 1986 when Representative Joe McDade (R–PA) amended the Omnibus Appropriation Bill to include funding for converting an abandoned rail yard into a historic site. As the ranking minority member of the House Appropriations Committee, McDade had enough clout to funnel significant funds back to his district for the conversion of the yard and purchases of various steam trains. The creation of Steamtown had little to do with historic preservation. Indeed, as documented elsewhere, justifying Steamtown on historical grounds has been difficult.[95] To give some sense of the money flowing to Steamtown, the total funds appropriated are well over four times the average annual operating budget for Yosemite.[96] Although McDade himself was under federal indictment for bribe charges during much of this time, he retained his position on the Appropriations Committee and Steamtown continued to receive funding well into the 1990s.

Steamtown is perhaps the most blatant example of congressional manipulation of site selection but hardly the only one. Representative Murtha (D–PA) and other officials have nurtured development of "America's Industrial Heritage" covering four units within the NPS system connected by a five-hundred-mile vehicular tour across nine counties. Between 1989 and 1993, Congress appropriated $63 million with the promise of significantly more to come.[97] The 1990 budget was so loaded with last-minute add-on projects that some NPS veterans were referring to their agency as the "National Pork Service." The budget included, for example, $4.5 million appropriated for renovating the historic Keith-Albee Theater in West Virginia at the behest of Senator Byrd (D–WV). Even then Senator Gore (D–TN) got into the act, securing $500,000 for the Cordell Hull (Franklin Roosevelt's secretary of state) NHS despite the fact that an anonymous NPS official said, "We don't do secretaries of state and never have. . . . We do presidents."[98]

One costly example of unplanned expansion is the Presidio. The 217-year-old military installation has been destined to become NPS responsibility since 1972 when Representative Burton amended the legislation establishing Golden Gate NRA to the effect that if the Defense Department ever abandoned the base, it would become NPS property. In 1989 the Base Closure Commission listed the Presidio to be closed. Representative Nancy Pelosi (D–CA), backed by Senator Diane Feinstein (D–CA) and others, then encouraged protection of the whole base: "Should we sell Yosemite? Should we sell the Grand Canyon? This is the same kind of national resource, and we have a responsibility to protect it."[99] Other members have questioned retention of the entire facility, bowling alleys and all. The NPS had no control over the final decision, although they did offer the revealing cost estimates cited earlier. The agency also estimates that future appropriations will not exceed $25 million annually.[100] Nevertheless, the Presidio officially joined the park system in September of 1994. Since then, the NPS has been forced to seek tenants and lessees for it that might use various structures to defray expenses.

In addition to consequences of site selection and cost, congressional manipulation of the expansion process also affects the timing of decisions. An illustrative example of the impact of politics on timing involves the Jazz Historical Park in New Orleans. The NPS had long pushed for some official recognition of this truly American art form. Finally in 1989, director of planning Galvin coordinated with the New Orleans Historical Society and drafted a bill for Senator J. Bennett Johnston to submit to Congress that would commemorate sites such as the Eagle Saloon and the Black Musicians' Hall. Johnston showed little interest in the legislation, however, until he was challenged by former KKK member David Duke in 1992. Needing the black vote for reelection, Johnston initiated the process for the new jazz site. Interestingly, Johnston did not win the white vote in Louisiana and thus owes his victory to black support. Attributing this support solely to the creation of the Jazz Historical Park would be an overstatement, but certainly such an action did not hurt Johnston's standing with many black voters. Galvin calls this a "textbook example of how new units are created."[101]

Finally, units that are created are compromised or incomplete. The most recent example of compromise involves the previously mentioned Tallgrass Prairie National Preserve in Kansas. Tallgrass prairies have been commonly cited as "the most significant missing element of the National Park System."[102] Less than 2% of these once vast prairies remains, much of it in the Flint Hills area of Kansas. Proponents of a park pushed for six decades to preserve some of this area but were opposed by local ranchers and farm groups. Even recent attempts in 1988 and 1991 were stopped.[103] Prospects in 1995 were strengthened largely because the bill was sponsored by most of the Kansas delegation, including Republican Senator Nancy Kassebaum and Senator Bob Dole, then Majority Leader. When the Tallgrass Prairie National Preserve was established in the Omnibus Parks Bill of 1996, the designation was not quite what earlier proponents had pursued. The National Park Trust will donate 180 acres to the NPS while the remaining 10,714 will stay in private hands. The 180-acre segment will include the historic buildings and an interpretive center and parking lot. The NPS will help manage the area, but local citizens will design the General Management Plan. When I visited the site in the fall of 1995, the plans were still in limbo. The caretaker of the Z Bar Ranch, the property in the middle of the proposed site, was quite realistic that if the site was approved, it would be much different than what was once envisioned.[104] Zurhellen and other supporters were well aware that current political conditions, not the existence of long-term plans, would determine the fate of these natural lands.

The failure to complete units is another problem. Over two million acres of private land, worth billions of dollars, exist within park boundaries.[105] As private land, these "inholdings" can be used, developed, logged, or mined. Political maneuvering has impeded purchase of inholdings, causing delays during which the price of land increases. For example, the NPS began purchasing lands within the Santa Monica Mountains NRA in 1978 only to be stopped by Secretary Watt's moratorium. Various areas within the park, such as the Currey-Riach Ranch, were instead taken over by real estate developers. Other areas came to the Park Service in subsequent years only at inflated prices or with significant strings attached.[106] Similar experiences occurred at urban parks, the Channel Islands, and even the Grand Tetons.[107] One factor making this record so frustrating is that money was available. The LWCF continued to pull in nearly $1 billion a year from fees and offshore oil leasing during the 1980s, but Congress was appropriating less than $250 million annually. Thus, over $5 billion built up in the fund by the end of the 1980s. That money does little good now at places like Santa Cruz Island. As Michael Wootton, chief of staff for local Representative Elton Gallegly (R–Simi Valley) says, "There was a time when these funds were forthcoming. It's highly unlikely now."[108]

The Future of System Expansion

The future for expansion of the national park system is very much in question. One possibility is a stop to most federal purchases. After taking over the majority in Congress in 1994, Republican lawmakers proposed legislation that would compensate landowners for regulatory actions that reduce property values by as little as 10%. Such a mechanism would make new units, purchases of inholdings in existing units, and establishment of buffer zones for parks prohibitively expensive. Members have also withdrawn money from the LWCF and used those funds for other purposes. Although the LWCF is supposed to consist of an annual pot of $900 million, little has been used in recent years for land acquisition. In 1996 and 1997, only about $140 million was appropriated each year to that end. Congress promised nearly $700 million in LWCF spending for 1998 but immediately designated much of that amount for purposes other than land acquisition.[109]

A second possibility is actual reduction of the system. Some members of Congress have recently expressed interest in proposals by conservative think tanks and interest groups to privatize the parks. Official action has been proposed on a broader attempt to close many units. In 1995 Republicans pushed legislation termed the National Park System Reform Act that was more often called the "park closure bill."[110] H.R. 260, sponsored by Representative Joel Hefley (R–CO), would have required the NPS to assess each unit for cost, national significance, and alternative management schemes. If the NPS did not comply within one year, then the bill would establish a park review commission of political appointees who could close park units.[111]

This proposal was abandoned after several objections were raised. First, although Hefley compared his commission favorably to the efficient military base closure commission, his was much more politicized in that the military has considerable input into base closures whereas the NPS would have little influence on the park commission decisions. Indeed, Section 103 (i) explicitly limited NPS involvement in preparation of the closure list. Second, according to Section 104 of the bill, the decisions of the park commission would be subject only to "appropriate" citizen input, and would be explicitly exempted from National Environmental Policy Act requirements.[112] Third, many suspected the whole procedure was a wolf in sheep's clothing, an elaborate effort to create the means to easily eliminate many units of the system. In July of 1995, Representative James Hansen (R–UT) suggested that 150 units of the system should be closed or privatized. Indeed, one piece of evidence that such a commission is a means to another agenda is that Congress already has the ability to terminate units of the park system. In fact, it has done so twenty-three times since the 1940s.[113]

One possibility for the future involves expansion in a different way. In 1993, at the urging of Interior Secretary Babbitt, the National Biological Service was created. The NBS merged biological scientists from seven different bureaus into a joint effort to conduct a national biological survey determining ecosystems that warrant protection. Those initial efforts received minimal political support in the next two years, leading to frustration among the scientists who found that members of Congress were generally interested in the national survey only in so far as it affected their own districts. In 1995 the NBS budget was cut significantly and the agency was renamed the Natural Resources Science Agency to be part of the U.S. Geological Survey.[114]

One other possibility involves a concept that director of planning Galvin and others in the agency are developing. This would designate entire areas with common themes as National Heritage Areas "containing natural, historic, scenic, and cultural resources and recreational and educational opportunities that are geographically assembled and thematically related."[115] For example, the proposed Essex NHA would encompass sites such as the Saugus Iron Works and Salem Historic Site in Essex County, Massachusetts. As of 1996, this concept had gained considerable bipartisan support, but not surprisingly among members whose districts would gain tourism benefits. The 1996 Omnibus Parks Bill authorized eight new Heritage Areas, most of them, as Clapper admits, "politically motivated."[116]

Assessment

The U.S. national park system in 1995 consisted of 367 units, including fifty-one national parks. The different kinds of units are listed in table 3-8. The existence of many of these units has little to do with long-term plans.

The national park system is, without question, larger and more diverse in 1995 than it had been in 1965. Growth has brought both important and questionable units into the system. In all cases, the details and timing and costs of the new units have been determined politically. Further, the merits of the diversification of the system are debatable.[117] The park system has been diversified for various reasons such as placing units in specific congressional districts, reaching out to new constituencies, and expanding the power base of the NPS. While many of the nontraditional units obviously warrant safeguarding, although some would say not by the NPS, the fact remains that the system as a whole was diversified more for these other reasons than to facilitate protection of previously unrepresented ecosystems and historic themes. Even now, proposals exist to add units that range from abandoned nuclear missile silos to the historic baseball parks at Yankee Stadium, Tiger Stadium, Fenway Park, and Wrigley Field.[118]

Internally, officials within the NPS are candid and critical. The agency has not attempted a systematic evaluation of progress on the

TABLE 3-8
National Park System Units As of 1995

Type of Unit	Number
International Historic Site	1
National Battlefields	11
National Battlefield Parks	3
National Battlefield Site	1
National Historic Sites	72
National Historical Parks	36
National Lakeshores	4
National Memorials	26
National Military Parks	9
National Monuments	76
National Parks	51
National Parkways	4
National Preserves	14
National Recreation Areas	18
National Reserves	2
National Rivers	6
National Scenic Trails	3
National Seashores	10
National Wild and Scenic Rivers	9
Other Park Units	11
Total System Units	367

1972 plan. However, in their self-examination of the NPS in 1992, agency personnel and outside experts included an assessment of system expansion. The report states, "As the National Park Service has expanded, units and programs have been added that arguably have lacked sufficient national significance to warrant National Park Service designation. Yet, such additions to the system have had sufficient constituent appeal and/or economic development benefits in selected regions to secure their inclusion in the Park Service portfolio."[119] Clapper says bluntly, "I don't think you could name a park that's been recently created that did not have strong political support."[120]

Past NPS officials are as candid as current employees about political manipulation of the expansion process. Former directors Hartzog and Ridenour have both published scathing reviews of recent expansion. Ridenour writes, "Many of the new parks and projects approved by Congress were unworthy of NPS status or support but got voted in anyway."[121] Former chief of policy development Dwight Rettie concludes, "There is no plan or planning process for the whole national park system. All planning is park or site specific."[122]

The clearest conclusion, not just from the current activity in Congress but also from the history of system growth, is that the NPS has little control over which units are added to the system, when, in what form, or how they might be removed. The growth of the U.S. national park system has been and will continue to be determined by political calculations, not by the goals of long-term planners.

ENHANCEMENT OF INDIVIDUAL UNITS

In addition to expansion, systematic preservation goals also include ecological restoration of individual units. The two processes are not unrelated. Indeed, many unit plans focus on alteration of boundaries or modification of practices that were authorized upon establishment of park units. As described earlier, boundary lines were initially drawn for political, not ecological, reasons. As Wright and his scientists wrote in 1933, "At present, not one park is large enough to provide year-round sanctuary for adequate populations of all resident species."[123] Between Wright's assessment and 1988, over five hundred boundary adjustments were made to nearly two hundred NPS units.[124] Were these adjustments ecologically responsive? When I asked NPS director of planning Galvin about this, he responded, "I can't think of an example of ecological input into a park boundary."[125]

Long-Term Planning for Ecological Restoration

In a survey published in 1994, NPS superintendents gave an average grade of only C+ to the natural resource condition of national parks.[126] Natural conditions in parks have suffered from both internal and external threats. Table 3-9 summarizes some of these threats identified in 1980.

Internal Threats
National park managers and observers have long been aware of the internal threats to natural conditions facing parks. The impacts of intensive visitation, for example, prompted the 1953 article advocating limits mentioned earlier. Many of these threats, such as traffic and congestion and the deterioration of park infrastructure, have since intensified.

Other studies describe some of these threats in considerable detail.[127] Several are shown in the left-hand column of table 3-9. To review briefly, natural conditions in parks suffer from severe development

TABLE 3-9
Park Threats by Category (1980)

Category	Internal	External
Air Pollution	83 (12%)	609 (88%)
Water Pollution	142 (30%)	324 (70%)
Aesthetic Degradation	423 (39%)	662 (61%)
Physical Removal of Resources	376 (59%)	262 (41%)
Exotic Encroachment	277 (46%)	325 (54%)
Visitor Physical Impacts	399 (79%)	106 (21%)
Park Operations	254 (71%)	103 (29%)

Source: U.S. NPS, 1980, *State of the Parks*: 4.

and commercialization in many places. Over one-third of the roads in parks are in need of repair. The U.S. General Accounting Office estimates a backlog of needed repairs to park infrastructure of at least $4 billion. Crime is a major problem in some parks, the total number of offenses per year for the whole system is well over forty thousand.

What is particularly problematic is that the agency has not received funding to keep up with even the most basic problems. Table 3-10 shows the total appropriations to the NPS over recent years in constant dollars. Put most simply, appropriations to the agency have not kept pace with inflation. Obviously, the NPS received more real dollars in 1983 than it did in 1993, while over that same decade, visitation increased by 36%. Different years can be substituted to get slightly different results, but the fact remains that funding has not been increased to allow the agency to keep up with more visitors and greater challenges.

Problems resulting from funding shortages are made worse by the fact that even the money that is appropriated to the parks is not necessarily available for priority projects. Table 3-11 shows congressional add-ons in the form of line-item funding for specific projects. In many years, add-ons dwarf agency requests. One might think this means more money overall is available to the agency. Instead, the add-on money is part of the total budget for the agency. Whatever money is committed to congressionally mandated projects is not then available elsewhere. Substitution leads to backlogs and delays in implementation of long-term plans. As Clapper says, "Had Congress not been doing add-ons and stuff like that, many of our needs would have been met."

External Threats

The last twenty years have brought increased awareness of external threats as well. In 1979 two organizations, the NPCA and the Conserva-

TABLE 3-10
Annual Appropriations to the NPS (in constant 1987 dollars)

Fiscal Year	Acquisition, Planning, & Development	Total Appropriations
1981	236.4	1100.8
1982	269.8	955.6
1983	291.1	1219.5
1984	224.3	1036.0
1985	217.7	1010.9
1986	146.3	871.0
1987	166.1	879.0
1988	158.6	943.2
1989	232.9	998.2
1990	248.1	990.6
1991	348.3	1190.5
1992	329.2	1229.9
1993	267.5	1146.8
1994	234.7	1174.9

Sources: U.S. D.O.I. *Budget Justifications:* FY1991, p. NPS–12; FY 1997, p. NPS–24.

TABLE 3-11
NPS Line-Item Construction Funding (in millions of dollars)

Fiscal Year	Requested	Appropriated	Add-ons (% of App)
1983	69.1	92.5	23.4 (25)
1984	61.6	95.2	33.6 (35)
1985	61.7	92.6	30.9 (33)
1986	50.0	94.8	44.8 (47)
1987	19.3	72.0	52.7 (73)
1988	19.3	77.1	57.8 (75)
1989	6.6	141.3	134.7 (95)
1990	23.2	156.7	133.5 (85)
1991	52.5	156.7	104.2 (67)
1992	84.2	216.6	132.4 (61)
1993	94.0	172.5	78.5 (46)

Source: U.S. NPS 1995, *Denver Service Center Annual Report:* 16.

tion Foundation, published reports describing the impacts from external activities, such as mining and logging in nearby areas, on lands adjacent to the parks.[128] As the right-hand column of table 3-9 shows, the NPS estimates that more than 50% of the threats to the parks arose outside of park boundaries.[129] Park boundaries are not adequate for redress of these threats. In 1988 the NPCA used maps, surveys, site studies, and interviews to describe the boundaries of nearly two hundred units as inadequate. As the study states, "The lack of a consistent process for determining boundaries based upon resource-oriented criteria means that economic and political concerns, albeit important, often override resource needs."[130] The historical record reveals several points.

First, even when planners try to draw natural boundaries for a park unit, defining the essential ecosystem may be difficult. The first park unit created explicitly to preserve natural conditions rather than just to present scenery is an example. Although the Everglades constitutes a good portion of the lower third of the state of Florida, the park is still only a fragment of the necessary ecosystem. In part, this is due to the fact that the park is in such a wet environment, where contaminants are quite mobile. For example, water-quality monitoring stations have detected phosphorous, a fertilizer used on farms sixty miles away, entering the park area at ten times the natural rate, affecting the algae that provides the food base for all Everglades species. Also, however, the original boundaries of the park left out several vital pieces of the ecosystem. These include river sloughs, such as the East Shark River, that provide major water sources for the park. The lack of management of these areas and their commercial use and development has altered water cycles in the park. As a result, the flow of freshwater from upland areas to the park has been reduced by as much as 90%.[131] In a massive study, a team of scientists concluded that restoring the Everglades ecosystem will be difficult and uncertain.[132]

Second, expansion advocates may sacrifice opportunities if they are too greedy in their efforts. In an attempt to expand Grand Canyon to more natural boundaries in 1975, Senator Barry Goldwater (R–AZ), with the assistance of environmental groups, attempted to create a buffer zone around the park. Natural conditions within the zone would be enhanced through prohibition of activities like mining in the buffer zone. This rather unlikely coalition fell apart before the bill could be passed when the environmentalists later insisted that the buffer zone lands actually be included in park area, a demand that Goldwater furiously rejected.[133] As a result, this expansion never occurred.

Third, even successful redraws may be achieved only with compromises. The original Grand Teton National Park encompassed only the

Teton range. When conservationists tried to redraw the boundary lines in the 1930s to include the Jackson Hole Valley, local hunters and their representatives resisted. In 1943 President Roosevelt declared part of the desired area a national monument to be added to the park, but Congress cut off funds. The solution, achieved in 1950, combined the two units, but only after Grand Teton became the first park to allow hunting.[134]

Fourth, even potentially significant redraws will not ameliorate certain severe external threats. Some external threats, such as air pollution and acid rain, arise from sources long distances from the parks. One prominent example involves Shenandoah. Shenandoah has a creative plan for park expansion involving a core area of 250,000 acres with another 135,000 acres designated for eventual acquisition.[135] Even if the park ever does attain these acres (at this point, the core has not been completed), the major threat to park resources will still be active. Air quality and visibility in Shenandoah have been drastically affected by air pollution from power plants that are miles away from the park.[136]

Fifth, getting other landowners to sell or cooperate with NPS efforts may be prohibitively expensive or unrealistic. According to Joseph Carlton, chairman of the Committee on the Bob Marshall Ecosystem, the Glacier–Bob Marshall area could be intact as an ecosystem except for "Forest Service reluctance" to cooperate with the NPS in their efforts.[137] At Point Reyes National Seashore, the owners of the Giacomini Ranch on the edge of the park claim they are willing to sell, but they want the NPS to lease back their property so that they can continue farming.[138] Finally, the strong opposition to Tallgrass Prairie Preserve reflected by local behavior and the signs along the highways mentioned earlier is a perfect example of lack of local endorsement.

NPS redress of external threats through boundary adjustments at historic sites has also been stymied by political actions. Commercial encroachment is perhaps even worse at historic sites than at natural areas since their boundaries are often less clearly marked. The most prominent example in recent years involved Manassas Battlefield in northern Virginia. In 1978 Senator William Scott (R–VA) stopped an expansion of Manassas in the Park Barrel Bill that might have precluded a major controversy in the 1990s. In that instance, preservation groups stopped plans by the Walt Disney Company to build a theme park nearby, but the land in question is still zoned for residential and commercial use. Also, the highway through the park, U.S. 29, has been proposed for expansion.[139] For another example, perhaps the most sacred site of the Civil War, Gettysburg, is also endangered by territorial encroachment. Certain portions of the battlefield were destroyed after a land deal turned over 7.5 acres to Gettysburg College.[140] Similar problems were avoided at Antietam only by expensive congressional purchase of lands slated for development.[141]

As a result of the failure to redraw park unit boundaries, the general conclusion has consistently been that external threats remain virtually unabated. General Accounting Office reviews in 1987, 1994, and 1995 report that most external problems remain unaddressed, if not undocumented.[142] The growing property rights movement may make federal acquisition or boundary adjustments even more difficult than in the past. Further, careful consideration of park boundaries is not yet a systematic procedure throughout the NPS. As NPS planner Galvin sadly concluded, "I don't know that we'll ever get to the point where you have a boundary that respects resource preservation, boundaries are political by nature."[143]

Need for Long-Term Plans

Long-term planning for individual units is obviously not limited to redrawing boundaries. Agency planners must attempt to address a variety of threats, both internal and external, that can affect natural conditions in the parks. These include such a wide range that they are best discussed in terms of individual parks. However, one general point should be reiterated. These restoration plans are subject to political manipulation just as are efforts to change park boundaries.

Yellowstone

When I first walked into Superintendent Mike Finley's office and told him that my research was on planning for the long term, he laughed. Later, when I told park planner Beth Kaeding that my research question concerned long-term planning, she laughed. When I asked chief planner John Sacklin about long-term planning, he also laughed. While the subsequent discussions with all three NPS employees were quite informative, the consistency of their initial reactions to my lead question had already told me volumes. Later, I spoke with Bob Ekey of the Greater Yellowstone Coalition. I told him that my research involved long-term planning by the NPS and he too laughed. So I asked him, "Why is planning for the long term such a funny idea?" His answer was succinct: "Things get politicized."

Background

The need for long-term planning at the world's first national park has been recognized throughout its history but rarely effectively acted upon. Although the 1872 establishing legislation calls for "preservation" of park resources "in their natural condition," little was done to that effect prior to the 1920s. In 1919, Superintendent Horace Albright hired biologist Milton Skinner as a "naturalist" to conduct research on natural processes within the area. As Skinner wrote in 1928, "Almost nothing has been written to show how unscientific, how careless, we have been in the Yellowstone National Park area in the past."[144] George Wright also found long-range prospects for the elk herds to be "deplorable."[145] Prompted by the studies of Wright, Skinner, Adolph Murie, and others, the NPS began implementing some fledgling proposals for restoration by altering the boundaries of the park in 1929 to include certain natural features and by physically manipulating the sizes of animal populations in the park. These efforts ultimately led to the creation of the Wildlife Division at the national level, headed by Wright, to oversee scientific projects at Yellowstone and elsewhere. Unfortunately, the momentum for this emphasis died with Wright in 1936. Long-term planning at Yellowstone then floundered for decades.

Prompted by increased environmental awareness, the Leopold Report, and a supportive political climate, the NPS released a Master Plan for Yellowstone in 1974. Publication followed a two-year process involving drafts, hearings, and solicitation of public input. The long-term emphasis of the plan was stated explicitly on the first page: "But, if Yellowstone is to survive the next 100 years, a new equilibrium must be achieved."[146]

A classic illustration of the fate of this plan concerns the Fishing Bridge area. A major proposal in the 1974 plan called for a compromise, the building of Grant Village in the South as a tourist center in exchange for the return to natural conditions of the Fishing Bridge area in the East.[147] Both locations are potentially prime grizzly bear habitat. The NPS has since tried to close down the campground, gas station, store, and recreational vehicle park at Fishing Bridge only to be stymied by what the park's superintendent called "policy consideration beyond Yellowstone."[148] Wyoming's senators, representing commercial interests in neighboring Cody, have prevented the agency from removing the commercial facilities and the 350-unit RV park. Meanwhile, Grant Village has grown to over seven hundred lodging units, three restaurants, and several stores. Efforts to restore either area to natural conditions have been stopped by the Wyoming and Montana congressional delegations.[149]

The 1974 plan also recognized that "if future demands to visit Yellowstone are to be met, an alternative to the private automobile must be provided" and called for development of a transit system that could use existing roads to bus visitors to the various sites in the park.[150] Implementation of this proposal was not as explicitly contradicted as at Fishing Bridge but rather was undermined by lack of funding. The money that has been available to the park has been used for stopgap measures, such as patching roads, rather than revising transportation through the purchase of buses and construction of terminals. By 1991 only 60 of the 410 paved road miles in the park were in good condition. The park thus has to devote nearly all of the $1 million/year in the Cyclic Road Program to immediate repairs rather than pursuit of long-range goals.[151] Further, with a backlog of over $28 million in repair work, future prospects for funding for alternative sources of transportation are in doubt.

The 1974 plan also formalized a fire policy to restore natural conditions over the long term. Prior to 1972, fire policy had been one of suppression of all fires. As the 1974 plan recognized, however, fire is a natural process that is vital to certain biological processes. The plan thus called for letting natural fires burn in certain areas and prescribed burning when necessary.[152] Prescribed burning was rarely implemented between 1974 and 1988, thus allowing a buildup of dry fuel in the forests. The summer of 1988 was the driest on record for Yellowstone. July and August brought twice the normal amount of lightning and winds gusting up to seventy miles an hour. Before the summer was over, roughly 36% of the park had been burned. Local interests and their representatives in Congress skewered the NPS for the let-burn policy. Overriding scientific consideration of the lack of prescribed burning and recommendations from the NPS and other federal agencies to continue a modified let-burn policy, politicians demanded a fire policy that puts so many requirements on NPS personnel that fire suppression is the likely result. As Senator Malcom Wallop (R–WY) boasted upon release of the new policy, "All the words about natural fire are in there, but the fact is they're now going to have to suppress the fires. You and I know that no bureaucrat is going to sign a certification that he will not be outwitted by God and a wildfire."[153]

Systematic Preservation Efforts

The focus of ecological restoration changed over the past two dozen years. Whereas the 1974 Master Plan began, "With each passing year, Yellowstone becomes more and more valuable as an *island of wilderness serenity* (emphasis added) in the midst of a world suffering from the pollution of air, water, and land; from the destruction of animal and plant life; and from overpopulation," current plans display a broader emphasis.[154] Today, many planning efforts consider the larger ecosystem of which Yellowstone is the base. The greater Yellowstone ecosystem includes eighteen to nineteen million acres.[155] This area includes Yellowstone (2.2 million acres) and Grand Teton (.3 million) national parks as well as six national forests, three wildlife refuges, Bureau of Land Management (BLM) areas, state and some private lands.

Figure 3-1 displays the Greater Yellowstone ecosystem. The map was produced by the Greater Yellowstone Coalition, an alliance of concerned citizens and groups headquartered in Bozeman, Montana. As the map shows, the area is threatened by a variety of developments that have real and potential impacts on the park. External activities include geothermal drilling, logging, private ranching, and commercial development just outside park borders. Indeed, the western boundary of Yellowstone is marked by clear-cut areas up to the exact edge of the park.

Aware of these external threats, planners have made some progress towards emphasis on the ecosystem. The House Interior Subcommittee on National Parks held hearings in 1985 to discuss possible coordination of federal agency actions throughout the Yellowstone ecosystem, concluding that current communication and coordination efforts were deficient.[156] Officials from the principal agencies formed a Greater Yellowstone Coordinating Committee and endorsed the concept of cooperative interagency efforts to scientifically manage the region. More specific efforts at coordination, such as the Interagency Grizzly Bear Study Team, were at least initiated. A 1989 symposium sponsored by the University of Wyoming called for management of this area as "an integrated ecological entity."[157]

Implementation of NPS plans for the greater ecosystem have, however, so far been frustrated by political obstruction. The NPS prepared a planning document, *Vision for the Greater Yellowstone Area*, in 1990 that called for more cooperative efforts by federal agencies managing surrounding lands, but the plan drew the wrath of Senator Alan Simpson (R–WY) and then White House Chief of Staff John Sununu. Political overseers demanded substantial revisions to the plan. The supervisor of the document, Lorraine Mintzmayer, later testified that political appointees rewrote the report, cutting it from sixty to ten pages. Mintzmayer was transferred by political superiors, and she ultimately resigned. An investigation later revealed Department of the Interior memos confirming political censorship of the report.[158]

Problems with subsequent implementation of even the revised *Vision* plan illustrate the difficulty of attaining some version of ecosystem management. Various proposals were met with severe criticism from other interests in the ecosystem and by reluctant cooperation from other agencies. Management plans were stymied by the lack of boundaries that conformed to any scientific definition of what constituted the ecosystem.[159]

Political winds can occasionally make agency efforts at implementing ecosystem emphases more likely. One major recent threat to the Yellowstone ecosystem was from a mining proposal. Noranda, a Canadian company, proposed building a massive gold mining facility just

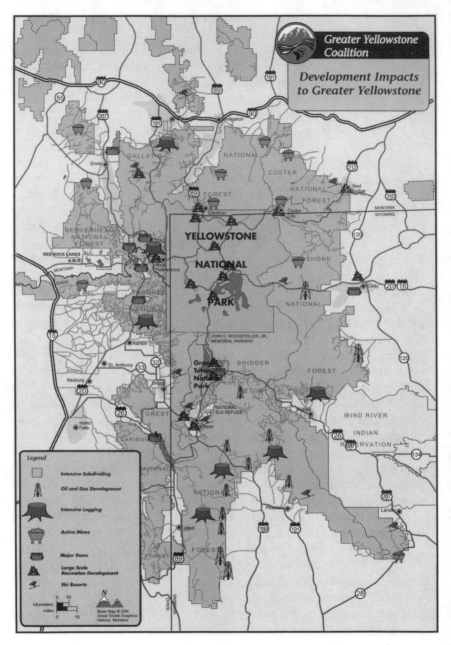

Figure 3-1   Development in the Greater Yellowstone Ecosystem

three miles northeast of the park in the Absaroka-Beartooth Wilderness. The area itself is rugged terrain serving grizzly bears and other wildlife that don't recognize where park boundaries start and stop. The immediate area and the entire region could have been affected. The mine area touched on watersheds for three Yellowstone rivers. Mine tailings would have been placed in an immense storage impoundment which, if breached, could drain toxic wastes directly upstream of the park. To make the scenario even more frightening, the area was classified as high risk for seismic activities. Superintendent Finley called it "putting acid waste in an envelope for perpetuity" and added, "They say it will last 100 years, but when I said 'then what' they didn't even answer."[160] Further, the Noranda company already had a devastating record of environmental violations and fines.

Fortunately for park planners, political circumstances favored stopping the mine. The public opposed it by strong majorities. Even a membership survey by the Cody Chamber of Commerce showed that over two-thirds of respondents opposed the Noranda mine.[161] Still, the mine proposal continued to move ahead until President Clinton struck a dramatic deal to shut down this mine in exchange for use of other federal land by Noranda. Clinton announced the deal on 12 August 1996, not coincidentally at the start of the Republican presidential convention, once again reminding voters of his environmental record. Actions affecting parks were again determined by political calculations, not by long-term planning for preservation of resources.

Like the Noranda case, many decisions at Yellowstone are not in agency hands. For example, because the mine would have been built on national forest land, the Forest Service wrote the Environmental Impact Statement (EIS). The Forest Service was receptive to Noranda's proposals and reluctant to do some of the tests, such as that for seismic analysis, requested by the NPS. Finley called the process "one of the poorest I've ever seen in terms of analysis or cooperation with surrounding agencies."[162] Many long-term projects face similar obstacles. Given that twenty-eight different public agencies exercise jurisdiction within the Greater Yellowstone ecosystem, coordination on Noranda and on many other long-term issues will remain problematic.[163] Many of these agencies are state and local. Finley says, "The only insulation parks have is that they are an instrument of the national government and that provides legal and political buffering from local politicians."

Other long-term threats to the Yellowstone ecosystem are pressing. Yellowstone planners are swamped with long-term projects awaiting implementation. Finley and the planning department track the various projects with a Priority List that categorizes according to timeframes and deadlines. Table 3-12 shows about half the list for summer of

TABLE 3-12
Yellowstone Priority List (1996)

Group I—Ongoing projects with nondiscretionary external (e.g., court-imposed) deadlines
    Bison Management Plan
    Madison-to-Norris Road Reconstruction
    Wolf Reintroduction
    Noranda Task Force
    Mammoth Housing Plan
Group II—Ongoing projects with nondiscretionary internal (NPS-imposed) deadlines
    Research Collecting Permits
    Lake Trout in Yellowstone Lake
    Grayling Restoration Plan
Group III—Ongoing projects with discretionary deadlines
    Backcountry Management Plan
    Abandoned Mine Lands Reclamation
    Snow Lodge Renovation
    Rehabitation of Turbid Lake Road
    Fishing Bridge Campsite Replacement
    Grizzly Bear Conservation Strategy
    Dunraven Pass Transportation Study
    Beartooth Highway Road Reconstruction
    Exotic Vegetation Control Plan
    Removal of Glen Creek Diversion
    Canyon Village Lodging Construction
    Archeological Site Monitoring Plan
Group IV—Projects to be started soon
    Historic Dump Evaluation
Group V—Future projects
    Boundary Lands Area Restoration
    Statement for Management
    Closure and Removal of Fishing Bridge Concessions
    Gardiner Service Center Redesign
    Bear Management Plan
    Backcountry Cabin and Lookout Inventory
    Prehistoric and Historic Trail Inventory
    Grant Village Marina Removal and Restoration

1996. Each project is assigned a leader (not printed here) to ensure coordination and accountability. Interestingly, removal of Fishing Bridge concession facilities is still listed as a future project.

Systematic, long-term planning is a luxury that can rarely be afforded. With limited funds and emergencies cropping up frequently, finding time is difficult. As planner Kaeding told me, "We go from crisis to crisis and can't, with government downsizing, devote resources to long-term planning."[164] Lack of attention to long-term planning is reinforced by funding procedures. Eric Compas, the NPS employee in charge of Geographic Information Systems for the park, said, "The way we get funded is on what we can show we did for a specific project for a specific time period, not for long-term systematic coordination even though there is a real need."[165] The park has not prepared a new General Management Plan (GMP) since 1974 nor a new Statement of Management since 1991. Finley intended to produce one for the 125th anniversary of the park in 1997, but he and others worried that the process itself would "bring controversies out of the woodwork."

While systematic implementation of long-term plans may be hard to find, Yellowstone personnel are making progress on some of the specific long-term projects listed in table 3-10. The project bringing the most pride to park employees currently is wolf reintroduction. The plan arose in the late 1980s. The long-term goal of the project was to restore Yellowstone's wildlife to a condition like that found when the park was first established. The gray wolf, eliminated from the ecosystem through hunting and government extermination between 1914 and 1926, was the only major wildlife component still missing in the 1980s. The NPS conducted studies on possible reintroduction of wolves to the area and, in 1990, received authorization to conduct an EIS for the idea.[166]

The current status of the wolf project illustrates both the promise for systematic preservation and the challenges. In spite of considerable local opposition from ranchers and others, the NPS successfully reintroduced packs of Canadian wolves into the area in the winter of 1995. While several wolves have since been killed when they wandered over park boundaries, even more have been born until now roughly forty wolves live in Yellowstone. Nearby communities remain split over the project, but Finley speaks for many when he says proudly, "I think it's been a success."[167] In spite of this "success," or perhaps because of it, a consortium of ranchers and farmers brought a lawsuit against the program. In late 1997, a federal judge ruled in favor of the lawsuit and, pending appeals, ordered removal of the reintroduced wolves from Yellowstone.

Counter examples to even tentatively successful stories are easy to find. During the same time the wolf packs were thriving in Yellowstone, the bison herds were suffering. The winter of 1996–97 was devastating. The bison, searching for grass under heavy snowfalls and enticed by roads packed down by snowmobiles, roamed outside park borders in vast numbers. Local authorities, fearing contamination of cattle herds by bison that might carry the disease brucellosis, shot the wandering animals. By the end of the winter, over a thousand animals or nearly one-third of the park's herd, had been killed. Finley and the other NPS employees were helpless to stop the killing, authorized by other political entities and occurring within the park's ecosystem but outside park boundaries.[168]

To summarize, some progress towards ecosystem management has been made in the first national park, but it remains limited. Agency personnel are dedicated to long-term efforts, but they remain constrained by low funding and political obstacles. Even a fairly optimistic compendium of research on the ecosystem published in 1991 concludes, "This evolutionary change in federal natural resource management policy is not coming easily in Greater Yellowstone."[169]

Grand Canyon

Someday the NPS would like the developed South Rim of the Grand Canyon to be more like the relatively pristine North Rim. Recently, Superintendent Rob Arnberger compared the two by saying, "People still talk in whispers as they approach the (North) rim."[170] I knew what he meant. In 1997 I visited the Grand Canyon by rail. As guest lecturer for the American Orient Express, I was travelling with a large group of people, many of whom had never seen this place that Theodore Roosevelt called "the one great sight that every American should see." The train pulled into the station just a short hike from the South Rim and my companions, having not been frustrated or hardened by fighting the traffic and congestion from intense automobile traffic on the road into the park, were able to approach the canyon in the early morning stillness. As we looked over the rim, the loudest sounds were sincere exclamations of awe. The NPS hopes to make such an experience more likely by removing cars from Grand Canyon and getting more people to visit by rail.

Background

Grand Canyon National Park contains over 1.2 million acres of canyons, side-canyons, rivers, mountains, and geologic history. The main canyon is home to a 277-mile stretch of the Colorado River that contains some of the world's most challenging whitewater. The exposed geologic strata on the mile-high canyon walls provide one of the most graphic displays of the earth's history to be found. The park's ecosystems range from desert to coniferous forests. When I hiked up Bright Angel Trail one March, the South Rim of the Grand Canyon was covered in snow while the campground at river level basked in seventy-five-degree sunshine.

The implementation of plans to maintain natural conditions within such a unique ecosystem is a challenging task. Significant political intervention has made the efforts of the NPS even more complex. Political involvement is pervasive at the Grand Canyon. Management assistant Mallory Smith says of canyon management, "Some people like to refer to us as apolitical, but politics is in everything we do, from some Congressman's visit to budget manipulation."[171]

The most obvious challenge facing park managers is providing services for the five million visitors per year without drastically altering the natural environment. Servicing these visitors has led to development of gift shops, restaurants, and hotels in Grand Canyon Village on the South Rim. For instance, more than two-thirds of the overnight visitors to Grand Canyon stay in lodges.[172] Park managers have historically lacked the political clout and funding to curtail much of the development along the South Rim or to provide a coordinated mass transportation system. As a result, the 1995 GMP admits, "The South Rim is too crowded during summer . . . The road system is heavily congested. . . ."[173] Recent development of the North Rim has stirred fears of alteration of natural conditions here as well.

Another obvious alteration to natural conditions in the park results from the Glen Canyon Dam on the Colorado River. The dam has controlled water levels and flows within the canyon since 1963. Despite the fact that the NPS called for "mitigat[ing] the influences of man's manipulation of the river" since the 1976 Master Plan, water flows have been determined largely for the benefit of power generation.[174] Through the mid-1980s, water was released in a rush in the mornings to provide power as customers began their days and then reduced dramatically at night. Water flows could vary between 1,000 and 31,500 cubic feet per second (cfs) within one day. As a result, many sandy beaches and shores were washed away by fluctuations in river levels and were not replaced due to the nutrient-rich sediment remaining behind the dam's walls. The released water comes from the bottom of Lake Powell and is cold and green rather than the natural warm and muddy Colorado. This shift has endangered native species of plants and fish while benefiting exotic species such as rainbow trout, tamarisk, and cottonwood trees. Only three of seven endangered species of fish living in the canyon before 1963 have survived.

The natural solitude of the canyon has been impaired by noise from two major sources. NPS moderation of both has been overruled by political actors. During the 1980s, airplanes and helicopters made over forty thousand flights each year over the canyon. In 1992 alone, 750,000 people toured the canyon from the air.[175] While these flights were not always audible, the noise was intrusive enough to inspire a congressional mandate to "provide for substantial restoration of the natural quiet and experience of the park . . . from adverse effects associated with aircraft overflight."[176] NPS attempts to do so in the 1980s, however, were directly countermanded by Interior Secretary Hodel and Assistant Secretary Horn, leaving flight restrictions largely up to the Federal Aviation Administration.[177] Aircraft noise has remained obnoxious enough that Grand Canyon has the highest priority among NPS units for the issue of airspace resolution.[178]

The second source of noise in the canyon is from motors on rivercraft. Nearly twenty thousand people traverse some or all of the Colorado River every year on rafts, dories, pontoon boats, and other craft. The NPS strictly limits the number of trips allowed each day on the river, but their efforts to control the types of trips have been stymied by political intervention. In the 1970s, independent studies showed that motorized craft on the river contributed to environmental problems such as noise and oil pollution and were less enjoyable for passengers and less cost effective per user day for concessionaires than oar-powered trips.[179] Using these studies as a base, the NPS proposed a phasing out of motorized watercraft from the canyon in the 1979 *Colorado River Management Plan.* This proposal inspired an amendment to a Department of the Interior (DOI) appropriations bill offered by Senator Orrin Hatch (R–UT), guaranteeing continued motorized use of the canyon by existing concessionaires. Many of these concessionaires operate out of Utah and are thus constituents of Senator Hatch. The NPS has subsequently revised its plans to allow motorized water travel.[180]

One final major threat to natural conditions in the canyon is from air pollution. Air pollution from urban areas as far away as Los Angeles and from coal-fired power plants on the Colorado Plateau can produce serious impairment of natural visibility at the canyon. The National Academy of Sciences estimates annual average visibility, free from manmade emissions, to be about 143 miles. Increased pollution, particularly sulfur dioxide emissions, dropped that annual average below 100 miles by the early 1970s. The NPS has been attempting to address this issue for years. A 1987 study used injected methane to trace emissions from Navajo Generating Station, located 110 km north of Grand Canyon Village. The experiment found significant concentrations at Hopi Point on the South Rim. These results were confirmed by the National Research Council.[181] Subsequent efforts to control emissions brought the annual average up to 112 miles by 1990, but further progress has been slowed by political reluctance to enforce the 1977 amendments to the Clean Air Act and a lengthy court process to bring recalcitrant polluters such as the Navajo Generating Station into compliance.[182] Visibility over the canyon is often significantly impaired.

Systematic Preservation Efforts

The 75th anniversary celebration of Grand Canyon National Park was held in October 1994. Speaking at the ceremony, Superintendent Arnberger said, "The future of Grand Canyon National Park is bright."[183] One year later, Arnberger and his staff were forced to repel a political intervention of a most dramatic kind. During the budget-induced shutdowns of the federal government, the governor of Arizona actively attempted to take over management of the canyon to keep it open for tourists. One attempt involved Governor Symington arriving at the Grand Canyon Airport with fifty members of the National Guard and thirty state park rangers. While political intervention into park affairs in the past has not been quite this dramatic, the future of natural conditions at Grand Canyon depends upon the ability of the NPS to implement proposed efforts without political contradiction.

The 1995 GMP accepts the existence of developed areas on both the South and North Rims but attempts to constrain their impact on the rest of the park. Over 90% of the park is zoned as wilderness. The GMP also recognizes that boundary modifications may be necessary to preserve resources but offers no specific plans in this document. The document calls for increased usage of the Grand Canyon Railway and various shuttles into the park to reduce the automobile congestion. Once there, the NPS promises a more extensive public transit system around park sites and the use of clean-burning fuels for park vehicles. New facilities will be constructed at Mather and at Tusayan to provide hubs for visitors and shuttle services. Further, a large parking area outside of the park will be constructed on Forest Service land from which visitors can find alternative means of transport into the park. By the year 2010, the GMP mandates that "Grand Canyon Village will only be accessible by transit, hiking, or biking."[184]

The most dramatic recommendation in the GMP is to limit visitors. The NPS promises to impose limits when the number of visitors on the South Rim at any one time reaches 22,500. Planners estimate that such an event will not occur until the year 2015. The number 22,500 is based on a detailed analysis of carrying capacity of park areas. The plan also states that should some of the proposed changes in transportation systems not occur, then limits "may need to be imposed much sooner."[185]

On 26 March 1996 the Grand Canyon was flooded. This flood did not occur naturally, but it was intended to restore some natural conditions along the river. The jet tubes on the Glen Canyon Dam were opened to allow a week-long flood of water released at 45,000 cfs, much higher than the usual flows but still lower than the historical floods of more than 120,000 cfs. During the rest of the year, the volume of water flows in the canyon are now mandated to range from 5,000 to 20,000 cfs with no daily variances greater than 8,000.[186] This "flood" was designed to lift the river level by ten to fifteen feet in the canyon. Scientists hypothesized that this flooding would replicate seasonal flows and move some sediment downstream to enhance sandy beaches and stimulate flora and fauna. If successful, similar floods were planned for future years. As of early 1997, the tests showed only mixed results.[187]

Efforts to address other threats are not as publicized. The GMP promises that the NPS will consider the use of motors in the canyon when the 1989 River Management Plan is revised.[188] Aircraft noise also remains a problem. In a 1994 report to Congress, the NPS admits that despite compliance with the 1988 regulations on airspace, "aircraft are still audible large percentages of the time in much of the park" and that without further changes, less than 10% of the park would enjoy "a substantial restoration of natural quiet" by the year 2010. The NPS thus makes explicit recommendations to expand flight-free zones and phase in quiet aircraft technology.[189] As of 1997, the FAA was still considering these proposals. Final recommendations of the task force considering air quality in the area are also pending, but the preliminary draft report issued in 1996 explicitly recognized the continuing existence of "significant adverse visibility impacts" from external sources.[190]

Given the past history of the NPS, the ability of the agency to implement recommendations in visitor control, continue efforts in river restoration, and make meaningful plans that will stick in noise and pollution issues is hardly guaranteed. Mindful of this history, Grand Canyon managers have created a new formal planning institution that recognizes the potential impact of political actors. The NPS has set up a three-person team located in Flagstaff, seventy miles from the canyon, precisely to concentrate on implementation of the GMP and other plans. Park managers recognize that successful implementation depends upon community support and effective liaisons with politicians at the state and federal levels. The team is established in the nearest large city precisely to effectuate those ends. As NPS official Smith says, "We're marketing in the political world."[191]

Yosemite

The emphasis on ecological restoration in Yosemite should have been apparent to any visitor to the park in the summer of 1996. Upon arrival, visitors were given a park guide with the front page story devoted to the plans for the twenty-first century. The story emphasized proposed changes to the famous Yosemite Valley, "The vision for the Valley is one of more extensive meadows and fewer roads and buildings." Such changes have been promised since 1980, leaving the obvious question: Will visitors in the twenty-first century be observing those changes or still seeing them in print?

Background

The focus of NPS planning in Yosemite has traditionally been and continues to be the Yosemite Valley. The mile-wide, seven-mile-long valley is home to famous sites such as El Capitan and Yosemite Falls as well as most of the lodging and campgrounds in the park. The valley is not only the most popular destination for visitors, but during much of the year it is one of the few that remains accessible. Since the All-Year Highway was built along the Merced River during the 1930s, automobiles have poured into the valley during all seasons. This occurred in spite of the warning British ambassador James Bryce offered early in the century, "If Adam had known what harm the serpent was going to work, he would have tried to prevent him from finding lodgment in Eden; and if you were to realize what the result of the automobile will be in that wonderful, that incomparable Valley, you will keep it out."[192]

Several forerunners to the 1980 GMP considered changes to management of the valley. One plan proposed in the late 1950s called for moving park operations and facilities to the nearby community of El Portal but was never implemented. In the early 1970s, NPS personnel working in conjunction with the Sierra Club proposed moving some management functions to El Portal and Big Meadow. When agency personnel began implementing preliminary parts of the plan, concessionaires exerted political pressure on NPS and DOI officials to stop the changes. The subsequent 1974 GMP, prepared with concessionaire involvement, called for increased development in the valley and was rejected for lack of public input. As Yosemite chief of cultural resources Jerry Mitchell told me, "History is littered with plans that went nowhere."[193]

Controversy over increased automobile usage and development in the valley led to the 1980 GMP. Dramatically increasing visitation, traffic jams, pollution from automobiles, smoke from campfires obscuring sites like Half Dome, and unnatural activities such as pushing burning wood off Glacier Point for an evening event stimulated demands for more careful NPS management of the park. Agency personnel held five years of meetings and public workshops involving more than sixty thousand people. When produced, the 1980 GMP made dramatic recommendations for the long term. On the first page, the GMP states explicitly, "The intent of the NPS is to remove all automobiles from Yosemite Valley and Mariposa Grove and to redirect development to the periphery of the park and beyond. . . . The result will be . . . nature uncluttered by piecemeal stumbling blocks of commercialism, machines, and fragments of suburbia."[194] The plan then outlined several general approaches, such as restoring natural processes and reducing traffic congestion, to achieve this goal.

How effective has implementation of this plan been? Critics describe improvements as only modest and point to new concession activities as evidence that the NPS is allowing "business as usual."[195] Some NPS personnel have acknowledged limited success over time. In 1984 Superintendent Robert Binnewies seemed resigned to existing levels of development: "I have worked very hard on the theme that a certain level of development has been achieved within the park and that *that level should now be held* (emphasis added) and no additional expansion or development in the park should occur."[196] By 1990 NPS Director Ridenour was calling the plan only "a concept, a good ideal."[197] This apparent lack of progress on implementation is attributed to two related factors. First, concessionaires have enough political clout to prevent dramatic alteration of their business concerns. Second, Congress has failed to appropriate funds with which to carry out significant plans.

Another perspective is somewhat less critical. NPS personnel knew implementation would be difficult and have worked incrementally to maintain progress. Mitchell said some incremental goals, such as a target of 7% removal of valley structures by the mid-1980s, had been met. Since 1980 the NPS has managed to expand shuttle bus service, rebuild the electrical system, revise the concessions contract, remove some parking areas, and move some facilities outside the park in spite of limited funding and concessionaire objections. Progress was slow but steady. According to chief of resources Hank Snyder, all these steps were necessary preparations to making larger changes: "You've got to build the foundation before building the house."[198] Snyder and other planners cite the 1980 GMP as still intact as the statement of general principles which allows them now to pursue dramatic changes according to specific detailed plans.

The most realistic assessment of implementation of the 1980 GMP is mixed. For those advocating a return to more natural conditions, the good news is also the bad news. Little really has changed in the valley. While that means major portions of the plan were not put in place, it also means that the NPS was able to slow the rampant development that had preceded the plan. Both Snyder and NPS strategic planner Chip Jenkins referred to the period between 1980 and 1995 as involving the least amount of change of any period in the park's history. Little change has occurred precisely because the NPS has been caught between the increasingly powerful environmental groups advocating restoration of natural conditions and the political forces at the national level emphasizing fiscal restraint and protection of private operators such as the Yosemite concessionaires.

Systematic Preservation Efforts

Numerous planning efforts are currently underway at the park. Indeed, the NPCA terms this "a time of unprecedented planning at Yosemite."[199] While the valley plan is the most crucial, other plans exist for Tuolumne, Glacier Point, and the wilderness areas.

Interestingly, the Valley Implementation Plan (VIP) grew out of one of the simple, incremental steps mandated by the 1980 GMP. NPS personnel wanted to tear down the old warehouse used by maintenance personnel and relocate those facilities to El Portal. To do so, they needed a plan. Once they began the planning process, they realized that one thing was connected to another. For example, if maintenance moved, so too could the grounds repair division, and the process snowballed. Now, the NPS has posed three alternative options for potentially major changes. All three involve returning more areas to natural conditions, moving some operations out of the valley, and requiring visitors to use the shuttle system rather than private vehicles while travelling in the area. The options range from an ambitious alternative restoring 130 acres to a moderate one restoring 80 acres to a minimal of 25 acres. Each involves different specifics, all based on moving visitor use to more resistant areas and away from less fragile sites.

As the planning process moved along, much of the discussion inevitably centered on transportation of visitors. Logically, the major obstacle to restoring natural conditions in the park is the movement of people, and most movement is by automobile. On average summer days in the early 1990s, nearly seven thousand vehicles entered the park. Roughly 37% of these visitors were making day trips into and out of the park. Over 70% of all visitors went to the valley during their trips.[200] These numbers, still growing, reinforce the perspective stated in the 1980 GMP that, "Increasing automobile traffic is the single greatest threat to enjoyment of the natural and scenic qualities of Yosemite."

The NPS has now come full circle to the Bryce warning and is considering several options to drastically reduce automobile traffic in the park. One option is to build a parking structure in the west end of the valley and then allow private cars to go no further. Another is a regional approach, parking cars in nearby communities like El Portal and having visitors then ride bus, light rail, or elevated trams into the valley. A third option involves requiring day-use visitors to make reservations to bring cars into the valley. The first option incites strong public opposition. The second depends upon regional cooperation and federal money to build transit systems. The third, restricting the number of visitors to the park, has never been done on this scale before. Table 3-13 displays the findings of park planners and private consultants on several of the options.

In 1997 some dramatic changes were made. Those changes followed a spring of severe flooding that inundated more than 350 campsites and 250 motel rooms and cabins. Rather than restoring them, the NPS used the flood damage as a reason to close some of these facilities. Further, park managers used the fact that the number of facilities had decreased to attempt to install a reservation system, even for day visits. That effort was stymied by the complaints of local businesses, but the NPS did resume utilization of a system that was in effect on the busiest days of the previous summer. When the park is full, one car is allowed to enter only when another car leaves.[201]

By the start of 1998, the NPS had made its choice. The official VIP mandates removal of all nonessential facilities (administration, employee housing, etc.) from the valley and restoration of nearly 150 acres of natural habitat. Day-use visitors will park outside the valley and then ride buses and trams to various sites. Campers and overnight lodgers can still drive into the valley but will then park and use trams, bicycles, or their own two feet. The plan is to be phased in by the year 2001.

TABLE 3-13
Yosemite Transportation Alternatives

System	Advantages	Disadvantages	Costs
Parking Lot	reduce cars not region-dept.	unsightly unpopular	moderate capital low operating
Bus Transit	reduce cars flexible routes	waiting time road repair	low capital high operating
Light Rail	remove traffic nature proximity	inflexible route construction impacts	high capital low operating
Elev. Trams	remove traffic novelty value	inflexible route obstruct views	high capital low operating
Reserved Day Use	reduce traffic already in place	inconsistent to mission inflexible visits	no capital some operating

Sources: U.S. NPS 1994, *Yosemite Transportation;* interviews with NPS.

Two related reasons make implementation of long-term plans perhaps more likely at Yosemite now than at other popular national parks.
First, Yosemite is more like an intact ecosystem than most parks. The
northern and eastern boundaries include the drainage basins for the
Tuolumne and Merced Rivers that flow through the parks. These two
watersheds are surrounded by parkland and national forest land in
relatively unaffected condition. Second, because the park is large and
fairly intact, the NPS does not have to deal with other federal agencies
nearly as much here as it does at places like Yellowstone and the
Everglades. Mitchell, who previously worked at Grand Canyon terms
the difference quite significant, stating, "Here, we control the variables." Stated another way, Yosemite planners are less susceptible to
the political manipulation through other federal agencies that is so
prevalent at other parks like Yellowstone.

The key political variables at Yosemite, then, are not external factors
or interagency coordination. Rather, one key is public trust. The park
is incredibly important to a lot of people and groups, all of whom want
a say in what happens, most with the political clout to make their
demands stick. Thus, the NPS planners have concentrated their efforts
on making public input easy as well as meaningful. The NPS hopes
that through this process, the public will understand the plans, have
some sense of ownership, and will trust the agency personnel to carry
them out.

The second key is money. Previous plans, including major portions
of the 1980 GMP have not been implemented precisely because supporting funds were not forthcoming. Today, the fiscal situation remains
tight. In Snyder's Resources Division, 97% of the operating funds go
toward wages and benefits. Thus, whereas superintendents in decades
past received a pot of money they could distribute, today's park managers have only a very limited amount of funds. Even if more money is
forthcoming, successful implementation is hardly guaranteed.

CONCLUSIONS

Systematic preservation for the U.S. national park system as a whole
and for individual parks such as Yellowstone is inevitably shaped by
the political desires of politicians, especially members of Congress.
Virtually every facet of expansion discussed in this chapter displays
the influence of immediate, individualized, political concerns. Plans
at individual units have been explicitly contravened and implicitly
underfunded. Thus, expansion is less than systematic and scientific
restoration of natural conditions is tenuous.

Agency personnel remain committed to long-term goals but are also aware of limitations on the ability to pursue them. The most recent strategic plan for the NPS stresses intergenerational delivery and states explicitly that the primary long-term goal is preservation of natural resources.[202] In the same 1996 document, however, the agency admits that because of funding and other constraints, the research and knowledge base to pursue effective preservation is not currently sufficient.[203]

4

Australia: Late in the Day

"... it is now very late in the day for obtaining anything like a full
and adequate representation of habitats and ecosystems."
—Committee of Inquiry into the National Estate, 1974.

The beach at Cape Tribulation in northern Queensland is widely recognized as one of the prettiest in the world. If you hike out along the shoreline to a point extending into the Pacific Ocean, you can look back at the puffy white clouds over Thornton Peak, the rain forests cascading down the sides of the mountains onto the beach, and the beautiful blue water rolling gently into the sandy alcove. I tried to get up and leave the spot where I had this view several times only to convince myself that I could stay just a little longer. It reminded me of lingering, mesmerized, in front of a Rembrandt self-portrait years ago. One surprising difference, however, was that few were around to share the view of Cape Tribulation. Parts of the Wet Tropics of northern Queensland are like that, spectacular and, so far, unspoiled. Whether or not the northern coast of Queensland will remain unspoiled in the future is a complicated question.

The question is complicated for reasons that have led to prominent controversies over protected lands in Australia in recent decades. Inspired by one such controversy, the Australian government initiated a study of its public lands in the early 1970s. Not only did the study find substantial gaps in representation of various ecosystems, as stated in the opening quote, the institutions to fill those gaps were largely nonexistent. Since then, some steps have been taken, but the national government's ability to implement long-term plans for preserved areas remains limited. This chapter describes the limited efficacy of Australian policymakers to provide intergenerational goods as the result of the two broad factors outlined in chapter 1. National efforts at systematic preservation are severely constrained by a dominant federal structure that retains state autonomy and by political intervention into bureaucratic behavior at all levels of government. Systematic preservation efforts for Australia are indeed "late in the day."

BACKGROUND

The flooding of Lake Pedder in 1972 was a seminal event in the history of Australian protected areas. Pedder was a beautiful mountain lake in Tasmania surrounded by a unique, pristine ecology. The area was flooded over when a new dam increased the surface area of the water from seven hundred to twenty-four thousand hectares.[1] Conservationists fought the dam, arguing that flooding the lake would destroy seventeen species of rare flora and fauna.[2] The official federal government inquiry afterwards concluded sadly, "It is clear that the lake was a place of outstanding beauty but that little weight was attached to this when the decision to flood it was made."[3] This conclusion was seconded by other policymakers and environmentalists who then committed to changing the decisions affecting other precious lands in the future.

Necessary Conditions

Certain essential conditions for systematic preservation are now in place in Australia. Ecological demands and official commitments were, however, slower to become effectual here than in Canada or the United States.

Increasing Demands for Ecological Protection

Though parks in Australia date to the nineteenth century, demands for systematic preservation have arisen in very recent decades, and then only slowly. These demands come from both domestic and international sources.

Most of the early parks were established largely as recreational areas. Boundaries were drawn to avoid interference with any economic activities. Further, these areas were often funded by sales of park resources such as timber. Mining and forestry were often permitted on parklands. Managing agencies in Queensland and Tasmania had little power and the parks existed as individual units rather than as parts of statewide systems.[4] As historian Colin Hall says, "The preservation of the ecological values of wilderness played only a minor role in the creation of the first Australian national parks."[5] The 1974 Committee of Inquiry into the National Estate summarized, "National Parks and other large reserves have generally been made only in areas unwanted for any other purpose."[6]

Perceptions of state-level neglect of ecological considerations stirred citizen activism in the late 1960s and early 1970s. The first of a series of "green bans" occurred in Sydney in 1968. Green bans consist of temporary alliances of local citizens and construction workers who attempt to stop development in green spaces. In 1968 many residents of the Kelly's Bush area of Sydney joined with local construction unions to stop development of twenty acres of virgin bushland that had been approved by the State Planning Authority. This incident marked the beginning of the "urban environmental revolution."[7] Quite a few of the green bans in New South Wales (NSW) and Victoria involved efforts to preserve historic sites and buildings as well as green spaces. Green ban supporters were concerned about what they saw as the "systematic destruction of the Australian heritage."[8]

Elsewhere, other perceived abuses also stimulated organized responses. The Lake Pedder case fostered creation of the world's first Greens Party in Tasmania. The United Tasmania Group became strong enough to nearly win a parliamentary seat in the state elections of 1972.[9] At Fraser Island, off the Queensland coast, several local conservation groups formed the Fraser Island Defense Organisation (FIDO) to protest accelerated sandmining.[10] Several different controversies led to dramatic growth of a nationwide organization, the Australian Conservation Foundation (ACF). As the middle two columns in table 4-1 show, membership was six times as large in 1972 as in 1967. These growing levels of environmental concern provided a new counterpoint to traditional pressures on land use.

Environmental activism by groups, rather than by individuals, was fairly new to Australia. Traditional resource extraction groups had previously dominated decisions about land and water usage. Agriculture and mining have generally been more important in Australia than in many other developed countries such as the United States. Further, as exports have become more important to the economy, the demand for access to land, particularly by miners, has increased. Between 1953 and 1982, mining as a percentage of exports jumped from 7% to 36%.[11] By 1975 Australia led the world in production of iron ore and bauxite, was third in lead and zinc, and fourth in nickel. Between 1968 and 1973 alone, nickel production increased by 500%.[12] The mining sector thus received considerable support from state policymakers. As one 1979 article noted, "At the opening of the decade, attitudes of earlier decades prevailed, and both federal and state governments saw the mineral industry as worthy of encouragement."[13]

These use sectors had prominent voices in state governments, particularly regarding park decisions. As Hall concludes, "Undoubtedly, the most pervasive form of opposition to the creation of national parks

TABLE 4-1
Australian Conservation Foundation Membership and Federal
Grants

Year	Total	Change	Grants
1967	1,017	—	$20,000
1968	1,392	+375	20,000
1969	n.a.	n.a.	20,000
1970	2,915	+1,523	50,000
1971	5,154	+2,239	50,000
1972	6,451	+1,297	50,000
1973	6,139	−312	150,000
1974	6,574	+435	150,000
1975	7,819	+1,245	150,000
1976	7,250	−569	150,000
1977	6,406	−847	150,000
1978	5,756	−650	150,000
1979	7,115	+1,359	100,000
1980	7,521	+406	100,000
1981	9,446	+1,925	75,000
1982	11,046	+1,600	75,000
1983	11,439	+393	77,000
1984	11,363	−76	120,000
1985	11,461	+98	140,515
1986	11,385	−76	140,000
1987	11,888	+503	145,000
1988	14,000	+2,112	149,300
1989	19,336	+5,336	157,800
1990	22,185	+2,849	167,268
1991	21,400	−785	175,631

Source: ACF Annual Reports; Papadikis 1993: 152, 118.

and wilderness reserves has been that based upon materialistic values."[14] For example, the Mines Department of NSW was blocking, at one point, over 120 reserve proposals.[15] Conflicts also occurred in the late 1960s over mining vs. parkland in Queensland (at Cooloola Sand Mass) and over agriculture vs. parkland in Victoria (Little Desert Lands) as well as other places.[16]

These early battles over parklands were intensified by the dismay of conservationists at what they saw as state recalcitrance. Spokespersons for the green bans described state authorities as retaining "the purpose for which they were created in the British colonial past, to be first and foremost development authorities."[17] Further, the growing export economy made states more likely to compete with each other through commodity development. As a result, many concerned citizens felt that state governments would give a higher priority to development opportunities than to land protection when the two were in conflict.[18] Indeed, cases such as Lake Pedder reinforced the view that state governments would inevitably favor use, rather than preservation, of land and water resources.[19]

In spite of some visible citizen activism, prospects for political support for environmentalism remained "bleak" in the early 1970s and only "gloomy" by the end of the decade.[20] First, politicians recognized, as mentioned above, that extraction industries were crucial to the Australian economy. Principal exports from Australia like coal ($5.3 billion in 1992), gold ($3.3 billion), and wool ($2.5 billion) are commodities that require intensive use, not preservation, of land.[21] Second, over two-thirds of the eighteen million Australians live in cities along coastlines. Because so much of their continent is undeveloped, many Australians traditionally did not worry about setting aside more. In contrast to the United States where many people have long perceived wilderness as disappearing, many Australians long thought that a considerable portion of their continent was quite wild. Indeed, relatively wild areas were abundant enough that the first nationwide assessment of wilderness areas in Australia did not appear until 1975.[22] One study concludes that park protection efforts have in fact suffered from the "sheer abundance" of natural land on the continent.[23] In a 1990 survey, only 6% of respondents expressed a "great deal" of concern about the lack of open spaces.[24] More were concerned about environmental problems affecting their cosmopolitan areas. Third, macroeconomic pressures are strong. While GDP growth rates have been similar to those in the United States since the 1970s, inflation and unemployment rates have actually been higher in Australia for much of that period.[25] Thus, sentiment for conservation is often diluted by concern over general economic conditions.

Also, strong national interest groups that could rally and focus public support on environmental issues were developing but only slowly. Early established groups showed reluctant leadership on parks issues. For example, the ACF was slow to protest the Lake Pedder dam.[26] Growth in membership levels was inconsistent. As the column for total members of the ACF shows in table 4-1, membership for this bellweather organization was actually lower in 1980 than it had been in 1975. Overall, Australians generally have been slower to join and participate in environmental groups than have citizens in other Western democracies.[27] The federal system also contributed to this fairly slow growth. Since the power to regulate the environment remained at the state level, most relevant groups retained their focus at that level. This phenomenon of interest groups focusing on the state level is not limited to environmental groups.[28]

Another factor contributing to the relatively slow growth of environmental demands relates to the major political parties. In Australia, the established parties reflect traditional cleavages in society. Labor represents trade-union-based social democracy. The National Party represents agriculture and the Liberal Party represents business, the two frequently acting in coalition. The Australian Democrats and the Labor Party have often been sympathetic to environmental issues, but none of the major parties is completely committed to environmental causes.[29] Various "Green" candidates have achieved success in recent elections, but no national Greens Party was operative before 1994.[30]

Despite this slow growth, domestic demand for systematic preservation has, since the 1970s, become increasingly noticeable. Even though controversies like that surrounding the Lake Pedder dam did not produce much in the way of results, they did increase public awareness. Support for environmental causes accelerated in the 1980s, stirred by specific issues like the Franklin Dam controversy. Although environmentalism remained fairly low in salience, a 1984 survey found 89% of respondents in favor of stronger measures to protect the environment.[31] In a 1990 survey, a strong majority of Australians remained concerned about environmental issues.[32] Salience also increased over time. Over a quarter of those surveyed in 1989 and 1990 listed the environment as one of the most important things about which the federal government should be doing something.[33]

In this increased environmental awareness, public support for the specific issue of parks has also grown. The answers to recent questions directly related to national parks are shown in table 4-2. They suggest significant support for preservation emphases. These widespread results are consistent with citizen reaction to specific issues. For example, a recent proposal by the Queensland government to replace Lindeman Island National Park with a resort inspired strong enough protest to abort the idea.[34]

As parks issues became more contentious in the 1980s, more conservation groups adopted a national posture. By late in the decade, international organizations such as Greenpeace and the World Wildlife Federation had achieved prominence in Australia. Membership in the former, for example, jumped from nine thousand in 1988 to forty-seven thousand two years later.[35] As table 4-1 shows, starting in 1979, membership in the ACF increased in ten of the next twelve years. By 1990 representatives of these groups had begun to achieve "insider status" in some political circles.[36]

TABLE 4-2
Survey Responses on National Parks

Statement	Strongly Disagree	Disagree	Neither	Agree	Strongly Agree
The greatest value of national parks and nature reserves is in recreation activities such as bush-walking, camping, or just taking photographs.	5	13	25	22	35
Jobs are the most important thing in deciding how to best use our natural resources such as mineral deposits and forests.	26	25	26	11	12
In deciding how to use Australia's natural resources, it is more important to consider the needs of future generations than our own.	2	2	9	22	65
If areas within national parks are set aside for development projects such as mining, the value of the parks are greatly reduced.	10	13	17	23	38
There should be more national parks created from state forests.	6	8	19	24	43

Source: Papadikis 1993: 147.

In general, environmentalism has now attained fairly wide support. An estimated eight hundred thousand Australians, or 4.4% of the population, are now members of the nearly one thousand conservation groups currently active in society.[37] With the caveat that the Australian figure includes subnational groups such as National Parks Associations of various states, this percentage is comparable to the 3.2% (eight million) of Americans belonging to major national environmental organizations.[38] In a 1990 survey, nearly three-fourths of the sample approved strongly of environmental groups.[39]

Increasing domestic demand for attention to public land also resulted from the boom in Australia's tourist economy. The Ecological Sustainable Development Working Groups concluded in 1991 that tourism has grown steadily in importance to the Australian economy in recent years to the point where it now contributes over 5% of GDP. The number of world tourist arrivals increased from about 120 million in 1965 to nearly 450 million in 1990.[40] Much of this tourism revolves around parks. The Working Group states, "The tourism industry is already reliant on protected areas and the experiences they offer and the growing trend in nature tourism to develop in remote places will intensify pressures on new areas."[41] Tourists want more parks, including more in remote areas.

Australians recognize the economic benefits of nature tourism. According to studies of individual areas, tourists bring far more into the local economy than it costs to run the parks. One study of Warrumbungle Park (NSW) in 1978 concluded, "[E]ven allowing for a considerable margin of error . . . the benefits of park use of land far outweighed the costs of that use."[42] Finally, the revenue from tourism is not just shifted from one sector or state to another, but rather much of it comes from outside the country. A survey of visitors to Kakadu (NT) in 1982 revealed that more than 11% of visitors were from overseas.[43]

International demands on Australian preservation efforts derive largely from the World Heritage Convention (WHC). Since ratifying the WHC in 1974, Australia has had more political and legal challenges related to the Convention than all other signatory countries combined.[44] As Graeme Marshall, a federal program director, told me, "World Heritage officials themselves say it's a much bigger deal in Australia than in other places." Marshall attributed that fact to "the chronic insecurity of Australians" and the visibility of fights like that over the Franklin Dam.[45]

The structural reasons for such an important role for international pressure emanate from the Australian Constitution and the system of federalism. Under the external affairs power specified in Section 51 of the Constitution, the federal government has the right to influence domestic policy in issues under the jurisdiction of state governments in order to meet international obligations as assigned under treaties or conventions. Section 51 enables the federal government, once it enters into an international treaty, to "legislate in respect of matters concerning which it would otherwise have no power at all." Australia is party to several international agreements that can affect preserved lands: the WHC, UNESCO's Man and the Biosphere Program, and the World Conservation Strategy.

The WHC has been a prominent part of land preservation decisions since the Franklin Dam case of the early 1980s. The groundwork for the Franklin Dam dispute was laid with the flooding of nearby Lake Pedder. Tensions remained from that dispute between the Tasmanian government, particularly the Hydro-Electric Commission (HEC), and the Tasmanian Wilderness Society (TWS), a coalition of interest groups and conservationists that evolved from the Lake Pedder Committee and the Greens Party. Bob Brown and several other founding members of the TWS, inspired by floats of the Franklin River in the mid-1970s, dedicated their organization to protection of the wild waterway and its narrow canyons. When the HEC proposed a $1.4 billion dam in 1979 that would flood much of the Franklin and Gordon River canyons, the TWS was ready. They initiated various efforts, such as publishing a book and taking people on floats, reminiscent of the fights in the United States to preserve wild rivers.[46]

The disagreement between the HEC and the TWS spread quickly. The TWS and other conservationists built a strong opposition to the dam, eventually constructing a coalition involving nearly eight hundred groups with half a million members. In an attempt to defuse the conflict, Tasmanian premier Lowe proposed a dam further upstream on the Gordon so that the Franklin could be spared. Neither the HEC nor the TWS approved of this compromise. In a 1981 state referendum held on the issue, two options were offerred to the citizens, one for each dam site. Instead of selecting either option, a remarkable 45% of voters wrote, "No dams" on their ballots. Though Lowe's mediation effort failed, he was successful in encouraging the federal government to nominate the Franklin area as a World Heritage site.[47]

The situation intensified in 1982. Lowe's Labor government was replaced by that led by Liberal Robin Gray, a strong proponent of the dam. Urged on by the TWS coalition, the federal Liberal government considered intervention but was reluctant since Gray's government was of the same party. Gray, terming the Franklin a "leech-ridden brown ditch," threatened to secede if the federal government intervened.[48] Gray promised his supporters, "I am not going to allow people on the other side of the Bass Strait (separating Tasmania from Australia) to come down here and dictate to you."[49] The federal Liberal Party refused to intervene, instead offering Tasmania $500 million to construct a coal-fired power plant instead of the dam.

The conflict began to receive national and international attention. In a nationwide poll, 42% of all Australians said they opposed the dam while only 28% favored construction. On 14 December 1982, the same day that much of Southwest Tasmania was listed as a World Heritage Area by UNESCO, conservationists from all over the world began a systematic blockade of dam construction. The blockade included nonviolent protests, disruption of equipment barges, and blockage of access roads. The blockade lasted three months and inspired supportive rallies throughout Australia, one in Melbourne drawing twenty thousand people.[50]

Resolution of the conflict came in the political arena. The lack of action by the federal Liberal government became a visible election issue in 1983. Leading the opposition Labor Party, Robert Hawke promised, "The dam will not be built."[51] After winning the election, the new Labor government passed the World Heritage Properties Conservation Act prohibiting damage to WHC sites in Australia. The bill specifically invoked the Commonwealth's external affairs power. The Tasmanian government protested the legislation in court, criticizing it as an unfair intervention into states' rights. Eventually, the High Court ruled 4 to 3 in favor of federal intervention, the majority basing their opinion on the federal government's obligation to honor international treaties under the external affairs power.[52] Justice Gibbs termed it, "a valid exercise of the power given by S. 51 of the Constitution to make laws with respect to external affairs."[53] Ultimately, the Tasmanian government received $277 million in compensation, but the dam was not built. Eventually, roughly 20% of Tasmania was listed as World Heritage. Tensions over the implications of that listing continue today.[54]

The Franklin Dam case generated recognition of the impact of international commitments on public lands in Australia. Almost immediately, individuals and groups concerned about other areas sought the extra protection that WHC listing seemed to afford. For example, in a 1982 editorial, the *Sydney Morning Herald* expressed concern about the Queensland government's efforts to drill for oil on the Great Barrier Reef: "The fact that the reef is on the World Heritage List could be as useful to its preservation as the Franklin River being on the World Heritage List."[55] Debates ensued at several natural areas with state-level policymakers vowing to fight WHC designation.

How does the WHC actually create international demands on Australian plans for protected areas? First, the 1983 World Heritage Properties Conservation Act is the only legislation in the world specifically committing a country to WHC obligations.[56] Thus, Australia has officially recognized the WHC as a mechanism for exerting international pressure. Second, the High Court's ruling on the Franklin Dam states that requirements on protected lands must be "reasonably appropriate."[57] Third, the WHC calls explicitly for "international assistance and co-operation" for member countries to ensure preservation of natural and cultural heritage for future generations.[58] Prime Minister Hawke stated in 1989, "With the honour of inscription on the World Heritage List comes the responsibility for preservation."[59]

This designated importance of an international body has served the federal government in numerous disputes with state authorities. Dr. Earl Saxon of the Wet Tropics Management Authority told me, "The Commonwealth government has used World Heritage listing as a means of asserting their view of conservation."[60] Further evidence that WHC presence is substantial is found in statements by critics of the proconservation impact.[61] In 1994, for instance, policymakers for the Federal Coalition of National and Liberal Parties criticized the WHC and promised to "ensure that Australian law is made in Australia, by Australians, and for Australians."[62]

By the mid-1990s, nine natural areas in Australia were subject to international demands through designation under the WHC. These areas are listed in table 4-3. WHC designation is quite noticeable at these places, pronounced boldly at entrance gates and in park brochures. WHC sites are subject to visits by international officials and occasional communications. Both federal and state officials denied that WHC representatives directly change the way parks are managed, but all agreed that a WHC listing was taken into account on individual planning decisions. For example, Great Barrier Reef legal officer Darin Honchin told me that a WHC listing leads to more explicit and thorough decisions.[63] The impact of international designation at the state level

TABLE 4-3
World Heritage Areas in Australia

Area	Region	Year Inscribed	Size (ha)
Great Barrier Reef	Queensland	1981	34,870,000
Kakadu National Park	Northern Territory	1981	1,307,340
Willandra Lakes	New South Wales	1981	600,000
Lord Howe Island	New South Wales	1982	1,540
Tasmanian Wilderness	Tasmania	1982	1,082,000
Temperate Rain Forests	New South Wales	1986	165,000
Uluru National Park	Northern Territory	1987	133,000
Wet Tropics	Queensland	1988	920,000
Shark Bay	Western Australia	1991	1,000
Fraser Island	New South Wales	1992	181,000

Sources: Hall 1992: 173–174; IUCN 1992: 302–303.

was noted by NSW parks manager Jeff Francis who said of WHC sites in his state, "We don't want to be embarrassed by delisting."[64]

Stable Democratic Processes

Increasing citizen and international demands for systematic preservation can have impact in the Australian political system. Political processes are stable and transitions of power frequent enough to promise responsiveness to voters.

The Australian system of government is often termed a hybrid, or a "Westminster ghost." The constitutional framework established in 1901 combines elements of both Westminster and American systems. The Parliament consists of a House of Representatives with seats proportional to population and an American-style Senate. Laws must be passed by both houses. The prime minister is the leader of the party or coalition of parties with the majority of seats in the House. The postwar prime ministers are listed in table 4-4. The prime minister uses a cabinet divided into "inner" and "outer" ministries. Cabinet decisions are given legal status by the Executive Council, headed by the governor-general who acts as a representative of the queen. The ultimate court of appeals is the High Court of Australia, made up of members appointed by the governor-general on recommendation of the cabinet.[65]

In general, Australians accept an active state but remain somewhat skeptical of its efficacy. Surveys show, for example, that twice as many Australians support government wage and price controls as do Americans. Indeed, over half of Australians surveyed in 1986 (54%) supported wage controls and over two-thirds (69%) supported price controls.[66]

TABLE 4-4
Postwar Australian Prime Ministers

Prime Minister	Tenure	Party
Ben Chifley	1945–1949	Labor
Robert G. Menzies	1949–1966	Liberal
Harold E. Holt	1966–1967	Liberal
John McEwen	1967–1968	Country
John G. Gorton	1968–1971	Liberal
William McMahon	1971–1972	Liberal
Gough Whitlam	1972–1975	Labor
Malcolm Fraser	1975–1983	Liberal
Robert Hawke	1983–1991	Labor
Paul Keating	1991–1995	Labor
John Howard	1995–?	Liberal

Still, Australians have long been noted for their independent nature compared to Canada, for example: "In both countries there has been an acceptance of a positive governmental role, but Canadians have been more deferential toward authority than the skeptical and self-assured Australians."[67] The classic example of wariness toward authority is evident on Australian roadways where, after seeing police cars on the side of the road, drivers flash their headlights to warn oncoming drivers to slow down.

Official Commitments

With increasing demands and an accessible political environment, official commitments to land preservation became more noticeable in the 1970s. Numerous institutions were created specifically to provide direction of park system efforts. State versions of National Parks and Wildlife Services preceded that at the federal level. Versions of these agencies were established in New South Wales (1967), Tasmania (1971), South Australia (1972), and Queensland (1975). Ministers in the different states increased communication and agreed on a common definition of national parks in 1970. The definition included "a relatively large area . . . protected from all interference other than essential management practices."[68]

Federal institutions designed to affect national parks issues were also established in the 1970s. One national environmental agency actually preceded Labor's ascension in 1972. Even though it was given little staff or budget, a new cabinet-level Office of the Environment was created in 1971 to enable the federal government to become involved in environmental issues. The new Labor government promised significant changes. Many in the Labor Party had been openly critical of Tasmania's behavior at Lake Pedder. Moss Cass, the new minister for the environment, vowed that the new government would adopt the slogan, "No More Lake Pedders," and then convened the offical inquiry that was so critical of the dam decision, thereby signalling a new emphasis on environmental concerns.[69] A new Department of Environment and Conservation was established in 1975. The Australian Parks and Wildlife Conservation Act of 1975 created the national Australian National Parks and Wildlife Service (ANPWS) that later became the Australian Nature Conservation Agency (ANCA). This agency was responsible for management of national parks in the Northern and Capital Territories, had the authority to deal with other countries through programs such as the WHC, and could recommend establishment of parks in the various states.[70] The Australian Heritage Commission (AHC) was created in 1975 to provide a register of the important scientific, natural, and historic places that comprise the national estate.

Recognition of the need for systematic expansion was voiced at high levels of society and government. Ecological pioneers began to use new techniques to identify critical ecosystems and to propose nationwide lists of places in need of protection. The Australian Academy of Science (AAS) study in 1968 calling for new parks in specific ecosystems and more ecological management of existing parks was seminal. The Academy even set up committees at the state level to advise state policymakers about potential new areas.[71] Many in the scientific community, such as J. D. Ovington, called explicitly for a long-term emphasis in plans: "Long term planning is essential if the management of national parks is to be placed on a rational basis."[72] Early planning efforts were generated by the AAS and by the Australian Subcommittee for Section CT of the Australian National Committee for the International Biological Program. One plan resulted from a survey organized by Professor Ray Specht and completed in 1971. A second study of ecosystems represented within the parks was completed in 1974. The major goal of these efforts was to open new areas in the interior, rather than just along the coast, of the country.[73] By the end of the 1970s, in fact, considerable progress had been made in arid zones in South Australia (Simpson Desert, Danggari) and Western Australia (Rudall, Collier Range).[74]

Calls for systematic expansion intensified through the 1970s. Labor's platform in 1969 had called for a coordinated, nationwide system of national parks.[75] The 1974 Committee of Inquiry into the National Estate called for a truly national park system administered by the federal government. In 1975 the ACF produced a review of wilderness areas in Australia along with a call for specific places needing protection in a national system.[76] At Australia's first National Wilderness Conference in 1977, the president of the ACF, Sir Mark Oliphant, endorsed the two goals of systematic preservation and called for "keeping the wilderness we have and expanding the wilderness areas so that they are adequate for the needs of the future."[77]

Constraining Conditions

Systematic preservation in Australia faces difficult challenges. Federalism is a dominant institution, affecting virtually all aspects of expansion and unit restoration. Agency efforts are subject to at least some political interference at both national and state levels.

High Vertical Constraints

The vertical dimension of federal-state, and lately international-federal-state, relations is extremely important in issues of Australian public policy. As Henry Albinski found in his comparison of Australian and Canadian policies, "A great deal of the actual course of policy is, however, determined by the kinds of arrangements, conventions, and political constraints which regulate relations among the state/provinces, and between them and the central governments."[78] What Albinski found in 1973 was still evident in a comparative study twenty years later when Campbell and Halligan described the pervasive presence of the "continuing imbroglios of Australian federalism."[79] This section suggests why this vertical dimension has been and is expected to continue to be so consequential to systematic preservation of lands.

Federalism is the crucial structural arrangement in Australian politics. Government exists on the three levels of federal, state, and local with policy responsibilities divided explicitly among them. Noted authority Brian Galligan says succinctly, "The central institution of Australian government around which other major political institutions and processes, including parliaments, parties, elections, and much of public policy, are structured is of course federalism."[80] The importance of federalism has been apparent throughout the history of the nation. Participants in all kinds of policy decisions believe that "the federal character of Australian politics is an important element in policy outcomes. . . . As a consequence they attempt to reshape it so that it matches their own policy vision."[81]

A prominent place for state governments was perhaps inevitable when the six established colonies formed the Commonwealth in 1901. The framers retained many powers for the states and reserved few exclusively to the federal government. For example, unlike Canada, each state retained some direct links to the British crown. Residual powers remain with the state governments.[82] The local level of government, made up of over nine hundred elected bodies, has few policy-making responsibilities besides the servicing of local development.[83]

Recent decades have witnessed numerous challenges to the traditional framework of federalism. Much of the stimulus for challenging the federal structure arose from the Australian Labor Party. Formally dedicated until the 1970s to abolishing federalism to achieve a more centralized government, ALP leaders continued to propose fundamental restructuring of traditional arrangements even after agreeing to work within the federal system.[84] Partly as a result of their efforts, the Commonwealth institutions have grown. The doubling of seats in the federal legislature and the growth of full-time staff as tools to assist a "bigger government operat[ing] across a progressively wider range of issues" are evidence of such changes.[85]

More specifically, each of the recent prime ministers listed in table 4-4 have brought a different emphasis to federal-state relations. The

Whitlam government's "New Federalism" was an attempt to centralize more policy responsibilities while recognizing the permanence of state institutions. Contentious battles over environmental issues like Lake Pedder, however, alienated many state policymakers. This alienation and the short tenure of Whitlam's government slowed the restructuring efforts.[86] Fraser's Liberal government promised more cooperation with the states but accomplished little in the way of intergovernmental changes. In part, Fraser's emphasis on states' rights seemed counter to many Australians' perception of the need for a stronger Commonwealth to deal with environmental issues.[87]

The Hawke government attempted some significant changes in the federal system. Hawke called for a new partnership with the states, promising cooperative federalism and holding a series of conferences with state premiers while his government was initiating centrally directed reforms in economic and environmental issues. To further his efforts, Hawke offered the possibilities of changing fiscal relations with the states, reworking the tax structure, and loosening some of the strings on federal grants. Yet, what might have been a broad restructuring of federalism did not occur. While many state officials welcomed potential changes in financial relations, other officials in the Labor Party viewed them as undermining central power. This inner-party dissension led to the replacement of Hawke by Paul Keating and a virtual end to the former's federalism initiatives.[88]

Federal policymakers have some significant means of influencing state behavior. Section 96 of the Constitution gives the federal government the right to provide grants to states. Further, the Commonwealth has monopolized collection of income taxes since World War II and now collects over three-fourths of the tax revenue. Over time, state governments have become increasingly dependent on the Commonwealth for financial resources and thus "subject to its influence about how that revenue will be spent."[89] Section 109 of the Constitution provides for supremacy of Commonwealth law when state laws conflict.[90] The federal government also can refuse to grant export licenses for certain commodities, thereby affecting state economic development projects.[91] Finally, the federal government has the external affairs power discussed previously, the ability to enter into international agreements that can affect specific state actions dramatically. The High Court has frequently upheld the shift of power to the Commonwealth in these and other issues.[92]

Some tools were created in recent decades that signalled a stronger federal presence in environmental issues in years to come. The most significant was the Environmental Impact Statement (EIS). The EIS was introduced in the 1960s to examine the consequences of new projects on environmental quality. The Commonwealth passed the Environment Protection (Impact of Proposals) Act in 1974 to strengthen this procedure by mandating more information gathering and utilizing more public input.[93] Federal policymakers showed occasional willingness to use the powers that they already had to intervene in what had previously been entirely state jurisdiction. Indeed, the Commonwealth's environment policy states explicitly that the federal government has "an obligation to develop appropriate environment policies and programs in co-operation with State, Territory and local governments."[94]

In spite of these various tools, however, state governments retain a powerful position in many policy areas. The states, as John Summers concludes, ". . . appear to be anything but powerless and irrelevant . . . often able to outmanoeuvre the Commonwealth."[95] As mentioned before, state governments kept responsibility for land and water resources within their borders. The failure of Hawke and others to make fundamental changes led observers to conclude that "federal-state relations had moved back considerably to the old fractious, fractured model."[96] State governments would not give up their powers easily. As one comparativist notes, "federalism is more insistent, immediate, and intractable in Australia than in the United States."[97]

Intractability is particularly apparent in systematic efforts involving the public lands. Officials at all levels of government and informed observers alike described to me the dominant influence of federalism on parks and preserved areas. Galligan, the prominent authority on Australian federalism, termed the impact of federal-state relations on parks issues "immense."[98] Noted park expert J. G. Mosley described federalism as of "tremendous importance."[99] National parks policy coordinator Alison Shepherd admitted that any federal efforts to affect state behavior in park management were difficult because "it really is an area they guard pretty jealously."[100] Rod Gowans, manager of Victoria's Parks and Reserves Branch, said increased federal control over state management of parks "just isn't likely to happen."[101]

To summarize the vertical dimension, state governments are important factors in virtually all policy areas in Australia. In terms of preserved lands, their behavior will be consequential to any efforts at long-term delivery.

Moderate Horizontal Constraints

Political control of park system bureaucrats is less likely in Australia than in the United States but is still quite possible. While less oriented to micromanagement, control does occur at the ministerial level of national government. Intervention from individual politicians into park affairs occurs more often at the state level, but then again, this is where most of the national parks are located.

At the federal level, since both the prime minister and the cabinet serve at the pleasure of the Parliament, one might expect this body to have considerable power. Conceivably, members can intervene in individual decisions such as park system expansion as do their American counterparts. In fact, however, such behavior is less noticeable in Australian politics. First, Parliament itself is not that strong an institution, meeting only sixty to seventy days a year and leaving most decisions to other actors.[102] Second, individual members are constrained by disciplined, well-organized political parties.[103] Similar to Canada, entreprenurial behavior by individual members is less likely than in the United States for many of the same reasons. Majority party members are reluctant to interfere in each other's affairs and minority members are unable. Further, the majority coalition in the House rarely has a clear majority in the Senate.[104] Thus, individual MPs rarely interfere with national agency behavior. Several federal officials told me that their only dealings with MPs occur once a year at budget time. Director of Protected Areas Development Unit David Phillips said, "Day to day, we're pretty well autonomous," and added that management plans for individual parks in the territories are never countermanded.[105]

The prime minister is also a potential source of strong control over the actions of public agencies. While this power was utilized more often in the 1970s, the recent emphasis has been on managerial discretion. Initiatives such as the Financial Management Improvement Program were established to, "in the jargon of the reformers . . . let the managers manage."[106] While most of these programs have not been realized to the same extent as in Canada, some delegation of authority has occurred and the influence of the prime minister and his cabinet over agencies has been reduced lately.[107]

Nevertheless, cabinet ministers are important players in park decisions. Portfolio ministers in charge of individual departments have some degree of autonomy from Parliament and the prime minister.[108] They, in turn, often develop strong parochial tendencies toward their own departments. As scholar John Wanna states, "Ministers, according to Westminster traditions of responsible government, are ostensibly in charge of departments and determine policy, yet Ministers have often become captives of the departments they were meant to administer."[109] In looking out for their own ministries, these high officials may well intervene in the affairs of another department.[110] Federal official Marshall termed the reputation of nonpolitical public agencies in a Westminster system as "largely true except at the highest level of

Ministers."[111] When I asked Wet Tropics manager Saxon if politicians got involved in their decisions, he answered emphatically, "They certainly do."[112] High-level intervention is particularly important for expansion. Agency decisions on creating new units at the federal and state levels must be cleared by other cabinet departments. Federal plans for parks must clear the Ministries for Primary Industry and Energy.

The High Court has taken a much more active role lately in many issues. Like the U.S. Supreme Court, the High Court has original jurisdiction in interpreting the Constitution and disputes between different governments as well as appellate jurisdiction. As discussed previously, the High Court has become much more involved in national parks issues since 1983. One particular means has been through interpretation of the powers of different levels of government.[113] A second line of cases that will affect parks and proposed parklands in the future involves the native claims of Aborigine tribes. In 1992 the High Court ruled in favor of such a claim by Eddie Mabo and his tribe. Though that case involved an area without national parks, the precedent was established that would affect parklands later.

Political intervention into park agency behavior is quite possible at the state level. Because federalism is such a dominant institution, state-level politicians have considerable control of their state agencies. The ministerial arrangement is similar to that at the national level. The consequences can be significant. As NSW official Jeff Francis told me, "We have a backlog of (nominated) areas that have been knocked back by Mineral Resources."[114] In addition to the impact of ministers, other state actors can also affect park decisions. Shifts in party control or ideology in state governments can have severe impacts on national parks in spite of the preferences of the national government. State courts as well can be consequential, but they have been so only very recently and only in specific cases. New South Wales established a new superior court in 1979 to deal specifically with environmental issues. However, this court's impact on parks has been small since national parks and wildlife matters were specifically excluded from court jurisdiction.[115]

Officials at the state level acknowledged the potential for political intervention. However, several also asserted that individual state MPs were not as intrusive as American members of Congress and attributed some of the difference to institutional arrangements such as funding procedures. In NSW, for example, revenues from fees are tracked by Treasury officials but returned to the parks for their use, a system much less susceptible to political manipulation than that traditionally used for fee revenue in the United States.[116]

To summarize, horizontal constraints on park authorities are not as severe as those facing the American NPS but are still consequential. Most noticeably, shifts in party control of governments at federal and state levels can lead to shifts in overall policy emphases, often manifested in the actions of influential cabinet offices.

Theoretical Expectations

Changes in certain conditions recently—domestic demand, international pressure, official commitments—increase the chances for systematic preservation in Australia. However, efforts at coordinated expansion and enhancement of individual units still managed at the subnational level will be significantly affected by the federalism dimension and the political influence afforded dominant state governments.

NATIONAL PARK SYSTEM EXPANSION

Many of the groups pushing for systematic expansion of preserved lands in Australia have now coalesced as the Australian National Parks Council. In 1995 I interviewed Nicky Esau, the coordinator of the group's program to achieve a representative system. When I asked her what the impact of federalism had been on their efforts, she answered succinctly, "bloody awful."[117] Even if one disagrees with Esau's personal assessment, her characterization of federalism as consequential to implementation of plans to pursue systematic expansion is consistent with the record over the past decades.

Origins

The early history of Australia's national parks reflects the dominant influence of the federal structure. Rather than one unified program, the collections of protected lands developed as several distinct systems. Because federalism is so entrenched, the Australian national parks developed not as one coordinated system but as distinct entities for the six states and two territories.

The history of Australia since European settlement in the late eighteenth century is one of independent behavior by separate colonies or states. In issues as fundamental as penal importation, each colony developed its own identity and practices.[118] This decentralization continued after federation in 1901 and throughout the history of park establishment.

Seeds of park systems were being planted independently in each of the colonies in the late nineteenth century. The Tasmanian legislature explicitly discussed scenic preserves as early as 1863. The NSW government created a reserve in the Blue Mountains in 1866. Victoria also designated a public park in 1866. Western Australian policymakers set aside an area of the coastal lowlands to protect wildflowers in 1872. These and other actions were encouraged by forerunners of modern environmental groups emerging within individual colonies during the nineteenth century, for example, the Royal Societies formed in Tasmania in 1842.[119] However, formal, long-term planning was virtually nonexistent. Only once during this period did any of these groups, the Australian Association for the Advancement of Science in 1893, propose a list of appropriate areas for a national system of parks.[120]

Most authorities date Australian national parks to the designation of "National Park" at what is now called Royal N.P. in 1879. This park was created at the insistence of NSW premier Sir John Robertson in response to the demands of early citizen groups. The groups demanded protected public parks as places to escape from the growing problems of overcrowding and disease in nearby Sydney. The NSW legislature agreed, suggesting "all cities, towns, and villages should possess places of public recreation." Indeed, the emphasis of this and other early parks was on providing recreation opportunities to balance the ills of urbanized life. [121]

During the first half of the twentieth century, individual states created their own collections of parks. Queensland established the first system of parks under a state agency in 1906. Tasmanian legislators designated the first political body, the Scenery Preservation Board, specifically to manage parks and reserves in 1915. Other states followed suit, setting aside many important areas during this time. Some of these are listed in table 4-5.

Several factors made the lack of systematic planning either by the Commonwealth or by the individual states almost inevitable. First, the Commonwealth of Australia, established in 1901, retained state control over land and water resources. Thus, the term "national park" actually refers, most often, to state-preserved land. To attempt any systematic national plans would have appeared to violate state prerogatives. Second, many areas were established at the behest of energetic individuals such as Romeo Lahey in Queensland and Myles Dunphy in NSW who could operate most effectively at the state level. With the exception of Dunphy, most of these individuals and the state-level National Park Associations they founded concentrated on specific park areas, generally near population centers, and not on any form of systematic expansion.[122] Third, any potential interest in national attempts at systematic expansion were doomed to inspire strenuous objections from resource user groups. Mining, timber, farming, and hunting interests questioned

TABLE 4-5
Early Australian Nature Conservation Areas

New South Wales	*South Australia*
Dorrigo	Morialta
New England	Naracoorte Caves
Morton	Flinders Chase
Warrumbungle	
Western Australia	*Tasmania*
Nornalup	Ben Lomond
Stirling Range	Cradle Mountain
Porongurup	Mt. Field
	Freycinet
Victoria	*Queensland*
Wilsons Promontory	Lamington
Mount Buffalo	offshore islands
Wyperfeld	
Mallacoota	

Source: Ovington 1980: 47.

preservation of natural conditions in even the most revered individual units, let alone systems of parks. For example, mining and timber operations continued in Royal N.P. until 1920.[123]

Starting in 1956, state governments initiated efforts to formally organize their collections of parks. In that year, the Victoria legislature passed the National Parks Act establishing the National Parks Authority with responsibilities for thirteen areas. NSW policymakers created the first National Parks and Wildlife Service in 1967, only after years of efforts by Minister for Lands Tom Lewis. In an interesting note related to this book, in a 1966 speech Lewis called for emulation of the systems in the United States and Canada.[124] This NSW agency became the model for the other Australian states and for the Commonwealth.[125] By the early 1970s, nearly 2% of Australian land had been set aside as national parks.[126]

These early efforts did little to produce representation of diverse ecosystems or any consistency nationwide. Many ecosystems were not represented at all. An Australian Academy of Science (AAS) study in 1968 described critical areas, notably the eastern coastline, the arid central zones, and marine ecosystems, as lacking representation.[127] The state systems expanded, though at different rates and with different priorities. Hall's assessment was of "nine different approaches, by the states, the territories, and the Commonwealth."[128]

Growth

By the late 1970s, expansion was well underway. Table 4-6 specifies the growth of national park areas throughout Australia in terms of number and size of area protected. As the final column shows, lands protected as national parks or nature reserves jumped from 1.2% of

TABLE 4-6
Growth in National Park Systems

State or Territory	Year	# Nat Parks	Area (ha)	# Nature Reserves	Area (ha)	% State Total as Reserves
New	1968	19	802,770	55	59,434	1.0
South	1978	46	1,734,630	126	338,602	2.6
Wales	1988	68	3,101,742	185	521,651	4.5
Victoria	1968	20	150,062	28	51,255	0.9
	1978	26	260,096	22	34,775	1.3
	1988	30	1,073,567	137	530,393	7.1
Queensland	1968	254	940,715	0	0	0.5
	1978	323	2,182,169	3	30,228	1.3
	1988	315	3,512,867			2.1
South	1968	6	208,392	98	961,192	1.2
Australia	1978	8	233,071	162	3,687,869	4.0
	1988	12	2,648,453	193	4,072,526	6.8
Tasmania	1968		288,259			4.2
	1978	12	653,048	24	28,099	10.0
	1988	13	851,046	93	49,426	13.3
Western	1968	35	332,478	127	818,442	0.5
Australia	1978	42	4,563,087	412	8,086,314	5.0
	1988	53	4,649,732	1,041	9,994,972	5.8
Northern	1968	4	195,123	5	4,647,400	3.6
Territory	1978	12	251,490	6	4,971,100	3.9
	1988	8	2,488,613	12	33,776	1.9
Australian	1968			1	4,858	2.0
Capital	1978			3	9,843	4.0
Territory	1988	1	94,000	2	10,020	43.3
Total	1968	338	2,857,799	314	6,542,581	1.2
	1978	469	9,877,591	758	17,186,830	3.5
	1988	500	18,420,020	1,663	15,212,764	4.4

Sources: Coveney 1993: 19; Mosley 1990: 46–47; Ovington 1980: 51.

Australian territory in 1968 to 3.5% in 1978 to 4.4% by 1988. Much of this growth occurred in the late 1970s. The percentage of area designated as national park or reserve increased from 2.46% in 1977 to 4.1% by 1981. In fiscal year 1978–79 alone, over 9.9 million hectares were added as protected areas.[129] A substantial amount of land (3.75 million ha) was subtracted from the total in 1982 when the Tanami Desert Wildlife Sanctuary was returned to aboriginal ownership.

Financial support for federal planning agencies increased during this same period. Funding for the ANPWS from Parliament increased from $1.885 million in 1977–78 to $3.035 million in 1980–81 (61% increase) to $5.948 million in 1983–84 (96% increase).[130] Similar increases funded AHC efforts. The AHC had been able to provide little direction early given that it employed only twelve staffers in its first five years of existence.[131] However, funding increased dramatically over the next dozen years, as shown in table 4-7, enabling the AHC to provide a significant presence.[132] That presence is reflected in the increasing amounts spent to inform and educate the public as shown in the right-hand column.

Growth slowed in the 1980s, however, and it will continue to get tougher. Many argue that enough land has been set aside. Those

TABLE 4-7
Appropriations to AHC and AHC Expenses

Year	Commonwealth/Parliamentary Appropriations	Expenses on Information, Publicity, Advertising $
1977	291,000	30,988
1978	446,225	61,109
1979	497,799	39,841
1980	519,200	51,184
1981	639,000	56,365
1982	719,000	41,123
1983	759,000	48,893
1984	1,200,000	171,295
1985	1,399,000	163,552
1986	1,592,000	178,263
1987	1,780,000	221,903
1988	2,243,600	192,439
1989	2,917,000	162,956
1990	4,484,000	327,916

Sources: AHC Annual Reports; Papadikis 1993: 110.

arguments are voiced often by extraction industries. Mosley notes, "Further expansion is likely to meet continuing opposition from mining and timber interests."[133] The timber industry has shown strong opposition to new parks in Tasmania and Western Australia. Miners have opposed new parks throughout the country. Finally, ongoing controversies regarding native claims on lands will add to the complexity involved in future expansion.

Systematic Expansion?

How systematic was this expansion? While significant growth occurred during this period, it did not attain certain ecological ideals.

First, many of the units added during the boom periods shown in table 4-6 were relatively small, too small to contain meaningful ecosystems. According to the IUCN definition, a national park should be over one thousand hectares. Of the 317 national parks in Queensland, 70% are smaller than this and forty of these are less than ten hectares.[134] One study concluded at the end of the growth period of the 1970s, "[M]ost parks are too small to guarantee the long-term conservation of wildlife."[135] Size of units caused another observer to worry, "The future of wilderness in Australia is very much an issue of uncertainty."[136] Subsequent expansion of these units has been difficult. Most parks have not achieved their ecological boundaries. As Mosley notes, "[M]ining, timber, and grazing interests pose serious obstacles to the expansion of the parks to their logical boundaries."[137] When I asked federal officials Phillips and Shepherd if boundaries were determined by what land is available, both agreed emphatically.[138]

Second, planning for expansion suffered from a lack of quality research. Lunney and Recher concluded in 1979, "The lack of information about the ecology and distribution of Australian plants and animals has resulted in the selection of poor sites for some parks."[139] Given economies of scale and the need for coordination, thorough research would be most possible at the national level. Indeed, the creation of national agencies in the 1970s increased the potential for national research efforts. Still, by the end of the expansion in the 1980s, Hall concludes, "Protection is usually the result of an ad hoc decision by government in response to political pressure from conservationists, often with loss of the original wilderness resource."[140] ANCA Director Phillips agrees: "We have approached expansion on an opportunistic basis, there has not been a systematic approach."[141] According to Mosley, "Not a great deal of attention has been paid in Australia to defining the biological objectives of park and reserve management."[142]

Rather than basing expansion on quality research, parks are usually created after "ad hoc decisionmaking and belated response to the push and pull of events whenever wilderness controversies have arisen."[143]

Third, new units were often sited to avoid conflicts with users more than to preserve specific ecosystems. The 1979 Lunney study cites too much emphasis on recreation as the primary value in park selection and too little consideration of ecological concerns.[144] Even into the 1990s, "the dominant attitude in Australia is that wilderness is worthless or unproductive land, which can only assume value to Australian society through the removal of timber or minerals, grazing, clearing for agriculture, or the onset of mass tourism."[145] The result was that most national parks and wilderness areas were designated only after the protected land was considered relatively useless for material reasons. NSW parks manager Francis says, "The land in national parks came to us because it wasn't needed for other purposes."[146] Marine areas were also difficult to establish due to conflicts over fisheries.[147] Thus, areas selected for ecological reasons were only likely to become protected if they didn't tempt other users. National parks are, Hall concludes, "in essence, worthless lands."[148]

Overall, planners were disappointed in the lost opportunities for more systematic expansion. At the end of the 1980s, the Australian national government launched a National Wilderness Inventory (NWI) as a "necessary first step" toward preserving appropriate lands out of what remained.[149] In 1995 ANCA published the *Interim Biogeographic Regionalisation for Australia* (IBRA) as a comprehensive assessment of representation by preserved areas. ANCA's systems planners state in IBRA: "It is widely acknowledged that the system of protected areas does not comprise a comprehensive sample of the variety of environments and landscapes."[150] Even regarding the terrestrial ecosystems that do have units, the adequacy of representation still leaves many deficiencies.[151] As noted authority Mosley concludes, ". . . the park systems of Australia are still far from complete."[152]

Impact of the Federalism Constraint

Though the NWI was scheduled to be completed by 1993, attainment of that goal was unlikely for one major reason, "the lack of cooperation" by certain state governments.[153] This outcome is only the most recent impact of the federal system on systematic expansion efforts.

Because of the intractable nature of Australian federalism, implementation of any major systemwide preservation plans must be achieved through consensus between the national and state governments. Two recent, thorough reviews of Australian public lands policies arrive at remarkably similar conclusions. Hall concludes that "The emphasis on 'consensus' between the Commonwealth and the states suggests that any wilderness system will be achieved as a lowest common denominator of government demands rather than as a rational environmental planning exercise."[154] Toyne describes preservation decisions as reflecting ". . . the painstaking process of building consensus between governments, a consensus often arrived at on the lowest common denominator of agreement."[155]

These characterizations do not suggest that state officials have been consistently negligent in pursuing systematic expansion. Indeed, many state agencies moved toward more long-term planning during this period. Both Victoria and Western Australia had developed conservation strategies by 1987. The Victoria plan calls explicitly for attention to preservation of diversity.[156] New South Wales, the state to pioneer creation of a national parks service, is also the state with the most growth in number of parks and number of total units as shown in table 4-6.

Most states use a dual system of national parks and nature reserves. Nature conservation is the paramount objective at both kinds of sites, but parks tend to offer more recreational and educational uses.[157] The NSW National Parks and Wildlife Act of 1967 combined parks and reserves under control of the NPWS and provided the first attempt at zoning of wilderness areas in Australia. Zones specify boundaries of areas, designations for uses, and the acceptability of roads within parks.[158]

Ecological considerations at the state level also benefit from the ideological perspectives of most agency employees. A survey of NSW personnel, for example, reveals most personnel regarding preservation of natural conditions as the primary goal of their agency.[159] NSW parks manager Francis says of his employees, "They are highly motivated to the cause of conservation."[160] These employees do, however, face political realities. One official told me that most of the employees were "green-minded" but that often led to conflicts with conservative state governments. This, he added, "causes enormous difficulties."[161]

Often, state decisions about usage when creating new areas determine conditions that inspire the "low common denominator" characterization used by Hall and Toyne. Some park areas in Victoria continue to be available to loggers, miners, and grazers. Grazing is allowed at remote parks in Queensland. Mineral exploration and grazing are allowed in South and Western Australian parks.[162] Governments in the Northern Territory and Western Australia have eased restrictions on mining in the parks.[163] South Australia is planning expensive hotels in some of its parks.[164]

The receptivity of state governments to World Heritage listings has also often been reluctant. Some Premiers, notably Neville Wran in New South Wales, have been quite interested. Others, notably Queensland, resist World Heritage intervention. For instance, Queensland's minister for tourism Bob McKechnie vowed in 1985 that "not one more square inch" would be added to the World Heritage List.[165] Prior to 1987, the Commonwealth always attained state consent to nominate an area for World Heritage listing. State opposition has been strong enough that the federal government abandoned the policy of seeking state approval before nominating areas for World Heritage listing in 1987.[166]

Most important, getting all state governments on board at the same time and moving in the same direction has been problematic. One study in 1984 found "considerable diversity in approach, manpower, and budget between the various states."[167] Many factors produce variance between states. As mentioned earlier, shifts in party control of state governments often lead to shifts of policy emphasis. Because state governments retain such a powerful role in national preservation efforts, a shift in any statehouse can complicate implementation of systemwide plans. Rarely in the last thirty years have all the state and federal governments been led by the same party. As one example, federal efforts to preserve alpine areas bordering NSW and Victoria were long stymied by "state government intransigence" in NSW under the Liberal–National government.[168]

Future Expansion

Several parks officials spoke with guarded optimism about future expansion in Australia. After speaking somewhat critically of past opportunism, NSW parks manager Francis told me that his agency was currently doing more systematic planning and greater consideration of ecosystem representation. Indeed, two systematic assessment projects commenced in 1994 for NSW. First, the Natural Resource Audit Council was created and then instructed to provide a comprehensive audit of public lands in northeast NSW. Second, the NPWS began a three-year project to gather information on biodiversity in western NSW.[169] The ultimate impact of such assessments has yet to be seen. As Francis added cautiously about state politicians, "I'll be interested to see if they will spend the money to purchase areas not yet represented."[170]

Queensland park planners have recently moved toward more systematic expansion. Planner Mark Gough spoke at length about the "worthless lands thesis." He agreed that it was historically accurate, that "many parks had been put in areas where the land was too steep for grazing," and acknowledged that "we ended up with the marginal stuff." But he also added that, in the last few years, his agency was using computer analysis and remote sensing to make decisions to maximize representation and diversity. "Now," Gough added, "if land is suffi-ciently valuable, we can compulsorily acquire it."[171] In fact, at least five recent purchases have been compulsory.[172] As of 1994, the Department of Environment claimed that recent efforts have "achieved representa-tion of about 67% of the State's ecosystem biodiversity."[173] Gough attrib-uted much of the shifting emphasis to a change in Queensland government from the conservative National Party to a more ecologi-cally receptive Labor administration that pushed through the Nature Conservation Act of 1992. Among its goals, this legislation mandates "the dedication and declaration of areas representative of the biological diversity, natural features and wilderness of Queensland as pro-tected areas."[174]

One big expansion issue in Queensland's future will center on setting aside significant portions of the Cape York Peninsula, as prom-ised by Premier Wayne Goss of the Labor Party in his successful 1995 reelection campaign.[175] Efforts to pursue this expansion have become quite complex. Much of the land on the Cape York Peninsula is wanted by livestock grazers, miners, conservationists, and the native Wik tribe. The latter claim received prominence in the mid-1990s and verification from the High Court in December 1996. The Howard government scrambled to find a compromise solution to these various demands in 1997 only to antagonize many of those involved.[176] Their efforts were complicated by the fact that the Queensland government allowed plans for a $200 million bauxite mine to continue. In August 1997, the Wik tribe reached agreement with the ALCAN mining company to allow development of the mine on peninsula land.[177]

The most advanced state effort in this regard is in Victoria. The Land Conservation Act of 1970 established the Land Conservation Council (LCC) to "carry out investigations and make recommendations to the Minister with respect to the use of public land in order to provide for the balanced use of land in Victoria."[178] The LCC has since become the advisory body for expansion decisions in Victoria, having made over five thousand recommendations for land use management. The LCC proceeds as follows. The Council announces intentions to investi-gate a specific area, provides a factual description of the area, invites public comment, and then publishes its recommendations that are subject to comment for another sixty or ninety days. The Council con-sists of a chairman, a deputy chairman, and fifteen members. The current board has expertise in biology, forestry, agronomy, mining, engineering, and conservation.[179] According to Rod Gowans of the

Department of Conservation, this diversity leads to "spirited discussions and informed decisions."[180] LCC recommendations are nearly always approved. As of 1994, the LCC had made 5,736 recommendations subject to government decision, of which 5,509 were approved as recommended.[181] The LCC has divided the state into seventeen regions to be studied for representation and had completed reviews on five of these by 1995.[182]

Change is also occurring, but slowly, at the federal level. Expansion plans on federal lands are currently fairly dormant. When I asked Graeme Marshall if any expansion was pending, he answered, "no, we're not actively looking for additional responsibilities."[183] On the other hand, self-appraisal is getting more sophisticated. The IBRA represents the most systematic effort at assessment of representation to date. An index of bias was created by ANCA to measure the "extent to which the existing system of protected areas fails to include examples of the most extensive ecosystems."[184]

Obviously, Australia has a long way to go to achieve coverage. According to the IBRA, the areas with moderate to high bias (little representation) are most numerous. In fact, the vast majority of the country is described in these categories. While applauding the IBRA effort, the World Wide Fund for Nature's review also concludes: "Progress in establishing a comprehensive and representative reserve system has been too slow."[185]

Further, while the federal government can provide assessments, the prospects for ANCA coordination of national planning are quite limited. While ANCA can use the IBRA process and other tools to encourage certain state behavior, the states will continue to act quite independently. The variance among state efforts remains quite large. In addition, state governments often reverse directions. For example, Tasmanian politicians have revoked parklands from protection nearly two dozen times.[186] The prospects for implementation of systematic expansion plans will continue to be affected by the federal dimension for the foreseeable future.

ENHANCEMENT OF INDIVIDUAL UNITS

Australia contains literally hundreds of sites bearing the title "National Park." Selection of a few units in order to analyze implementation of planning is facilitated by three issues. First, given the importance of the vertical dimension, units should be used that reflect different jurisdictions within the federal structure. Thus, one park described below is purely federal, one is purely state-managed, and the other two are different versions of joint federal-state operations. Second, the latter three are all located in the state of Queensland. This enhances comparison as they differ according to how the federal and state governments interact rather than as a result of being governed by entirely different state governments. Third, considering the important historical role of international affiliations in park affairs, all four sites discussed below are World Heritage sites.

Kakadu

On the bus ride into Kakadu National Park, in the Northern Territory of Australia, tour companies often show a video of recent crocodile attacks on humans. My sense was that this had as much to do with building anticipation as it did with encouraging caution. Indeed, spotting these creatures that have refused to accept human supremacy in Kakadu's river systems is a thrilling experience. Kakadu can provide such thrills, but the fights over protection of the park have been nearly as fierce as the park's toughest residents.

Background

Kakadu is one of only sixteen sites in the world that are listed as World Heritage for both natural and cultural significance. Others include Tongariro in New Zealand, Machu Picchu in Peru, and Mt. Athos in Greece. Kakadu's cultural significance derives from the continuing occupation of the park by aboriginal people, the Jawoyn tribe, an occupation that dates back some twenty thousand years. The Aborigines own much of the area and lease it back to the federal government for operation as a national park. The natural significance is obvious in the park's nineteen thousand square kilometers of rainforests, rivers, waterfalls, and wetlands teeming with one-third of Australia's bird species and wildlife such as the aforementioned crocodiles.

Kakadu is also home to rich mineral deposits. Uranium and gold have been the most sought-after commodities, but other minerals include tin, copper, and diamonds. Some accounts estimate that up to $100 billion in minerals exist within park boundaries.[187] Recently, a Canadian named Tony Gray found what was reported to be the largest uranium deposit in the world here.[188] Demands for these minerals have shaped political interactions affecting the park since the 1970s. Indeed, although the Whitlam government announced plans to form a national park in 1973, the Fraser government approved the opening of the Ranger Uranium Mine in 1977 before the park could be formally established.[189]

The park area is all within the Northern Territory. Thus, establishment and management have been subject to deliberations between the federal and territorial governments as well as between the governments and the Aborigines. Toyne terms the Northern Territory reaction to Commonwealth protection as "vitriolic," adding, "no tolerance is shown to those who hold or represent views contrary to the mainstream white, conservative Territorians."[190] Since the park is not on state land, however, implementation of federal plans for the park has not been severely constrained by the federal dimension. Rather, federal actions have been more affected by the interaction between ministers at the highest level of Australian government.

Systematic Preservation Efforts

The total protected area was declared in three stages between 1979 and 1989. World Heritage recognition has also occurred in phases beginning in 1981.

Political interaction between officials at the national level regarding these developments has been significant. In 1986 federal Minister for Environment Barry Cohen released a new management plan for Kakadu. The plan called for exclusion of mining within Stages I and II, World Heritage listing for Stage II, and creation of a new Stage III area to the south that would include an unspecified Conservation Zone (CZ) within which mining could occur. The CZ was deemed essential by mining interests since it would presumably include gold-deposit-rich locations such as Coronation Hill. Such a compromise was arguably justified by language recognizing that mining claims existed "prior to proclamation of the park."[191]

This plan created considerable controversy at the federal level. The lack of specific boundaries on the CZ invited differing proposals from other political actors. Minister for Resources and Energy Gareth Evans called for a large area to be available for mining, criticizing the Stage III area as "clapped out buffalo country."[192] Cohen responded that in fact mining and exploration should be prohibited in Kakadu and offered amendments to that effect in late 1986. Evans' support from the mining community was countered by Cohen's support from the ACF and other environmental organizations. The proposal to prohibit mining in Stage II was successfully challenged in Federal Court by a mining company with an existing lease.

Propreservation forces fought back. Cohen and supporters successfully passed the National Parks and Wildlife Conservation Amendment Act of 1987 in May to prohibit mining even in areas where interests already existed.[193] The Commonwealth further appealed the previous court ruling allowing mining to continue and won, using the World

Heritage agreement, in Full Federal Court in September 1987. The court declared the cabinet decision to be a valid exercise of power.[194] National park officials, backed by World Heritage designation, pushed for greater preservation efforts.

However, implementation of these plans stalled. Mining interests, prodevelopment forces in the Northern Territory, and the federal Ministry for Primary Industries lobbied intensely on behalf of development. When Stage III was officially designated in June 1987, roughly half of the 4,500 square kilometer expansion was designated as CZ, available for exploration.[195] Mining continued at spots in the other stages, such as at the Ranger Uranium Mine. Operations at Ranger continue to this day. When I asked a spokesman for the mine if park officials were trying to stop operations, he replied, "No, they really can't, it's all in the lease, and the mine was here before they were."[196] Several billion dollars worth of uranium have been mined at Ranger over the last two decades.

Temporarily stymied, largely by its own internal divisions, the Labor government took two major actions. First, in late 1989, they reduced the CZ to a narrow strip of less than fifty square kilometers. This step was largely a response to public opinion polls showing roughly 75% support for greater protection at Kakadu.[197] Second, they appointed a Resource Assessment Commission (RAC) to make long-term recommendations. The inquiry lasted a year and included hearings, field trips, and written submissions. In 1991 the RAC concluded that the economic contribution from the mine would be less than estimated by its advocates, but also environmental damages would be less than predicted by conservationists.[198] The RAC also attempted to assess the Jawoyn position on mining. While various spokespersons offered somewhat conflicting views, ultimately the Aborigine position was viewed as one of opposition to mining in Kakadu.[199]

In 1991 Stage III was extended to include the CZ and the area at Coronation Hill. In 1992 all three stages were inscribed on the World Heritage List. As a result of these various expansions and the associated arrangements with each, the management plan for Kakadu is fairly complex. The ANPWS uses management zones as shown in figure 4-1. Park officials explicitly acknowledge that tourism and other uses of the park should not take priority over aboriginal rights and the natural and cultural heritage.[200] Further, the current management plan for the park states that "recovery of minerals will continue to be prohibited."[201]

The future for preservation of Kakadu is promising, but prospects could change quickly. Mining companies are anxious to pursue various opportunities within the park.[202] The Liberal-National coalition promised to open mining at Coronation Hill if they won control of the

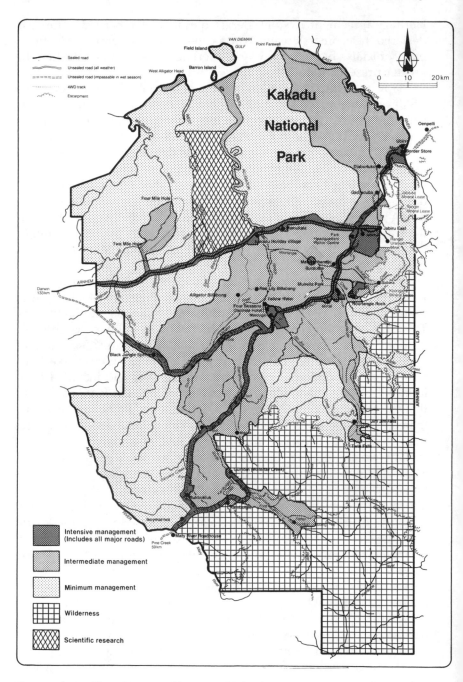

Figure 4-1   Management Zones at Kakadu
(Source: Kakadu Plan of Management: p. 18)

federal government.[203] Aborigine support for preservation is somewhat tenuous.[204] In 1994 the Jawoyn tribe entered into an agreement with a mining conglomerate and the Northern Territory Chamber of Mines to search for gold in their jurisdiction.[205] Considering the importance of the Jawoyn position on the Coronation Hill decision and the role of the Aborigines in comanagement of the park, this recent arrangement may have serious effects on the future of preservation at Kakadu.[206] In general, events at Kakadu illustrate the importance of political forces, even without a dominant federalism constraint, on the implementation of planning decisions. As one observer states, "The major challenge for the federal government has, therefore, been to gain some control of the agenda."[207]

The Great Barrier Reef

When snorkelling in the waters of the Great Barrier Reef, one can't help but feel immersed in one of the true natural wonders of the world. The colors, sizes, and shapes of the coral and the fish are simply stunning. Ironically perhaps, but not surprisingly, this natural beauty has made preservation for future generations anything but a sure thing.

Background

When nominating the area for World Heritage designation in 1981, the Great Barrier Reef Marine Park Authority (GBRMPA) asserted: "The GBR is by far the largest single collection of coral reefs in the world. Biologically, the GBR supports the most diverse ecosystem known to man."[208] The area plays host to 1,500 species of fish, 350 species of coral, and nearly 250 species of birds. The GBR is the largest protected area in the world, encompassing nearly 3,000 individual reefs and 350,000 square kilometers of continental shelf off northeastern Queensland.

The GBR is also one of the most heavily used areas in the world. Annually, the GBRMP hosts over two million visitors. As table 4-8 shows, tourism is much higher here than at other popular Australian destinations.[209] Tourism has increased dramatically in recent years until it now far surpasses other uses of the area in terms of financial value.

The table also indicates, however, that the presence of other users is substantial. Historically, the area contained prime targets for commercial fishing, recreational fishing, and oil exploration.[210] As of 1967, over half of the GBR had been leased for oil exploration by the Queensland government. Oil pollution and spills led to conservationist demands for Commonwealth attention to state leasing practices. Following public hearings and debates, the Commonwealth government used its participation in the international Convention of the Terri-

TABLE 4-8
Tourist Expenditures at Australian Parks (1991–92) ($ million)

Park	Tourists	Other Users	Mgmt. Budget
Great Barrier Reef	776	147	18.1
Wet Tropics	377	25	12.1
Kakadu	122	NA	10.8
Uluru	38	NA	2.9

Source: Driml 1994: vi.

torial Sea to pass the Seas and Submerged Lands Act in 1973, claiming sovereignty over the territorial waters off Australia, and declared a new marine park encompassing the Great Barrier Reef. The GBR has been and continues to be a "multiple use" marine park.[211] The Queensland government, concerned about losing access to offshore oil, challenged the Seas and Submerged Lands Act but lost in the High Court in 1975.[212] The Great Barrier Reef Marine Park Act of 1975 effectively put an end to future leasing.[213] Mining and oil exploration are now only allowed in the portion of the World Heritage Area (about 2.5% of total) outside of the GBRMPA. While this sounds promising for preservation, natural conditions are increasingly affected by other human uses. The growth in tourist operations remains remarkable. In 1993–94 alone, the GBRMPA granted 341 tourist program permits (for flights, fishing trips, diving, etc.), a 113% increase over the previous year.[214]

Systematic Preservation Efforts

Though the 1994 twenty-five-year Strategic Plan for the GBR includes a joint promise from Prime Minister Keating and Queensland premier Goss to "ensure the long term health of the Reef," the ecological protection of the GBR is subject to many factors.[215] Implementation of this plan is and will be heavily affected by federalism.

First, the management structure has a significant impact. Stated in simplest terms, the Commonwealth government manages the water portions of the GBR while the Queensland government manages the land portions including most of the islands, but both coordinate through the GBRMPA.[216] As legal services officer Darin Honchin told me, "We have two separate agencies working together under one decision-making body."[217] The top level of the MPA consists of three appointees: one chair, one scientist, and one representative of the Queensland government.

This arrangement often leads to complex decisions. For example, which level of government decides the fate of birds that migrate from sea to shore? Even the boundaries are subject to dispute. When deciding the Seas and Submerged Lands case, the High Court did not specify if the waterline starts at the mean of low waters, the lowest astronomical tide (often claimed by Queensland), or the low water line of ordinary tides.[218] The Commonwealth provides most of the capital budget, but funds for daily operations are split on a 50-50 basis between the Commonwealth and Queensland.[219]

The rhetorical cooperation between levels of government evident in the twenty-five-year planning document may not last beyond the next elections, at either federal or state levels. Virtually every aspect of park management is affected by federal-state relations. Activities on shore, in areas governed by the state, affect all parts of the GBR. According to the MPA, "[T]he greatest threat to the Reef arises from the long-term effects of run-off [of nutrients and sediment] from the mainland."[220]

Second, current funding levels are adequate but not growing. In 1993–94, both Queensland and the Commonwealth governments appropriated $3.058 million for operating funds. This matched the 1992–93 appropriation.[221] Should Queensland cut funding for daily operations, the Commonwealth is bound to do the same in order to maintain the 50-50 matching arrangement. This is a classic illustration of the low common denominator factor described earlier.

Third, ecological management of this multiple-use park is implemented through extensive zoning. The categories include preservation zones (all use prohibited), scientific research (only research allowed), marine park (recreation allowed), and general use zones (fishing permitted). Developing zone plans usually requires two years of proposing draft outlines and soliciting public comments on proposed uses. The final zoning plans are approved by the GBR Ministerial Council made up of federal and state officials and then authorized by the Federal Parliament. Zones are generally set for five-year periods.[222] As a result of the collective planning for zones, currently less than 1% of the marine park is restricted from tourists. Less than 5% is restricted from fishing and collection.[223] Further, the MPA admits that these percentages may not grow in the future as competition for areas increases.[224]

One situation where these complex relations have recently been manifest is in the Hinchinbrook Channel area near Cardwell. Development of the area to provide accommodation for two thousand guests and a marina with two hundred berths was first proposed in 1987 by a company called Resort Village. Before either the Queensland government or the MPA could react, the local Cardwell Council approved a special zone allowing Resort Village to begin removing mangroves and excavating the marina basin at Oyster Point. Resort Village started and then stopped work, due to financial problems, before either the Commonwealth or Queensland governments could even require an environmental impact assessment. The site was left degraded.

In 1991 the Commonwealth Attorney General's office advised the MPA that the Oyster Point site was part of Queensland's internal waters and outside the MPA's jurisdiction. Thus, when a new developer purchased the site with intent to build a "Port Hinchinbrook," the MPA could only advise the Queensland authorities on approval. During 1994 the Commonwealth government expressed concern about impact on the World Heritage Area even if the marine park was outside World Heritage boundaries. Despite public protests, Queensland authorities approved the project in late 1994 and development of what was to be the largest integrated resort and marina in Australia resumed without substantial environmental impact assessment.

The Hinchinbrook project was subsequently suspended to consider the threat to seagrass, but both critical observers and the MPA think resumption is likely soon.[225] Professor David Haigh explicitly worried that "World Heritage is merely a gold plated tourist plaque, directed to economic return rather than the lofty, yet attainable, ideals of the Convention."[226]

In general, the management arrangement for planning and implementation at GBR has had mixed results. Management of day-to-day operations is generally fairly smooth. Working relations between federal and state employees are usually cooperative. Implementation of long-term plans is more difficult. The most fundamental issue is expansion of protected areas. Though the twenty-five-year Strategic Plan calls for more areas with reduced "human access and/or impacts, and which are free from structures and extractive uses," GBR planners admit that expansion of preserved zones has been, as Honchin says, only "level" in recent years.[227] They are also quite explicit about the primary reason for slow progress. An entire section of the Strategic Plan is devoted to "Integrated Planning" between levels of government. As the document states, plans must be "coordinated across geographical boundaries and stakeholders."[228] When I asked Honchin if federalism issues were getting any closer to being settled, he answered quite emphatically, "No, we will still see political conflicts."

Wet Tropics

Standing on the beach at Cape Tribulation, one can imagine that all the surrounding land is equally unspoiled and protected. In fact, the

Wet Tropics constitute a patchwork of pristine and unprotected areas that defies consistent management efforts.

Background

The Wet Tropics is an area constituting roughly one million hectares of northeastern coastal area between Townsville and Cooktown. The area includes most of the remaining wet tropical rainforest found in Australia and perhaps the oldest continuously surviving rainforest on earth. The wildlife includes 30% of Australia's marsupial species, 18% of bird species, and over 60% of bat and butterfly species. Mountains climb to over 1,600 meters. Some of the trees date to three thousand years old.[229] The Wet Tropics contain areas like Mossman Gorge and the Daintree River that are treasures of biodiversity. Even Captain Cook must have marvelled at the beauty of the area despite the problems with grounding his ships that led him to give Tribulation its name.

The Wet Tropics area has been subjected to a wide range of demands that have not received a coordinated response largely due to the Australian federal system. Uses have included real estate development, mining, agriculture, tourism projects, road-building, and especially logging.[230] Throughout the 1980s, local governing councils and the Queensland government of Joh Bjelke-Petersen welcomed these demands, often approving projects without even soliciting ecological advice. As Joh said one time, "You can do so much with a bulldozer."[231]

Protection of the Wet Tropics became quite contentious in the early 1980s when the Queensland government turned bulldozers loose on building a road north from Cape Tribulation. The road corridor cut through dense rainforests and up and down steep hillsides. Environmental protests and blockades ultimately led to Commonwealth consideration of the situation. As in the Kakadu case, however, the initial federal response from the environment minister was weak, constrained by pressure from the transport, finance, and other ministries at the federal level and Queensland bureaus of logging and mining at the state level.[232] Road-building continued despite perennial washouts during the wet seasons.

When the controversy continued, members of the Commonwealth government proposed listing the area as World Heritage. The prodevelopment Queensland government fought listing of the Wet Tropics, despite the fact that well over 70% of the Australian public and over 90% of visitors to the area wanted it preserved in natural condition.[233] In spite of this pressure, the Commonwealth failed to nominate the area for World Heritage status between 1984 and 1986, cowed by arguments of "states' rights." In the federal elections of 1987, the Hawke government promised to nominate the area for World Heritage if re-

elected. After winning the election, the government successfully inscribed the Wet Tropics in 1988 and fought off subsequent challenges
from Queensland in the High Court.[234]

Systematic Preservation Efforts

Because of these bitter disputes between levels of government,
long-term planning for the Wet Tropics was nonexistent before 1990.
Only then was an agency established with the potential to engage in
systematic decision making. Even that agency, however, is severely
constrained by the compromises that have resulted in a complicated
management structure for the area.

The Wet Tropics Management Authority (WTMA) was established
as the result of an agreement between the Commonwealth and Queensland governments in 1990. Even in 1995, when I asked Dr. Earl Saxon,
manager of the WTMA, and his colleague Ian Garvin about the structure, both joked about how unique and unsettled it remains. The basic
structure is depicted in figure 4-2. The important point to note is that
responsibilities are divided between federal and state officials at each
level of the planning agency. For example, the Ministerial Council
consists of two federal and two state nominees. The WTMA includes
a part-time chair, a nonvoting executive director, two Commonwealth
nominees, and two Queensland nominees. Funding is divided strictly

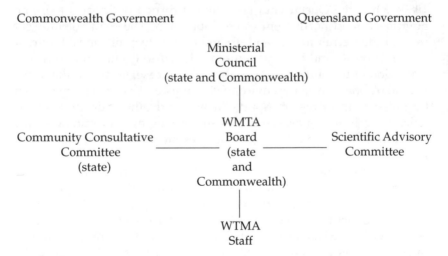

Figure 4-2 Wet Tropics Management Authority Structure
(Source: WTMA document 1995)

on a 50-50 basis. The WTMA has been criticized as excessively con-servation-oriented by the Queensland government, slow to provide protection by conservation groups, and unwieldy by other parks offi-cials. As Queensland NPWS official Mark Gough said regarding the arrangement, "Ministerial Councils are a pain in the ass, they're for-ever fighting."[235]

The legacy of these intense disputes and their complex resolutions is patchwork protection of public lands in the Wet Tropics ecosystem. The area contains more than eight hundred separate land units, both privately and publicly owned, under the jurisdiction of the WTMA and fourteen separate local authorities. Only 29% of the land is national park with the rest state forest (44.4%), timber reserve (11.6%), or miscel-laneous ownership. As the WTMA admits, "Day to day management of the World Heritage Area is the responsibility of individual land holders."[236] Commercial logging has been stopped on the state forests, but these areas are still much more accessible than parks and more open to tourist development. In some areas, the commercial development is rampant. Parks manager Garvin told me that when the minister of lands visited the Daintree area in 1993, he was "so appalled that he put a moratorium into effect."[237] Figure 4-3 shows how World Heritage protection is fragmented throughout this area.

Like the structure of the WTMA, plans for the future preservation of the area are quite unsettled. When I talked to Saxon and Garvin in 1995, they were negotiating with state authorities over jurisdiction of the state forests. The forest managers were willing to abdicate, but central authorities had not promised any more resources to the WTMA to manage these areas as parks. These WTMA officials expressed some frustration at the fact that they had a plan to make sensible, ecosystem-oriented boundaries but that "the state government mostly wants to just move lands from one agency to another."[238]

Plans will continue to be affected by politicians at both the federal and state levels. Preservation of the area could receive an immense boost in coming years if the Goss state government follows through on its promise to set aside the entire Cape York Peninsula as protected area. Saxon and Garvin showed me the proposal they have prepared for the Cape York expansion and then Saxon added pointedly, "The politicians will decide whether to put it into effect or not."[239]

Fraser Island

Like nearly everyone else who visits Fraser Island, we got stuck in the sand at one point. It's easy to do, since Fraser is all sand. Being stuck

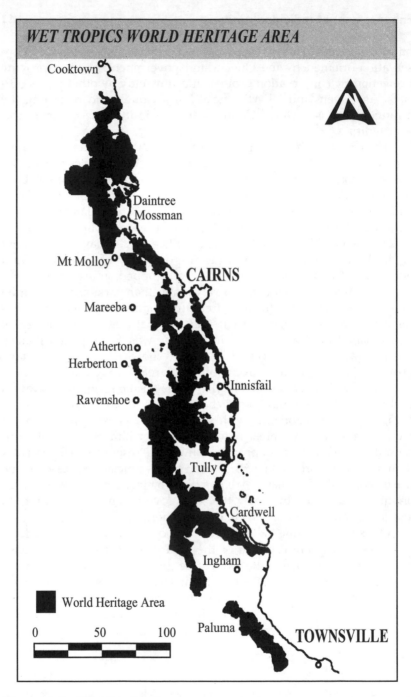

Figure 4-3 Wet Tropics Area
(Source: WTMA document, 1995)

isn't really so bad, however, as it provides more time to appreciate the beauty of the sand formations, the massive trees, the clear freshwater lakes, and the Pacific Ocean crashing on the beaches.

Background

Fraser is the world's largest sand island. It is also the site of one of the more memorable historical incidents of the penal settlement years. The island gained its name when shipwrecked survivors, including Eliza Fraser, washed up on shore. Many were killed by Aborigines, but Mrs. Fraser survived and became a celebrity. Fraser Island and the surrounding Great Sandy Region were formed by sand deposits from rivers in northern NSW and southern Queensland over thousands of years. Fraser is over 120 km in length, up to 25 km in width, and covering an area of over 160,000 hectares. Fraser contains the oldest and greatest number of distinct dune systems in the world, many of them arrranged in brightly colored, exotically shaped formations. The freshwater lakes are the world's largest and highest perched dune lakes, with some of the purest water on the planet. Vegetation is remarkably varied and includes impressive stands of satinay and brush box. Rare, precious species range from ground parrots to acid frogs.[240]

These natural features have drawn people to Fraser Island over recent decades for a succession of reasons that long prevented ecological preservation. Timber companies logged the island for decades, beginning early in the nineteenth century. Their lucrative but destructive operations inspired the Australian Association for the Advancement of Science to recommend making the whole island a national park in 1893. Most of the valuable rainforest species were cut and removed by World War II, at which point loggers shifted to the hardwoods. Fraser Island's sand beaches are tempting for their minerals. Specifically, rutile, zircon, and ilmenite are valuable components in the production of titanium steel and paint pigments. In the 1950s and 1960s, sand mining companies began large-scale mining operations through intensive scouring of Fraser's beaches.

State planning and management of the island had little to do with long-term ecology and everything to do with short-term economic opportunities. Thus in 1965, when the Queensland state government declared one-fourth of the island as national park, boundaries were drawn to avoid including any exploitable land. The new park did not contain a single ocean beach, any of the rainforest, any of the forty perched lakes, or any of the colored sand formations. In short, the park contained only "the least appealing and least important features on the island."[241] The Queensland government granted leases to mining companies in 1971 and 1973, despite the growing opposition of local citizens in the Fraser Island Defense Organisation (FIDO) led by John Sinclair. Throughout these and subsequent years, as Sinclair stated, "The advocacy for environmental protection has been persistently resisted by both vested interests and the Queensland government."[242]

Some change occurred in the 1970s and 1980s but only slowly. The Commonwealth government, lobbied by FIDO and other environmental groups, used its export restriction powers to end sand mining in 1976, but refused to provide further protection to the rest of the island as a national park. The Queensland government continued to allow sawmilling and encouraged the next wave of usage by approving questionable tourist operations. Boundaries of protected areas were continually drawn to include only those areas not desired by economic interests.[243] Further, management was divided among six different agencies. As Sinclair said, "This had the effect of reducing the level of management to something approaching anarchy."[244] Efforts to list Fraser as World Heritage were thwarted by the Joh government in Queensland. Through the 1980s, Queensland NPWS official Mark Gough told me, Fraser Island was subject to "terrible abuse."[245]

Systematic Preservation Efforts

The management situation for Fraser Island changed dramatically in the 1990s. After winning the Queensland elections in 1989, the Goss Labor government initiated an inquiry into Fraser Island, led by Tony Fitzgerald, that made several serious recommendations for greater protection. Though both state and federal governments dragged their feet at various stages, one recommendation was implemented when Fraser was listed as World Heritage in 1995.[246]

In 1994 the Queensland NPWS produced the first management plan for the region. Gough, one of the architects of the plan, spoke with pride of the new management structure for Fraser. The structure is displayed in figure 4-4. As Gough pointed out, this structure is much simpler than that for the WTMA. This structure should help planners avoid some of the delays that have affected the Wet Tropics and, to a lesser extent, the GBR. The plan prohibits sand mining, logging, and oil exploration on the island, and closes some areas to vehicular traffic.[247] The ultimate goal, stated in the management plan, is to provide "a place where nature's evolutionary processes can continue unimpeded, a bequest to all humanity."[248]

Plans for Fraser Island's future will be affected by certain realities, not the least of which is the continuing influence of the Queensland government. Fitzgerald's inquiry recommended that the entire island be managed as a national park, but Queensland officials limited national park coverage to roughly half. The current park boundaries are

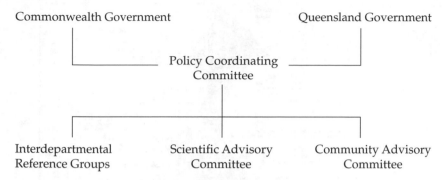

Figure 4-4   Fraser Island Management Structure
(Source: Queensland NPWS planner Mark Gough, 8/4/1995)

displayed in figure 4-5. As the map shows, many of the most important areas, including beaches and perched lakes, are not within park boundaries. The inquiry also called for protection of the entire Great Sandy Region, but again, much of the area remains unprotected. Petroleum exploration is still allowed five hundred meters off shore and elsewhere throughout the Great Sandy Region. The 1994 plan still allows considerable four-wheel drive access, commercial and recreational fishing, and increasing tourist traffic.[249] Gough spoke of the Queensland government's role in this decision: "We think if it's a national park, you shouldn't be allowed to do anything like this, but they've changed it."[250]

Ultimately, Gough and other managers are optimistic about Fraser's future. Fittingly perhaps, the World Heritage listing that the Joh government opposed so strongly may be one of the strongest safeguards for the island. As Gough said, "World Heritage is not a promise of intervention by an international body but rather a recognition and demanding of high standards."[251]

CONCLUSIONS

Systematic preservation of natural areas in Australia is inextricably intertwined with political factors, to some extent the influence of other political actors and to a greater degree the impact of the federal structure. Establishment of a national system of preserved lands has been and will continue to be dependent upon state cooperation. In terms of individual sites, some have existed in Australia for over a century, but long-term plans to restore ecological conditions are a relatively recent phenomenon. Implementation of those plans will vary according to

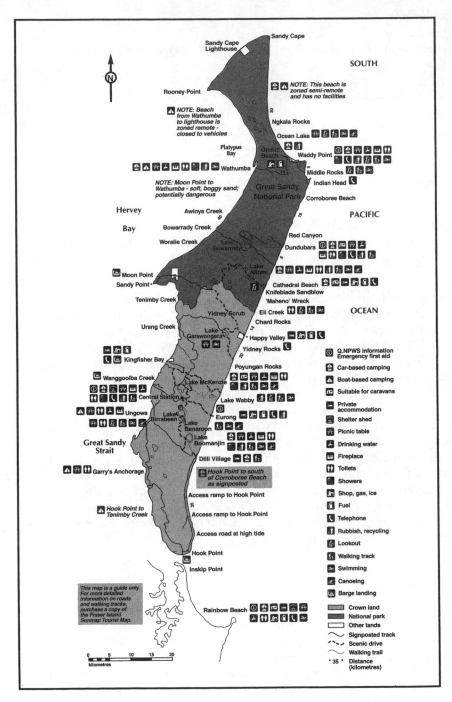

Figure 4-5 Fraser Island *(Source: Queensland News, 1995)*

placement of the site in the federal structure. The Commonwealth government has had the upper hand in decisions at parks located in territories such as Kakadu and Uluru, and while plans here are subject to some obstruction from other federal ministeries, the arrangement does lead to more optimism than at sites located within states. Recently, Australian national planners have met with their New Zealand counterparts to form an Environment Conservation Council that may provide greater national coordination of preservation efforts. Making extensive changes will be difficult, however. As historian Hall concludes, "The creation or continued protection of a national park is not a rational process. It is a political battle, a process which involves the values of interests in the struggle for power relative to government decisions."[252] Those battles have been shaped by the federal structure throughout Australian history and will continue to be so in the future.

5

Canada: A Lot of Negotiating

> We haven't done that much good except for a lot of studying and a lot of negotiating.—Murray McComb, chief of planning, Parks Canada

In 1996 the Canadian government released a major study to reconsider management of Banff and the other Rocky Mountain national parks. The study was motivated in large part by criticisms of Banff's dramatic commercial growth. Many people called for limits on building and development and much greater emphasis on restoring natural conditions in Canada's most famous national park. Yet, as I walked to the park service offices to review the study with planners, I walked past several new construction sites and plots of land recently cleared for more development. I couldn't help but recall the quote from chief planner McComb. Would this be just one more case of studying?

This chapter describes Canadian efforts to expand the national parks system and to enhance individual units for future generations. The first section provides some background by discussing the conditions in Canada that hypothetically affect systematic preservation. The second section examines the empirical record of system expansion. The third section discusses efforts at individual units, Banff and the mountain parks in particular.

BACKGROUND

I walked about a mile through mud and short-grass fields before I found the trailhead, indeed the only trailhead currently in operation in Grasslands National Park in southern Saskatchewan. The trail looked inviting, in an undeveloped kind of way, leading into vast tallgrass prairies under a big blue sky with dark clouds looming off to the west. While Grasslands has its own kind of beauty, many people would not initially think of the area as a national park. The trail leads into a virtually untouched flat area of native plants and grasses. Much of the rest of the park is crossed by roads and split by private property. Grasslands exists to represent an ecosystem niche in a long-term expansion plan that Parks Canada takes quite seriously. It exists in the condition that it does, still only about half complete, because of the institutional context in which implementation of that plan takes place.

In many important ways, the Canadian political environment is conducive to intergenerational concerns. Yet, progress towards systematic preservation at places like Grasslands is not as rapid as many desire, slowed by negotiations between levels of government necessitated by traditional institutions of land ownership.

Necessary Conditions

Much of the history of Canada's national parks reflects an emphasis on short-term benefits through economic development and use. Prior to 1970, little attention was given to long-term planning or systematic ecological preservation. Since then, however, systematic preservation efforts have benefitted from substantial demands for ecological attention, relatively stable political processes, and repeated official commitments to land preservation. As noted in all three sections below, however, developments in the mid- to late 1990s make the impact of these conditions increasingly less predictable.

Demands for Systematic Preservation

A visible symbol of a shifting attitude toward parks occurred in 1966. Early in that year, the Canadian government and the provincial government of Alberta were making a concerted effort to land the 1972 Winter Olympics. The games would bring considerable development to Banff National Park. Just prior to the vote by the International Sports Federation, however, environmental groups such as the Canadian Wildlife Federation voiced their concerns about alteration of natural conditions in national parks. The voting delegates were reportedly affected by the protests and the games were awarded to Sapporo, Japan.[1]

The actions regarding the Olympics were typical of an increased awareness regarding environmental issues throughout Canada in the late 1960s and 1970s. According to a Gallup poll in 1970, pollution was the issue ranked highest as deserving more government attention, with 65% putting it in the top spot.[2] In response, the Canadian Parliament enacted nine major environmental statutes between 1968 and 1972 such as a Clean Air Act and the Canada Water Act. While the salience of environmental issues declined somewhat through the 1970s, public opinion surveys at the end of the decade showed that 89% of respondents still considered deterioration of the environment to be a major concern, outranked only by inflation, unemployment, and crime.[3]

Demands specific to expansion and enhancement of the national parks were particularly apparent at the National Parks Conference meeting in Banff in 1968. Noted authorities from inside and outside of government made strong criticisms of past behavior and explicit recommendations for the future. Criticisms included the lack of system planning, stagnant expansion over the previous forty years, lack of ecological research on appropriate sites for new parks, and obstructionist behavior by provincial governments. Conference attendees strongly recommended accelerated expansion according to systematic ecological plans and enhancement of existing units through more awareness of ecosystem boundaries and needs.[4]

These demands were echoed and reinforced in subsequent years by a range of observers and environmental groups.[5] Several commented specifically on the need to improve relations with provincial governments in order to speed the process.[6] One study played on the economic concerns of provincial governments by encouraging more receptivity to park expansion "as a means of assisting economic development in depressed areas."[7]

Interest groups have not historically been as noticeable in Canada as in her southern neighbor. The Canadian political culture has traditionally been more consensual and less adversarial in Canada than in the United States.[8] Recent years, however, have seen a significant increase in political activity by interest groups.[9] Notable among these increasingly active participants are indigenous groups such as the Canadian Parks and Wilderness Society (CPWS) as well as Canadian branches of international organizations such as Greenpeace and the World Wildlife Fund. Over recent decades, these groups have voiced noticeable demands for land preservation.

The Canadian public has been generally supportive of systematic preservation goals. A 1987 poll showed 70% of respondents agreeing that logging, mining, and hydro-electric development within parks is harmful.[10] Further, such support can also be found at the provincial level. Table 5-1 shows the public response to a survey about protected lands in the British Columbia provincial park system.

This public support has become somewhat more tenuous in the late 1990s, however. Assessments at the national and provincial levels show that economic concerns in particular have dampened the enthusiasm of many Canadians toward the most ambitious environmental goals.[11] Levels of demand for systematic preservation are certainly high enough to meet criteria as a necessary condition, but they are not sufficient in themselves to effectuate responsive behavior.

TABLE 5-1
Public Priorities for British Columbia Park Programs

Program	First Priority	Second Priority
	(percent of respondents)	
Protecting natural resources	37	54
Acquiring more parkland	27	42
Ensuring clean facilities	25	34
Expanding overnight accommodations	8	17
Improving security services	7	14
Upgrading structures and roads	6	12
Providing more information	4	11
Wider range of recreation programs	2	9

Sources: Survey of 2,565 respondents by British Columbia Ministry of Parks, 1990. Reprinted in CEAC 1991: 23.

Stable Political Processes

Canada's political processes are quite stable and designed to be accessible to demands for goals such as those of systematic preservation. The Westminster-style parliamentary system utilizes single-member districts with elected members of the majority party serving as prime minister and other cabinet ministers. Political power has been turned over frequently in recent years, but the process for doing so remains stable and peaceful. Table 5-2 lists the recent governments.

Two recent developments make the future less predictable. First, the ongoing controversy regarding the possible secession of Quebec has been visible and contentious. Obviously, no one knows what the consequences of secession would be, but analysts fear a significant loss

TABLE 5-2
Recent Governments of Canada

Years	Prime Minister	Party
1963–1968	Lester Pearson	Liberal
1968–1979	Pierre Trudeau	Liberal
1979–1980	Joe Clark	Conservative
1980–1984	Pierre Trudeau	Liberal
1984	John Turner	Conservative
1984–1993	Brian Mulroney	Conservative
1993–?	Jean Chretien	Liberal

of political stability.[12] Second, while political parties have traditionally been more disciplined than those in the United States and campaign on platforms that presumably express the party's response to public demands, the party system is increasingly unpredictable. Even prior to the rise of the Reform Party in the 1990s, Canadians showed an increasing disaffection with the traditional powerful Liberals and Progressive Conservatives. Some shifted allegiance to the New Democratic Party and others dealigned from any affiliation.[13] Major gains were made by the Reform Party in the 1990s. This party has attracted strong support in the west and among conservatives with a message of reducing the role of the central government and increased reliance on market-based decision making. For example, one survey reports over 95% of party members as agreeing that "Big government increasingly is a major problem."[14]

These developments are not meant to suggest that political processes will lose the necessary stability to support long-term efforts such as systematic preservation. Rather, such efforts will be increasingly challenging in future years, particularly in times of constitutional changes and increased party volatility.

Official Commitments to Systematic Preservation

One early official commitment to system expansion occurred in a quite informal way. Under Prime Minister Trudeau, Parks Commissioner John Nicol and then Minister of Indian Affairs and Northern Development Jean Chretien were strong advocates of expansion. In 1968 Minister Chretien made a bet that he would create ten new parks while minister. The five-dollar bill is now framed in his prime minister's office. Between 1968 and 1974, ten new national parks were established, virtually doubling the area in the system. By 1978, when Nicol retired, national parks existed in every province and territory.[15]

Canadian parks officials, like their American counterparts, forwarded ideas for new emphases in planning in the 1970s. By the end of the decade, official guidelines for long-term provision of preserved natural areas had changed to reflect a commitment to systematic preservation. The 1979 Parks Canada Policy Statement called for representation of diverse ecosystems, greater reliance on zoning in individual park plans, and full consideration of ecological integrity.[16]

Those principles have been consistently restated over the years since. Those reiterations culminated in the "Green Plan" released by the Mulroney government in 1990. Regarding parks, the Green Plan made official commitments to ecological emphases, systematic expansion, and fiscal support in promises of billions of dollars. Later in the 1990s, even after Parks Canada was moved into the Department of

Canadian Heritage in 1994, the agency's purpose remained steady. The 1994 Parks Canada Guiding Principles state the agency's purpose as to "encourage public understanding, appreciation and enjoyment of this heritage, while ensuring long-term ecological and commemorative integrity."[17]

The political climate in which the parks agency operates changed significantly in the mid-1990s. Like so many other countries, Canada's government is now emphasizing fiscal restraint. Fiscal deficits have grown dramatically in recent years, forcing at least rhetorical attention to fiscal austerity. The 1995 National Business Plan calls upon the agency to become increasingly entreprenurial and self-sufficient by streamlining operations, privatizing certain services, raising revenues, and adopting other new techniques.[18] This emphasis on economic priorities was consistent with the reported shift in public opinion among many Canadians. To reiterate, where environmental concerns had been somewhat dominant before, the economic problems of the 1990s led many to rethink perceived tradeoffs between the economy and the environment. Arguably, jobs and trade are now viewed as having a higher priority.[19]

Constraining Conditions

Between the environmental awakening of the early 1970s and the complicating developments of the late 1990s described above, momentum existed for an emphasis on systematic preservation of public lands. Awareness of ecological concerns was increasing and many in positions of authority seemed ready to seize the opportunity. What institutional constraints would shape relevant behavior?

Low to Moderate Horizontal Constraints

In the 1970s, the agency known as Parks Canada and later the Canadian Parks Service was assigned responsibility to provide systematic preservation for the national parks system. (Parks Canada became the Canadian Parks Service from 1986 to 1993 at which time it reverted to the Parks Canada designation.) The agency had not been known previously for an ecological emphasis. Rather, the agency, and its predecessors, had a reputation for "a pioneer mentality of unlimited forests, lakes and wildlife" that was consistent with the views of many Canadians.[20] However, many with authority in the agency had adopted the new environmental awareness. Agency personnel expressed concern about ecological preservation, and agency policymakers committed to a long-term focus.[21] Would they enjoy the autonomy to pursue such a focus?

Most comparative analyses suggest that political manipulation of agency behavior is relatively low in Canada compared to many democracies. Comparisons to the United States emphasize fundamental differences between parliamentary systems like Canada and the American presidential system.[22] Party members in parliamentary systems are more disciplined and thus less likely to intervene in agencies headed by their colleagues. Back-benchers have less entreprenurial freedom to interject their own preferences into agency affairs in parliamentary systems. Indeed, several studies and surveys reveal that legislators are less likely to intervene in agency affairs in Canada than elsewhere.[23] The interviews I did with members of Parliament and their staffs were consistent, all respondents asserting that intervention into agency affairs was not that frequent. This response may sound self-serving, but it was in fact quite different from the response I received from U.S. congressional staffers.

Importantly, the relative autonomy of Canadian bureaucrats has increased in recent years. While American politicians have shown increasing tendencies to micromanage bureaucratic affairs, Canadian officials have stressed delegation to public agencies.[24] Throughout the 1980s, Canadian authorities emphasized deference to bureaucratic expertise, granting agencies "considerable freedom in their fields of jurisdiction."[25] One 1988 study concludes: "The Government of Canada has made efforts in recent years to achieve a greater degree of managerial deregulation and administrative decentralization."[26]

These efforts climaxed in 1990 with the highly visible document titled *Public Service 2000*, with a goal simply summarized as "let the managers manage." This document calls on policymakers to give bureaucrats "the tools and the authority to perform effectively."[27] Though this document could be dismissed as pure rhetoric, a number of public servants I interviewed in the early 1990s said they felt real change had occurred. As one park superintendent stated, "I've heard this stuff before, but for the first time, action is backing up the words."[28]

Relevant to environmental issues, one procedural difference from the United States has reinforced official efforts to achieve relatively greater insulary of Canadian agencies. American public actions affecting the environment must go through a detailed Environmental Impact Statement process whereby the relevant agency is subject to intense scrutiny from courts, interest groups, and others. Canadian agencies began using the Environmental Assessment and Review Process (EARP) in 1973. The EARP relies heavily on self-assessment by public agencies, particularly reviewers from the relevant agency and the Department of the Environment. The procedure was changed in 1984 to mandate public input, but agency decisions continue to be more insulated in Canada than are those in the United States. Further, unlike those in the United States, most Canadian interest groups have not focused substantial efforts on the judicial branch, thus diminishing a potentially powerful source of intervention into agency affairs.[29]

Specific to the national parks agency, one means of providing greater insularity was structural. In 1979 the Government Organization Act moved the agency out of the multifaceted Department of Indian Affairs and Northern Development and into the new Environment Canada. Unlike the U.S. Department of the Interior in which the American National Park Service is housed, Environment Canada was clearly focused on an environmental mission uncomplicated by side missions of resource development and extraction. The absence of conflicting missions made contradictory interventions from sister agencies less likely for Parks Canada than they were for the American NPS.[30]

Parks Canada was shifted again in 1994, from Environment Canada to the newly created Department of Canadian Heritage. This department includes a variety of programs, such as Canadian Identity and Status of Women, that reflect a national identity. The parks agency may lose some of the coherence that was fostered by placement in Environment Canada, but agency officials were determined to retain the sense of identity that had developed. Senior planner Judy Otton told me that the move was done basically for cost-cutting, but added that it should not affect the department's relative insularity since Parks Canada brought with it the strong sense of mission it had developed while in Environment Canada.

One final factor shaping horizontal constraints on Parks Canada in the future is the National Business Plan. Mentioned above, this 1995 plan mandates that the 1995 funding for the agency be reduced by $98 million from 1994–95 to 1998–99, or roughly one-fifth of the agency's budget. In addition to this direct reduction, corporate functions providing support services will be cut by 24%. Many functions, such as maintenance, will be turned over to private companies allowing the agency to cut roughly one-fourth of its full-time employees. Further, the agency is to become more self-sufficient, with projected revenues increasing from $35 million in 1994–95 to $70 million in 1999–2000.[31]

How will these changes affect the relative insularity of the parks agency? The National Business Plan is intended to make the agency even more autonomous from other political actors, particularly in terms of fiscal independence. Fiscal independence may be, however, a double-edged sword for long-term planning and delivery. Federal authorities promise that the agency will continue to pursue the same mission, but assert that it may have to change the way it proceeds.[32] In a fiscal crunch, long-term goals usually have considerably less priority than more immediate concerns. The impact of fiscal limitations will be exaggerated in negotiations with provincial and other relevant authorities that are often necessary to pursue preservation goals.

Aside from the changes that could result from greater fiscal independence, the characterization of bureaucratic autonomy from other federal entities should not be carried too far. Members of Parliament, the courts, and appointees of the prime minister still have the ability to intervene in agency affairs. Indeed, they still do so.[33] Imposition of tight fiscal controls is only the most obvious means of control political authorities enjoy. In terms relative to other national park agencies, however, these constraints can be classified as perhaps no longer low but still in the moderate range.

Moderate to High Vertical Constraints

The Canadian system of federalism provides a potentially powerful institutional constraint on agency behavior. Canadian provincial governments are generally considered more powerful, more independent, and more influential than American state governments.[34] As one authority notes, "The provincial governments are more active participants in the national political system than are state governments."[35] The provinces are arguably as strong in some policy areas in Canada as the states are in Australia.[36]

The roots for decentralization are deep. In 1867 the four federating provinces (Ontario, Quebec, Nova Scotia, New Brunswick) retained their rights over many policy areas, including natural resources. At the Inter-Provincial Conference of 1887, the premiers of the existing provinces met to criticize the power of the federal government. Since then, many have subscribed to a "compact theory" stating that since the colonies created the confederation and federal government, they have the right to change it.[37] When the provinces of Manitoba, Saskatchewan, and Alberta were created, the central government attempted to retain control over certain issues and large tracts of unused lands. However, the 1930 Constitution Act authorized arrangements similar to those in the original provinces, thereby leaving control over natural resources with provincial governments.

Recent procedural changes have institutionalized provincial involvement in much decision-making. Similar to the Australian states, the Canadian provinces relinquished their income-taxing powers to the central government in World War II, but unlike the Australian experience, the provinces were able to restore this power by the early 1960s.[38] In the 1960s, Prime Minister Pearson used a version of cooperative federalism to consult with premiers at regular meetings on policy issues. This practice has grown into what is termed "executive federalism" wherein major policy decisions require the unanimous consent of provincial premiers and the prime minister at regularly held conferences. The recent Meech Lake Accord is an example of the use of this procedure in one attempt to address the constitutional crisis with the province of Quebec.

While the emphasis on decentralization has not always been consistent, recent shifts have been toward more power for provincial leaders. Despite the centralizing efforts of Liberal Party leaders, notably Prime Minister Trudeau, recent decades have witnessed an emphasis on greater delegation to subnational levels.[39] In 1982 a new section (92A) was added to the Constitution that substantially increased provincial power over natural resource decisions. Consistent with such sentiment, the Mulroney government made decentralization a prominent plank in its successful platform of 1984. As a result of these efforts, federalism, while always an important factor in Canadian public policy, has become an even more visible institution.[40] Provincial governments have retained and, in some cases, increased their authority in many policy areas.[41]

This trend toward decentralization is not likely to be reversed in the near future and, in fact, may be further institutionalized. According to one review in 1995, "The federal government will increase its attempts to hand down responsibility for managing and funding different government programs to the provinces."[42] As one observer notes, federalism will not be easily ignored for it is "a way of life" for many Canadians.[43]

This strength of provincial governments is certainly true in environmental policy and especially so in public lands management. Today, provinces continue to "dominate" most areas of environmental protection.[44] With regard to lands, most public land in the United States belonged originally to the federal government whereas most in Canada belongs to provincial governments. At the end of the 1980s, less than 6% of American land was owned by state governments whereas provincial governments owned more than half of Canada's land.[45] "One way in which Canada is unusual as a federation," notes one comparative appraisal, "is the degree of power of the provincial governments over natural resource policy."[46]

Thus, complications in negotiations between levels of government are somewhat inevitable. Provincial emphases on resource extraction and maintaining tax bases were principal reasons that expansion prior to the system plans of the 1970s slowed to a crawl.[47] Even after federal plans were formalized, negotiations between levels of government intensified.[48] While advocating the completion of a representative system at the 1978 Conference on Parks, Minister of Indian Affairs and

Northern Development Hugh Faulkner admitted that provincial negotiations would be difficult: "I am still optimistic that new national
parks may be established through agreements whereby the provincial
governments transfer the control of resources to the federal government. I am aware that this approach is sometimes difficult for provinces
to accept."[49]

This characterization of provincial demands as consequential is
not meant to be perjorative. Certainly, policymakers must necessarily
be concerned about the economic health of their provinces. In many
economic aspects, the western provinces, where so many of the most
famous parks are located, are at some disadvantage to their eastern
counterparts. Federal spending is less in these provinces, unemployment is often higher, economic activity is more resource dependent.[50]
Objectively, however, the depiction of provincial concerns as being
more economically oriented than goals often prioritized at the federal
level is realistic. One strong piece of evidence for this is that the Business
Council on National Issues, the mouthpiece for business interests in
Canada, has strongly advocated continued decentralization to provincial levels.[51]

Theoretical Expectations

I thus expect that systematic preservation according to systemwide
and individual unit plans for the national parks in Canada will be only
partially successful. The Canadian parks authorities will be able to
formulate plans but putting them in place will be constrained by provincial demands and, somewhat ironically, by the fiscal realities that come
with increased financial independence for the central parks agency.

NATIONAL PARK SYSTEM EXPANSION

In their 1995 review of endangered spaces, the Canadian World Wildlife
Fund is quite critical in their assessment of Canada's national park
system expansion, giving the federal government grades of C– for
terrestrial parks and D– for marine parks (WWF 1995). When I asked
Parks Canada chief of planning Murray McComb about these grades,
he pointedly admitted, "Their assessment is right."[52] Why have they
scored so low?

Early Growth

Canada's first national park remains a reminder of the early focus of
park developers and managers. Banff, the park, was established in 1885
as "a public park and pleasure ground for the benefit, advantage, and

enjoyment of the people." The emphasis on tourism, not preservation, is evident in that the park consisted first of just a ten-square-mile reserve around a hot spring to which the Canadian Pacific Railroad could deliver tourists to see the scenery and bask in the springs. Early on, the focus on Banff and its hot springs was to develop a tourist center for wealthy travelers comparable to European spas. Over a century later, Banff, the village, was officially recognized as a town in 1990 when the Canadian Parks Service (CPS) turned over civic responsibility to local residents. In between these dates, the park developed as a tourist resort where decisions were based largely on the economic demands of local residents.[53]

The Canadian national park system developed in ways consistent with the emphasis seen in the first park. Most national parks were established as tourist destinations. Largely due to the fact that so much of Canada was already undeveloped, parks were established not to preserve wilderness but to provide wilderness settings for visitors, especially railroad passengers, to enjoy "scenic resorts, recreation areas, and tourist attractions."[54] The Dominion Forests and Parks Act of 1911 was the first attempt to put the national parks, at that time numbering five, in some kind of system. The act authorized a more active federal role by creating a national parks agency and, at least rhetorically, encouraged more caution in decisions affecting resource depletion. Thirteen national parks were created between 1887 and 1930, most as land surrounding townsites for railroad destinations.

The early importance of federal-provincial relations is noticeable in the location of these parks. On one hand, under the Canadian Constitution of 1867, control of natural resources of western provinces belonged to the federal government. On the other hand, federal policymakers needed provincial agreement to establish parks in the eastern half of the country. Not surprisingly, ten of the pre-1930 national parks were designated in western areas.

The process for adding new parks changed dramatically in 1930. In that year, the National Parks Act formally authorized the national system and provided enabling legislation for the establishment of new parks. The emphasis of long-term planning shifted from making parks accessible to the railroads to making them accessible to automobiles.[55] Also in that year, the western provinces assumed ownership and control of natural resources within their borders. Since then, provincial governments must either have or attain rights to desired lands before the federal government can purchase them for national park establishment.

With provincial governments responsible for lands throughout the country, park system expansion slowed perceptibly. Only six new parks were established between 1930 and 1968. As one account notes,

"Because regional objectives were not always coincident with national objectives, achievement of the agreement necessary for the formation of new national parks was a slow process."[56] In contrast to the statistic on location cited above, only three of the fifteen national parks established since 1930 are located in the west.

What were the objectives of regional policymakers that might slow national park establishment? During the twentieth century, Canada intensified efforts at resource extraction, becoming, for example, the world's leading exporter of forest products.[57] Provincial agreement for new national parks generally occurred only if the area was lacking in resources such as timber or oil, or if the resources had already been extracted or boundaries drawn so that they still could be removed.[58] The federal government could sweeten the pot for assuming control of the land but only by promising certain economic advantages through such means as the building of roads within the province, thereby drawing tourists and providing infrastructure for development.[59]

Even when natural areas included significant recreation potential, provincial policymakers were often reluctant to turn lands over to the federal level. Provincial governments frequently created their own parks, areas that could ensure outdoor activities such as hunting and fishing while still allowing logging and mining to continue.[60] Provincial parks date to Ontario's Algonquin established in 1893. The provincial park systems grew to over sixty million acres by the early 1990s. Provincial administrators have now banned resource extraction from many of these parks, but they still constitute land unavailable to federal planners. Table 5-3 displays the amount of land set aside as provincial and territorial parks throughout Canada.

As a result of previous tendencies to emphasize recreational aspects of parks and the reinforcement from provincial demands, ecological planning for Canadian parks was minimal in the period between 1930 and the mid-1960s. Some participants at the 1961 Resources for Tomorrow Conference argued for more parks in more diverse locations, but theirs was a minority voice. Commercial recreation and resource development dominated the decision-making processes for areas formally designated as protected.[61]

Greater Emphasis on Long-Term Planning

In the 1970s, Parks Canada initiated a long-term plan for national park system expansion. Starting with the 1971 National Parks System Planning Manual, the agency identified nine marine and thirty-nine terrestrial regions differentiated according to biologic, oceanographic, physiographic, and geographic features. This approach resulted from

TABLE 5-3
Provincial and Territorial Protected Areas

Province/Territory	Areas	Sq. Km.	% of Province/Territory
British Columbia	415	51,900	5.5
Alberta	172	7,908	1.2
Saskatchewan	31	5,050	0.8
Manitoba	76	43,088	6.6
Ontario	490	56,980	5.3
Quebec	22	4,866	0.3
New Brunswick	29	3,402	4.1
Nova Scotia	35	1,331	2.4
Prince Ed Island	6	29	0.5
Newfoundland	17	1,287	0.3
N.W. Territories	14	173,090	5.1
Yukon Territory	2	5,918	1.1
Total	1,237	354,849	

Source: Eidsvik and Henwood 1990: 68.

recognition that past expansion had been haphazard and politically determined and from the increasingly prominent demands that future growth should be based on ecosystem representation.[62] The plan was later expanded to include priority historic themes and the number of marine regions warranting representation increased to twenty-nine.[63]

At the time the plan was being developed, the system had significant gaps in terms of regions represented. Some regions, such as the Rocky Mountains, were thoroughly covered with various parks. However, as participants at the 1978 Conference on Parks and others pointed out, less than half of the terrestrial regions were represented.[64] The terrestrial regions are displayed in figure 5-1.

The plan was well received. Environmental organizations voiced guarded optimism about future growth.[65] Members of Parliament expressed confidence when formally authorizing the plan in 1979 even while admitting that such expansion would require serious negotiations between levels of government as "the administration and control of most Crown lands is vested in the provinces."[66] Observers were impressed with the development of a national plan at the same time that Parks Canada was getting a new institutional home in the Environment Canada.[67] Scientists applauded the fact that "system planning in the past few years has developed a sound ecological basis" even while withholding judgment on likely implementation.[68] The plan also

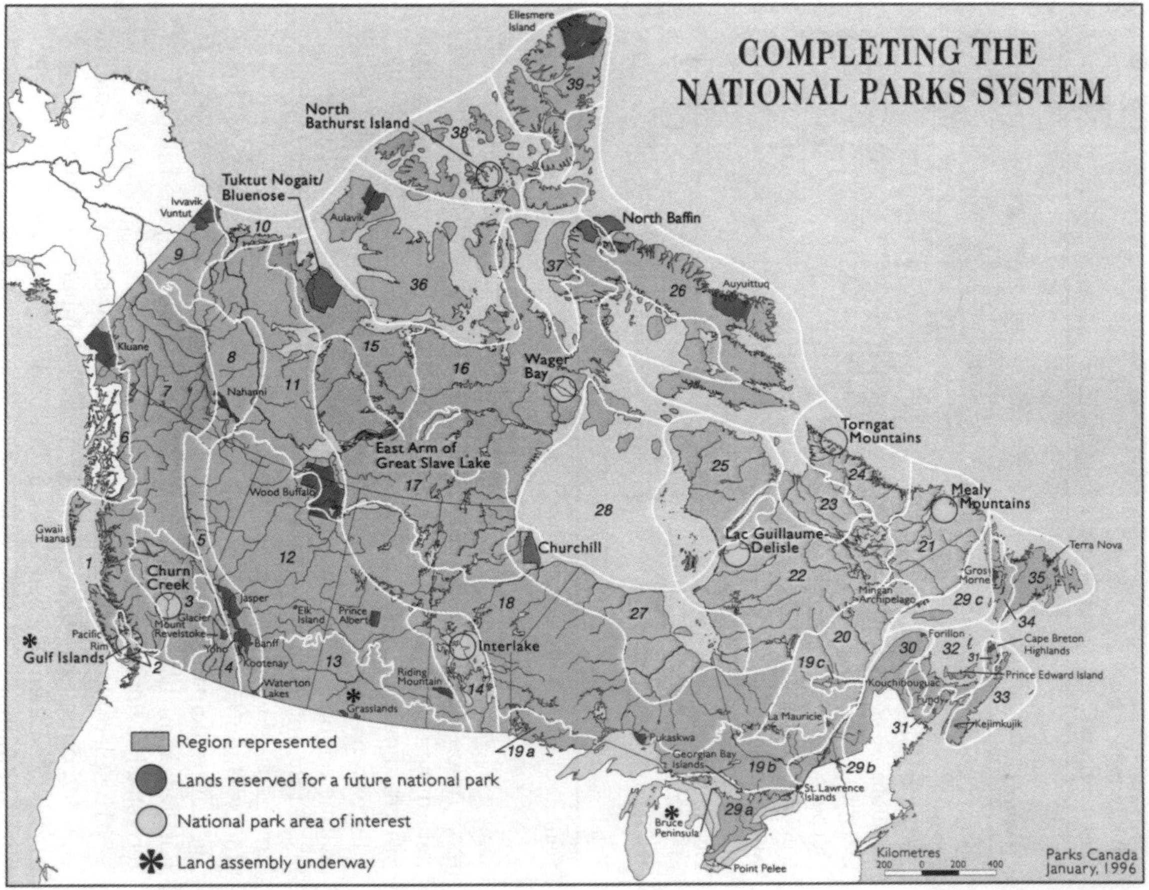

Figure 5-1 Plan for Completing the Canadian Parks System

received public support. A 1990 Angus Reid poll revealed 60% of Canadians in favor of at least doubling the area designated for wilderness in the country and three-quarters of respondents critical of the government for not setting aside enough natural habitat for threatened species.

Federal authorities have continually referred to and reiterated support for this plan. Released in 1990, the Green Plan committed the government to official timetables. Goals included setting aside as protected space 12% of the country (an increase from 3.4%), with roughly one-third of that as national parks. This goal is consistent with Brundtland Commission recommendations. The Green Plan promised that the federal government would establish five new national parks by 1996 and negotiate agreements for thirteen more by the year 2000 to complete the system. Three new marine parks would be established by 1996 and three additional sites identified by 2000.[69] In the 1990 *State of the Parks* document, the minister of the environment restates these goals with specific timetables for new units and future agreements.[70] Further, agency personnel continue to regard the scientific emphasis as crucial. When asked to compare the Canadian plan with the American, Canadian Parks Service senior analyst Jay Beaman said with pride, "We use scientific grounds for expansion rather than political reasons."[71] Indeed, the first Strategic Objective listed in the 1991 CPS Strategic Plan distributed to employees is "Protect through Science."[72]

The process is supposed to work as follows. Efforts to add new units are concentrated on regions that remain unrepresented. Parks Canada conducts studies to identify possible new areas that are deemed worthy if they represent natural features of the region and display minimal human impact. The second step is to select one of these areas for a park site by assessing candidates against a dozen criteria of practicality, appropriateness, and availability. Parks Canada then does a full feasibility study with direct involvement by provincial or territorial authorities and representatives of local communities. If this assessment reveals feasibility and public support, then the federal government negotiates transfer of administration and control of the land from current managers, usually subnational governments.[73] These negotiations resolve such issues as boundaries, acquisition costs, and regional integration. Finally, the federal government formally places the land under the authority of the National Parks Act.[74]

Implementation

Implementation of the Canadian system plan proceeded quickly for a while but then slowed perceptibly. The process of expansion has been significantly affected by political institutions, notably the prominent role of federalism.

Progress

Since establishing the new emphasis in the early 1970s, Parks Canada made some progress in filling out the system. By 1978 the number of parks had increased from eighteen to twenty-eight, while the acreage covered had nearly doubled. Between 1978 and the early 1990s, eight new parks or park reserves were added to the system, all but one in regions not previously represented. That one, Bruce Peninsula, surrounds Canada's first marine park at Fathom Five. Areas have been selected for study in fourteen of the remaining eighteen regions and active proposals exist in seven of them.[75] Further, the number of historic sites and large historic parks within the system has grown fairly dramatically.[76]

Much of this progress was achieved during the late 1960s and 1970s. Several of the new parks were areas that had been awaiting establishment for years. For example, support for designation of Kejimkujik in Nova Scotia had grown since 1945 only to achieve fruition in 1968. At the 1978 Conference on Parks, Parks Canada planner John Carruthers attributed these successes to "a fortuitous combination of factors" including the environmental movement, a supportive public climate, the strong economy of the nation, motivated authorities (such as Chretien), and the momentum provided by the national parks agency.[77]

Carruthers and park historians also describe two other factors that diminished potential provincial roadblocks. First, federal cost-sharing on land acquisition made national park establishment more tempting. In a 1992 interview with this author, Carruthers termed the early negotiations "less complex and expensive" than they were in the 1990s.[78] Second, three of the new parks were located in the Northern Territories where regional authorities were less obstructive.[79] These three parks were located in areas previously unrepresented according to the 1971 plan. Thus, the northern strategy proved a fruitful means of making progress without excessive complications.[80]

Progress on systematic expansion slowed in the 1980s. Assessments during this time period were increasingly critical. In the mid-1980s, an independent task force headed by John Theberge expressed frustration with the slow pace of expansion and cited obstacles such as protracted negotiations with provincial governments.[81] A summary assessment in 1990 applauded the efforts to protect a variety of natural regions but criticized ". . . the inordinate amount of time it now takes to establish a park," citing ongoing negotiations at proposed sites throughout the country as evidence.[82] In their official 1990 review, the Canadian Parks Service admitted that expansion is "becoming increasingly complex, expensive, and time-consuming."[83]

During the 1990s, observers and environmental groups have become increasingly skeptical of chances for the successful completion of the system. Growing weary of stated intentions, the Canadian Nature Federation concluded in 1991 that "The real question . . . is how the good intentions of parks policy will be implemented."[84] Other groups were explicitly dubious as to the ability of the CPS to finish the system by stated deadlines.[85] Referring again to the 1995 WWF report, the C– grade was based on the fact that "no new national parks have been designated in southern Canada since 1988" and signals for the future were not encouraging.[86] All told, in addition to the eighteen terrestrial regions still awaiting completed units, only two of the twenty-nine marine regions are currently represented. Table 5-4 breaks down the evaluations offered by the WWF for different components of the expansion process. Obviously, policymakers have had more success with planning (stages 1 and 2) than with implementation.

Reasons for Slow Progress

In part, efforts by the Canadian parks agency were complicated by political constraints at the national level. As described earlier, the parks agency was not completely autonomous to pursue its system plan. Taking power in 1984, the Mulroney government displayed a lack of enthusiasm for maintaining the momentum of the process. Minister of the Environment Suzanne Blais-Grenier did not advocate creation of new parks, particularly not in remote areas where tourism potential was low. In the new parks that were established, she expressed

---

TABLE 5-4
WWF Grades for Park System Expansion (1995)

Stage	Terrestrial	Marine
Use of ecological criteria for selection of new areas	C	C
Strategy for completing system	B	C
Completion to date	D	F
Annual rate of progress	F	F
Adequacy of standards for maintaining integrity of existing areas	D	D
Average Grade	C–	D

Source: Canadian WWF 1995: 51.

a willingness to allow logging and mining to continue.[87] Even after Blais-Grenier was replaced, largely due to her lack of commitment to natural areas, the new minister, Tom McMillan, offered mixed messages, promising new parks at Ellesmere Island and South Moresby even while emphasizing the need for a focus on tourism interests and provincial demands.[88] The complications affecting the political system in the 1990s described earlier, notably the Quebec issue and a volatile party system, have made concentration on expansion in this period difficult. Finally, the current emphasis on fiscal restraint does not bode well for expansion efforts.

The primary reason for slow implementation, however, has been the impact of the federal system. The combination of increasing delegation to Parks Canada and increasing decentralization to provincial leaders meant that any actions by the former would have to be negotiated through the latter. Provincial authorities have often been reluctant partners, as "the loss of revenue that would be derived from resource exploitation" has fostered provincial reluctance to cooperate with attempts to set up new national parks in their jurisdiction.[89] Negotiations for desired land and marine areas between levels of government have been slow, complex, and costly.

The importance of the federalism institution for the expansion process was recognized early by many in the policy community. For instance, at the 1978 conference, Deputy Minister A. T. Davidson stated the issue presciently: "When transferring administration and control of lands to the federal government, provinces generally seek a clear commitment that benefits will accrue to the provincial and local economy in the short term. This has led to large-scale capital developments in and near many new national parks within the first five years of park establishment. One may question the appropriateness of certain of these developments, such as golf courses or access roads; however, they are part of the price paid to gain the necessary provincial government agreement to create a national park. How far we can or should go in this regard in the future is a fundamental concern."[90] It was and remains a fundamental concern.

Retrospective judgments also cite federal-provincial negotiations as a major stumbling block. In the 1990 agency review, the first reason listed by the CPS for slow expansion is that "Land-use and jurisdictional conflicts will have to be resolved in co-operation with the provinces and territories."[91] The Canadian Environmental Advisory Council, a group of knowledgeable and visible experts on land-use, stated in 1991, "The main task related to the completion of the national parks system is the selection of potential sites within these regions and the negotiation of agreements between the federal government and other jurisdictions and with aboriginal people where appropriate."[92] While asserting that the plan was still on track in 1992, Minister of the Environment Charest admitted that expansion was getting to be more difficult precisely because of reluctant provinces.[93]

What, exactly, are the consequences of federal-provincial interactions? Several consequences are quite significant. Each is illustrated by real-world examples.

Time

The first consequence of most federal-provincial interactions is time. The expansion process can become quite lengthy and protracted, leading to greater costs and more alteration of natural habitats before protection occurs.

Establishment of the Grasslands area in Saskatchewan has taken decades. After years of consideration, authorization for a federal-provincial agreement occurred in 1981. This led to extended negotiations. Policymakers attained an explicit arrangement in 1988 to purchase land from provincial and local landowners creating a nine-hundred-square-kilometer park. When I first visited the site in 1992, the park was only 40% finished. Land acquisition slowed even more after that, Parks Canada receiving virtually no funding for this project between 1993 and 1995, leaving the park only half completed by the time I returned in 1996.[94] While this process drags on, the potential parkland is altered by farming and grazing. The agency admits that "many of the lands yet to be acquired have had significant modification of natural vegetation."[95] When I visited, the Parks Canada personnel were still optimistic about filling in the gaps in the grasslands ecosystem, but admitted that the current owners of the proposed additions were in no hurry to sell.

Grasslands is only one recent example of how delays can lead to alteration of natural conditions. Establishment of many of the fully operational parks took longer than anticipated due to provincial reticence. For instance, Pacific Rim was established in 1970, but only after the British Columbia government delayed official designation so that the area under consideration could be logged.[96]

Cost

The second major consequence of federal-provincial negotiations is cost. Increasing land values become even more inflated as provincial negotiators realize that certain areas are specifically targeted by expansion plans.

A recent illustration involved areas on Moresby Island in British Columbia. Parks Canada was interested in these areas as representative of the Pacific Coast Mountains terrestrial region and two marine regions. Debate over the issue intensified after 1974, following submission of a logging plan from a timber company that would drastically affect some of the natural areas. Environmental groups responded, focusing much of their pressure on federal authorities to designate the area for preservation.[97] Following nearly thirteen years of debate, British Columbia provincial authorities, realizing the strategic worth of the land, requested nearly $200 million for the area. One noted authority, writer Margaret Atwood, spoke for many when she termed the British Columbia demands "ransom."[98] British Columbia settled for over $100 million in 1987, more than nearly all the other national parks had cost together. The province received several goodies, including compensation for effects on the logging industry. British Columbia premier VanderZalm proudly hailed the emphasis on provincial concerns in the negotiations: "I am pretty happy now with what's been concluded in that I believe sufficient protection has been given British Columbia."[99]

Compromise

A third consequence of federal-provincial interactions is that new areas often come only with substantial compromises.

In negotiations over establishment of Ellsmere Island, a pristine but fragile ecosystem, Northwest Territory authorities demanded development of the proposed park in ways that would increase jobs and revenue, encouraging planners to pursue the "love boat market."[100] Park officials ultimately agreed to higher visitation levels and more tourist activities than it would have preferred.[101] Part of the reason the federal government acquiesced to these demands was that Ellsmere Island is in a strategic location. In 1985 an American ship traversed this section of the Northwest Passage without the permission of the Canadian government. By creating the park at Ellsmere, the government could more easily protest such actions on the basis of national sovereignty.[102]

Other national parks have come only with significant strings attached. Forillon's status is significantly affected by the strained relations between the Quebec and federal government. The province refused to turn over permanent title to the land to the federal government, thus necessitating a ninety-nine-year lease at the end of which the land will revert to provincial control.[103] The boundaries of Kluane and other parks were drawn to avoid inclusion of areas with high mineral value.

Inaction

A fourth possible consequence of the impact of federalism is inaction. Park proposals remain dormant when negotiations become sticky.

A proposed park at Churchill in Manitoba remains in the planning stage as federal-provincial bargaining is mired in concerns over the opposition of local residents. While some residents welcome the idea of increased tourism, others fear lost use of the tundra for hunting, trapping, and other activities. As one trapper said, "If it becomes a national park, it belongs only to the tourists."[104] The CPS readily admitted that establishment of the park would "require the support and cooperation of the residents of the Churchill region and the government of Manitoba."[105]

Summary

Long-term system planning is not only feasible but has been pursued quite visibly for the Canadian national park system. Implementation of plans, however, has been constrained to some degree by political influence on the bureaucracy and, to a more severe extent, by the role of provincial governments.

ENHANCEMENT OF INDIVIDUAL UNITS

In one day in the Canadian Rockies, I experienced the legacies of two very different approaches to managing national parks. I woke up in the backcountry campground at Lake O'Hara, an astonishingly beautiful alpine area in Yoho National Park, accessible only by foot or by buses that run just four times per day. Even in July, the morning air was cold and invigorating, and the snowfall from the previous day stretched up the mountainsides into the pine forests surrounding the clear, blue lake. Parks Canada decided in the 1970s to manage the area to restore its natural beauty and prohibited automobile traffic. The area today remains quite pristine. The presence of brilliant scenery, pure air, and numerous grizzly bears makes camping authentic enough that saying good-bye even to your temporary neighbors is like bidding farewell to close friends. Upon returning to the parking lot eleven kilometers away, I drove down to Lake Louise. Obviously, also a beautiful mountain lake setting, this area has been managed, as has much of Banff National Park, to attract as many visitors as possible. The congestion and short tempers, both on the roads leading into the parking lot, and on the trails leading out from the Chalet, were overwhelming. Cars raced for parking spaces, tourists with cameras jostled for strategic positions. The contrasting settings at the two mountain lakes represent two results of management of Canadian parks that now face reconciliation in one large effort at long-term planned preservation.

Background

While many of the demands concerning national parks focused on expansion, some interested parties called for enhancement of existing units. Even the most renown of the Canadian parks have been characterized as mere islands of habitat, with boundaries drawn for political reasons, that could not be sustained as natural ecosystems.[106] Observers criticized activities within those islands as lacking ecological justification and as too focused on economic development.[107] National policy statements of 1979, 1988, and 1994 emphasized the need for management plans at parks to be written or renewed at five-year intervals with an emphasis on protecting ecosystems. The current policy guidelines for Parks Canada state explicitly that "maintenance of ecological integrity must be the first consideration in management planning."[108] The document further states, "In keeping with park management plans, Parks Canada will establish measurable goals and management strategies to ensure the protection of ecosystems in and around national parks."[109]

How has this increased emphasis on systematic preservation affected the most prized units of the system? The most appropriate units to examine are the mountain parks of Banff, Jasper, Kootenay, and Yoho. Designated together as a World Heritage site in 1985, these parks are the most famous, most visited, and most prestigious part of Canada's natural heritage. While I will discuss important differences between these parks, much of the following analysis considers these units as part of a larger ecosystem. Indeed, such an approach is consistent with one of the major tenets of current long-range planning for these areas.

Planning for Tourists

Banff is Canada's first, most famous, and most visited national park. Situated a mile high in the Canadian Rockies, the park includes the town of Banff and the surrounding six thousand square kilometers. This area contains some of the prettiest mountains and waterways of the world, including the renowned Lake Louise. This beauty has attracted increasing numbers of visitors since the arrival of the Canadian Pacific Railroad (CPR) in the late nineteenth century until today when roughly five million people come each year.

The townsite of Banff has grown in proportion to the numbers of visitors. The village was first managed by the railroad for its passengers and then by Parks Canada. During these years, town residents settled in, encouraged by long-term leases and nearly perpetual renewal. These residents developed close ties, and considerable political clout with policymakers at the provincial and federal levels.[110] The impact of the town on natural conditions extends beyond the obvious issues of development. The town is located in the warm valley bottoms that are also prime wildlife areas. Pollution from activities in the town, such as smog from automobiles, extends well beyond the townsite. Planes flying in and out of the town's airstrip are noticed throughout the park. Rivers were dammed to form artifical lakes for water supply and recreation. Property owners in town demanded consideration in management planning that resulted in policy decisions such as the suppression of natural fires.

As at so many parks, early management efforts focused on economic concerns. Early federal plans consisted mainly of surveys of geology and topography. Planning goals were consistent with the interests of the CPR. Plans focused on bathhouses and facilities that would attract wealthy visitors to ride the trains to the spas. For years, park officials allowed and even encouraged growth of the townsite and nearby facilities such as the golf course. When natural concerns conflicted with economic demands, the latter were usually given priority. Over the decades following discovery of the hot springs in 1880, plans for park boundaries were redrawn numerous times to allow the province of Alberta to use land for grazing, mining, and other activities.[111] For example, in 1930 Banff was significantly reduced in size in order to exclude a river that was to be used for hydroelectric development.[112]

As the popularity of parks increased following World War II, planning efforts concentrated on promotion of tourism in different ways. Much attention was given to building more roads, notably the completion of the Trans-Canada Highway through the park. Satellite areas for development, such as that at Johnston Canyon, were developed. Ultimately, planners worked on making Banff a year-round destination with ski facilities and winterization of the Banff Springs Hotel in 1968. By the mid-1990s, Banff was bringing well over $4 billion in tourist money into the province of Alberta.[113]

The historical background at the other mountain parks was similar to Banff's in some ways. Jasper, Kootenay, and Yoho all date back nearly as far as Banff. Like Banff, Jasper also has a townsite and was an early destination of railroad tourists and later the junction between two well-traveled highways. The Grand Trunk Pacific Railway line was built in the early twentieth century to try to achieve some of the success of the rival CPR to the south. The railroad company demanded government assistance similar to that provided to the CPR at Banff, and thus the park was established in 1907. Kootenay was designated in 1920 to protect hot springs similar to those at Banff and make them accessible to the wider public. Yoho dates to 1886 when a small area was set aside as a reserve near Mount Stephen, British Columbia. Like Banff and Jasper, Yoho also contains a townsite and sits on a major rail line.

The early emphasis of planners in these parks was also to make them more accessible to tourists. Plans focused on opening roads to automobiles, even at a fairly high cost to natural conditions. A highway to Jasper from Edmonton 220 miles to the east was opened in 1931. The Yellowhead Highway has become a major east-west access road between Alberta and British Columbia. The Banff-Jasper Highway from the south was opened in 1940, later expanded to become the Icefields Parkway. The prioritization of accessibility comes with a high price along this corridor. Between 1970 and 1980 alone, approximately one thousand animals (mostly elk, mule deer, and bighorn sheep) were killed on this highway.[114] Yoho is bisected by Route 1, the Trans-Canada Highway. Since this is the major cross-country thoroughfare, more than three million people drive through the park each year. Road kills of wildlife are extremely common.

While the planning emphasis at Jasper, Kootenay, and Yoho was similar to that at Banff in the early decades, one difference has been noticeable. Parks Canada personnel have remained aware of both the successes and the problems achieved in the most famous of Canadian parks.[115] In their planning decisions, the managers of the other parks have used Banff as a model to either emulate or avoid. Jasper superintendent Gaby Fortin told me in an interview in 1992, "There's nothing in the rules stopping Jasper from becoming another Banff," and then he added with emphasis, "But we aren't going to let that happen."[116]

A Shifting Emphasis

Beginning in the 1960s, the relations between Parks Canada and commercial interests in the mountain parks started to change. Outside planners, Vancouver architect Peter Oberlander and others, encouraged consideration of limits on development. As early as 1962, Parks Canada called for limits on townsite growth. Local residents had little interest in curtailing growth, however. Recommendations from the agency and critics like Oberlander were thus denied by politicians acting in response to residents' concerns. If federal politicians were slow to respond to growth advocates, residents always found a receptive ear in Alberta policymakers. Indeed, in 1963, the Banff Park Citizen's Association called for transfer of park management from the federal to the provincial government.[117] Park managers had little ammunition with which to fight back on specific demands, as the park lacked any kind of formal planning document.[118] The 1964 Parks Canada Policy Statement for Banff set some controls but created no real mechanisms to prevent continued approval of new facilities.[119]

The growth of environmental concerns during the 1960s had substantial effects on the planning process in Banff. The intense debate over the Winter Olympics fueled environmental group involvement with the 1970 Master Plan for the park. Parks Canada continued to be somewhat inconsistent in its shift toward preservation values, caught between their own preferences for ecological restoration and the politically supported economic demands of residents. The agency favored the Olympics and then proposed a master plan that approved many new roads into the mountain parks. Groups like the National and Provincial Parks Association weighed in heavily against the proposal and Parks Canada eventually adopted lower growth options. By the late 1970s, the shifting emphasis of agency personnel was becoming apparent. The 1978 Parks Canada Policy Statement regarding townsites called for higher rents on leaseholders and limits on expansion.

Subsequent discussions led to the public participation process regarding the "Mountain Parks Planning Program." Parks Canada offered the public several options: A) prevent further expansion, B) expand existing facilities but do not allow new ones, C) allow high-growth with new facilities. Nearly half of the respondents (49.4%) chose A, 33.4% preferred B, and 16% opted for C. In spite of this apparent support for restrictions, the federal government responded with a somewhat vague compromise. Further development within existing boundaries would be allowed, but expansion beyond townsite limits was to be prohibited. Unfortunately for conservationists, townsite limits were not explicitly defined at all.[120]

Not surprisingly, since the 1970s, tension between national park managers and the Banff residents has continued to grow.[121] Disputes often involved the provincial government who always acted on the side of the local residents. For one mundane example, in 1985 Alberta policymakers tried to allow alcohol consumption at all picnic sites whereas Parks Canada had previously limited such activity to overnight areas.[122] The 1984 Canada-Alberta Tourist Agreement fueled considerable development in Banff with commercial facilities and twinning of the Trans-Canada Highway. Much of the money for new construction came from the $12 million contributed by the federal government to the agreement.[123] Park plans to restrict flights by dramatically closing the airstrip in Banff were overruled.[124]

The most heated battle over preservation efforts in the 1980s concerned ski facilities. Again, pressure was exerted by the Alberta provincial government and again Parks Canada officials were outranked by federal policymakers. In 1986, responding to demands by ski operators and the Alberta government, Minister of the Environment Tom McMillan removed park restrictions on competitive skiing in the mountain parks. Provincial arguments were based on the presumed loss of ski business to British Columbia and the United States as well as the need to offset the impact of low world oil prices on Alberta's petroleum-based economy. This initial allowance by McMillan led to subsequent efforts to expand operations at Sunshine Village and elsewhere in the park. During this controversy, environmental groups and observers noted and were critical of the fact that park officials had been "muzzled" by higher authorities and were unavailable to discuss environmental threats.[125]

In the ski case and in many others, whatever Banff managers planned, implementation could prove to be quite difficult. As Perry Jacobson, a park manager at Banff for eighteen years, told me, "If you did something someone there didn't like, you could bet you'd be hearing from Ottawa a half hour later."[126] Or, as Yoho superintendent Ian Church said, "The old joke about Banff was, if the super turned down your building permit, you could just fly to Ottawa and get the MP to approve it."[127] Outside analysts concur. One summary is illustrative: "In a few cases Superintendents have stood up to the pressure from local entrepreneurs only to have their decisions reversed in Ottawa."[128]

Meanwhile, planners in the other mountain parks were fighting their own battles. Partly because of its own internal pressures and partly because the park is contiguous with Banff, plans for Jasper are also subject to political interference. In 1982, for example, planners proposed closing the Banff-Jasper Highway during winters to save on snow-clearing costs. The plan was aborted when Chambers of Commerce in both townsites complained to provincial and federal politicians.[129] George Andrew, the president of the Chamber of Commerce for Jasper, told me in 1992: "Relations have always been a roller coaster ride with the Park Service."[130] Historian Hildebrandt says, "Banff *and* Jasper have felt unrelenting pressure from developer and business interests to exploit commercial opportunities and expand tourist facilities."[131]

In many ways, Jasper's potential for development is as great as Banff's. In 1988 the townsite had about half as many permanent residents, 3,500, as did Banff. In the early 1990s, park service expenditures were about half of what they were at Banff. Roughly one-third the number of visitors come to Jasper, although recent growth rates in visitor totals have been higher at Jasper than at Banff. Since 1979 visitor totals at Jasper grew at a rate of about 1% per year until over two million visitors arrived annually in the late 1980s.[132] Further, the Jasper residents may not have as much political clout as their Banff neighbors, but they have shown the ability to exert influence.

Still, Jasper managers enjoyed somewhat more freedom to implement plans than did their Banff counterparts. By any measurement,

Jasper managers were more successful restricting townsite expansion. Table 5-5 shows the value of all building permits in the two parks for the period 1984–89. While one could argue that Banff's totals are higher simply because more pressure and opportunities exist there, two factors undermine this argument. First, in raw numbers, the Banff totals are magnitudes higher than those for Jasper considering the smaller differences in number of residents and visitors. Second, consider the percentages. A much higher percentage of Jasper's permits have gone toward the "Other" category, basically public-sector development such as schools and hospitals, whereas over three-quarters of Banff's permits are residential or commercial.

At Yoho, one major focus of long-term planning was the aforementioned Lake O'Hara backcountry. By the 1970s, the Lake O'Hara area was, like many popular destinations in the Rockies, becoming overrun and overdeveloped. The largest meadow in the area actually served as a parking area for guests to the lodge and hiking trails. Parks Canada personnel then implemented plans to return the area to its natural condition, closing the road to vehicular traffic and putting strict limits on the numbers of overnight visitors. To get to the lake and its numerous trailheads, visitors must either walk the eleven kilometers or ride a bus that runs twice in the morning and twice at night. They may only stay in the lodge or in the primitive, thirty-site backcountry campground. Park personnel track movements of wildlife, particularly the grizzlies, and regularly put even the most popular hiking areas off limits to any human traffic. Human impact on the natural area is kept to a strict minimum.

For the mountain parks in general, the shifting emphasis to systematic preservation has been formally documented and authorized. For example, by the time the 1979 Parks Canada Policy Statement for the mountain parks was written, Parks Canada opted for no expansion of

TABLE 5-5
Total Value of Building Permits 1984–89
(in millions of constant 1988 dollars)

	Residential	Commercial	Other	Total
Banff	26.5	93.2	39.6	159.3
	17%	59%	25%	101%*
Jasper	1.65	5.4	4.7	11.8
	14%	46%	40%	100%

*numbers don't add to 100% due to rounding

Source: CPS 1989, "Private Sector Construction": pp. 5, 9.

park boundaries, no more ski areas, and no more golf courses.[133] In the 1994 Parks Canada Guiding Principles, Parks Canada states formally that "no new golf courses will be constructed in national parks and expansions to existing golf courses will not be considered."[134] Further, the agency prohibits new ski areas and mandates that existing facilities "be managed within their legislated boundaries according to long-range development plans."[135]

Current Status of Systematic Preservation Efforts in the Mountain Parks

Current plans to provide for preservation of natural conditions in the mountain parks are affected by the same political environment that affects systemwide expansion plans. Parks Canada personnel remain focused on a mission of long-term preservation and continue to enjoy some relative autonomy to pursue implementation, but the agency operates under increasingly tight fiscal budgets and actions must be sensitive to provincial concerns.

The 1988 Management Plans

In 1986 Parks Canada released the planning document titled, "In Trust for Tomorrow: A Management Framework for Four Mountain Parks." The title is significant in that it signals a major planning change that continues today. Plans for Banff, Jasper, Kootenay, and Yoho are coordinated and, in many ways, consistent. This provides the agency with the ability to think in terms of a larger ecosystem.

In 1988 Parks Canada published management plans for all the mountain parks. The plans are intended to provide fifteen-year guidelines with formal reviews every five years. The process leading up to the plans, pictured in figure 5-2, took six years. As shown, public input was incorporated at numerous steps along the way. The plans include environmental and social impact analysis as required under the EARP procedure. The plans were ultimately approved at the highest levels of government (Approved by Minister) and tabled in the House of Commons. This helps prevent subsequent political manipulation. Plans for the different parks share basic features such as Purpose and Objectives Statements emphasizing long-term ecological preservation and heavy reliance on zoning but differ in some specifics beyond that.

The 1988 Banff Management Plan emphasizes ecological principles but in somewhat more guarded tones than those for the other parks. To some degree, this moderation is inevitable. As Judy Otton, senior planner for the mountain parks, told me, "Because Banff is the flagship of the system, everything here is scrutinized quite intensely."[136] Otton

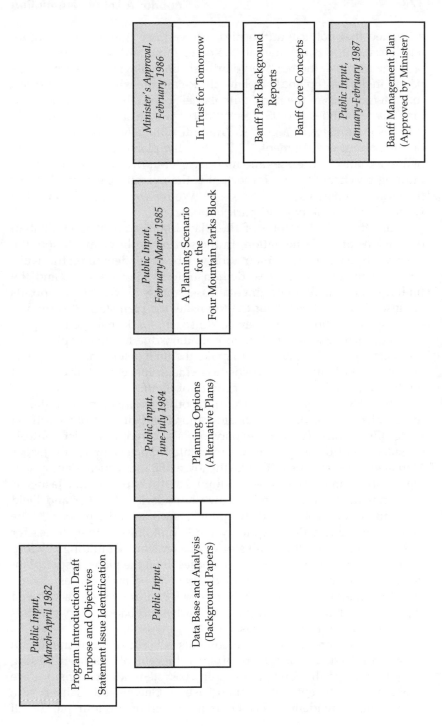

Figure 5-2 The Planning Process for the 1988 Banff National Park Management Plan

177

estimated that political authorities received one hundred times more letters regarding Banff than all the other mountain parks combined.

Nevertheless, the renewed emphasis on ecological concerns is apparent in the Banff plan. The plan calls for an extensive system of zones for different uses of the park, with 4% as Special Preservation with no man-made facilities and 93% as Wilderness with specific limits.[137] The plan also mandates as a goal to "minimize the effects of the townsite on the natural environment."[138] Further, the plan calls for recognition of fires as natural processes and mandates let-burn as well as prescribed burning practices.[139] More important is the overall tone of thinking of the mountain parks as an ecosystem. "We realized," says Otton, "that we needed to think beyond park boundaries."

Still, the guarded tone of the planning document is evident in discussions of implementation. In the section on Implementation, the agency admits that "implementation will be dependent upon the availability of financial resources, demonstrated visitor demand, and the findings of detailed environmental assessments."[140] Specific proposals are also cautious. Regarding the townsite, the plan states, "Although the original intention had been to do so, the park management plan does not include a detailed town boundary due to the complexity of the issue and the time needed to make the final determination."[141] The lack of specific limits on the townsite is a major concern to those worried by the continued pressures for growth of Banff.

The 1988 management plans for the other mountain parks reiterate the emphasis on ecological considerations and differ from Banff on some dimensions. Townsite expansion is allowed, but strict controls on subsequent development are mandated. For example, the Jasper Management Plan states: "Unlike the town of Banff, which is approaching its acceptable environmental limit, careful expansion of Jasper is environmentally acceptable."[142] Town boundaries at Jasper and Field are made quite explicit with techniques such as aerial photos.[143] The Yoho Management Plan explicitly limits buildings to two stories for residential and two-and-a-half stories for commercial buildings.[144] Zoning is emphasized for ecological purposes in all the plans. Jasper planners, for instance, call for 98% of the park to be managed as Zone 2 areas and another 1% as Zone 1. The need for natural fires is recognized explicitly in all the plans. All establish fairly strict backcountry controls in terms of permits and quotas.

While these are impressive documents, subsequent implementation has been mixed. The most important achievement has been finding ways to manage the four parks as an ecosystem. Many decisions are now made for the entire Mountain District. One person, Gaby Fortin, former superintendent of Jasper, is in charge of the four parks. All superintendents answer to him. Thus, objectives for park issues, such as backcountry plans, are consistent for all four parks. Research is also coordinated. For example, Parks Canada has one aquatic resources manager for the whole ecosystem. Otton is in charge of planning for the whole district and has been able to implement considerable ecosystem analysis using GIS and other techniques. Otton expressed confidence that because of these changes, the next plans will be stronger, more strategic, and more ecological than previous ones.[145]

Other specific efforts at implementing the 1988 plans have made slower progress. In an outside review, the Coopers & Lybrand consulting firm suggested several reasons. A substantial number of the monitoring activities described in the 1988 plans still await implementation. Many proposals are quite broad and not specific enough to set measurable guidelines. Because the plans are approved at very high levels, changing specifics is difficult and flexibility is diminished.[146] Fiscal restraint has meant salary freezes and staff reductions. Thus, Parks Canada personnel are overworked and often discouraged. Personnel lack business and marketing skills that are needed to implement cost-saving and efficiency efforts. The review process for proposed projects lacks clarity and interproject coordination. Funds are budgeted on an annual basis, making long-term consistency difficult. Ultimately, the consultants concluded that progress is slow due to "political factors and traditional federal-provincial issues."[147]

To be fair, complete evaluation of implementation of the 1988 plans at this point is not completely possible for two reasons. First, Parks Canada has not had sufficient time to implement several of the longer term projects. Second, implementation efforts for all the parks, particularly at Banff, have been somewhat superseded by two subsequent events, the incorporation of Banff and the Banff-Bow Valley Study, both described below. Indeed, the 1993 five-year review of the 1988 management plans was completed but never published due to the importance of the second of these events.

Incorporation of Banff

Implementation of long-term plans at Banff remains challenging for many reasons, not the least of which is the product of a decision in 1990. After extensive federal-provincial negotiations, Banff was formally recognized as a town, responsible for its own services and with the power to levy taxes. The Incorporation Agreement is between the province of Alberta and the federal government. Basically, the town of Banff has authority over all services and operations characteristic of Alberta municipalities.[148] For instance, Parks Canada will no longer be responsible for functions like sewage treatment and fire protection.

The town must pay $550,000 each year (plus tax) to the federal government to lease lands for the municipality.

The potential impact of incorporation on systematic preservation efforts is complex. Parks Canada retains control over all management plans, zoning agreements, and lease conditions. Environmental impact assessments are still required for developments in the town. Parks Canada has attempted to increase efficiency of the review process for proposed developments while still meeting the requirements of the Canadian Environmental Assessment Act (CEAA). Further, Parks Canada and the town did reach agreement on acceptable boundaries.

However, the agency will not have control over many of the processes that are involved in implementation of long-term plans. Much of Banff's development is intended to attract more visitors, an aspect not technically covered by environmental impact assessments. The new development review process remains complex, paperwork-intensive, and closed to meaningful public participation.[149] Future town bylaws not directly related to land use planning or the environment are beyond the scope of Parks Canada's jurisdiction. No systematic lists of acceptable or unacceptable projects is available to screen proposals. Finally, even within existing town boundaries, the ultimate usage for many areas is not yet determined. As of 1996, Parks Canada personnel said negotiations over the use of certain housing reserves, such as Mineral Spring, were fairly contentious.

Opinions concerning the impact of incorporation on long-term preservation efforts have been and remain mixed. Shortly after the transfer of power, Yoho superintendent Ian Church expressed concern about incentives for the residents: "It won't be long before they [Banff residents] panic over losing market share to Aspen."[150] Likewise, Perry Jacobson, then at Kootenay, stated that he was "never convinced that making it autonomous was a good move."[151] Banff superintendent Charlie Zinkan, on the other hand, was confident that residents would be careful with their decisions: "There is a sense that Banff must be a sustainable community."[152] This mixture of opinions has not diminished even with several years of perspective. On the optimistic side, current Banff mayor Ted Hart says development decisions are now much more controlled where they had previously been chaotic. Former superintendent Dave Day is also high on the switch. Of course, both these observers are residents and actively pro-growth. Harvey Locke, president of the Canadian Parks and Wilderness Society, is quite critical, terming "control" just another word for development.[153] Occupying the middle ground, agency planner Otton sees both benefits, such as a greater sense of pride amongst Banff residents, as well as downsides such as strained relations between town managers and Parks Canada personnel. Overall, however, Otton says, "I think it's more efficient for Parks Canada to not run the townsite."[154]

The Banff-Bow Valley Study

The major current plan potentially affecting future decisions at Banff is the Banff-Bow Valley Study. Bow Valley refers to the watershed of the Bow River as it runs through Banff and surrrounding areas. Michel Dupuy, Department of Canadian Heritage minister, commissioned the study in 1994.

The impetus for overhauling planning for the parks, just years into the fifteen-year cycle established by the 1988 management plans, was the abundance of questions and criticisms about current conditions at Banff arising from all quarters. The ministers of the environment and later the Department of Canadian Heritage received hundreds of letters each year questioning existing practices at the park. Parks Canada personnel continued to propose changes to existing practices and to express frustration with political interference. A 1993 survey by the Angus Reid Company revealed "overwhelming" opposition to more development in the parks with, by far, the most complaints directed at Banff. In a major cover story on Christmas Eve 1994, the *Globe and Mail* cited serious concerns about Banff's future from dozens of experts and outside observers. Even the IUCN threatened to remove World Heritage listing for the park.

Perhaps most revealing are opinions of the citizens of Banff and Alberta. In a 1996 survey of Banff householders, public opinion firm Praxis showed strong concern for diminishing natural conditions in the area. When asked about levels of desired commercial growth, only 6.2% preferred higher commercial growth whereas 21% were content with the status quo and an impressive 69.2% wanted lower growth rates. In another question, of seventy-four possible future priorities ranging from garbage collection to daycare services, the one receiving the most support was "preserving environmentally sensitive areas and open spaces in town."[155] Recent surveys of Calgary residents showed a majority (58%) describing development in Banff (the park) and nearly two-thirds (64%) describing development in Banff (the town) as at least "slightly high."[156]

The Banff-Bow Valley Study was mandated to develop a long-term vision for the park that balances preservation of ecological conditions with economic development. Specifically, the minister called for planners to develop comprehensive goals, analyze existing information, and provide direction "in a manner which will maintain the ecological integrity of the Banff-Bow Valley and provide for sustainable tourism."[157] The scope of the project was thus immense. The process of the study was also ambitious as the commission was mandated to utilize heavy public input. The commission included many notable authorities from biological, engineering, and other fields and was headed by Robert Page, a dean at nearby University of Calgary. The study concentrated on Banff, but Parks Canada intends to use it for planning at all of the mountain parks.

The fact that the study was done external to Parks Canada requires explanation. In fact, Parks Canada personnel were involved in the deliberations, often as "shadow members" as one consultant termed them.[158] They provided input and information when needed. However, the study was done externally precisely to retain independence and to reinforce public perception of impartiality. As Parks Canada planner Otton says, "We stayed out to keep it objective. We thought there would be more faith in an outside study."[159]

An indication of the potential importance of the study was the intense scrutiny it received during deliberation. Verbal battles over the study between groups with opposing views of the preferred future of Banff flared after the process commenced. Major participants include the prodevelopment Association for Mountain Parks Protection and Enjoyment headed by former Banff superintendent Day and the anti-development CPWS headed by Calgary lawyer Locke. At points, Day and Locke had such heated exchanges that Page was prompted to request they "lower the volume and eliminate what I like to call unparliamentary language."[160] The commission's deliberations drew attention from groups in other countries, such as the Sierra Club.

Given the intense level of interest, the Study Task Force attempted to be as inclusive as possible in deliberations. From the outset, the Task Force invited public involvement through written statements or verbal presentations, ultimately receiving over 261 submissions and eleven deputations.[161] Continuous input was provided via a Round Table involving as many interest sectors as possible. The Round Table met on a regular basis, compared ideas, and sought to find common ground for recommendations. The Task Force kept the public informed through newsletters, press releases, and even opened an office in downtown Banff.

Perhaps surprisingly, the Alberta government did not get heavily involved in the study except as observers. Chairman Page encouraged their full participation, and they did sit in on the Round Table meetings, but they were reluctant to fully endorse the process. In part, this reluctance reflects a Conservative provincial government whereas the study was mandated by a Liberal Party running the federal government. More than that, however, relations between federal and provincial authorities have been strained for some time. Planner Otton says relations between field personnel are good, but not at higher levels, thus affecting their participation in the study. She says, "They were afraid the federal government would railroad them."

The commission worked for two years, utilizing a variety of experts and consultants.[162] During that time, Sheila Kopps replaced Dupuy as Department of Canadian Heritage minister, but she, an outspoken former minister of the environment, announced her full support for the project. Over the two years of deliberation, the study received over $2.5 million federal dollars in support. The Task Force utilized research from Parks Canada, provincial governments, and the commercial sector.

The Task Force released the study in the fall of 1996. The major conclusion of the study was that the Banff area was in serious ecological trouble. The *Summary Report* (p. 14) states that "ecological integrity has been, and continues to be increasingly compromised." Looking ahead fifty years, the report predicts (p. 27): "If current trends and pressures are allowed to continue, they will threaten the qualities that make Banff a national park."

These dramatic conclusions are supported by an abundance of evidence in the *Technical Report*, probably the most detailed and thorough planning document ever prepared for a national park. The forecast includes as many as nineteen million tourists by 2020, dramatic regional development of nearby areas, expanded transportation corridors, fragmentation of the entire ecosystem, severe damage to wildlife and aquatic systems, elimination of remaining cultural heritage, and alteration of Parks Canada's priorities from one of preservation to one of revenue generation. Further, because Banff is the cornerstone of Canadian parks, the Task Force predicts that such growth will eventually contaminate the rest of the system leading to "the failure of the second oldest system of protected areas in the world."[163]

To prevent such a future, the study offers over five hundred specific recommendations. Table 5-6 provides summaries of several key areas of recommendations. Underlying all of them are the needs to think long term about ecological integrity and for Parks Canada to provide the necessary leadership. Indeed, the report states that ecological integrity will be "the primary mandate in all zones."[164] Yet, one should notice how the Task Force tried to find some balance between current growth trends and complete restoration of wilderness conditions. For example, they call for modifying the golf course, not removing it. They recommend altering the ski areas but not closing them down.

Official reactions to the study came quickly. Heritage Minister Kopps reacted to publication with the comment, "If we don't get our act together today, this park may not exist in 50 years."[165] The

TABLE 5-6
Banff-Bow Valley Study Recommendations

Aquatic Ecosystems
- set specific limits on pollutants from specific sources
- monitor and reduce nonpoint source pollutants
- identify species needed to restore biodiversity
- integrate research for entire ecosystem
- Parks Canada take lead for integrated management

Terrestrial Ecosystems
- prescribe exact areas and amounts for prescribed burns
- prescribe exact areas and amounts for natural flooding
- restore wildlife linkage zones to other areas in four mountain parks
- reintroduce wildlife such as free-roaming bison
- remove nonnative species of plants and animals
- integrate research for entire ecosystem
- Parks Canada take lead for integrated management

Human Usage
- combine rail and highway corridors into single multiuse transportation corridor
- close sections of highways where animal mortality high
- reduce speed limits on other highways
- convert some existing roads to hiking/cycling trails
- develop more public transit for commuters from cities
- restrict periods of use of ski areas
- restrict number of skiers on ski areas
- stop plans to expand golf course and, if need be, reduce the number of holes
- provide incentives for tourism operators to use ecologically sound practices
- adopt current zoning system to site-specific limits
- establish ecological carrying capacity limits for trails, campgrounds, waterways, etc.
- impose limits on use in sensitive areas

Towns
- no commercial expansion in Lake Louise hamlet
- no commercial expansion in Banff town
- no residential expansion in Lake Louise hamlet
- only residential fill-ins within existing Banff town
- plan model ecological communities for Banff and Lake Louise

Source: Parks Canada 1996, *Banff-Bow Valley Technical Report.*

Department of Canadian Heritage put several proposals into effect immediately, including a prohibition on further commercial development in the park and prioritization of biodiversity restoration throughout terrestrial and aquatic ecosystems. Further, the department promised considerably more action to soon follow.[166]

The obvious question regarding the Banff-Bow Valley Study, as with any long-term plan, concerns implementation. Several factors promote optimism. First, the inclusiveness of the process established certain levels of cooperation and consensus that did not previously exist. Parks Canada's Otton says, "The people involved in those round tables developed strong relations, they won't let it fall through." Second, the study has been highly visible and well-publicized. Broken promises will be apparent. Mel Wilson, one of the outside consultants hired by the Commission, expressed confidence. "The Ministers have made solid commitments to implementing this study," Wilson said, "and they have spent a lot of money on it. This is a big, high-profile undertaking."[167] Third, public opinion remains supportive.

Then again, implementation will not be easy. Some of the recommendations, such as strict limits on trail usage and moratoriums on townsite growth, elicited strong criticisms from prodevelopment groups.[168] Others, notably those designed to enhance ecosystem restoration, depend upon activities in areas outside the immediate park. Table 5-7 displays the categories of lands in the Central Rockies ecosystem. By far the largest category consists of private lands in Alberta available for extraction and other uses. The second largest category consists of multiple use and private lands in British Columbia. The limited

TABLE 5-7
Land Jurisdiction in Central Rockies Ecosystem

Land Jurisdiction	Area (sq km)	% CRE
British Columbia Provincial Parks	452.4	1.06
British Columbia Wilderness Areas	650.5	1.53
British Columbia Multiple Use & Private Lands	10,645.3	25.06
Parks Canada	9,537.9	22.45
Alberta Provincial Parks	611.1	1.44
Alberta Wilderness	948.9	2.23
Alberta Multiple Use & Private Lands	19,177.3	45.13
Native Reserves & Misc. Federal Lands	470.5	1.10
Total	42,493.9	100.0

Source: Parks Canada 1996, *Banff-Bow Valley Technical Report:* 40.

involvement of provincial policymakers in the study's deliberations does not bode well for future cooperative efforts. The study itself admits that Alberta authorities promote economic activities without input from Parks Canada and summarizes potential federalism impacts this way: "Federal/Provincial jurisdictional issues limit the ability to progress in this area (ecosystems)."[169]

The Future of Park Planning?

Does the current situation in the mountain parks represent the future for long-term planning in Canadian ecosystems? Most of those involved in the Banff-Bow Valley Task Force are guardedly optimistic. Mountain park planners incorporated much of the Banff-Bow Valley Study into their revised management plan released in 1997. In April of that year, two days before the country's elections, Minister Kopps filed the plan with Parliament. The timing was important, guaranteeing that the plan had been approved (it only has to be filed, not voted on) at the highest levels of government even if Kopps and her party lost the elections. In fact, the Liberals retained power and Kopps was reappointed minister of the Department of Canadian Heritage.

The plan has also received significant support from the community. Task Force chair Robert Page told me, "It has been a better reaction than we expected" and attributed much of that to the high-profile involvement of Kopps and others.[170] Many private operators were working with parks personnel to make their activities more ecologically oriented. Perhaps even more surprising has been the reaction among some provincial authorities. Page has been appointed to a provincial consulting body on their parks, thus allowing greater communication between federal and provincial authorities. Further, the premier of Alberta referred explicitly and positively to the Banff study in his successful reelection campaign in 1997.

Is the planning experience in the mountain parks atypical of efforts elsewhere in the Canadian national parks? Certainly, the scope is smaller at other individual units. The long-term goals of planners are consistent, however. For example, personnel at Prince Albert concluded an intensive planning process with publication of their management plan in October 1995. The document followed years of study, proposals, and public comment. The emphases in the plan on preserving ecological integrity and using ecosystem approaches to management are quite apparent.[171] Still, moving toward these goals will be difficult here just as it is in the mountain parks, especially given the current budget constraints.

What of ecosystems outside of national parks? The mixed success of the planning process at the national level may yet be a model for similar efforts at provincial levels. Policymakers in British Columbia have undertaken a vast land-use plan with a goal of setting aside one-eighth of its area as protected space. The process began with the election of the Mike Harcourt government in 1991 and came in part as a response to international protests over extensive timber harvesting in the province.[172]

CONCLUSIONS

Canadian policymakers recognize the need for and the realities involved in long-term planning for delivery of intergenerational goods. As historian Walter Hildebrandt says, "Management planning is the central and crucial process for administering a national park. . . . It cannot, however, deal with political questions that affect park administration." As a result, says Hildebrandt, "Effective implementation of comprehensive management plans is also lacking."[173] Both aspects of Hildebrandt's comments, the crucial role of planning and the frustration of implementation, are evident in long-term efforts at the system and individual unit levels. Both the systemwide expansion plan and the Banff-Bow Valley Study constitute sincere efforts to emphasize ecological care for intergenerational goods. Both are also subject to significant delays and complications in implementation due to fiscal constraints and provincial demands.

6

Costa Rica: Making the Transition?

We wanted to regrow the forest and that was a breeze. Making
the administrative transition was and still is a bit more difficult.
—Dan Janzen, 23 May 1997

On my first hike in Costa Rica, on the Sendero Natural in Santa Rosa
National Park in the northern part of the country, part of the area
where biologist Janzen and others have "regrown" the forest, I almost
stepped on a three-foot-long iguana. The creature's camouflage and
lack of movement made him relatively imperceptible, but once I spotted
him, I appreciated the opportunity. Iguanas are not what most people
think of as beautiful, and they are certainly not warm and fuzzy creatures. Yet, to me, they look oddly stoic and unflappable. Their stoicism
is odd because many species of these descendants of the dinosaurs are
also severely endangered. Thanks to the efforts of Janzen and others
who have preserved some of Costa Rica, I was able to see part of our
distant past in the wild. Whether travelers in the future will also be
able to see that past depends largely upon the transition to which
Janzen refers.

BACKGROUND

Costa Rica contains a remarkable system of protected areas. The system
is remarkable for the inclusion of all types of ecosystems, from volcanoes to rainforests to the last intact stand of tropical dry forest in
Central America. The system is also remarkable for the recent efforts
to protect immense conservation areas where species really can be
preserved. The Costa Rican system is the envy of many other nations
where systematic preservation is preached but often not achieved,
nations with longer traditions and more material resources. Why has
"regrowing" the forest in Costa Rica been possible? For much of the
period since the early 1970s, Costa Rica has enjoyed circumstances
quite favorable to preservation efforts.

188

Necessary Conditions

Costa Rica is unique among developing nations for a variety of reasons such as peaceful transitions of power and a widely literate population. One result of these factors is the presence of favorable conditions for intergenerational concerns. Systematic preservation efforts have been facilitated by public support from various sources, stable democratic processes since 1948, and official commitment to these efforts since the early 1970s. However, recent changes in all of these conditions make the future less certain.

Public Support

In many respects, the idea of protecting natural areas in Costa Rica is a recent phenomenon. Public support for this idea arose from very different sources.

One obvious stimulus to support for long-term preservation of natural areas is the impressive array of biodiversity to be found in this nation. Costa Rica is not a large country, yet several biogeographic features produce numerous ecosystems. This fairly compact nation is bordered by both the Atlantic and Pacific Oceans and divided by a mountain range of over ten thousand feet in elevation. Further, the country is part of the isthmian link between North and South America. Thus, Costa Rica contains ecosystems found in different climates, at different elevations, and on different continents. Biologists estimate that the country contains over half a million different species, including eight hundred of birds and eight thousand of higher plants. The total variety of species constitutes roughly 7% of the world's biodiversity.[1]

Historically, the immense richness of biodiversity attracted the attention of one particular group of scholars. Biologists began migrating to Costa Rica in substantial numbers in the 1950s and 1960s. Once there, they contributed immensely to the nurturing of institutions of science and learning. The Universidad de Costa Rica (UCR) was re-formed in 1955 largely at the behest of Archie Carr and other scientists. The Tropical Science Center was established in 1962 by three Americans as a private consulting institute. The Organization for Tropical Studies (OTS), consisting of seven North American universities and the UCR, was created in 1963. A center for the study of agronomy and forestry (CATIE) became an independent entity in 1972, subsequently becoming a host to many biologists. The presence of biologists in Costa Rica was so strong by the end of the 1960s that they formed their own professional association. As one analyst states, "In short, the scientific base and the scientific culture to support a healthy conservation ethic were solidly in place in Costa Rica by the 1970s."[2]

The scientific community has provided strong support for preservation efforts. Between its founding in 1963 and the early 1980s, for example, the OTS produced hundreds of papers on ecological issues affecting the country. Janzen was one of the biologists involved in these efforts. As he writes, the actions of OTS and other intellectual centers provides Costa Rica with "an awareness of ecological problems and the proper attitude" to face environmental dilemmas.[3] Whereas scientific input into establishment and management of natural areas in the United States has almost been an afterthought, the scientific community in Costa Rica was in the forefront of preservation efforts.

A second stimulus for public support for preservation derives somewhat ironically from Costa Rica's history of deforestation. Between 1940 and 1960, vast areas of forests were cut, clearing the ground for timber, cattle ranching, or increased agricultural production. The Costa Rican economy has long been dependent upon exports of coffee, bananas, beef, and sugar. By the late 1960s, what remained of the original forest cover was being removed at rates of roughly 1% per year.[4] In the 1970s, nearly sixty thousand hectares per year were cut. Flying in or out of the country now, one can't help but notice vast deforested areas. Recent satellite images estimate that Costa Rica's early forest cover of roughly 75% is now down to 17%. Amazingly enough, the country has lost so much forest that it will become a timber importer in years to come.[5] Concerns over deforestation fueled persistent and successful demands for ecological protection of the natural areas that remained in this developing nation.

This devastation inspired international as well as domestic concern. Various immigrants and visitors increased demands on more public protection of lands or began raising international money in order to do it themselves. For example, one pioneering couple from Sweden, the Wessbergs, purchased the last stand of forest on the Nicoya Peninsula in 1963, an area that became the Cabo Blanco Biological Reserve.[6] Other expatriates living and working in Costa Rica would continue to see this country as providing a chance to emphasize an ecological orientation throughout the development of the park system. This awareness has led to significant amounts of international support in numerous preservation efforts.

A third major source of support came from the Costa Ricans themselves. This support was not manifested as a large "environmental movement" as in the United States or Australia. Rather, individuals such as Mario Boza and Alvaro Ugalde developed interests in conservation while they were students in Costa Rica's impressive education system. Since the present Constitution of Costa Rica was adopted in 1949, policymakers made a concerted effort to sponsor social reforms and to foster educational growth in the country. Indeed, the Constitution mandates that at least 10% of the budget be allocated to education. In part, this emphasis was facilitated by the money that would no longer be spent on armed forces, these having been abolished in 1948. Much of the educational emphasis contained a biology component. Both Boza and Ugalde were graduates of the reformed UCR and its school of biology.

Boza and Ugalde wrote academic and editorial pieces on national parks and began to influence Costa Rican president Jose Figueres and his wife Karen. Interestingly, many of their ideas about national parks grew out of visits to American parks, particularly the Great Smokies and the Grand Canyon. Boza's reaction to U.S. parks was typical: "I think the U.S. Park Service is more oriented toward recreation than the protection of the biological resource. They're more interested in having nice highways and picnic areas."[7] Boza and Ugalde took many lessons from their visits to the United States. For example, they decided that a park system should build tourist facilities outside the park, not only to protect the natural conditions within but also to allow local entrepreneurs rather than corporate concessionaires to benefit from increased economic activity.

Years later, Boza stated the principles which guided the system through its evolution: "Yes, parks are for people. We need to develop facilities. But the principal reason for parks is the need to protect nature. The real reason for parks is to protect species."[8] Boza and Ugalde nurtured fledgling Costa Rican conservation efforts in the early years. Their actions benefitted from the simple fact that they could learn lessons from previous protection efforts in the United States and elsewhere.

While the efforts of some Costa Ricans were essential, the idea of preservation for future generations is not an easy one to grasp for many people in this developing country. Still, even the less affluent Costa Ricans are generally literate and relatively worldly. Though not always informed on specific details, surveys have shown that the Costa Rican people are at least environmentally aware and concerned about issues such as deforestation.[9] When asked why a developing country displayed such concern for wilderness values, Ugalde stated, "The way I used to explain it was that parks were part of the Costa Rican soul." Other locals also described the parks in near-religious terms.[10] In many environmental issues, including those that might affect parks through external threats, Costa Ricans have made impressive progress. Most notably, the country is being weaned away from fossil fuels and has, particularly in recent years, developed aggressive energy policies focusing on conservation and renewables.[11]

Even if widespread sentimental attachment to the land seems somewhat amorphous, others supported the parks for more material reasons.

Though not always called by the same term, recognition of the value of "ecotourism" has existed in Costa Rica for decades. By 1988 tourism accounted for 13% of Costa Rican export income. Further, three-fourths of foreign visitors said they came to the country for its natural beauty.[12] In the 1990s, foreign tourism was growing at a rate of 27% per year as opposed to a 3% growth rate for internal tourism.[13] Those dependent upon tourism have been vocal supporters for the addition and management of ecological areas throughout the country.

The future of public support for parks in this country will depend to a significant extent on the cultivation of widespread interest among the population. Policymakers are attempting to do this through regionally managed conservation units, the most notable being the Area de Conservacion Guanacaste (ACG) in the northern part of the country. When I asked Juan Carlos, one of the staff at the ACG, why local people were supportive of protected areas, he responded without hesitation, "Because they are involved in it."[14] This involvement was and remains the next essential step in preservation of many areas in Costa Rica. Without such involvement, Costa Rican support for natural areas may become diluted by concerns for other problems.

Stable Political Processes

Demands for systematic preservation are more likely to be heard in Costa Rica than in many developing nations. The country has been politically stable since just after World War II.

The Costa Rican government is unitary, popular, and representative. The executive branch is headed by a popularly elected president, a cabinet, and two vice presidents. The Legislative Assembly consists of fifty-seven deputies (in 1983) elected on the basis of proportional representation. Table 6-1 lists the ruling parties of the government since the new state was born in 1948. The dominant party in much of this period has been the Partido Liberacion Nacional (PLN), a multiclass-based party with an emphasis on economic and social reforms.

While political processes in Costa Rica are stable, the specific political environment of the managing parks agency is not. Parks management has gone through several phases even in a relatively short duration in this country. Parks agencies enjoyed considerable stability through the 1970s and into the 1980s, the period of much expansion of the system. However, since the late 1980s, the park service has been changing, part of the transition to which Janzen refers. Policymakers have attempted to shift many responsibilities to the local level, leaving Costa Rica without a centralized parks agency but rather a collection of semiautonomous regional units loosely coordinated by the Ministry of Natural Resources, Energy, and Mines.

TABLE 6-1
Costa Rican Governments (1949–1998)

Term	President	Party
1949–1953	Otilio Ulate Blanco	Union
1953–1958	Jose Figueres Ferrer	Liberacion
1958–1962	Mario Echandi Jimenez	PUN
1962–1966	Francisco Bolmarcich	PLN
1966–1970	Jose Fernandez	Unificacion
1970–1974	Jose Figueres Ferrer	PLN
1974–1978	Daniel Oduber Quiros	PLN
1978–1982	Rodrigo Carazo Odio	Unidad
1982–1986	Luis Alberto Alvarez	PLN
1986–1990	Oscar Arias Sanchez	PLN
1990–1994	Rafael Calderon Fournier	Unidad
1994–1998	Jose Maria Figueres Olsen	PLN

Official Political Commitment

Official political commitment to systematic preservation in Costa Rica was quite prominent during the 1970s and the early 1980s. Since then, rhetorical commitment remains although the goals have become more complicated.

Public protection of natural places in Costa Rica occurred only through intermittent efforts preceding the late 1960s. In 1913 the government declared the area around Poas Volcano in the central mountains as "inalienable."[15] In 1939 the government called for conservation of areas of land along coastlines and river bottoms and established small reserves around Poas and Irazu Volcanoes. The term "national park" was first used in regards to an area along the Panamerican Highway in 1945, but proposals to protect the site were not implemented. Subsequent actions included the creation of a few protected areas on paper and statements of intent by the Costa Rican government. As late as 1966, the Legislative Assembly was only finally getting around to formally declaring plans to set aside the area at Santa Rosa, site of the important 1856 battle with invader William Walker, as a national monument. Federal authorities had neither the money nor the ability to manage any of these places as real parks.

In 1969 the Forestry Law established the General Forestry Directorate (DGF) and authorized executive establishment of national parks, the boundaries to be specified in congressional decrees. In 1970 the government of Jose Figueres established a Department of National Parks within the Ministry of Mines, Agriculture, and Livestock "as a response to the Costa Rican people's demand for a park system dedicated to preserving the natural areas of Costa Rica."[16] President Figueres appointed Boza to run it. Though initially slowed by civic unrest and a lack of funds, Boza and Ugalde began to work on creating a system. In 1977 Law No. 6084 elevated the status of the parks department to that of a separate general directorate termed the National Parks Service—Servicio de Parques Nacionales (SPN).

In the mid-1980s, many facets of protected area management began to change. In 1986 the Arias administration made several alterations. To begin, they appointed an experienced biologist named Luis Mendez as director of the parks. They shifted the agency from Agriculture into the newly formed Ministry of Natural Resources, Energy, and Mines (MIRENEM) and appointed an energetic engineer named Alvaro Umana as head. Umana promptly pronounced a renewed emphasis on sustainable development and made it official policy to encourage local activities that do not impair natural conditions, such as ecotourism and sustainable agriculture.[17]

Under Umana and his successors, the National Parks Service entered a transition period. The transition was motivated by concern for local involvement. For years, no explicit policy regarding the impact of conservation decisions on rural people was formulated, and, in some cases, those decisions unfairly harmed long-time residents.[18] Umana and others encouraged decentralization of power to local people. Policymakers have attempted to replace the central coordinating agency with a much more fluid, decentralized form of governance in the regional conservation units discussed later in the chapter. This decentralization, however well intentioned, has caused some concern about the loss of central direction from a strong parks agency.[19]

Political commitments to preservation ideals have wavered in the mid-to-late 1990s. A massive government deficit makes commitment of resources difficult, especially as the country faces numerous other challenges. The current overseer of the nation's protected areas, Carlos Manuel Rodríguez, says quite pointedly, "The politicians have recognized that national parks have attracted a lot of foreign currency because of ecotourism, and they use the environmental issue in every political campaign, but there is not the political will to really work to resolve our problems."[20]

Constraining Conditions

For all of the progressive aspects of Costa Rica, it is still a third world country. One need only drive on even the best of roads there to be reminded of this fact. The government has enough money to mark some of the many craterous potholes but not enough to fill them. Systematic preservation efforts benefitted from a lack of vertical and horizontal constraints for many years, but they are increasingly affected by different forms of vertical influence, one that arises at the higher level of global affairs and the other from the need to involve subnational levels in administration. Reliance on international money creates a potentially unfavorable and unpredictable system of funding. Decentralization makes coordination of efforts much more complicated.

Low But Increasingly Evident Vertical Constraints

For most of the period of Costa Rican park system expansion, intervention from other levels of government into park system processes was not a problem. Current efforts to enhance natural conditions, however, are becoming more affected by other levels of policymakers, those outside of Costa Rica and those involved in local management.

The limited power of local government was certainly true in land issues for Costa Rica for decades. This limited role dates substantially to 1961 when the Legislative Assembly enacted an agrarian law that declared much of the land in the country as belonging to the national government. This included unoccupied land, lands of the political agencies, zones along rivers, and borders of forest reserves and parklands.[21] Most of the government powers have traditionally been centered in San Jose. The country is divided into 7 provinces, 81 cantons, and 415 districts. These subnational entities have their own political officials, but they have few administrative powers. In addition, the local governments lack the means to raise much revenue.[22] Further, studies have shown that Costa Ricans are more likely to contact their Assembly deputies than they are to call on local officials to solve problems.[23] As one analyst states, "Local government is very limited."[24]

Costa Rican preservation efforts also remained fairly autonomous from potentially influential outside actors such as funding organizations and international conventions. Though money for parks was coming in from outside Costa Rican borders, it was not pervasive until more recently. For many of the early years of expansion, funding was not typically a problem. Costa Rica experienced significant economic growth between 1960 and the end of the 1970s, annual growth rates of GDP averaging 6% before the economic crisis of the 1980s. While the national economy was good, most of the park service agency's funds came from the central government.

However, many involved with preservation efforts in the country correctly anticipated that not only might the economy turn, but also that the public funds that were available would not be enough for much of the planned land acquisition. They thus began to aggressively pursue funding from international organizations such as the Nature Conservancy. Early solo efforts at this fundraising were later supplemented by more concerted attempts through nongovernmental organizations such as the National Parks Foundation.[25] The Foundation was established in 1979, largely by Boza, with a five-person Board of Directors to coordinate foreign donations. The transition toward more external sources of funding accelerated during the 1980s. Between 1987 and 1990, the SPN budget consisted of $27 million (U.S. dollars) from the state and $19 million from private foundations.[26]

The increasing inability of the government in San José to provide adequate funding created a more complicated financial situation. First, international funds were often directed at a specific area or solicited by an aggressive fundraiser such as Janzen. Thus, financial resources for protected areas dependent upon international sources could vary considerably from one unit to the next. This lack of consistency makes planning for the future much more challenging, particularly if the flow of international funds slows dramatically as it appears to be doing in the latter part of the 1990s.[27] Indeed, complications involving environmental issues other than land preservation have already been attributed to dependence on international funds.[28]

A second concern involves dependence on ecotourism. Certainly, the money and support from many ecotourism activities has been helpful to some natural areas. For example, tourist dollars have been quite helpful in saving the leatherback turtles at Las Baulas Marine National Park.[29] As at other places, however, the increased tourism is a double-edged sword. More tourists means more development. Further, as private interests have become more involved in parks, the government has welcomed them and used them to supplant public funding for preservation efforts. As a result, park personnel are few, usually not well-paid, and often relatively untrained. In addition, while private entrepreneurs have become increasingly visible in or near parks, government regulation of their activities has not kept pace with this growth.[30]

Third, international money for tourism is not always directed at ecologically sound activities. In recent years, the Costa Rican tourism industry has grown to become the nation's largest moneymaker with revenues over $700 million per year. Much of this money is spent on activities that hardly constitute ecotourism. In particular, golf courses are becoming a booming business. According to the American Society of Travel Agents, golf-related visits to Costa Rica have increased by 10% per year since 1990. The number of courses has grown to six with nine more on the way by the end of the decade. Plans exist to cut some courses directly out of the rainforests.[31]

Fourth, a relatively poor economy can foster local resentment to protected areas unless local people share in revenue from visitors and ecotourism. Changing the system to meet this problem was not easy. Delegation of park management to subnational governments was not really an option. As described earlier, provincial and local governments have little authority. In recent years, some policymakers have pursued an increased role for local people in park planning. This position, advocated by Janzen, Ugalde, and others, has aroused substantial disagreement from, among others, Ugalde's former partner Boza.[32] The fact that the two main founders of the Costa Rican park system disagree on this trend is illustrative of the controversy surrounding this development.

The results of decentralization of parks management are not yet clear as the Costa Rican system remains in transition from one form of governance to another. Many feel that local involvement is essential to maintain local support, but others fear that, indeed, local participation may complicate implementation of national plans. As the opening quote suggests, effectively implementing this transition has not been easy and will not become any easier with growing fiscal problems.

Low Horizontal Constraints

The governing parks agency has gone through several versions, including the current transition, but for much of the period since the early 1970s, the agency was quite important in preservation decisions. Consistent with the respect shown other bureaucracies in Costa Rica, park system managers pursued many plans without severe political manipulation.

Deference to public agencies in Costa Rica dates at least to the reforms of the late 1940s when policymakers wanted a less political and more expertise-oriented style of government. Bureaucratic institutions have been awarded enough autonomy for it to be reflected in their unofficial title. As Ameringer states in his oft-cited account of political processes in Costa Rica, "The autonomous institutions are truly autonomous.[33]

Intervention from members of the Assembly is rare for several reasons. First, because Costa Rica does impose term limits on representatives, deputies serve only one four-year term. While Assembly deputies, perhaps surprisingly, do still attempt to deliver favors to constituents, extensive micromanagement of public agencies is less possible with such a short term of service.[34] Second, legislative power exists in standing committees where members serve one year and are then rotated to other committees. Thus, these bodies lack the expertise that could lead to many forms of intervention. Third, the Assembly does not have the ability to remove cabinet ministers such as the heads of natural resource departments and though it can censure them, this power is rarely exercised.[35]

Presidents have little power over the agencies once ministers are appointed. For instance, presidential appointments are staggered so that terms for agency officials overlap presidential and legislative terms. Again, the autonomous institutions were designed to be so precisely to prevent extensive political control from one central authority.

Political parties are historically quite weak.[36] Whereas weak parties in the United States facilitate manipulation of agencies by individual American congressional entrepreneurs, Costa Rican deputies are constrained by the term limits mentioned above. In fact, term limits keep the parties weak since they have no formal sanctions on individual members.[37] Thus, parties are unlikely to be able to develop any kind of cohesive effort to crack the professional insularity of agencies.

Interest groups are increasingly active participants in Costa Rican politics, but none have developed anything near the potential clout needed to capture political agencies. One might expect the agricultural sector to be quite influential. Indeed, it is prominent, constituting nearly one-fifth of the GDP, but the political clout of the sector is diminished by the fact that farming interests are divided along crop-type and regional lines.[38] Besides the agricultural sector, other business entities also have less power than might be expected. Costa Rican versions of business-oriented Chambers of Commerce remain "relatively ineffectual."[39]

Some changes were made in the 1970s to check autonomous agency behavior, but political control remained low. As one study concludes, "the autonomous agencies have continued to issue rules, adopt policies, and embark on new forms of activity without being obliged to secure executive and legislative sanction."[40] Many of the autonomous institutions are even constitutionally guaranteed a fixed percentage of the national budget. Political scientist Jack Hopkins summarizes: "Thus major policy decisions are made by autonomous agencies without legislative control."[41]

Perhaps partly because of the discretion they enjoy, the motivation of most parks personnel has traditionally been high. In contrast to common perceptions of corrupt agency officials in many developing nations, the employees involved with management of protected areas that I met while in Costa Rica were intelligent and dedicated. Evidence is necessarily anecdotal, but just as one example, while on a hike with a staffer at Poas Volcano, I asked her if she thought her job, at the time picking up litter on the trail, was a good job. She replied with a wave of her hand at the surrounding vegetation, "I work hard, but I do it in a place like this."

Much of this motivation has to do with factors discussed earlier. Costa Ricans are generally literate and informed. Parks personnel are aware that they are responsible for presenting their country's finest areas to foreign visitors. On the one hand, pride is reinforced by the knowledge that their livelihood may depend on making positive impressions. On the other hand, some analysts report that many in the agency are less than enthusiastic about the current transition to decentralized management.[42]

One cloud on Costa Rica's horizon reflects a potentially important change in the characterization of horizontal constraints as low. With the current fiscal problems facing the nation, park areas have become a tempting source for revenue. One 1998 report suggests that much of the money raised within the parks was raided by legislators for use on other projects in 1997.[43] Such behavior, if it continues, is reminiscent of problems faced by the U.S. NPS for so many years and troubling for the future autonomy of Costa Rican parks even if they do become self-sufficient.

Theoretical Expectations

For much of the period of park system growth, conditions in Costa Rica were conducive to significant success with efforts at systematic preservation. This success will hypothetically be manifest in representation of diverse ecosystems as well as restoration of natural conditions at some units. The future is less clear, however, as the system shifts in new directions.

SYSTEM EXPANSION

I was parked just off the Siquiries Highway in Braulio Carrillo National Park, in the mountains east of San Jose, listening to the sounds of the surrounding rainforest. Even the fairly heavy rainfall did not diminish the singing of the various birds in the area. Occasionally, those natural sounds were interrupted by the guttural roar of a logging truck rumbling toward San Jose. This was the bad news for those seeking natural conditions in the park. The good news was that those trucks don't stop in Braulio Carrillo. Other than the highway that bisects this immense area, the rainforest remains undeveloped, mainly due to the ecological goals emphasized in expansion of the Costa Rican system.

Planning

Planning in Costa Rica was never as formal a process as elsewhere, yet the goals were often much more clear. As Mario Boza once said,

"Nothing was planned. We had no experience, although the basic idea of what we wanted to do was clear."[44] In an interview with David Wallace in 1982, system founder Ugalde stated the issue of ecosystems as the guiding principle of expansion. Ugalde said, "Management of the ecosystems in parks in perpetuity is the Park Service's main goal."[45] In his book on Costa Rican parks, cofounder Boza echoed the emphasis on preservation of diverse ecosystems.[46]

The idea motivating system expansion was representation. That idea was developed by biologists and ecologists working with a system termed Holdrige Life Zones. In 1947 L. R. Holdridge suggested classifying areas according to vegetation, climate, latitude, elevation, and other data to describe diverse "life zones" on the planet.[47] In 1964 a biologist at UCR named Rafael Caballero utilized such a system to publish a list of natural areas warranting some form of protection. That list would "serve as a kind of agenda" for park system expansion.[48]

In one sense at least, Costa Rican planners benefitted from the relative youth of the system. Ugalde acknowledged the difference between their intentions and those motivating U.S. expansion, "The world was different when the U.S. started its park system than when we did. It's my impression that Yellowstone was created to protect the landscape and give citizens a place for recreation. We started with a system to protect biodiversity. The world was speaking more about biodiversity than recreation. We were influenced by biologists, not just a few park planners from the U.S. So recreation and scenery were secondary."[49] With scenery taking secondary importance, Costa Rican policymakers could emphasize other goals. In particular, they set out to establish protected areas in all of the diverse areas of the country.

Implementation

The system expanded quickly. The number of units jumped from just a few in 1971 (including Cabo Blanco, Poas, and Santa Rosa) to sixteen national parks and biological reserves by 1978. By 1992 the system had grown to thirty-four national parks and reserves, covering 12.2% of the nation's total land area.

Maintaining the Emphasis on Representation

As the national parks agency grew beyond just the efforts of Boza and Ugalde, the academic community and the parks agency together continued to emphasize expansion to achieve systematic representation. Throughout the next two decades, the academic community advocated preservation of diverse ecosystems. In addition, the SPN cultivated this interest, commencing a program of environmental education with conferences and other activities immediately after establishment of the agency.[50] As Wallace describes, "From its hasty beginnings, and despite the huge cost of acquiring land not in the public domain, the Costa Rican park system tried to acquire land throughout the country, in every type of landscape and ecosystem possible. It was evolving toward a new kind of park system that would be a repository of a nation's biodiversity, of its ecological capital, as well as a showcase of its scenery."[51]

As the system grew, so too did the administrative apparatus to govern it. The number of personnel involved in planning and managing protected areas increased from Boza and Ugalde in 1970 to approximately six hundred by 1992. The SPN also developed ties with several nongovernmental organizations (NGOs), the most prominent being the National Parks Foundation, the Neotropical Foundation, and the National Biodiversity Institute. The NGOs contributed funding and advice for protected area planning.

The emphasis on systematic expansion diminished somewhat in the early 1980s with the economic crisis but was revitalized later in the decade. Many suggested that without consistent care the system had become too fragmented and that planning lacked coordination.[52] This renewal of concern was apparent at the highest levels of government with the changes made by the Arias administration in the mid-1980s. The academic community, led by biologists at UCR, also reasserted their leadership role in many system decisions.[53]

Contentious Areas

During the 1970s and 1980s, areas were set aside, often in spite of demands for logging or development, in order to preserve precious ecosystems. Many of the new units did not come without a fight and the most contentious areas were often somewhat compromised, but the representation goal was not sacrificed when proposals stimulated controversy.

Braulio Carrillo is a forty-four-thousand-hectare block of wilderness located, amazingly enough, just twenty kilometers northeast of the congested metropolis of San José. The park includes five Holdridge Life Zones and numerous habitats at different elevations as well as a volcano and acre after acre of rainforest containing ferns, mosses, palms, and the large leafy plant referred to as "poor man's umbrella."

When proposed as a park in the early 1970s, the idea for Braulio Carrillo aroused opposition from both loggers and advocates of an improved highway between San José and the Caribbean coast. The proposed park area was located in the logical place to build a highway over the mountains to Limon. Park proponents persisted, however, in their support for protection of the rainforest. A compromise was reached in 1978 whereby a vast area of rainforest was declared off limits to timber and development, but a direct highway to the coast was allowed through the forest. The new Siquiries Highway was built during the 1980s. Both parts of the park, on either side of the highway, are immense and unspoiled, large enough to sustain numerous ecosystems.[54] Little wonder that one spot here was used for the 1997 visit by President Bill Clinton of the United States to talk about the need to preserve ecosystems.

Another fierce battle over land deemed priceless by preservationists occurred when Corcovado National Park was established in the southern part of the country in 1975. Boza called it "without a doubt the most important wilderness to be conserved of the country's national heritage."[55] Others have referred to it as "the crown jewel" of the system.[56] The importance of the scientific basis for its establishment is evident in the fact that other demands for its creation were largely absent. Much of the local population neither wanted nor welcomed the park. Many continued to resent the intrusion of the central government and the subsequent emphasis on conservation and foreign tourists to the neglect of local interests and concerns.[57]

Corcovado was designated a national park only after an intense dispute over protection of the ecosystems on the Osa Peninsula. In the 1960s and early 1970s, the fastest disappearing forests in Costa Rica were those on the Osa. Biologists and other visitors were particularly concerned because those same forests contained as many species as perhaps any land area in the world. Advocates of setting some of the area aside, however, found President Figueres and the Legislative Assembly initially reluctant to support park proposals. The situation received considerable media attention when conservationist Olof Wessberg disappeared, with rumors of murder, in 1975. Even with the increased attention, only after months of debate did President Oduber sign a decree establishing Corcovado in October.[58]

Preservation at Corcovado was never easy. Even after establishment, the park was infiltrated by gold miners. The Management Plan of 1983 called for their removal but eviction did not occur until Ugalde obtained a court order in early 1986. Still, parks personnel pursued their goals. Typical of the lack of intervention into park agency affairs, no one else in the government attempted to interfere with the park service evictions, despite the protests of the mining community.[59] Park officials, however, continued to face local opposition to their presence from farmers, loggers, and other locals.

One apparent exception to a pure emphasis on representation of diverse ecosystems is Manuel Antonio, located on the western coast. This beautiful rainforest beach became a park as a result of local demands as well as ecological value. In the early 1970s, commercial developers began to plan for a private resort in the area. Local citizens first protested and then committed several acts of civil disobedience to try to stop the development. Park planners became aware of the area partly as a result of the civil actions and began to learn more about its diversity of species. They then began pushing for acquisition of the area. The Costa Rican government purchased the land in 1975. The park has become the system's most popular, to the extent that park personnel now close it one day a week to attempt to limit overuse.[60]

Results

By many measures, the efforts to provide protection for a wide range of ecosystems have been quite successful. Today, a considerable portion of Costa Rica is under some protected status. Roughly 10% is in forest reserves. Another 6.6% lies in indigenous reserves. About 12% of the land cover in Costa Rica is under total protection in areas that do not allow extractive uses. The protected areas now include nineteen of the twenty life zones that have been identified in the country.[61] Protected areas are described in table 6-2. The national parks are listed in table 6-3. As the right-hand column in the table shows, nearly all have been established since 1970.

By other measures, these efforts could not be termed a complete success by the late 1990s. Many of the protected areas were not large enough to protect entire ecosystems for various species. Many units

TABLE 6-2
Federal Protected Areas in Costa Rica (1989)

Category	# Units	Area (km²)	% Nation	Agency*
National Parks	14	4,047	7.93	SPN
Biological Reserves	8	177	0.35	SPN
National Wildlife Res.	11	1,302	2.55	SVS
Protected Zones	20	1,250	2.45	DGF
Forest Reserves	12	3,780	7.42	DGF
Indian Reserves	19	3,146	6.17	CONAI
Total	84	13,702	26.87	

*agency abbreviations:
SPN—Servicio de Parques Nacionales
DGF—Direccion General Forestal
SVS—Servicio de Vida Silvestre
CONAI—Comision Nacional de Asuntos Indigenas

Source: Hopkins 1995: 46.

TABLE 6-3
National Parks of Costa Rica

Area	IUCN Category	Size (ha)	Year Notified
National Parks			
Arenal	II	2,000	1991
Ballena	IV	4,200	1990
Barra Honda	V	2,295	1974
Braulio Carrillo	II	44,099	1978
Cahuita	V	1,067	1970
Chirripo	II	50,150	1975
Corcovado	II	54,568	1975
Guanacaste	II	32,512	1991
Isla del Coco	II	2,400	1978
La Amistad (Talam)	II	193,929	1982
Palo Verde	II	13,228	1982
Rincon de la Vieja	II	14,083	1973
Santa Rosa	II	37,217	1971
Tortuguero	II	18,946	1975
Volcan Irazu	V	2,309	1955
Volcan Poas	I	15,600	1971
Biological Reserves			
Cabo Blanco	I	1,172	1963
Carara	I	4,700	1978
Hitoy-Cerere	I	9,154	1978
Isla del Cano	IV	200	1978
Islas Guayabo	I	143	1973
Lomas Barbudal	IV	2,279	1986

Source: IUCN 1992: 134.

contained private inholdings. As of 1998, one study estimated that 17% of parklands were still held by private landowners.[62] Most areas remained understudied, and information necessary for management planning was often unavailable. Funding for protection was, occasionally at least, inadequate. Because management of areas was not completely integrated into local economies, many protected areas remained somewhat isolated from communities and public support.[63] To address these problems would require significant changes.

ENHANCEMENT OF INDIVIDUAL UNITS

I found Dan Janzen at home, literally and professionally, deep in the tropical dry forest of Costa Rica. His house's small front porch is littered with old furniture and the remnants of biological studies. The battered Toyota out front sports a bumper sticker proudly stating, "I Brake for Penguins." Janzen himself was clothed only in slacks, no shoes, no shirt in spite of the flies that would light whenever the wind relented. As might be expected in the house of the world's leading tropical biologist, the phone rings quite often for him or Winnie Hallwachs, calls from sources as diverse as a local school teacher or the British Broadcasting Company. Janzen's voice carries the ring of authenticity and the wisdom of experience from three decades as the most important figure in changing Costa Rican preservation efforts. The quotation that opens this chapter tells the story of those efforts in a nutshell.

Background: Conservation Areas as an Idea

By the latter part of the 1980s, most of the people involved in the expansion of Costa Rica's parks system recognized that they had not only accomplished most of their goals but also that they wouldn't be able to get much more land anyway.[64] Further, realization of expansion goals was only half of the motivation for a shift in emphasis. The other half involved recognition of greater attention to restoration and maintenance of natural conditions in the units that had been created. In a speech in 1983, Boza foresaw the need for such a shift and anticipated how it would have to be done when he said, "Creating a park on paper is easy. . . . Preserving it is another story. We have to teach the people what conservation is."[65] Writing in 1986 about the system expansion that had already occurred, Janzen prophesied, "Within the next five to ten years the wildland component of Costa Rican society will be forever fixed in place. What Costa Rican habitat is not in preserves will be dead, and the next stage (which we have already entered) is that of improving the quality of both wildland preserves and agriculture in the ecosystem."[66]

Many people involved in Costa Rican parks developed a similar attitude as the 1980s progressed. For preservation and sustainability to occur, the parks would have to be managed in ways that paid more attention not just to the animal and plant species therein but also to the humans that were affected. Similar to the demands for expansion in the early 1970s, much of this thinking was stimulated by academics, scholars like Pedro Leon and Rodrigo Gamez. Gamez and Ugalde envisioned much more interaction between parks and local communities and planned an organization focused on that relationship similar to the way that the National Parks Foundation concentrated on relations with foreign donors. In 1985 Neotropical Foundation was created. At the same time, biologist Janzen was working on an idea for the next phase of Costa Rican parks. He published the idea in 1986 in a book entitled *Guanacaste National Park: Tropical Ecological and Cultural Restoration.*

The idea for the next stage hatched by Janzen and the others was of conservation areas large enough to protect entire ecosystems and decentralized enough to involve the maximum participation of local people. They recognized the problems facing the parks: inadequate funds, fragmented areas, inconsistent management practices, local indifference if not opposition. The emphases on ecosystem boundaries and integration into general society evolved into a proposal for nine conservation areas in Costa Rica, each containing the different landforms listed in table 6-2 and managed by a combination of local residents and government personnel. "The truly unique thing about this," Janzen says, "is the pooling of what Americans call the National Park Service, the Forest Service, and the Fish and Wildlife Service, give them one budget, and then let them do different things for different hectares as long as all those things protect the biodiversity."[67]

The new approach received formal backing as the National System of Conservation Areas (SINAC). SINAC would integrate the management of various protected and private areas into regional units that addressed issues of biodiversity as well as socioeconomic needs of local communities. This proposal was formally supported within the Ministry of Environment as early as 1989.[68]

The area in Guanacaste province, in the northern part of Costa Rica, soon became the pilot program for the concept for several reasons. First, the area already contained three national parks (Santa Rosa, Guanacaste, and Rincon de la Vieja) preserving rare ecosystems such as tropical dry forest, nesting sites for sea turtles, and the location of several historic battles (including the defeat of Walker's invaders in 1856) that are important in Costa Rican history. Second, the Guanacaste cattle industry was in decline in the early 1990s and ranchers were thus more willing to sell their property to expansion advocates.[69] Third, the area is near Nicaragua. When the political situation in Nicaragua is unsettled, this proximity can be discouraging to other potential competing investors. Fourth, the area is so far north that, as Janzen says, "We're like the North Slope of Alaska to people in San Jose. They didn't care that much if we wanted to experiment up here." Fifth, the area was home to Janzen himself.

Janzen saw the project as essential and pushed hard for its realization. He and other biologists understood that species need different habitats in different seasons. Santa Rosa Park consisted mainly of low dry forests. Guanacaste Park stretched up into the highlands and mountains to the east. Combining the lowlands of Santa Rosa with the changing elevation in Guanacaste would enable the species to maintain their natural migration patterns, including routes that go from mountain to sea and back.

When Janzen proposed the idea to the government, he received a mixed reaction until he made a crucial commitment. Some, including President Arias, liked the idea but refused to appropriate public funds. They endorsed the idea only after Janzen convinced them that he would raise the money for land acquisition and would not impose severe financial demands on the government. Janzen, with the help of the World Wildlife Fund and others, would raise the $11.8 million considered necessary, and the project would not cost the Costa Rican government any additional money.[70]

Systematic Preservation Efforts: Conservation Areas in Practice

The SINAC idea was put into practice in the 1990s. One major step occurred in 1995 when the various forestry, wildlands, and wildlife agencies were merged to pursue Regional Conservation Units—Unidades Regionales de Conservacion (URCs)—under the same banner. A second step was formal recognition that local communities would be in control of most of these units.[71] Not surprisingly, implementation of this program moved most rapidly in the Guanacaste area.

ACG as Pilot

By the time I visited in 1997, the "megapark" at Guanacaste was officially referred to as Area de Conservacion Guanacaste (ACG). This title was conferred by the Costa Rican government in one of three different official decrees for the project. A map of the area is reproduced in figure 6-1. As the map shows, what had been numerous separate areas are now contiguous.

Funding for the ACG works as follows. The money that Janzen and others raised through donations, gifts, and a major debt-for-nature swap sponsored by Sweden is now a $12 million endowment. The ACG is financed by income generated from the endowment, entrance fee revenue (the ACG keeps 75% of the money that comes in—about $6 U.S. per visitor in 1997), and 100% of the income from direct services supplied in the area such as the cafeteria and educational programs. Inconsistent or inadequate funding from the government is no longer a problem.

Management of the area is, to use Janzen's term, "maximally decentralized." A federal office in San Jose no longer directly manages the area. Decisions are made by the local staff of 120 members. All these people are local professionals involved with the ACG as teachers,

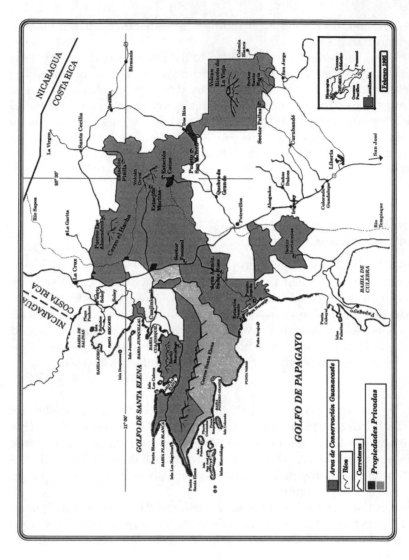

Figure 6-1 Land Area of the ACG. *(Source: ACG document, 1997)*

police, firefighters, cleaners, and other occupations. The staff elects a Directorate and a Board of Directors, called the Local Committee, on a rotating basis. This ACG Directorate is officially recognized in San Jose as part of the Ministry of Natural Resources. A formal depiction of the management structure for Regional Conservation Units is shown in figure 6-2. As the earlier quote from one of the ACG staff, Juan Carlos, suggests, local involvement has dramatically increased local support of long-term preservation efforts.[72]

In addition to self-sufficient funding and maximum local participation in management, the real success story at the ACG is ecological. The staff are involved in countless ecosystem restoration and maintenance programs.[73] The different habitats that are being served include grasslands, deciduous forests, evergreen forests, tropical dry forests and tropical rainforests.[74] Ecotourism is thriving both inland and on the beaches of the Nicoya Peninsula. The ACG offers a wide variety of educational and training programs that will foster continued care into the future. Biologists and other scientists have flocked to the ACG for their own studies that can contribute to preservation efforts elsewhere. The former Guanacaste park area is home to no less than three biological stations. In short, just as Janzen said, the forest(s) at the ACG have been and are being regrown.

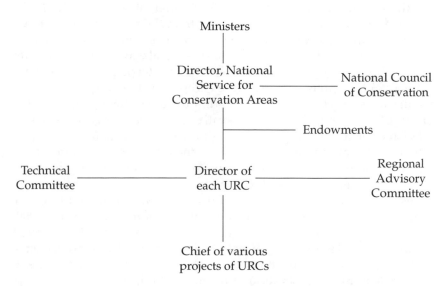

Figure 6-2 Organization Structure for Regional Conservation Units
(Source: Costa Rican government, 1989, reprinted in Hopkins 1995: 59; IUCN 1992: 129)

General Progress

The second half of the quote that opened this chapter demands attention. How complete is the administrative transition? Has the success at ACG been replicated elsewhere? Is it likely to be? Even Janzen admits, "This has become a lot bigger and more complicated than we envisioned."

Ten regional conservation areas have been established and are managed under the SINAC governance structure. Like the ACG, these units involve ecosystem protection through coordination of parks and other public areas, creative fundraising, and community involvement in decision making. The conservation areas contain a core zone strictly protected by the state surrounded by contiguous forests and reserves managed in zones according to ecological characteristics and community needs. Private lands are allowed, but these lands are expected to be used in ways that facilitate them serving as buffer zones for ecosystems. Each area is to be administered by a director and management committee, with input from scientists and others. All areas are expected to include educational programs in their management plans which will foster community involvement and support. The goal for each is to be approaching relative self-sufficiency by the year 2000.[75]

The shift to concentrate conservation efforts at these areas required major administrative changes in San Jose. Before 1995 protected areas in the country were managed by four different agencies: the Parks Service, Forestry, Wildlife, and Indian Affairs. During the 1990s, SINAC evolved within the Ministry of Environment as a means to consolidate management efforts. SINAC is unique in several ways. First, it is heavily decentralized. The ten conservation areas are territorial units that are largely autonomous from San Jose except that they are all governed under the same development and administrative strategy. Second, the focus of decision making is democratization. Local, civil society has "a decisive role in the decision-making process."[76] Figure 6-2 shows that the Director of each regional unit depends upon advice from a local advisory unit.[77] Finally, SINAC calls for all of the conservation areas to develop financial self-sufficiency. In the early years of the regional conservation areas, roughly 30% of the funds came from tourists, 30% from the government, and 40% from outside sources. By the year 2000, these areas are to raise 50% of their revenue through funds generated within the wild areas (tourism, entrance fees, hydroelectric power, etc.), 15% from endowments and trust funds, 15% from international aid, and 20% from the Costa Rican government budget.[78]

Progress at the different units has been somewhat uneven. Some, such as the area called Cordillera Volcanica Central, involving Braulio Carrillo and the Poas and Irazu Volcanoes, are moving along in fundraising and implementation.[79] Many of the others have not yet gotten much past the planning stages. When I asked Randall Garcia, an official with the Ministry of Natural Resources, how the other areas compared to the ACG, he laughed and said, "The situation is very different at each."[80] Those working at the ACG know they are the pilot program. As ACG staffer Juan Carlos says, "We are much farther along than the other areas."[81]

One of the other regional units that has seen considerable progress is the one on the Osa Peninsula. As described earlier, preservation efforts here have always faced some opposition. In the mid-1980s, a team of international scientists proposed managing Corcovado in ways that involved locals in planning for use of the park and sharing in revenues. Out of this proposal and the cooperation of the World Wildlife Fund, the Neotropical Foundation, and government officials came the Osa Peninsula Forest Conservation and Management Project (BOSCOSA). BOSCOSA called for the utilization of local community organizations in planning the management of area resources and development of activities in the region such as sustainable agriculture. Proponents of the BOSCOSA plan persevered even though they faced "a difficult struggle."[82]

By 1997 implementation of plans for the Osa area were well underway. The Osa Conservation Area (ACOSA) contained over 4,100 square kilometers and over 100,000 human inhabitants. Management of this large area was pursued under three major sectors. The Promotion Sector coordinates private enterprise activities and the conservation of resources. The Control Sector concentrates on natural resource control programs. The Protected Areas Sector oversees biodiversity and ecological programs in the wildland areas. Observers cite ACOSA as having been able to "avert an ecological disaster while allowing for sustainable human presence on the peninsula."[83]

Difficulties

With such a unique transformation, difficulties are inevitable. Problems in Costa Rica have been magnified in the late 1990s by the fiscal crisis affecting the government.

One source of complications for implementing the megapark idea was the presence of extant land managers. Because of the regional concept, the formal structure for management of protected lands has changed dramatically. Such a dramatic administrative transformation could not be done without some resistance. As Janzen says, "Imagine if you tried this in the U.S. You would run into a lot of opposition from people who already have interests." The establishment and institutionalization of SINAC has removed some of this complexity, but administration is still not on a secure basis at many areas. For example, Baulas National Marine Park has no permanent staffers, making patrolling or collection of entrance fees impossible.[84]

A second source of problems has been uneven funding. Umana and others were quite adept at bringing money into the system through the latter part of the 1980s and early 1990s. The areas at Guanacaste and Osa have done fairly well in fundraising efforts. However, in recent years, not all of the areas have been as aggressive or as successful as the ACG in raising international money. One aspect making this difficult is competition among units. Some have criticized the ACG for using up funds that might have been available elsewhere. A second aspect involves control. Once raised, the finances for each regional unit are managed, at least in part, by an NGO such as the National Parks Foundation. Working out the arrangements between local managers and international organizations like the NPF is not easy.[85] Finally, the "looting" of park revenues in 1997 by federal legislators mentioned earlier makes self-sufficiency a tenuous goal.

A third source of friction regarding progress at the conservation areas is almost inevitable within the political process. Some, many of whom hold high positions or respect in policy-making circles, have either had second thoughts or have maintained reservations about conservation areas. Mario Boza is one of the former and has questioned the wisdom of attempting to put so much of the country's land area, over 25%, within these units.[86] Others worry about consistency across different political administrations, and, indeed, three official decrees in one decade is somewhat illustrative.[87] When I asked Janzen if he was worried about reversals in the future, he admitted some concern but then stated confidently, "but it's so logical and it works so well, it provides its own bulwark against reversal."

One other concern that must be addressed involves the very decentralization that is so crucial to the success at ACG so far. Will such extreme decentralization facilitate a loss of focus that could perhaps only be enforced through central direction? In other words, might some area decide to pursue timber production or commercial development or some goal other than preservation? Other observers, notably David Wallace, have expressed concern that URCs will be managed to accommodate the lowest common denominator. The preservation focus of national parks could be lowered to meet the goals for the other units included in the regional area.[88] Janzen admits that some role for the central government is necessary, if for no other reason than to ensure adherence to the agreed upon goal of long-term biodiversity protection. "Then," Janzen says, "the key is to give local people enough resources and trust them to do the job."

Summary

The fact that Dan Janzen is a true believer in the system utilized to enhance the ecosystem at Guanacaste is probably not a surprise. After all, he has played a key role in the transition to this new form of protection. Thus, when I asked him if such conservation areas were the future for preservation efforts in Costa Rica and the rest of the world, his answer was predictably emphatic: "My opinion is that it's totally the future."

Other assessments are mixed. Participants in the process, such as SINAC officials and university advisers, remain enthusiastic, citing the "remarkable" pace at which progress is occurring.[89] Carlos Crespi, president of Fundacion Neotropica, proudly says that URCs are "where I think a lot of visionary planning has crystallized."[90] Others remain noncommittal. Joseph Franke, author of one the most-cited texts on Costa Rican parks, terms the current situation as "fluid and complex."[91] John Burnett, a correspondent for U.S. National Public Radio, expresses serious concern about future finances.[92] Even the strongest supporters admit that the system remains one in transition.

Is the ACG the preservation model for the future throughout the world as well as in Costa Rica? Similar efforts are underway elsewhere in different forms, but none are as far along as in Costa Rica. The rest of the world will be watching Costa Rica to learn the final results of this very important experiment. As one recent appraisal of progress at the URCs concludes, "The U.S. and other developed countries could learn a great deal from Costa Rica about how to develop effective national and regional resource management policy."[93] However the conservation area concept evolves, that statement is certainly true.

CONCLUSIONS

In a short period of time in 1997, I was able to visit ocean beaches, tropical dry forests, volcanoes, and rainforests all in a country about the size of the state of Kentucky. Even more notable than the fact that so many diverse ecosystems exist within such a small landmass is the fact that many exist in well-preserved natural condition. Further still, that country is setting a trend for the rest of the world in what may be the future of ecosystem management. What makes these facts truly remarkable is the relative lack of wealth in this country, ironically, the very reason that even here in Costa Rica, the future of long-term systematic preservation is not guaranteed.

7

Free-Riding on the Future?

> Sustainability is a problem precisely because each of us knows or realizes that we can profit at the expense of the future rather than at the expense of our contemporaries and the environment. We free-ride on each other and we free-ride on the future.—Robert Solow

Are national governments capable of providing intergenerational goods? Within the context of public lands, will future generations be able to see a representation of diverse ecosystems? Will natural conditions be restored in coming years in individual units? More specifically, are plans to remove automobiles from Grand Canyon and Yosemite in place? Will the Cape Tribulation and Cape York Peninsulas be managed as pristine areas? Are Banff and Grasslands both manageable as ecosystems? Will management of Guanacaste and other regional units in Costa Rica succeed?

These questions are important to many of us, but the answers are elusive. Politicians often promise concern for future outcomes, but observers like Solow are skeptical. In this book, I have argued that the answers lie somewhere in between benign promises and compelling skepticism. Systematic preservation efforts are only partially effective, success varying from nation to nation according to societal factors such as public demand and the institutional constraints shaping the behavior of people and agencies responsible for parks. This chapter reviews the theoretical argument and summarizes the empirical evidence. I then extend the discussion both theoretically to make the model more dynamic and empirically to consider other intergenerational goods besides preserved lands.

THE ARGUMENT AND THE EVIDENCE

How willing and able are nations to provide intergenerational goods? I offered a theoretical explanation for the variance in national behavior

214

and then examined the empirical evidence in the context of pre-served lands.

Reliance on the Public Sector

Intergenerational goods are goods and services promised for delivery to future generations. These can be some item like a balanced budget twenty years hence or some condition like a sustained yield of timber in the distant future.

Behavior of the public sector is often the key to provision of intergenerational goods. Even the most noted of free-market economists have recognized the greater potential for concern for the long term from the public rather than the private sector. Recall the quote from Adam Smith in the first chapter. Or, consider the following from noted economist Arthur Pigou: "It is the clear duty of Government, which is the trustee for unborn generations as well as for its parent citizens, to watch over, and if need be, by legislative enactment, to defend, the exhaustible natural resources of the country from rash and reckless land spoliation."[1]

One policy perspective gaining considerable attention in the American West emphasizes increased usage of the marketplace in public lands decisions. Often called the New Resource Economics, this school suggests that mismanagement of public lands could be remedied through greater use of property rights, financial incentives, and market structures that would motivate bureaucrats to be more accountable and more oriented to efficiency in their decisions. While the NRE makes compelling arguments about the need to coordinate economic and ecological principles regarding the use of many public lands, their recommendations are less persuasive regarding preservation of pristine lands for generations to come. Further, these economic instruments provide tools that can be used by public officials, but ultimately the public sector plays a crucial role in providing intergenerational goods. Compelling reasons such as the focus on short-term profits make markets unlikely providers of intergenerational goods.[2]

Other analyses describe effective provision of intergenerational goods such as sustained yields of certain fish species, but those efforts are generally limited to common-pool resources where access is controlled and the livelihood of users depends upon long-term supplies.[3] A variety of intergenerational goods remain dependent upon the public sector for delivery.

What determines public sector behavior in this regard? The theoretical argument posed in chapter 1 offers an answer to that question. First, considerable variance is to be expected among national governments in the provision of intergenerational goods. Second, certain factors are necessary conditions for future-oriented behavior: significant demand, stable democratic processes, and some degree of official commitment. These factors vary from nation to nation, thus affecting the variance in public sector behavior. Third, the presence of these factors is necessary for at least minimal behavior, but even when all are readily apparent, national efforts at providing intergenerational goods will still be constrained by institutions shaping the behavior of actors within the political system.

Policymakers at the national level attempting to provide such goods will be significantly affected by other actors who can be thought of in both vertical and horizontal dimensions. The vertical dimension involves actors conceptually below and above the national government. The involvement of subnational governments and international bodies can create challenging complexities and pressures affecting delivery of intergenerational goods. The horizontal dimension refers to other actors located at the same level as those pursuing future goods but who are more focused on the short term than on the long term. The potentially constraining impact of these other actors will strongly determine the variance among nations in their efforts to provide intergenerational goods.

National Efforts toward Systematic Preservation

As the Pigou quote suggests, one intergenerational good is preserved natural land. For decades, citizens have demanded that governments provide public spaces in preserved natural condition for future generations. They continue to do so today. For example, the renowned Lincoln Institute for Land Policy in the United States stated in a 1995 document, "Policies should aim to preserve long-term ecological processes, including processes of change, over broad areas."[4] The continued call for such emphasis provides some indication of the general lack of success so far.

Chapter 2 provides broad historical and statistical overviews of national efforts to preserve lands. Preservation is a complex concept. What does it mean to demand preserved lands for future generations? The historical account summarizes the progression of the ideas regarding preserved lands. The goals of many national efforts in this regard have evolved to a focus that I term systematic preservation. This focus emphasizes representation of diverse natural environments and restoration of natural ecosystems. The statistical analysis displays the initial steps taken by over one hundred nations to protect public lands and then examines the variance between the extent and degree of land protection. The statistical analyses support the designation of certain conditions as correlated to higher amounts of preserved lands. These include domestic demand, stable political processes, and official commitment generally through the continuing presence of a relevant public agency. However, these econometric analyses are limited in several ways, not the least being that measuring diverse representation and ecosystem restoration is statistically impractical. To consider efforts toward those goals requires indepth case studies.

The case studies in chapters 3 through 6 discuss preservation efforts in four nations that meet necessary conditions for providing intergenerational goods but differ in terms of constraining conditions. Table 7-1 summarizes some of the key characteristics of each nation and some of the indicators of land preservation efforts. While obviously different in many regards, the four nations are similar in the existence of stable political processes, a history of demands for systematic preservation, the presence of diverse ecosystems, the high motivation of park managers and planners, and formal authorization of stated goals of ecological attention. Even under these high levels of the conditions identified in chapter 2 as correlated to responsive behavior, however, the ability of public agencies to pursue intergenerational goods is constrained by political institutions. The ability to provide systematic preservation has been and continues to be affected by other political actors in two broad dimensions.

Vertical Constraints

First, national efforts may be constrained by the requirements, or needs, to involve different levels of government in land preservation. True to the characterizations of political scientists from Madison to

---

TABLE 7-1
Characteristics of Studied Nations

	U.S.	Canada	Australia	Costa Rica
GNP per capita	22,356	20,740	17,068	1,841
% Protect (92)	10.74	5.36	10.65	12.16
% Preserve (92)	4.22	2.91	8.62	9.48
Years Protect	123	110	116	40
Years Preserve	123	110	116	32
Vertical Constraint	Low	Moderate	High	Low
Horizontal Constraint	High	Low	Moderate	Low

Wildavsky, involvement of state and provincial policymakers, even when their intentions are consistent with national goals, complicate implementation of long-range plans.[5] These complications, most apparent in Australia but also evident in Canada, include making the acquisition of valued lands difficult and the application of ecological principles to restoring natural conditions contingent upon local political circumstances. Interestingly, the two nations designated as relatively low on vertical complications are currently experiencing changes that may increase subnational involvement in future efforts. In the United States, property rights advocates and state policymakers are demanding decentralization of many policy issues, including those that involve national parks. In Costa Rica, the recent emphasis on greater involvement of local constituencies necessitates an entirely new model of land preservation, one whose future effectiveness is not yet entirely clear.

One might also think of this vertical dimension as going the other direction, outside the nation rather than down to lower levels. International involvement can also complicate efforts. The dependence of some Costa Rican programs on external funding makes consistent systematic preservation efforts within the country less predictable.

Horizontal Constraints

Second, intergenerational efforts are subject to, and often contradicted by, the actions of elected politicians and their appointees at the national level who are more concerned with short-term electoral gains than with long-term goals. Again consistent with much of the political science literature, especially that regarding political control of the bureaucracy, implementation of long-range programs by relevant agencies is often cut short.[6] The effect of political constraints on agency behavior has been particularly noticeable in the case of the U.S. National Park Service where long-term plans have been underfunded, ignored, and frequently cancelled.

Such impact is not limited to the United States, however. Australian parks planners must contend with political intervention at both national and state levels. Canadian parks officials as well have been forced to deal with political involvement in agency decisions, especially in the high-profile environment of Banff and its surrounding areas. In general, efforts at systematic preservation face a seemingly inevitable tension between the long-term focus of many parks agencies and the short-term concerns of elected officials. Again, the perspective of the Lincoln Institute is consistent, describing land officials from all over the world agreeing that one major obstacle to implementation of ecological plans is that politicians must ". . . start thinking in 20- to 100-year time spans beyond their current terms of office . . . politicians must put off present crises in order to help future contituents who would at best vote for [the same politicians'] grandchildren."[7]

Advocating such behavior is much different than witnessing it, however. As stated in chapter 1, not all politicians behave the same in this context. Some, Representative Vento in the United States and Costa Rican president Figueres for examples, have been quite supportive of systematic preservation efforts. However, the incentives facing elected officials all over the world necessitate electoral attention to the short term. Intervention into long-term projects such as system expansion may be moderated by bureaucratic capabilities, but preserved lands will always tempt political manipulation.

Seeing Patterns in Specific Cases

What do patterns of behavior in response to constraining conditions tell us about specific cases? Variance in institutional constraints on both vertical and horizontal dimensions has fostered different experiences in systematic preservation efforts.

United States

Efforts by the American NPS to expand into relatively unrepresented ecosystems and to enhance ecological conditions in parks, described in chapter 3, have often been stymied by political manipulation. Pork concerns have frequently outweighed park concerns in the creation of new units. The fact that certain ecosystems such as tallgrass prairies previously lacked representation provides a less powerful motivator for expansion decisions than do electoral incentives such as bringing home construction dollars. Similarly, efforts to restore natural conditions in individual units depend upon political calculations. Long-term plans at even revered units such as Grand Canyon and Yellowstone have been explicitly countervened by politicians to satisfy certain constituencies. In response to the question at the start of the chapter regarding automobiles in Grand Canyon and Yosemite, such plans are in place but will remain so only if the necessary conditions of public approval and official commitment remain at high levels and potentially constraining conditions do not become dramatically manifest.

Australia

Efforts to achieve systematic representation and ecological enhancement of Australian national parks have long been fragmented by the dominance of the institution of federalism. The Australian parks, as described in chapter 4, continue to constitute many different systems rather than one unified entity. Largely as a result of federalism, planning for individual units is done in a variety of ways with a variety of intentions. Further, those plans are affected by political factors at both state and national levels. Will national support for preservation at Cape Tribulation, Cape York, or even the Great Barrier Reef result in increased attention to ecosystem protection? The answer is only if political forces in Queensland support these goals as well as do the policymakers in Canberra.

Canada

Canadian national park agency employees have used their relative autonomy to pursue systematic expansion and more emphasis on ecological concerns within some of their parks. Chapter 5 discusses how efforts to achieve the former goal, at places like Grasslands, have been slowed by protracted and expensive negotiations with provincial authorities for desired lands. Plans to move toward the latter goal have centered on Canada's most revered park units. Preservation efforts at Banff and the mountain parks have, however, been stymied by local and provincial objections that are voiced and heard loudly in Ottawa. The current high-profile attempt to preserve a Rocky Mountain ecosystem around Banff and Jasper parks will be more successful than past efforts only if historical trends at Banff can be overcome.

Costa Rica

Costa Rican parks planners have achieved considerable success in creating a system protecting diverse ecosystems and are moving towards broader ecological restoration of some units. As chapter 6 explains, Costa Rican parks planners were relatively insulated from other political actors and other levels of government for much of the expansion period. Costa Rican policymakers are not immune to political forces that affect their behavior, however. Recent emphases on decentralization and regional cooperation are major components in a significant transition in park management. These changes can enhance pursuit of some preservation goals, but they also contain certain risks. Will ecosystem management at Guanacaste and the other regional units be successful? The answer is only if commitment to the goals of systematic preservation is not altered by either local or international pressures.

THEORETICAL EXTENSIONS

The theoretical framework regarding provision of intergenerational goods can be extended to make it both more nuanced and more realistic. Logically enough, given that the model assesses long-term behavior, these extensions are necessitated by the need for dynamism over periods of time. The dimensions and categories proposed in the cases and in table 7-1 are portrayed as static when in fact change can occur in several major ways. First, policymakers can become aware of the constraints that will affect systematic preservation efforts and can change their behavior to anticipate them. Second, conditions affecting those policymakers can change. Third, the goals emphasized as systematic preservation may also change.

Changing Behavior

Many of the instances in the chapters suggest that the people who often know preserved lands better than anyone are the employees of the government agencies assigned to manage those lands. Not surprisingly, these people also understand factors that constrain their long-term efforts. They may thus attempt to adjust behavior to address those constraints.[8]

Political intervention into the U.S. NPS is pervasive and visible. NPS officials recognize this and are attempting to find ways to adjust. For example, planners at Yosemite are being extremely careful to involve the public in every phase of the current planning operation so that eventual decisions to restore more natural conditions in the valley will be more likely to receive support and less likely to be vetoed by other political actors. Grand Canyon planners have moved their office to the largest nearby community to be able to develop more cooperative political relations with local constituents.

The importance of federalism to preserved lands in Australia is obvious. Australian parks planners are learning, however, from their own varied experiences and making some moves to moderate the impact of federalism. The recently developed GIS-based framework for systematic expansion throughout different jurisdictions and the Australia-New Zealand Environment Conservation Council, both mentioned in chapter 4, represent two recent innovations that might lead to more unified and cohesive efforts at long-term preservation of diverse natural places.

Canadian parks personnel have long understood that political demands from both the provincial and national levels can affect the most prominent units. At Banff, particularly, policymakers have learned from past problems. The agency now attempts to treat the Rocky Mountain parks surrounding Banff as one large ecosystem, rather than separate entities, less susceptible to provincial demands on any one unit. Further, the long-range plan for the area relied upon outside, scientific input to further insulate subsequent implementation.

Planners in Costa Rica have been able to learn not just from their own experiences but also by witnessing what has occurred in other nations. Awareness of other national experiences by Costa Rican policymakers is evident in my interviews with Dan Janzen and in the writings of Mario Boza. For instance, as Boza wrote of the American experience, "U.S. park policymakers aren't concerned with protecting the biological resource. The rangers and researchers are, but the policymakers aren't."[9] Many aspects of the regional conservation units constitute attempts to address problems seen in other nations, such as conflicts between different public lands agencies, before they cause severe damage to ecosystem protection efforts.

The ability of personnel to share ideas across international lines offers some promise for learning and adaptation. In talking to agency planners in different countries, I learned that these individuals were often aware of behavior by their counterparts in other settings but also that they wanted to learn more. Certainly, international exchanges of ideas have not reached the ease of diffusion often witnessed between states in the same country.[10] However, the presence of international conferences on parks like those mentioned in chapter 2 and the existence of institutions devoted to the sharing of knowledge about lands issues such as the Lincoln Institute and the Banff Centre for Management provide hope for increased diffusion of ideas.

However, awareness does not guarantee remedial action. In many cases, parks agency personnel are not capable of overcoming traditional constraints on behavior. The U.S. NPS, for example, has long been criticized for its political naivete. Congressional staffers have told me that NPS personnel are, for the most part, less skilled in dealing with Washington politics than are their counterparts in other agencies.[11] NPS employees themselves recognize this problem. The Vail planning document describes how NPS personnel are often "dropped" into managerial or leadership roles without adequate training, thereby inviting constant monitoring and oversight from higher levels or outside sources.[12] This naivete of personnel is in part the result of a lack of prioritization within agencies to emphasize certain kinds of training. Further, the lack of such skills among agency employees in any nation is not surprising. Indeed, parks personnel need expertise in so many other areas that expecting them to possess strong political skills as well is unrealistic. Finally, institutions such as federalism in Australia are much more entrenched than can be challenged by any single agency.

Still, even marginal adjustments can have impacts. Those adjustments arise from understanding. Prominent documents such as the ones generated by the 1991 Vail Symposium in the United States and the 1995 IBRA in Australia can help facilitate the awareness among agency personnel that can lead to more effective adjustments to institutional constraints on preservation-oriented behavior.[13]

Changing Conditions

A second element that necessitates thinking of the model in more dynamic terms is that societal conditions can change. If those changes are significant enough, conditions designated as necessary for systematic preservation may diminish or constraining conditions may also be altered.

In terms of the former, levels of necessary conditions such as domestic demand and political stability remain at fairly high levels in all four nations, although issues as universal as fiscal stress and as country-specific as Quebec secession may have impacts in the future. Official commitment to some form of preservation is not likely soon to be dramatically revised, at least not explicitly. Openly questioning the future of preserved lands in any of these nations is simply bad politics, as the experiences of U.S. Secretary of the Interior Watt and Canadian Minister of the Environment Blais-Grenier illustrate. Constraining conditions, however, may become even more severe in all of the nations studied.

Evidence already exists for increased tensions between national and subnational actors even in the countries categorized in table 1-3 as low on this dimension. Ironically enough, the regional units in Costa Rica make coordination and implementation of long-term plans more complex than before. In purely theoretical terms (refer to table 1-3), Costa Rica may be shifting into the cell marked by high tensions with other levels of government.

Conflictive relations between political actors are also likely to increase in all nations in coming years, even those designated as lower on this dimension, if for no other reason than fiscal restraint. In Canada, for example, the parks are being asked to become much more self-sufficient in the future. This emphasis will inevitably affect relations between the parks service and the Parliament and ultimately alter agency behavior. Again referring to table 1-3, one may not be able to characterize the Canadian system as low in conflictive relations if the self-sufficiency trend leads to a dramatic diminution of funds for Parks Canada.

Changes such as these are not insignificant. Further, they are not limited to Canada and Costa Rica. Privatization and decentralization are goals that are increasingly prominent, at least rhetorically, throughout many nations in recent years. What were already challenging goals of representation and ecosystem restoration will become even more so under these emphases unless new ideas to respond to these trends are generated and attempted. Some new ideas are already being tested. These include revenue generation through ecotourism in Costa Rica, more competitive bidding for concessions contracts in Canada and some places in the United States, joint federal-state management techniques such as those seen in Australia, and regional management like that being tried on a large scale in Costa Rica.

The dynamic nature of these conditions suggests restraint in stating definitive conclusions about current preservation efforts, however. One could argue that what may happen to systematic preservation efforts in these four nations in coming years will approximate some regression to the mean. In other words, with both Canada and Costa Rica transitioning into more difficult periods and Australia and the United States showing signs of improvement, the variance in efforts among the four nations may be diminishing rather than increasing. The troubling fact for preservation advocates is that the ultimate mean may not be too high. To restate the point, provision of intergenerational goods will remain difficult.

Changing Goals

How secure is the emphasis on systematic preservation goals? Will the goals of representation and restoration of diverse ecosystems be manifest in coming years? After all, as chapters 1 and 2 described, preservation has been an evolving concept over time.

One major reason that systematic preservation may lose favor follows directly from the analysis in this book. Achieving goals of representation and restoration has proven to be elusive, if not extremely difficult. Even the most systematic planning documents, grounded in science and logic, such as the Canadian system *Strategic Plan* and *Vision for the Greater Yellowstone Area,* await implementation. Difficulties lead to criticism, vulnerability, and lack of continued public legitimation. As one observer of failed efforts at Yellowstone asserts, "What remains unanswered is whether or not ecosystem management will lead to changes in policy."[14]

If the concept of preservation evolves significantly due to these problems of implementation, it may be to a more narrow and perhaps more attainable definition. Perhaps political realities will dictate a less ambitious agenda for future generations. Such a change would provide strong testimony for the impact of political forces and institutions on the ability of governments to provide intergenerational goods.

If those interested in national parks and related areas want to maintain goals of systematic preservation, certain steps could be pursued more consistently in all the nations studied to enhance the emphases on representation and restoration. One step would involve systematized topographic mapping, similar to that done by the U.S. Geological Survey, of each park area in each system that specifies land ownership, topography, hydrography, vegetation, and significant resources. Long-term plans would then have a systematic and comparable formal foundation. Advocates of expansion in all nations considered have to recognize that parks services or other relevant agencies don't have to manage all lands adjacent to preserved areas if they can at least influence activities upon them. A second step would thus involve drawing zones of influence around preserved units wherein the relevant authority has some input into decisions that affect resources in the park unit. A third step, advocated by some resource economists, encourages charging market prices on all commodities within an ecosystem thereby reducing certain uses, such as subsidized timber cutting. Adoption of such a procedure would negate short-term changes to adjacent lands that impede implementation of restoration plans.

EMPIRICAL EXTENSIONS

Preserved lands are just one intergenerational good that public sectors are asked to provide. Others include everything from retirement pensions to space exploration to future defense systems. What lessons have been learned here that can apply to provision of these other goods?

Impact of the Lack of Necessary Conditions

The essential presence of conditions identified in this work as necessary but not sufficient for provision of intergenerational goods is made evident in case after case. Insufficient levels of public demand, stable processes, or official commitment provide a ready explanation for failed delivery of many possible intergenerational goods.

Commitment Without Demand

Official commitment to a future outcome without correlated levels of public demand will not likely produce significant results. One illustration involves fiscal deficits in the United States. In the Balanced Budget and Emergency Deficit Control Act of 1985, also known as Gramm-Rudman after its sponsors, Congress officially committed the nation to a balanced budget by 1991. The act set explicit targets with the goal of balancing the budget so that future generations would not be burdened with a growing national debt. By 1991, however, with little public support for such a goal, the deficit was not zero but rather over $280 billion. In public opinion polls, reduction of the deficit traditionally received little attention as a pressing problem. Meaningful progress toward a balanced budget did not occur until the mid-1990s when public support for deficit reduction achieved unprecedented levels. For example, in 1995 Americans cited the deficit as the #3 problem facing the nation, behind only crime and unemployment. Further, 82% of those asked by Gallup demanded that Congress give deficit reduction a high priority (second only to anticrime legislation).[15] Immediately following the 1996 elections, the public asserted that a balanced budget should be the top priority for President Clinton, the first time such a ranking had happened, by double the amount demanding attention to the economy or health care or education.[16] This increased demand, along with a strong economy, made attainment of a balanced budget much more likely than in any previous year.

Inconsistent Demand

A similar inability to provide intergenerational goods can occur if public support fades even after official commitment. One case illustrating diminishing provision of an intergenerational good was that of the Strategic Defense Initiative (SDI), also known by its critics as "Star Wars." President Reagan proposed SDI in 1983 as a space-based anti-missile defense system that would render nuclear missiles "obsolete" in future generations. The public supported the program in its initial years, a 1985 Gallup survey showing a majority (52 to 38) in favor of development.[17] Between fiscal years 1985 and 1991, funding for SDI from Congress grew, albeit at slower rates than Reagan requested, and over $23 billion was authorized in this period. Questions regarding efficiency and efficacy dogged SDI, however, and by 1988, a majority (50 to 38) opposed the program.[18] Not surprisingly, funding trends reversed as well. Eventually, the SDI program was scaled down to be more ground-based and ultimately replaced by the Ballistic Missile Defense Program. Without consistent demand, commitment to this intergenerational good failed.

International Demand Without Domestic Commitment

The need for demand *and* official commitment is also quite evident in the international arena. Thomas Princen's study of the ivory trade ban describes how an international agreement, the Convention on International Trade in Endangered Species (CITES), can be immensely strengthened by the manifestation of demand through the actions of nongovernmental organizations facilitating education, public awareness, and pressure for species protection. Even with this concerted action, the ivory trade ban is not totally effective, but without both demand and official commitment acting together, the effort to sustain elephant populations for future generations would be noticeably ineffective.[19]

Political Instability
The impact of the loss of political stability can also be devastating to provision of intergenerational goods. One tragic example involves attempts to preserve the species of mountain gorillas found in the African nations of Zaire and Rwanda. This story was made famous through the work of Dian Fossey who studied these gorillas in the 1970s and early 1980s. Official commitment to protection was evident in that nearly all the gorillas lived in habitat presumably protected as parks, Parc National des Virungas in Zaire and Parc National des Volcans in Rwanda. Nevertheless, Fossey and the gorillas suffered from political turmoil in the region, particularly the revolution in Zaire. The lack of stability contributed to increased poaching of the gorillas, the loss of protective habitat, and eventually to Fossey's death in 1985.[20]

Lack of Demand, Commitment, or Stability
Potential provision of important intergenerational goods has not even achieved the political agenda in many nations. In some cases, none of the necessary conditions are present. One example involves renewable water supplies that can sustain future generations. More than two dozen nations are already considered water-scarce, where renewable water supplies are less than 1,000 cubic meters per person per year. In many of these nations, political instability is quite apparent, often in fact due to tensions over water shortages. Only in a handful of these nations has the issue attained levels of public demand and official commitment that any efforts are underway to conserve supplies or find alternative sources. In nearly all of these nations, projections are that this precious good will become even more scarce for future generations.[21]

Importance of Necessary Conditions in General
Does this argument thus mean that provision of intergenerational goods will never occur without certain levels of public demand, political stability, and official commitment? Certainly, some intergenerational goods are passed along within families or even larger units within societies but without much assistance from governments or public agencies. The literature on common-pool resources cited in chapter 1 gives numerous examples of sustainability over generations.[22] For several reasons, however, that literature does not contradict the stated

importance of the necessary conditions posited in this work for provision of many intergenerational goods.

First, common-pool resources constitute only a subset of impure public goods. Other impure public goods include toll goods such as private roads and libraries as well as many of those intergenerational goods such as national parks and renewable energy sources described in this book. Few counter examples exist to describe many of these intergenerational goods as sustainable.

Second, many of the common-pool resources described in the empirical literature as sustainable benefit from certain conditions that make intergenerational delivery more possible. For one, the people using the resource, lobster fishermen for example, depend upon sustainable amounts of the good in question for their livelihood. For a second, the users are able to establish "perimeter-defended areas (wherein) access to the resource is highly controlled."[23] Many of the intergenerational goods discussed in this project, preserved lands and others, enjoy neither of these beneficial factors, at least not in their current form. Park users, with a few exceptions like myself, do not depend upon such places for their livelihood. Further, parks are generally supposed to bring people in, not keep them out.

Third, even the common-pool resources that are described as sustainable depend upon the presence, albeit in different forms, of the conditions (demand, stability, commitment) described in this work as important.[24] Those conditions are not easily achieved. Thus, I maintain that intergenerational provision of many goods remains a challenging prospect.

Effects of Constraining Conditions

Even when the potential provision of other intergenerational goods does benefit from relatively high levels of the conditions described as necessary, delivery is still not guaranteed. Elected officials in stable national governments will continue to be subject to and at least verbally responsive to demands for provision of such goods. Further, politicians will likely authorize plans and delegate responsibility for implementation to a designated national public agency. More responsibility than resources may be forthcoming to the agency, however. Instead, agency efforts to provide intergenerational goods will face institutional constraints precisely because they are national and public. Because efforts are national, they will often require cooperation from policymakers at different levels of government. These actors will cooperate with implementation efforts when those efforts are in their interests. When goals are not consistent, subnational policymakers or international organizations will attempt to modify long-term plans to fit their own needs. Because the effort is public, bureaucratic efforts will be dependent upon political actors for funding and support and subject to political pressure for short-term utility rather than long-term results.

Vertical Constraints

As the current evolution of the Costa Rican parks situation shows, complications across different levels of governments are not limited to nations that are easily identified as federal systems. Vertical constraints are most apparent, however, when federalism is an integral component of the political system. A nonpark example of provision of an intergenerational good that meets the necessary conditions but is seriously affected by subnational behavior involves forestry in Canada. To make timber available for future generations requires attention to sustained yields, a goal espoused by policymakers for decades. Actual forestry decisions, however, are made almost entirely at the provincial level. In British Columbia, for example, the province owns 85 to 95% of forest lands. For centuries, these lands were cut at rates that could not be sustained. Despite provincial attempts at restraint in the 1970s and federal involvement in the 1980s, meaningful revisions to policies did not occur until the 1990s, particularly with the Forest Renewal Plan of 1994. Until then, international and national demands for sustained yields were stymied by the dominant influence held by logging interests over provincial policymakers.[25]

Horizontal Constraints

As an illustration of the impact of conflicts between institutional actors at the national level on intergenerational goods, consider the variable progress in nations throughout the world in supporting the development of renewable energy sources. Many people have long recognized that renewable sources such as solar and wind could provide significant amounts of clean energy for future generations. Further, citizens have increasingly supported and many governments have verbally committed to research and development, subsidies, and incentives for further creation and delivery of these sources. Actual provision, however, has been slowed by the lack of support, if not explicit antagonism, given agencies with responsibility for such programs. In the United States, for example, Department of Energy renewable programs have been regularly underfunded, criticized, and targeted for elimination by hostile Congresses. Even when a commitment to renewables was offered prominently by President Carter, the lack of congressional support made the weak foundation for a renewable energy program readily susceptible to dismantling by the subsequent Reagan administration.[26] Such halting progress has been evident in many nations throughout the world. As one recent compendium summarizes, "Indeed, unless the industrialized countries make renewables a central part of their domestic energy programs and back this commitment with resources and policy reforms, a world commitment to renewable energy would have little credibility."[27] Again, commitment to provision of intergenerational goods is a necessary but not sufficient condition for provision, implementation of that commitment being subject to demands from many political actors.

Recommendations

Obviously, provision of intergenerational goods is a daunting task for public as well as private sectors. Yet, people in modern societies continue to express concern about the delivery of certain goods to future generations. If that concern is sincere, how then can provision be made more likely?

This study suggests that one key is public demand. Referring to chapter 1, most scholarly models of public opinion consider its impact in the short term. Sustained and substantial public support is essential, however, for commitment to and meaningful delivery of intergenerational goods in the long term as well. Just as the statistical analysis in chapter 2 asserted, public concern over future outcomes is correlated with higher levels of education. Thus, a more educated society is one more likely to care about future generations. One recommendation to enhance public sector responsiveness over the long term, then, is to encourage and support education, literacy, and public awareness of factors affecting the future.

A second recommendation derives from the need for official commitment to some intergenerational good even while recognizing that such commitment will not be sufficient on its own. One implication easily inferred from the analysis is to free bureaucratic agencies from political or subnational control entirely so that they can pursue long-term delivery of some good. Such a course of action could then, however, result in dominance of agency actions by certain interest groups that may well be focused solely on the short term, similar to that described by certain "capture" theorists.[28] Avoiding such an outcome motivates the need for official commitment. With an explicit mission, even if the public agencies are given more autonomy, they are not entirely removed from political control. Indeed, they will have been given a specific mandate—in this context official commitment to systematic preservation of some good like diverse ecosystems—that belies the vague delegations of power that inspired so many characterizations of interest group dominance of agency behavior. Official commitments may be cheap talk, but they are necessary.

A final broad recommendation is the logical followup to the previous one. Given a specific mission and enough public support for a mandate, agency personnel need enough autonomy and discretion to pursue effective delivery of intergenerational goods. Efforts to affect the long term will be more effective if less constrained by actors motivated almost entirely by the short term. Further, agencies should be given the slack and the resources to learn from past mistakes and to thus adjust to institutional constraints that might undermine their long-term efforts.

CONCLUSIONS

The delivery of intergenerational goods to future citizens is one of the most important and demanding tasks facing governments. Most nonmaterial rewards and long-term benefits can only reasonably be expected to be important to the public, rather than the private, sector. Responsive public sector behavior is not guaranteed, however. Rather, it is affected by institutional tensions between those pursuing long-term results and those whose behavior is shaped by short-term incentives. While difficult to realize, implementation of plans to achieve delivery of such goods may provide the greatest legacy for any government. Politicians could do much worse. For example, Teddy Roosevelt will always be remembered as the president who created Grand Canyon National Monument. National parks are the most striking example of a good that exists as a monument to past efforts, a treasure to current users, and a gift to future generations.

Notes

CHAPTER 1

1. Buchanan 1968; Hanson 1978; Loehr and Sandler 1978; Ruys 1974; Samuelson 1954; Schmanske 1991.
2. Ruys 1974: 6; Schmanske 1991: 19.
3. Buchanan 1968: 49–50; Schmanske 1991: 45.
4. Buchanan 1968: 187; Samuelson 1954.
5. Loehr and Sandler 1978: 33.
6. Solow 1993: 182.
7. Nelson 1982: 66.
8. Olson 1965: chapter 1; Smith 1776.
9. North and Weingast 1989: 832.
10. Chase 1987, 1995; Herman 1992; Sax 1980.
11. Wright and Mattson 1996: 6.
12. Smith 1776: 306.
13. Acheson 1987; McCay and Acheson 1987; Netting 1997; Ostrom 1990; Ostrom, Gardner, and Walker 1994.
14. Ostrom and Schlager 1996: 129.
15. Ostrom, Gardner, and Walker 1994: 7; Ostrom and Ostrom 1977: 12.
16. Ostrom and Ostrom 1977: 12.
17. Campbell et al., 1960; Converse 1964; Zaller and Feldman 1992.
18. Key 1966; Downs 1957; Fiorina 1981.
19. Achen 1975; Sullivan, Piereson, and Marcus 1978.
20. Nash 1982; Roosevelt 1908; Thoreau 1851.
21. Downs 1957.
22. Lowi 1979; Schattschneider 1960.
23. Olson 1965; Rothenberg 1988; Walker 1983.
24. Keohane, Haas, and Levy 1993; Magraw 1988; Princen 1994.
25. Fenno 1978; Mayhew 1974.
26. Heinz et al., 1993: 412.
27. Cain and Ferejohn 1987; Franks 1987.
28. Neustadt 1980.
29. Kingdon 1984; Lindblom 1959; Lowi 1979.
30. Ostrom and Schlager 1996: 128.
31. For recent examples, see Boix 1997; Booth and Richard 1996; Sobel 1994; Volgy and Schwarz 1996.
32. Ostrom and Schlager 1996: 128.

33. Berger 1981; Hall 1986; Katznelson 1981; Leithner 1997; McGillivray 1997; Vogel 1990.

34. Ostrom and Schlager 1996: 128.

35. This argument was stated most forcefully by Lowi 1979.

36. Derthick 1979; Heclo 1977; Kingdon 1984; Moe 1985; Nathan 1983; Pfiffner 1987, 1990; Rourke 1991.

37. Aberbach, Putnam, and Rockman 1981; Peters 1988.

38. This perspective has recently been considered by Bates and Shepsle in Nie and Drobak 1997.

39. Halperin 1974; Ripley and Franklin 1976; Warwick 1975; Wilson 1989: 83–89.

40. Eisner and Meier 1990; Ringquist 1995; Sabatier, Loomis, and McCarthy 1995.

41. Bardach 1982; Derthick 1970; Pressman and Wildavsky 1984.

42. Keohane, Haas, Levy 1993; O'Neill 1996; Parson 1993; Princen and Finger 1994.

43. Halperin 1974; Ripley and Franklin 1976; Lowry 1994; Warwick 1975; Wood and Waterman 1991.

44. Alesina and Summers 1993; Rogoff 1985.

45. Noss 1996: 98–100; Wright and Scott 1996.

46. Agee 1996: 32–33; Keiter 1997; Noss 1996: 107.

47. Baden 1977; Enloe 1975; Kitschelt 1986; Lundquist 1980.

48. Vogel and Kun 1987: 161.

49. Examples include Bella 1987 on Canada; Frome 1992 on the U.S.; Toyne 1994 on Australia.

50. Harrison, Miller, and McNeely 1984; Harroy 1974; Nicholson 1974.

51. Bella 1987; Hartzog 1988; Toyne 1994.

52. Foresta 1984: 111–116; Hall 1992: chapter 8.

53. Machlis and Tichnell 1985; Allin 1990; Lowry 1994.

54. Chase 1987; Eidsvik 1990; Hall 1992; Runte 1979.

55. Hall 1992; Runte 1979.

56. Aberbach, Putnam, and Rockman 1981; Durant 1992; Lowry 1994; Wood and Waterman 1991.

57. Albinski 1973; Campbell and Halligan 1992; Cullen 1990; Galligan 1993.

58. Davis 1994; Wanna 1994; Zifcak 1994.

59. Cairns 1992: 57; Cullen 1990; Weaver 1992: 44.

60. Aberbach, Putnam, and Rockman 1981; Campbell 1983; Franks 1987.

61. Ameringer 1982: 41; Tartter 1983: 200; Wallace 1992.

CHAPTER 2

1. The language of the 1 March 1872 act is repeated in U.S. NPS, 1991, *Yellowstone Statement for Management*: 5.

2. For a review, see Caulfield 1989.

3. Quoted in Allin 1990: 10.

4. IUCN, 1971.

5. Nicholson 1974.

6. CEQ, *Environmental Quality: The First Annual Report*, 1970: 5.

7. Harf and Trout 1986: 13; Keohane, Haas, and Levy 1993: 6.

8. Risser and Cornelison 1979: 1.

9. Ibid., 2.

10. NPCA, 1988, *Investing*: 23.

11. World Heritage Convention, Article 1.

12. World Heritage Convention reprinted in UNESCO, 1982.

13. IUCN, 1993: 29.

14. Chase 1995: 113–115.

15. Agee 1996; Keiter 1997; Noss 1996; Wright and Scott 1996.

16. Freemuth 1997; Keiter 1997.

17. The presidential proclamation is reprinted in *The Final Report of the National Parks Centennial Commission*: 18.

18. Unfortunately, the Categories I–V currently applied were not utilized in 1970. To calculate preserved land, therefore, we had to identify the areas in each nation now listed in Categories I–III and determine which existed in 1970. This may not be completely accurate, but it does provide the most realistic estimate possible.

19. Sabatier and Jenkins-Smith 1993.

20. Sabatier, Loomis, and McCarthy 1995: 236.

21. Lertzman, Rayner, and Wilson 1996; Sabatier and Jenkins-Smith 1993; Sabatier, Loomis, and McCarthy 1995.

22. Berger 1981; Enloe 1975; Heidenheimer, Heclo, and Adams 1990; Katznelson 1981; Vogel 1986.

23. Heidenheimer, Heclo, and Adams 1990; Janda 1980; Kitschelt 1986.

24. Keohane, Haas, and Levy 1993.

25. O'Neill 1996.

26. Parson 1993: 68.

27. Princen 1994.

28. Erskine 1972; Mitchell 1984; Moore 1995.

29. The exact specification is (literacy*urbanization)*(1/Free category). This is done because Freedom House assigns lower numbers to the more free societies and higher numbers to the less free societies.

30. O'Neill 1996.

31. Hall 1992.

32. Norris 1992.

33. Obviously, development of commercial facilities in national parks is a controversial subject and challenging to measure (Bella 1987; Frome 1992; Toyne 1994). Suffice it to say that the tension between preservation and development makes the impact of tourism complicated.

34. Arnold 1990; Fenno 1978; Mayhew 1974.

35. Clarke and McCool 1996: 5; Eisner and Meier 1990; Meier 1985: 15; Ringquist 1995; Rourke 1984; Sabatier, Loomis, and McCarthy 1995.

36. Immergut 1992; Kitschelt 1986: 63.

37. Clarke and McCool 1996.

38. Two different individuals coded this variable with an intercoder reliability rate of 93%.

39. Not surprisingly, the two measures for agency presence are highly correlated. The Pearson correlation coefficient is .58.

40. Culhane 1981: 10; Frome 1971: 141; Clarke and McCool 1996: 82.

41. Survey by Daniel McCool cited in Foresta (1984: 104).

42. Dye 1966; Game 1979; Vogel 1990: 276.

43. Daly 1991: 9.

44. Daly 1991; Solow 1993.

45. These are just examples of why comparison of these UN lists over time should be done with care. As the IUCN admits, much of the apparent expansion is due to improved data collection (IUCN, 1994, *UN List of National Parks*: xii).

46. Allin 1990: 12.

47. IUCN, 1994: 246. For calculations, 1,000 ha = 10 sq km = 2471 acres = 3.86 sq miles.

48. Several potential methodological complications were checked. Multicollinearity is not a problem. The variables for domestic environment and alternative use are correlated, but running the equation with either one omitted does not change the results. A second concern involves having total area on both sides of the equation: as an independent variable and in the denominator of the dependent variable. Running the equation without total area on the right-hand side does not change any of the relationships. Finally, heteroskedasticity could be a problem, for example, if the dependent variable measure is bunched geographically. For instance, France might be likely to have a similar amount of preserved lands to Belgium, etc. This is not the case. Individual country amounts are independent.

49. When the extractive industries measure was used, the alternative use variable was not significant, but all other relationships in the equation remained intact.

50. When using raw numbers rather than percentages, the Pearson's correlation coefficient between total area and protected area is .72, between total area and pristine area is .68.

51. The relationships described below are consistent when the nations examined have other varying amounts of RGDPC. The overlap in the displayed analyses is necessary to retain enough cases for statistical purposes.

52. The results for protected lands were quite similar.

53. The Ecuador number is somewhat misleading as the Galapagos Islands constitute nearly eight of the eleven million hectares of protected land.

54. I tested two versions of such a variable: one measuring the presence of a plan for systematic expansion of park systems and the other reflecting participation in the Montreal Protocol. Both were positive but not significant, and neither changed the fundamental relationships in the displayed model.

55. Foresta 1984; Hartzog 1988; Lowry 1997; Wallace 1992.

56. Clarke and McCool 1996; Khademian 1996; Ringquist 1995; Rourke 1984.

CHAPTER 3

1. Galvin interview by author, 21 December 1995.
2. Deruiter and Haas 1995: 12.
3. Wright, Dixon, and Thompson 1933, *Fauna of the National Parks*: 19, 38.
4. Leopold 1963.
5. NAS, 1963, *A Report by the Advisory Committee.*
6. Sellars 1997.
7. Devoto 1953.
8. Nash 1982: 231.
9. Mapes 1966: 1.
10. Quoted in McPhee 1971: 62. See also Swem 1970.
11. Foresta 1984: 111.
12. Erskine 1972; Mitchell 1984; Moore 1995.
13. Vaske and Haas 1996: 5.
14. Albright and Cahn 1985: 32.
15. NPS Organic Act, U.S. Code Annotated, Title 16: sec. 1: 66.
16. Cheever 1997.
17. Wirth 1980: 237.
18. Schlesinger 1965: 659, 1016.
19. Chubb 1985: 276.
20. Lowi 1979: 276; Reagan 1982.
21. Chubb 1985; Conlan 1988; Lowry 1992.
22. U.S. NPS, 1994, "Restructuring Plan for the NPS."
23. Wise and Emerson 1994.
24. Lowry 1996; U.S. GAO, 1997, "Similarities and Differences."
25. Sundquist 1981: 367; Smith 1985.
26. For an example, see Ferejohn and Shipan 1989.
27. Campbell 1983: 295; Franks 1987: 98.
28. Foresta 1984: 75–78; Hartzog 1988; Mazmanian and Nienaber 1979.
29. Douglas 1972.
30. Lowry 1994: 211–212.
31. Moe 1985: 268; Nathan 1983: 7; Rourke 1991: 133.
32. Freemuth 1997: 703; Lowry 1994.
33. Kanamine 1995: A3.
34. Greve 1997: A1.
35. Sellars 1997.
36. U.S. NPS, 1992, *National Parks for the 21st Century*: 28.
37. Kriz 1995: 2151.
38. Lancaster 1990: A8.
39. U.S. NPS, 1972, *National Park System Plan*, Part 1: vii.
40. Galvin interview.
41. Runte 1987: 48–64.
42. Everhart 1983: 95; Quote from Rep. Lehlbach (R-NJ) in *Congressional Record*, 24 May 1934: 9497; Ise 1961: 371–378.
43. Albright and Cahn 1985: 33.
44. Runte 1987: 138–154.

45. Quoted in Miles 1995: 77.

46. Miles 1995: 77 and generally 71–95.

47. Wirth 1980: 349.

48. Hartzog 1988: 137–139.

49. Conservation Foundation, 1985: 42–43; Hartzog 1988: 173; Runte 1987: 149–150.

50. Quoted in Frome 1992: 28.

51. Hartzog 1988: 174.

52. Graves 1974.

53. Conservation Foundation, 1985: 43; Runte 1979: 152–153.

54. Conservation Foundation, 1985: 43; Frome 1992: 17; Hartzog 1988: 175.

55. U.S. Congress, Senate Subcommittee on National Parks, 1971: 44.

56. Freemuth 1991: 49.

57. U.S. NPS, 1972, *National Park System Plan*, Part 1: 81.

58. U.S. NPS, 1972, *National Park System Plan*, Part 2: 1.

59. Ibid.

60. Foresta 1984: 111, 116.

61. U.S. NPS, 1976, *Guadalupe Mountains Master Plan*: 1–2.

62. U.S. NPS, 1972, *National Park System Plan*, Part 2: 12, 14, 109–115.

63. Clapper interview by author, 2 January 1997.

64. Foresta 1984: 81.

65. Clapper interview; see also Foresta 1984: 81.

66. NPCA, 1979, "NPCA Interviews Philip Burton": 22.

67. Kihss 1972: 42.

68. Morris 1972: 1; Everhart 1983: 71; Smith 1972.

69. Quoted in Everhart 1983: 70.

70. Foresta 1984: 174.

71. Conservation Foundation, 1985: 61.

72. Adams 1993: 10; Philip 1991: 1A.

73. Everhart 1983: 71; Foresta 1985: 218–222.

74. Foresta 1984: 280–282.

75. Everhart 1983: 129.

76. Quoted in Runte 1987: 251.

77. As quoted in Runte 1987: 254.

78. Cahn 1982: 29–32; Runte 1987: 255–257; Shanks 1984: 257–261.

79. Quoted in Cahn 1983: 52.

80. Cahn 1983: 52; Lash 1984: 280–285; Zielenziger 1988.

81. Ridenour testimony in U.S. Congress, 1995: 36.

82. Everhart 1983: 29.

83. Russakoff and Barringer 1982.

84. Ridenour testimony in U.S. Congress, 1995: 10.

85. Galvin interview.

86. Reid 1987: A1, A11; Editors of the *Washington Post*, 1987: A22.

87. NPCA, 1988, *Investing*: 35.

88. Zarafonitis 1991.

89. NPCA, 1988: 35.

90. Wright and Mattson 1996: 11.

91. Galvin interview.
92. Testimony of Rick Gale in U.S. Congress, 1995: 15.
93. Testimony of Robin Winks in U.S. Congress, 1995: 40.
94. Foresta 1984: 151.
95. Hinds 1992: 12; Lancaster 1990a: A8.
96. U.S. GAO, 1991: 1, *Status of Development at the Steamtown Site.*
97. U.S. GAO, 1993, *Scope and Cost of AIHP*: 2.
98. Lancaster 1990a: A1.
99. Quoted in Spolar 1993: A3.
100. U.S. GAO, 1993, *Transfer of the Presidio*: 2.
101. Galvin interview.
102. NPCA, 1995, "Tallgrass Prairie": 11.
103. Estes 1995; Linn 1995; NPCA, 1995, "Tallgrass"; Tyson 1994.
104. Zurhellen interview by author, 25 September 1995.
105. NPCA, 1988, *Investing*: 28.
106. Lash 1984: 280–283; NPCA, 1991, "NPCA Opposes."
107. Associated Press, 1995, "The Last Private."
108. Quoted in AP 1995, "The Last Private."
109. McManus 1998: 35.
110. NPCA, 1995, "Congress Takes Aim": 10.
111. Camia 1994; Hefley 1995; Pritchard 1995.
112. U.S. Congress, H.R. 260, Sec. 103 (a).
113. Kriz 1995; Pritchard 1995, "260"; Winks 1995.
114. Allen 1995; Babbitt 1995.
115. Draft amendment H.R. 1280 as proposed on 15 November 1995.
116. Clapper interview.
117. The Conservation Foundation, 1985, *National Parks for a New Genera-tion*: 32.
118. Krayna 1995; Smith 1993, "Writing."
119. U.S. NPS, 1992, *National Parks for the 21st Century*: 12.
120. Clapper interview.
121. Ridenour 1994: 97.
122. Rettie 1995: 105.
123. Wright, Dixon, and Thompson 1933: 37.
124. NPCA, 1988, *Investing*: 20.
125. Galvin interview.
126. Layden and Manfredo 1994: 7.
127. Frome 1992; Lowry 1994; U.S. NPS, 1992, *National Parks.*
128. NPCA, 1979, "NPCA Adjacent Lands Survey": 4–9; Shands 1979.
129. U.S. NPS, 1980, *State of the Parks*: viii, 4.
130. NPCA, 1988, *Investing*: 21.
131. DiSilvestro 1993: 12–18.
132. Davis and Ogden 1994: 794.
133. Comments of Goldwater in *Congressional Record*, 2 August 1973: S. 27539; Freemuth 1991: 28.
134. Shanks 1984: 217.
135. NPCA, 1988, *Investing*: 21.

136. Lowry 1994: 183–187.

137. Fahrling 1986.

138. Martin 1994: A19.

139. Fordney 1994.

140. Forstenzer 1995; NPCA, 1995, "NPS Works."

141. Ayres 1988: A18; Deford 1988: MDI.

142. U.S. GAO, 1987, *Limited Progress*; 1994, *Activities*; 1995, *Information*.

143. Galvin interview.

144. Skinner cited in Chase 1987b: 235.

145. Wright, Dixon, and Thompson 1933: 85.

146. U.S. NPS, 1974, *Yellowstone Master Plan*: 1.

147. Ibid., 17, 31.

148. Letter from Superintendent Townsley, reprinted in U.S. NPS, 1988, *Yellowstone Fishing Bridge EIS*: 342.

149. Chase 1987: 206; Lowry 1994: 158–159.

150. U.S. NPS, 1974, *Yellowstone Master Plan*: 19.

151. U.S. NPS, 1991, *Yellowstone Statement for Management*: 49.

152. U.S. NPS, 1974, *Yellowstone Master Plan*: 24.

153. Quoted in Reid 1989: A3.

154. U.S. NPS, 1974, *Yellowstone Master Plan*: 1.

155. Keiter 1991: 4; Leal 1990: 25.

156. U.S. Congress, House Committee on Interior, 1985, *Greater Yellowstone*.

157. Keiter 1991: 5.

158. Mintzmayer 1992; NPCA, 1992, "New Evidence"; Rauber 1992.

159. Freemuth 1997: 713; Keiter 1997: 658–666.

160. Finley interview by author, 15 July 1996.

161. Cody Chamber of Commerce survey of 1995.

162. Finley interview.

163. Greater Yellowstone Coordinating Committee 1994: 2.

164. Kaeding interview by author, 16 July 1996.

165. Compas interview by author, 16 July 1996.

166. U.S. NPS, 1991, *Yellowstone Statement of Management*: 29.

167. For an excellent review of the first year of the program, see Ferguson 1996.

168. Keiter 1997: 660–662; U.S. GAO, 1992 "Many Issues"; Wilkinson 1997.

169. Keiter and Boyce 1991: 381.

170. Quoted in Glick and Murr 1997: 61.

171. Smith interview by author, 6 March 1996.

172. Based on 1990 figures of 908,000 overnighters with 614,000 staying in lodges, or 68%. Figures available in U.S. NPS, *Statistical Abstract*, 1990: 32.

173. U.S. NPS, 1995, *Grand Canyon GMP*: 24.

174. Long 1997; U.S. NPS, 1976, *Grand Canyon Final Master Plan*: 23.

175. U.S. NPS, 1994, "Report on Effects of Aircraft Overflights": E20.

176. U.S. Public Law 100–91, 1987, Section 3.

177. Lowry 1994: 167.

178. U.S. NPS, 1994, "Report on Effects of Aircraft Overflights": E25.

179. Parent and Robeson 1976; Shelby and Nielsen 1976; Thompson, Rogers, and Borden 1974.
180. Lowry 1994: 158–170.
181. National Research Council, Committee on Haze 1990; 1993.
182. Mathai 1995; NPCA, 1991, "Relief in Sight."
183. Quoted in NPCA, 1995, *National Parks*: 47.
184. U.S. NPS, 1995, *Grand Canyon GMP*: 16–17, 23–25.
185. Ibid., 23.
186. Associated Press, 1996: A1. NPCA, 1991, "Relief in Sight": 8; U.S. GAO, 1996, *Assessment*.
187. Long 1997; Stevens 1997.
188. U.S. NPS, 1995, *Grand Canyon GMP*: 57.
189. U.S. NPS, 1994,"Report on Effects of Aircraft Overflights": E9.
190. Mathai 1995.
191. Smith interview.
192. Quoted in Everhart 1983: 65.
193. Mitchell interview by author, 27 August 1996.
194. U.S. NPS, 1980 *Yosemite General Management Plan*: 1.
195. Interview with park historian Al Runte 28 July 1992; U.S. Congress, Senate Subcommittee on Public Lands, 1990: 110.
196. Cited in Conservation Foundation, 1985: 298.
197. Cited in Nolte 1990: A20.
198. Snyder interview by author, 27 August 1996.
199. NPCA, 1996, "Transit": 24.
200. U.S. NPS, 1994, *Yosemite Alternative Transportation*: ES–2, ES–5.
201. Glick and Murr 1997.
202. U.S. NPS, 1996, *Strategic Plan*: 22.
203. Ibid., 40, 42.

CHAPTER 4

1. Johnson 1972; Montgomery 1995.
2. Johnson 1972; Roddewig 1978: 131.
3. Lake Pedder Committee of Enquiry, 1974: 257.
4. Mosley 1990: 39–40; Ovington 1980: 47–48; Roddewig 1978: 82.
5. Hall 1992: 101.
6. Lake Pedder Committee of Enquiry, 1974: 77.
7. Roddewig 1978: 4.
8. Ibid., 80.
9. Brown 1987; Hay 1994; Montgomery 1995; Sewell et al., 1989.
10. Toyne 1994: 19, 33.
11. Head 1986: 12; Australian Overseas Information Service, 1994.
12. Roddewig 1978: 119.
13. Bambrick 1979: 21.
14. Hall 1992: 67.
15. Ovington 1980: 49.

16. Mosley 1990: 41; Ovington 1980: 49.
17. Roddewig 1978: 40; also Papadikis 1993: 341.
18. Head 1986: 39, 46.
19. Johnson 1972; Lake Pedder Committee of Enquiry, 1974: 256.
20. Papadikis 1993: 106.
21. Statistics from Australian Overseas Information Service, 1994.
22. Hall 1992: 7.
23. McMichael and Gore 1984: 258.
24. McAllister 1994: 28.
25. Gregory 1991: 119–121.
26. Papadikis 1990: 343.
27. Hall 1992: 242.
28. Matthews 1991: 206, 193.
29. Christoff 1994; Warhurst 1994.
30. Christoff 1994: 132; McAllister 1994: 35.
31. Papadikis 1990: 345.
32. McAllister 1994: 28.
33. Papadikis 1993: 43.
34. Mosley 1990: 57.
35. Papadikis 1994: 388.
36. Kellow and Moon 1993: 248; also Papadikis 1994: 391.
37. Australian Overseas Information Service, 1994: 5.
38. Rosenbaum 1995: 27.
39. Papadikis 1993: 149.
40. ESD Working Groups, 1991, *Tourism*: xvii, 139.
41. ESD Working Groups, 1991, *Tourism*: xix.
42. Ulph and Reynolds 1981: xv.
43. Gale and Jacobs 1987: 41.
44. Suter 1991: 4.
45. Marshall interview by author, 21 July 1995.
46. Brown 1984; Kendell and Buivids 1987: 84; Thompson 1984.
47. Toyne 1994: 38.
48. Green 1981.
49. Editors of the *Sydney Morning Herald*, 22 December 1982, "Tasmania Tells 'Other Island' It's Our Business": 1.
50. Kendell and Buivids 1987: 85; Papadikis 1990: 343, 1993: 114; Sewell, Dearden, and Dumbrell 1989: 154.
51. Quoted in Kendell and Buivids 1987: 100.
52. Commonwealth v. Tasmania (1983) 46 A.L.R. 625; Lumb 1984; Papadikis 1993: 114–115.
53. High Court, 1987, *Summary of Proceedings*: 13.
54. Hay 1994; Saunders 1992.
55. Editors of the *Sydney Morning Herald*, 10 December 1982, "Fraser's Cave": 14.
56. Boer 1989: 142.
57. Quoted in Hall 1992: 202.
58. WHC, Articles 4 and 5.

59. Hawke 1989: 22.
60. Saxon interview by author, 26 July 1995.
61. See Slatyer 1989: 4.
62. Quoted in Jagger 1994: 23.
63. Honchin interview by author, 31 July 1995.
64. Francis interview by author, 6 July 1995.
65. Davis 1994: 45; Parkin and Summers 1994; Solomon 1994.
66. Bean 1991: 84.
67. Albinski 1973: 129.
68. Lunney and Recher 1979: 185; Mosley 1990: 55.
69. Roddewig 1978: 131.
70. Mosley 1990: 42; Papadikis 1993: 108.
71. Mosley 1990: 44; Ovington 1980: 52.
72. Ovington 1969: 41.
73. Mosley 1990: 44.
74. Ovington 1980: 53.
75. Papadikis 1993: 187.
76. Hall 1992: 7–9.
77. Oliphant 1978: 12.
78. Albinski 1973: 367.
79. Campbell and Halligan 1992: 236.
80. Galligan 1993a: 288.
81. Davis et al., 1993: 48.
82. Fleiner-Gerster 1992: 14; Fletcher 1992; Head 1986: 32–33; Saunders 1985: 26.
83. Keen, Mercer, and Woodfull 1994: 44; Roddewig 1978: 41.
84. Galligan 1993a: 291.
85. Collins 1991: 76.
86. Galligan 1993a: 291; 1993b: 179; Gruen and Grattan 1993: 221.
87. Galligan 1993b: 180; Kelly 1992: 528.
88. Fletcher 1992: 596; Galligan 1993a: 292; 1993b: 180; Milik 1989: 32; Rees 1991: 12
89. Summers 1994: 84; Fletcher 1992: 593–596.
90. Honchin 1994: 3.
91. Bambrick 1979: 115; Coveney 1993: 20.
92. Cullen 1990.
93. Papadikis 1993: 111–112.
94. Australian Department of Arts, Heritage, and the Environment, 1987, *Environment Conservation and Heritage:* 1.
95. Summers 1994: 94.
96. Gruen and Grattan 1993: 232; also Fletcher 1992: 611.
97. Collins 1991: 79.
98. Galligan interview by author, 13 July 1995.
99. Mosley interview by author, 12 July 1995.
100. Shepherd interview by author, 11 July 1995.
101. Gowans interview by author, 12 July 1995.
102. Uhr 1994: 27.

103. Warhurst 1994.

104. Parkin and Summers 1994.

105. Phillips interview by author, 11 July 1995.

106. Zifcak 1994: 93.

107. Campbell and Halligan 1992: 166; Davis 1994: 58; Wanna 1994: 62; Zifcak 1994: 110.

108. Davis 1994: 58.

109. Wanna 1994: 62.

110. Albinski 1973: 355.

111. Marshall interview.

112. Saxon interview.

113. De Jersey 1985; Solomon 1994.

114. Francis interview.

115. Ryan 1981: 18.

116. For the U.S. case, see Lowry 1994: 58–59.

117. Esau interview by author, 11 July 1995.

118. Hughes 1986.

119. Papadikis 1993: 65.

120. Hall 1992: 95; Mosley 1990: 38.

121. Quoted in Ovington 1980: 45; Mosley 1990: 38; Papadikis 1993: 63.

122. Mosley 1990: 43.

123. Hall 1992: 93; Papadikis 1993: 66.

124. *NSW Parliamentary Debates*, 1966, Vol. 67: 3049.

125. Mosley 1990: 41.

126. Lunney and Recher 1979: 184.

127. Ovington 1980: 52.

128. Hall 1992: 25.

129. Johnstone 1984: 308; Papadikis 1993: 112.

130. Figures from ANPWS *Annual Reports*.

131. Coveney 1993: 20; Papadikis 1993: 110.

132. Papadikis 1993: 111.

133. Mosley 1990: 57.

134. Coveney 1993: 39.

135. Lunney and Recher 1979: 185.

136. Stankey 1980: 323.

137. Mosley 1990: 54.

138. Phillips and Shepherd interviews.

139. Lunney and Recher 1979: 185.

140. Hall 1992: 155.

141. Phillips interview.

142. Mosley 1990: 57.

143. Davis 1989: 113.

144. Lunney and Recher 1979: 187.

145. Hall 1992: 156.

146. Francis interview.

147. Ovington 1980: 53.

148. Hall 1989: 454.

149. Hall 1992: 20.
150. ANCA, 1995: 6.
151. Mosley 1990: 45.
152. Ibid., 54.
153. Hall 1992: 21.
154. Ibid., 23.
155. Toyne 1994: 2.
156. Coveney 1993: 18.
157. Mosley 1990: 56.
158. Ibid., 56.
159. Wearing and Brock 1991: 33.
160. Francis interview.
161. Marshall interview.
162. Coveney 1993: 39; Mosley 1990: 55.
163. Mosley 1990: 57.
164. Ibid., 56.
165. Quoted in Hall 1992: 178.
166. Figgis and Mosley 1988: 18; Mosley 1990: 57.
167. McMichael and Gore 1984: 258.
168. Hall 1992: 39.
169. Both projects are discussed in the NSW NPWS *Annual Report 1993–94*: 24–25.
170. Francis interview.
171. Gough interview by author, 4 August 1995.
172. Haslen 1995: P6.
173. Queensland Dept. of Environment, *Annual Report 1993–94*: 7.
174. *Nature Conservation Act 1992*, Act No. 20 of 1992: 11.
175. Haslen 1995: P6.
176. Emerson and Windsor 1997.
177. Sproull 1997.
178. *Land Conservation Act of 1970*: 1.
179. Victoria LCC, *Annual Report 1993–94*: 2–3.
180. Gowans interview.
181. LCC, *Annual Report 1993–94*: 11.
182. LCC, *Annual Report 1993–94*: 7.
183. Marshall interview.
184. ANCA, 1995, *IBRA*: 6.
185. World Wide Fund for Nature, 1995, "The Application of IBRA."
186. Mercer and Peterson 1986: 134.
187. Papadikis 1990: 348.
188. "Land of the Apocalypse," Discovery Channel, 10 April 1995.
189. Toyne 1994: 129–130.
190. Toyne 1994: 62; see also Hall 1992: 187.
191. ANPWS, 1991, *Kakadu Plan of Management*: 91.
192. Quoted in M. Steketee, "Cabinet Rules," *Sydney Morning Herald,* 17 September 1986: A1.
193. ANPWS 1991, *Kakadu Plan of Management*: 91.

194. Hall 1992: 208–210; Papadikis 1990: 349.

195. Coveney 1993: 43; Toyne 1994: 133.

196. Quinten interview by author, 20 July 1995.

197. Toyne 1994: 139.

198. Ibid., 142.

199. Lea 1992: 9/9; Toyne 1994: 147.

200. ANPWS, 1991, *Kakadu Plan of Management*: 6.

201. Ibid., 91.

202. "Land of the Apocalypse," Discovery Channel, 10 April 1995.

203. Coveney 1993: 44.

204. Strider 1984: 97.

205. Toyne 1994: 150.

206. Hill and Press 1994.

207. Papadikis 1990: 349.

208. GBRMPA, 1981: 5.

209. Driml 1994: vi.

210. Price 1978; Wright 1977.

211. Craik 1993: 91.

212. Roddewig 1978: 83.

213. Hall 1992: 140–141; Wright 1977: 32–33.

214. GBRMPA, *Annual Report 1993–94*: 30.

215. GBRMPA, 1994, *Keeping It Great*: Foreword.

216. Kelleher 1987: 28.

217. Honchin interview.

218. Honchin 1994: 8.

219. Craik 1993: 95; Honchin interview.

220. GBRMPA, *Annual Report 1993–94*: 4.

221. GBRMPA, *Annual Report 1993–94*: 117.

222. Craik 1993: 94; Kelleher 1987: 31.

223. Hawkes and Williams 1993: 55; Honchin interview.

224. GBRMPA, *Annual Report 1990–91*: 2; *Annual Report 1993–94*: 2.

225. Haigh 1995: 13; Trinder and Sparkes 1995: 11.

226. Ibid., 22.

227. GBRMPA, 1994: 15.

228. Ibid., 31.

229. Hall 1992: 217–218; Rainforest Conservation Society, 1986: 79; Toyne 1994: 65–67.

230. Hill and Graham 1984: 13–14; Russell 1985: 241; Toyne 1994: 66.

231. Quoted in Toyne 1994: 65 from the NBC *Today Show*, 1987.

232. Hill and Graham 1984: 14–17; Papadikis 1990: 347; Toyne 1994: 71–72.

233. Toyne 1994: 76.

234. Hall 1992: 220–221; Mosley 1990: 43; Papadikis 1990: 347–348; Toyne 1994: 80–83.

235. Gough interview; Saxon interview; Toyne 1994: 85.

236. WTMA, 1995, "Backgrounder": 2; WTMA, 1992, *Wet Tropics Plan: Strategic Directions*: 20.

237. Garvin interview by author, 26 July 1995.

238. Saxon interview.
239. Ibid.
240. Queensland NPWS, 1994, *Great Sandy Region Management Plan*: 28.
241. Roddewig 1978: 125; Mosley 1990: 41; Toyne 1994: 16–18.
242. Sinclair 1990: 219; see also Roddewig 1978: chapter 12.
243. Hall 1992: 145; Sinclair 1990: 236; Toyne 1994: 25.
244. Sinclair 1990: 238.
245. Gough interview.
246. Sinclair 1994: 158; Toyne 1994: 29.
247. Queensland NPWS, 1994, *Great Sandy Region Management Plan*; Toyne 1994: 31.
248. Queensland NPWS, 1994, *Great Sandy Region*: 3.
249. Ibid., 30–31.
250. Gough interview.
251. Ibid.
252. Hall 1989: 453.

CHAPTER 5

1. Reuters 1966.
2. Gallup poll of 2 December 1970 cited in Hoberg 1992: 31.
3. Editors of *Nature Canada,* 1979. Concern for environment alive and well. *Nature Canada,* Vol. 8, No. 3: 3.
4. Brooks 1970; Fuller 1970; Marsh 1970; Nelson 1970.
5. Bryan 1973: 276; Nelson 1979: 17.
6. Davidson 1979: 26; Nelson 1979: 17.
7. Canadian Outdoor Recreation Research Committee, 1975: 1.
8. Lipset 1989; Rabe 1994: 23.
9. Gray 1992; Howlett 1994; Sears 1992.
10. Survey results cited in CEAC, 1991: 23.
11. Blake, Guppy, and Urmetzer 1997; Schneider 1997.
12. Banting 1992: 168; Dion 1995: 536.
13. Clarke and Kornberg 1993; MacIvor 1996.
14. Archer and Ellis 1994: 295; Laycock 1994; Sigurdson 1994.
15. Editors of *Nature Canada,* 1981. Beginnings. *Nature Canada,* Vol. 10, No. 2: 10–13.
16. Parks Canada, 1979.
17. Dept. of Canadian Heritage, 1994: 13.
18. Dept. of Canadian Heritage, 1995.
19. Blake, Guppy, and Urmetzer 1997; Schneider 1997.
20. Hummel 1985: 585.
21. Carruthers 1979; Galbraith 1989.
22. Aberbach, Putnam, and Rockman 1981; Campbell 1983; Harrison and Hoberg 1994: 12–13; Sutherland and Doern 1985.
23. Campbell 1983: 295; Campbell 1988: 309; Doern and Phidd 1983: 30; Franks 1987: 98; Harrison and Hoberg 1991: 22.

24. Durant 1992; Lowry 1994; Pross 1985; Schwartz 1986.

25. Pross 1985: 246.

26. Aucoin and Bakvis 1988: xiv; also Aucoin 1988: 346; Cook 1982: 6.

27. Tellier 1990: 124.

28. Interview with Pukaskwa superintendent Mike Murphy, 9 June 1992.

29. Howlett 1994.

30. Hoberg 1993: 114.

31. Dept. of Canadian Heritage, 1995, "Parks Canada's Mandate for Change"; Parks Canada, 1996, *At the Crossroads Technical Report*: 297.

32. Dept. of Canadian Heritage, 1995, "Parks Canada's Mandate for Change": 4.

33. Pross 1985: 266; Weaver 1992: 39.

34. Cairns 1992; Hoberg 1992: 20; Lubin 1986: 564; Nemetz, Stanbury, and Thompson 1986: 591.

35. Gibbins 1982: 108.

36. Cullen 1990.

37. Bercuson 1990: 9.

38. Cullen 1990.

39. Aucoin and Bakvis 1988: 1–2.

40. Bakvis and Chandler 1987: 5; Doern and Phidd 1983: 29.

41. Bakvis 1989: 131; Gibbins 1982: 45; Lubin 1986: 564; Watts 1991: 171.

42. Coopers & Lybrand 1995: 9.

43. LaSelva 1993: 220.

44. Hoberg 1992: 20.

45. Leman 1987a: 29; Weaver 1992: 44.

46. Cairns 1992: 55.

47. Brooks 1970: 316; Lewis 1979: 69.

48. Cairns 1992: 67.

49. Faulkner 1979: 8.

50. Kilgour 1991.

51. Laurie 1991.

52. McComb interview by author, 5 February 1996.

53. Begin 1989: 2; Bella 1987: 29.

54. Nicol 1970: 25; Stephenson 1983: 1.

55. Hildebrandt 1995: 14.

56. Eidsvik and Henwood 1990: 65; see also Bryan 1973: 248.

57. Barney, Freeman, and Ulinski 1981: 92; Brown 1970: 47.

58. Bella 1987: 38; Bryan 1973: 250.

59. Begin 1989: 7; Bella 1987: 72.

60. Leman 1987: 29; Marsh 1985: 1362.

61. Bryan 1973: 253; Theberge 1976: 195.

62. Faulkner 1979: 6; Theberge 1976: 205.

63. CEAC, 1991: 55.

64. Carruthers 1979: 647; Reid 1979: 108.

65. Mondor 1981: 14.

66. Parks Canada, 1979: 15.

67. Nelson and Patterson 1979: A1.

68. Theberge 1979: 678.
69. Environment Canada, 1990, *Canada's Green Plan*: 13.
70. Ibid., 3.
71. Beaman interview by author, 3 June 1992.
72. CPS, 1991: 9.
73. CPS, 1990: 7–8.
74. This process is formally reiterated in Dept. of Canadian Heritage, 1994: 26–27.
75. CPS, 1990.
76. Taylor 1990: 169–190.
77. Carruthers 1979: 651.
78. Carruthers interview by author, 3 June 1992.
79. Carruthers 1979: 651; Eidsvik and Henwood 1990: 65.
80. Foresta 1985, "National Parks for Northern Canada."
81. Lowey 1987; McLaren 1986.
82. Nikiforuk 1990: 39–41.
83. CPS 1990: 9.
84. CNF, 1991: 3.
85. CNF, 1992; McNamee 1992; Walker 1992.
86. WWF, 1995: 18.
87. Bella 1987: 150; Canadian Press, 1985; Lowey 1985.
88. Bella 1987: 151; Huff 1985.
89. Begin 1989: 6.
90. Davidson 1979: 26.
91. CPS, 1990: 9.
92. CEAC, 1991: 55.
93. Charest cited in Walker 1992: A13.
94. WWF, 1995: 18.
95. CPS, 1991: 164.
96. Bella 1987: 170.
97. Sewell, Dearden, and Dumbrell 1989: 158.
98. Munro 1987b: A7.
99. Canadian Press, 1987: B1.
100. Fenge 1979; Gardner and Nelson 1980.
101. CPS, 1991: 175.
102. Bella 1987: 151.
103. Bella 1987: 170.
104. Brue 1989; Canadian Press, 1988.
105. CPS, 1991: 76.
106. Reid 1979: 108; Theberge 1976: 201.
107. Bella 1987: 2; Nikiforuk 1990: 32; Theberge 1976: 673.
108. Dept. of Canadian Heritage, 1994: 29.
109. Ibid., 34.
110. Becker 1979; Bella 1987: 113; Patterson 1979; Scace 1968.
111. Brown 1970; Hildebrandt 1995: 9, 14.
112. Bella 1987: 163.
113. Depalma 1997: 5.

114. CPS, 1988, *Jasper Management Plan*: 113.
115. Lothian 1987: 55–56.
116. Fortin interview by author, 25 June 1992.
117. Bella 1987: 117.
118. Nelson 1970b: 89.
119. Hildebrandt 1995: 47.
120. Bella 1987: 119–121; Editors of the *Calgary Herald*, 1984.
121. Bella 1987: 119–121; Leighton 1985; Seale 1979.
122. Masterman 1985.
123. Hildebrandt 1995: 69–70.
124. Ovenden 1992.
125. Bergman 1986; Canadian Press, 1989; Howse 1989.
126. Jacobson interview by author, 30 June 1992.
127. Church interview by author, 3 July 1992.
128. Hildebrandt 1995: 79.
129. Purser 1982: D7.
130. Hildebrandt interview by author, 26 June 1992.
131. Hildebrandt 1995: 79.
132. CPS, 1988, *Jasper National Park Management Plan*: 14–15.
133. Hildebrandt 1995: 67.
134. Dept. of Canadian Heritage, 1994: 41.
135. Ibid., 42.
136. Otton interview by author, 22 July 1996.
137. CPS, *Banff National Park Management Plan*, 1988: 23–27.
138. Ibid., 143.
139. Ibid., 40–41.
140. Ibid., 20.
141. Ibid., 145.
142. CPS, *Jasper National Park Management Plan*, 1988: 132.
143. CPS, 1988, *Jasper*: 133; CPS, 1988, *Yoho Management Plan*: 127.
144. CPS, 1988, *Yoho*: 125.
145. Otton interview.
146. Coopers & Lybrand 1995: 31.
147. Ibid., 36.
148. Hodgins 1996: 13.
149. Taylor 1996: 24–25.
150. Church interview.
151. Jacobson interview.
152. Zinkan interview by author, 2 July 1992.
153. All three were interviewed by Hildebrandt 1995.
154. Otton interview.
155. Praxis, 1996: 31, 62.
156. Angus Reid Survey, 1996: 3.
157. National press release on "Background" for study dated July 1994.
158. Wilson interview by author, 19 July 1996.
159. Otton interview.
160. Quoted in Adams 1994: A17; see also DePalma 1997.

161. Parks Canada, 1996, *Banff-Bow Valley Summary*: 10.

162. I should note that I was consulted during this process.

163. *Summary Report*: 27.

164. Parks Canada, 1996, *Technical Report*: 235.

165. Quoted in DePalma 1997.

166. "Highlights of Minister's Response to the Bow Valley Study Report."

167. Wilson interview.

168. See comment by Brad Pierce in DePalma 1997.

169. Parks Canada, 1996, *Technical Report*: 284.

170. Personal communication of 20 June 1997.

171. Parks Canada, 1995, *Prince Albert Management Plan*: 9, 19.

172. *Seattle Post-Intelligiencer* as reprinted in the *St. Louis Post-Dispatch,* 10 December 1994.

173. Hildebrandt 1995: 33.

CHAPTER 6

1. IUCN, 1992: 130; Janzen 1983: 9.

2. Hopkins 1995: 24.

3. Janzen 1983: 10.

4. Rovinski 1991: 43.

5. Franke 1993: 58; Hopkins 1995: 22.

6. Franke 1993: 112; Wallace 1992: 1–11.

7. Quoted in Wallace 1992: 126.

8. Quoted in Wallace 1992: 125.

9. Hopkins 1995: 73.

10. Wallace 1992: 126–127.

11. Lovejoy 1997.

12. Wallace 1992: 119–120.

13. McCanahay 1993: 47.

14. Carlos and staff interview by author, 25 May 1997.

15. Hopkins 1995: 42.

16. Janzen 1983: 7–8.

17. Rovinski 1991: 45; Wallace 1992: 146.

18. Kutay 1991.

19. Wallace 1992: 182–183.

20. Quoted in Burnett 1998: 2.

21. Whitaker 1983: 138.

22. Wilson 1997: 81.

23. Wilson and Lehoucq 1997: 32.

24. Wilson 1997: 81; see also Tartter 1983: 198.

25. Wallace 1992: 102.

26. IUCN, 1992: 129.

27. Burnett 1998: 2.

28. Thrup 1990: 20.

29. Desimone 1997.

30. Rovinski 1991: 52–55.
31. Boncompagni 1997.
32. Wallace 1992: 184.
33. Ameringer 1982: 41.
34. Carey 1996: chapter 4.
35. Wilson 1997: 81.
36. Carey 1996: 136; Wilson 1997: 87.
37. Carey 1996: 146.
38. Hopkins 1995: 19; Wilson 1997: 106.
39. Wilson 1997: 106.
40. Tartter 1983: 202; see also Ameringer 1982, 57–77.
41. Hopkins 1995: 28.
42. Wallace 1992: 183.
43. Burnett 1998: 3.
44. Quoted in Wallace 1992: 37.
45. Ibid., 118.
46. Boza 1992: 11.
47. Franke 1993: 42; Rachowiecki 1991: 20.
48. Wallace 1992: 13.
49. Quoted in Wallace 1992: 126.
50. Hopkins 1995: 28.
51. Wallace 1992: 45.
52. Hopkins 1995: 56.
53. Wallace 1992: 150.
54. Franke 1993: 168; Rachowiecki 1991: 112.
55. Quoted in Wallace 1992: 128.
56. Donovan 1994: 217.
57. Donovan 1994: 218.
58. Wallace 1992: 53–69.
59. Ibid., 140.
60. McCanahay 1993: 47.
61. IUCN, 1992: 130.
62. Burnett 1998: 2.
63. IUCN, 1992: 130; Vaughan and Rodriguez 1997: 2; Wallace 1992: 148–150.
64. Boza 1992: 11; Franke 1993: 10.
65. Quoted in Wallace 1992: 150.
66. Ibid., 159.
67. Janzen interview.
68. Vaughan and Rodriguez 1997: 3.
69. Wallace 1992: 162.
70. Ibid., 161–162.
71. Vaughan and Rodriguez 1997: 3.
72. See also Hopkins 1995: 57; Rachowiecki 1991: 145.
73. For a summary of recent activities, see ACG, 1997.
74. Boza 1992: 17.
75. Franke 1993: 58; IUCN, 1992: 131; Vaughan and Rodriguez 1997: 4–5.

76. Vaughan and Rodriguez 1997: 4.
77. Hopkins 1995: 59.
78. Vaughan and Rodriguez 1997: 7–8.
79. Wallace 1992: 178.
80. Personal communication, 18 June 1997.
81. Carlos interview.
82. Donovan 1994: 232.
83. Vaughan and Rodriguez 1997: 7.
84. Burnett 1998: 3.
85. Wallace 1992: 171–176.
86. Ibid., 180.
87. Franke 1993: 58.
88. Wallace 1992: 179.
89. Vaughan and Rodriguez 1997: 8.
90. Quoted in Wallace 1992: 175.
91. Franke 1993: 58.
92. Burnett 1998.
93. Vaughan and Rodriguez 1997: 9.

CHAPTER 7

1. Pigou 1920: 29.
2. Anderson and Hill 1994; Baden and Dana 1987; Power 1997; Sagoff 1997.
3. Acheson 1987; Ostrom 1990.
4. Lincoln Institute 1995: 1.
5. Madison 1787, "Vices of the Political System of the United States"; Pressman and Wildavsky 1984.
6. Derthick 1979; Lowry 1994; Moe 1985.
7. Lincoln Institute 1995: 9.
8. Lertzman, Rayner, and Wilson 1996 also found adaptive learning in their analysis of advocacy coalitions affecting British Columbia forestry policy.
9. Quoted in Wallace 1992: 126.
10. For one oft-cited source on this subject, see Walker 1969.
11. See also Clarke and McCool 1996: 81; and U.S. NPS, 1992, "National Parks": 28.
12. U.S. NPS, 1992, "National Parks": 58.
13. U.S. NPS, 1992; ANCA 1995.
14. Freemuth 1997: 726; also Keiter 1997: 687.
15. *Gallup Report*, January 1995: 3, 7.
16. *Gallup Report*, December 1996: 2–3.
17. *Gallup Report*, March 1985: 12–13.
18. *Gallup Report*, July 1988: 10.
19. Princen 1994.
20. Fossey 1983.
21. Postel 1993.

22. Acheson 1987; McCay and Acheson 1987; Ostrom 1990; Ostrom, Gardner, and Walker 1994.

23. Acheson 1987: 63; McCay and Acheson 1987; Netting 1997.

24. Ostrom and Schlager 1996: 128.

25. Bryner 1997; Marchak 1995.

26. Davis 1993: 248–250;

27. Johansson et al., 1993: 43.

28. Most noticeably Lowi 1979.

Bibliography

Aberbach, Joel D., Robert D. Putnam, and Bert A. Rockman. 1981. *Bureaucrats and Politicians in Western Democracies*. Cambridge: Harvard University Press.

Aberbach, Joel D., and Bert A. Rockman. 1988. Mandates or Mandarins? Control and Discretion in the Modern Administrative State. *Public Administration Review*, Vol. 48, No. 2: 606–612.

Achen, Christopher. 1975. Mass Political Attitudes and the Survey Response. *American Political Science Review*, Vol. 69: 1218–1231.

Acheson, James M. 1987. The Lobster Fiefs Revisited. In B. J. McCay and J. M. Acheson, eds., *The Question of Commons*. Tucson: University of Arizona Press, 37–65.

Adams, Gerald D. 1993. The Presidio Puzzle. *Image*, Vol. 3, No. 38: 9–15.

Adams, Jeff. 1994. Banff Battles Keep Flaring Up. *Calgary Herald*, 20 October: A17.

Agee, James K. 1996. Ecosystem Management. In R. G. Wright, ed., *National Parks and Protected Areas*. Cambridge: Blackwell, 31–44.

Albinski, Henry S. 1973. *Canadian and Australian Politics in Comparative Perspective*. New York: Oxford University Press.

Albright, Horace M. 1971. *Origins of National Park Administration of Historic Sites*. Philadelphia: Eastern National Park and Monument Association.

Albright, Horace M., and Robert Cahn. 1985. *The Birth of the National Park Service*. Salt Lake City: Howe Brothers.

Alesina, Alberto, and Lawrence Summers. 1993. Central Bank Independence and Macroeconomic Performance. *Journal of Money, Credit, and Banking*, 25 (May): 151–162.

Allen, William. 1995. Playing Politics with Environment. *St. Louis Post-Dispatch*, 23 October: C1.

Allin, Craig W. 1987. Wilderness Preservation as a Bureaucratic Tool. In Philip O. Foss, ed., *Federal Lands Policy*. New York: Greenwood Press, 127–138.

Allin, Craig W. 1990. Introduction. In Allin, ed., *International Handbook of National Parks and Nature Reserves*. New York: Greenwood Press, 1–20.

Ameringer, Charles D. 1982. *Democracy in Costa Rica*. New York: Praeger.

Anderson, Terry L., and Peter J. Hill. Rents from Amenity Resources. In Anderson and Hill, eds., *The Political Economy of the American West*. Lanham, Md.: Rowman and Littlefield, 113–127.

Angus Reid Group. 1996. Identifying Appropriate Activities for Banff National Park. Paper for Banff-Bow Valley Study.

Aniskowicz, B. T. 1990. Life or Death? *Nature Canada*, Vol. 19, No. 2: 35–38.

Archer, Keith, and Faron Ellis. 1994. Opinion Structure of Party Activists. *Canadian Journal of Political Science*, Vol. 27, No. 2: 277–308.

Area de Conservacion Guanacaste. 1997. *Bulletin Informativo*, Vol. 3, No. 1.

Arnold, R. Douglas. 1990. *The Logic of Collective Action*. New Haven: Yale University Press.

Associated Press. 1993. Coalition Urges $1 Billion Plan for Park Land. *St. Louis Post-Dispatch*, 14 February: 7A.

Associated Press. 1992. GAO: Sweetheart Deals in U.S. Parks. *Washington Post*, 22 May: A4.

Associated Press. 1995. The Last Private Landowner in the Channel Islands. *San Francisco Chronicle*, 21 February: A18.

Associated Press. 1996. Water Shed. *St. Louis Post-Dispatch*, 27 March: A1, A8.

Aucoin, Peter. 1988. The Mulroney Government, 1984–88: Priorities, Positional Policy and Power. In Andrew B. Gollner and Daniel Salee, eds., *Canada under Mulroney*. Downsview, Ont.: University of Toronto Press, 335–356.

Aucoin, Peter, and Herman Bakvis. 1988. *The Centralization-Decentralization Conundrum: Organization and Management in the Canadian Government*. Halifax, Nova Scotia: The Institute for Research on Public Policy.

Australian Department of Arts, Heritage, and Environment. 1987. *Environment, Conservation and Heritage*. Canberra: ADAHE.

Australian National Parks and Wildlife Service. *Annual Report 1977–78*. Canberra: ANPWS.

Australian National Parks and Wildlife Service. *Annual Report 1980–81*. Canberra: ANPWS.

Australian National Parks and Wildlife Service. *Annual Report 1983–84*. Canberra: ANPWS.

Australian National Parks and Wildlife Service. 1991. *Kakadu National Park Plan of Management*. Canberra: ANPWS.

Australian National Parks and Wildlife Service. 1991. *Uluru National Park Plan of Management*. Canberra: ANPWS.

Australian National Parks and Wildlife Service. 1982. *Uluru Plan of Management*. Canberra: ANPWS.

Australian Nature Conservation Agency. 1995. An Interim Biogeographic Regionalisation for Australia. Canberra: ANCA.

Australian Overseas Information Service. 1994. Fact Sheet on Australia. Canberra: AOIS.

Ayres, B. Drummond, Jr. 1988. House Passes Bill to Enlarge Park at Battlefield in Virginia. *New York Times*, 11 August: A18.

Babbitt, Bruce. 1995. Science: Opening the Next Chapter of Conservation History. *Science*, Vol. 267: 1954–1955.

Baden, John. 1977. A Primer for the Management of Common Pool Resources. In Garrett Hardin and Baden, eds., *Managing the Commons*. San Francisco: W. H. Freeman and Company, 137–146.

Baden, John, and Andrew Dana. 1987. Toward an Ideological Synthesis in Public Land Policy. In P. O. Foss, ed., *Federal Lands Policy*. New York: Greenwood, 1–20.

Bakvis, Herman. 1988. Regional Ministers, National Policies and the Administrative State in Canada: The Regional Dimension in Cabinet Decision-Making, 1980–1984. *Canadian Journal of Political Science*, Vol. 21, No. 3: 539–567.

Bakvis, Herman. 1989. Regional Politics and Policy in the Mulroney Cabinet, 1984–88: Towards a Theory of the Regional Minister System in Canada. *Canadian Public Policy*, Vol. 15, No. 2: 121–134.

Bakvis, Herman, and William M. Chandler. 1987. Federalism and Comparative Analysis. In Bakvis and Chandler, eds., *Federalism and the Role of the State*. Toronto: University of Toronto Press, 3–11.

Bambrick, Susan. 1979. *Australian Minerals and Energy Policy*. Canberra: Australian National University Press.

Banks, James T. 1988. The Clean Water Act: Still Vital to the Parks. In David J. Simon, ed., *Our Common Lands*. Washington, D.C.: National Parks and Conservation Association: 243–251.

Banting, Keith G. 1992. If Quebec Separates: Restructuring Northern North America. In R. K. Weaver, ed., *The Collapse of Canada?* Washington, D.C.: The Brookings Institution, 159–178.

Bardach, Eugene. 1982. *The Implementation Game*. New York: Harper.

Barney, G. O., P. H. Freeman, and C. A. Ulinski. 1981. *Global 2000: Implications for Canada*. Toronto: Pergamon Press.

Bartlett, Richard A. 1985. *Yellowstone: A Wilderness Besieged*. Tucson: University of Arizona Press.

Bates, Robert H., and Kenneth A. Shepsle. 1997. Intertemporal Institutions. In J. Nie and J. Drobak, eds., *The Frontiers of the New Institutional Economics*. New York: Academic Press, 197–211.

Bean, Clive. 1991. Are Australian Attitudes to Government Different? In F. G. Castles, ed., *Australia Compared*. Sydney: Allen & Unwin, 74–100.

Bean, Michael J. 1988. The Endangered Species Act: Protecting Living Resources of the Parks. In David J. Simon, ed., *Our Common Lands*. Washington, D.C.: National Parks and Conservation Association: 253–259.

Becker, A. F. 1979. The Resident in a National Park. In J. G. Nelson, ed., *The Canadian National Parks: Today and Tomorrow Conference II*. Waterloo, Ont.: University of Waterloo, 593–602.

Begin, Patricia. 1989. *Use of Canada's National Parks from Resource Protection to Tourism*. Ottawa: Library of Parliament.

Bella, Leslie. 1987. *Parks for Profit*. Montreal: Harvest House.

Bercuson, David J. 1990. The Failure of Executive Federalism. *Parliamentary Government*, Vol. 9, No. 2: 9–10.

Bercuson, David, J. L. Granatstein, and W. R. Young. 1986. *Sacred Trust?* Toronto, Ont.: Doubleday Canada Limited.

Berger, Suzanne. 1981. Introduction. In Berger, ed., *Organizing Interests in Western Europe*. Cambridge University Press, 1–23.

Bergman, Brian. 1986. National Parks Going Downhill? *Equinox*, No. 29: 115–116.

Blake, D. E., N. Guppy, and P. Urmetzer. 1997. Canadian Public Opinion and Environmental Action. *Canadian Journal of Political Science*, Vol. 30, No. 3: 451–472.

Boer, B. 1989. Natural Resources and the National Estate. *Environmental and Planning Law Journal*, Vol. 6, No. 2: 131–143.

Bohn, Glenn. 1985. Logging Urged in Pacific Rim National Park. *Vancouver Sun*, 24 August: A3.

Bohn, Glenn, and Tom Barrett. 1987. BC Tourist Industry Calls for National Park in Charlottes. *Vancouver Sun*, 19 June: B1.

Boix, Cales. 1997. Political Parties and the Supply Side of the Economy. *American Journal of Political Science*, Vol. 41, No. 3: 814–845.

Boncompagni, Tatiana S. 1997. Costa Rica: Beauty, Beasts—and Golf? *Wall Street Journal*, 15 August: B11.

Booth, J. A., and P. B. Richard. 1996. Regression, Participation, and Democratic Norms in Urban Central America. *American Journal of Political Science*, Vol. 40, No. 4: 1205–1232.

Boza, Mario. 1992. *Parques Nacionales*. San José, Costa Rica: Editorial Incafo.

Brooks, Lloyd. 1970. Planning a Canadian National Park System—Progress and Problems. In J. G. Nelson, ed., *Canadian Parks in Perspective*. Quebec: Harvest House, 313–320.

Brown, Bob. 1987. Greening the Conservation Movement. In D. Hutton, ed., *Green Politics in Australia*. North Ryde, NSW: Angus & Robertson, 35–48.

Brown, Bob. 1984. Wilderness versus Hydro-Electricity in South West Tasmania. In J. G. Mosley, ed., *Fighting for Wilderness*. Melbourne: Australian Conservation Foundation, 59–68.

Brown, Robert Craig. 1970. The Doctrine of Usefulness: Natural Resources and National Park Policy in Canada, 1887–1914. In J. G. Nelson, ed., *Canadian Parks in Perspective*. Quebec: Harvest House, 46–62.

Brue, Mike. 1989. National Park Plan Concerns Townsfolk. *Calgary Herald*, 23 December: F7.

Bryan, Rorke. 1973. *Much Is Taken, Much Remains*. North Scituate, Mass.: Duxbury Press.

Bryner, Gary. 1997. Balancing Preservation and Forestry. Unpublished manuscript.

Buchanan, James. 1968. *The Demand and Supply of Public Goods*. Chicago: Rand McNally.

Burford, Anne M. 1986. *Are You Tough Enough?* New York: McGraw-Hill.

Burnett, John. 1998. Once an Eco-Paradise, Costa Rican Parks Are Falling on Hard Times. *Ecocentral: Central American Economy & Sustainable Development*, Vol. 3, No. 1: 1–4.

Burton, T. L. 1979. The Promises and Problems of Coordination in Parks Development and Management. In J. G. Nelson, ed., *The Canadian National Parks: Today and Tomorrow Conference II*. Waterloo, Ont.: University of Waterloo, 313–327.

Cahn, Robert. 1982. *The Fight to Save Wild Alaska*. Washington, D.C.: National Audubon Society.

Cahn, Robert. 1983. The National Park System. *Sierra*, May/June: 46–56.

Cahn, Robert. 1993. Science and the National Parks. *Environment*, Vol. 35, No. 2: 25–27.

Cahn, Robert, and Patricia Cahn. 1987. Disputed Territory. *National Parks*, May/June: 28–33.

Cahn, Robert, and Patricia Cahn. 1992. Parallel Parks. *National Parks*, Vol. 60, No. 1–2: 24–29.

Cain, Bruce, and John Ferejohn. 1987. *The Personal Vote*. Cambridge: Harvard University Press.

Cairns, Robert D. 1992. Natural Resources and Canadian Federalism: Decentralization, Recurrent Conflict, and Resolution. *Publius*, Vol. 22, No. 1: 55–70.

Calvert, Randall, Matthew D. McCubbins, and Barry R. Weingast. 1989. A Theory of Political Control and Agency Discretion. *American Journal of Political Science*, Vol. 33: 588–611.

Camia, Catalina. 1994. Panel Approves Plan to Detail Expansion of Park System. *CQ Weekly Report*, 28 May: 1383.

Campbell, A., P. Converse, W. Miller, and D. Stokes. 1960. *The American Voter*. Chicago: University of Chicago Press.

Campbell, Colin. 1983. *Governments under Stress*. Toronto: University of Toronto Press.

Campbell, Colin. 1988. Mulroney's Broker Politics. In Andrew B. Gollner and Daniel Salee, eds., *Canada under Mulroney*. Downsview, Ont.: University of Toronto Press, 309–344.

Campbell, S. J. and John Halligan. 1992. *Political Leadership in an Age of Constraint*. Pittsburgh: University of Pittsburgh Press.

Canadian Assembly on National Parks. 1986. *Heritage for Tomorrow*. Ottawa: Environment Canada.

Canadian Environmental Advisory Council. 1991. *A Protected Areas Vision for Canada*. Ottawa: Minister of Supply and Services.

Canadian Heritage. 1995. *National Business Plan*. Ottawa: Dept. of Heritage.

Canadian Heritage. 1994. *Parks Canada Guiding Principles and Operational Policies*. Ottawa: Dept. of Heritage.

Canadian Heritage. 1995. *Parks Canada's Mandate for Change*. Ottawa: Dept. of Heritage.

Canadian Nature Federation. 1979. Concern for Environment Alive and Well. *Nature Canada*, Vol. 8, No. 3: 3.

Canadian Nature Federation. 1979. Major Changes in Parks Policy. *Nature Canada*, Vol. 8, No. 3: 21.

Canadian Nature Federation. 1991. National Parks Policy Review: Paralysis through Analysis. *Nature Canada*, Vol. 1, No. 1: 3.

Canadian Nature Federation. 1992. Oil Companies Relinquish Rights. *Nature Canada*, Vol. 2, No. 2: 1.

Canadian Nature Federation. 1980. Twinning the Trans-Canada Highway in Banff National Park. *Nature Canada*, Vol. 9, No. 2: 26.

Canadian Outdoor Recreation Research Committee. 1975. *The Economic Impact of Parks*. Toronto: Ontario Research Council on Leisure.

Canadian Outdoor Recreation Research Committee. 1976. *Park and Recreation Futures in Canada: Issues and Options*. Toronto: Ontario Research Council on Leisure.

Canadian Parks Service. 1992. *An Economic Statement and a Visit Profile of Atlantic Region*. Ottawa: Environment Canada.

Canadian Parks Service. 1988. *Banff National Park Management Plan*. Ottawa: Environment Canada.

Canadian Parks Service. 1990. *Final Report of the Parks and People Task Force.* Ottawa: Environment Canada.

Canadian Parks Service. 1988. *Jasper National Park Management Plan.* Ottawa: Environment Canada.

Canadian Parks Service. 1990. *National Parks System Plan.* Ottawa: Environment Canada.

Canadian Parks Service. 1989. *Private-Sector Construction in Banff, Jasper, and Waterton National Parks in Alberta.* Ottawa: Environment Canada.

Canadian Parks Service. 1992. *Proposed Policy.* Ottawa: Environment Canada.

Canadian Parks Service. 1991. *Revenue Profile.* Ottawa: Canadian Parks Service.

Canadian Parks Service. 1990. *State of the Parks.* Ottawa: Environment Canada.

Canadian Parks Service. 1990. *Strategic Plan.* Ottawa: Environment Canada.

Canadian Parks Service. 1988. *Yoho Management Plan.* Ottawa: Environment Canada.

Canadian Press. 1988. Churchill Residents Disagree over Plan for National Park. *Toronto Star,* 10 December: G7.

Canadian Press. 1989. Ontario Natives Vow to Stop Transfer of Land to National Park. *Montreal Gazette,* 17 April: A8.

Canadian Press. 1987. Ottawa, BC Make a Deal on National Park for South Moresby. *Montreal Gazette,* 7 July: B1.

Canadian Press. 1985. Parks Pass Fee Triples. *Winnipeg Free Press,* 18 May: 11.

Carey, John M. 1996. *Term Limits and Legislative Representation.* Cambridge University Press.

Carruthers, J. A. 1979. Planning a Canadian National Park and Related Reserve System. In J. G. Nelson, ed., *The Canadian National Parks: Today and Tomorrow Conference II.* Waterloo, Ont.: University of Waterloo, 645–670.

Caulfield, Henry P. 1989. The Conservation and Environmental Movements. In James P. Lester, ed., *Environmental Politics and Policy.* Durham: Duke University Press, 13–56.

Chase, Alston. 1987a. How to Save Our National Parks. *The Atlantic Monthly* (July): 35–44.

Chase, Alston. 1995. *In a Dark Wood.* Boston: Houghton Mifflin.

Chase, Alston. 1987b. *Playing God in Yellowstone.* San Diego: Harcourt Brace Jovanovich.

Chase, Alston. 1991. Unhappy Birthday. *Outside* (December): 33–40.

Cheever, Federico. 1997. The U.S. Forest Service and NPS: Paradoxical Mandates, Powerful Founders, and the Rise and Fall of Agency Discretion. *Denver University Law Review,* Vol. 74, No. 3: 625–648.

Chen, Ingfei. 1992. U.S. Park Plan for Presidio Moves Ahead. *San Francisco Chronicle,* 2 September: 7.

Christoff, Peter. 1994. The 1993 Australian Elections—A Fading Green Politics? *Environmental Politics,* Vol. 3, No. 1: 130–139.

Chubb, John E. 1985. Federalism and the Bias for Centralization. In Chubb and P. Peterson, eds., *The New Direction in American Politics.* Washington, D.C.: The Brookings Institution, 273–306.

Clarke, H. D., and A. Kornberg. 1993. Evaluations and Evolution: Public Attitudes toward Canada's Federal Political Parties, 1965–1991. *Canadian Journal of Political Science,* Vol. 26, No. 2: 287–311.

Clarke, Jeanne Nienaber, and Daniel McCool. 1996. *Staking Out the Terrain*, 2d ed. Albany, N.Y.: State University of New York Press.

Cochran, Clark E., Lawrence C. Mayer, T. R. Carr, and N. Joseph Cayer. 1990. *American Public Policy*. New York: St. Martin's Press.

Collins, Hugh N. 1991. Central Power in the Australian Commonwealth. In R. W. Baker, ed., *Australia, New Zealand, and the United States*. New York: Praeger, 73–87.

Conlan, Timothy. 1988. *New Federalism*. Washington, D.C.: The Brookings Institution.

Conservation Foundation, The. 1985. *National Parks for a New Generation*. Washington, D.C.: The Conservation Foundation.

Converse, Philip E. 1964. The Nature of Belief Systems in Mass Publics. In D. E. Apter, ed., *Ideology and Discontent*. New York: The Free Press, 206–261.

Cook, Earl. 1982. The Role of History in Acceptance of Nuclear Power. *Social Sciences Quarterly*, Vol. 63, No. 1: 3–15.

Coopers & Lybrand. 1995. A Review of the Governance Model of the Banff-Bow Valley. Calgary, AB. Prepared for the Banff-Bow Valley Study of 1996.

Council on Environmental Quality. 1970. *Environmental Quality*. Washington, D.C.: CEQ.

Coveney, Janet. 1993. *Australia's Conservation Reserves*. Cambridge: Cambridge University Press.

Craik, Wendy. 1993. The Great Barrier Reef Marine Park. In *What Makes a Successful Marine and Estuarine Protected Area?* Townsville: GBRMPA.

Culhane, Paul J. 1984. Sagebrush Rebels in Office: Jim Watt's Land and Water Politics. In Norman J. Vig and Michael E. Kraft, eds., *Environmental Policy in the 1980s*. Washington, D.C.: CQ Press, 293–317.

Culhane, Paul J. 1981. *Public Lands Politics*. Baltimore: Johns Hopkins University Press.

Cullen, Richard. 1990. The Encounter between Natural Resources and Federalism in Canada and Australia. *University of British Columbia Law Review*, Vol. 24, No. 2: 275–305.

Daly, Herman E. 1991. *Steady-State Economics*. Washington, D.C.: Island Press.

Davidson, A. T. 1979. Canada's National Parks: Past and Future. In J. G. Nelson, ed., *The Canadian National Parks: Today and Tomorrow Conference II*. Waterloo, Ont.: University of Waterloo, 23–37.

Davis, Bruce. 1989. Wilderness Conservation in Australia: Eight Governments in Search of a Policy. *Natural Resources Journal*, Vol. 29, No. 1: 103–113.

Davis, David Howard. 1993. *Energy Politics*, 4th ed. New York: St. Martin's Press.

Davis, Glyn. 1994. Executive Government. In A. Parkin, J. Summers, D. Woodward, eds., *Government, Politics, Power and Policy in Australia*, 5th ed. Melbourne: Longman Cheshire, 44–60.

Davis, G., J. Wanna, J. Warhurst, and P. Weller. 1993. *Public Policy in Australia*, 2nd ed. St. Leonards: Allen & Unwin.

Davis, Steven M., and John C. Ogden. 1994. Toward Ecosystem Restoration. In Davis and Ogden, eds., *Everglades: The Ecosystem and Its Restoration*. Delray Beach, Fla.: St. Lucie Press, 769–796.

Deford, Susan. 1988. Preservationists Hope to Protect Antietam from March of Development. *Washington Post,* 18 August: MD1.

De Jersey, Paul. 1985. The Inherent Jurisdiction of the Supreme Court. *Queensland Law Society Journal,* Vol. 15, No. 5: 325–332.

DePalma, A. 1997. Popularity Brings a Huge Canadian Park to Crisis. *New York Times,* 5 January: 5.

Department of the Environment. 1994. *Renomination of Uluru.* Canberra: Dept. of Environment.

Derthick, Martha. 1979. *Policymaking for Social Security.* Washington, D.C.: The Brookings Institution.

Derthick, Martha. 1970. *The Influence of Federal Grants.* Cambridge: Harvard University Press.

Deruiter, Darla, and Glenn Haas. 1995. National Public Opinion Survey on the National Park System. Washington, D.C.: NPCA.

Desimone, Bonnie. 1997. Tourism Plays Role in Saving Turtles. *Arizona Republic,* 25 May: T5.

Devoto, Bernard. 1953. Let's Close the National Parks. *Harper's Magazine* (October), Vol. 207: 49–52.

Dion, Stephane. 1995. The Dynamic of Secessions. *Canadian Journal of Political Science,* Vol. 28, No. 3: 533–557.

DiSilvestro, Roger L. 1993. *Reclaiming the Last Wild Places.* New York: John Wiley & Sons.

Doern, G. Bruce, and Richard W. Phidd. 1983. *Canadian Public Policy.* Toronto: Methuen.

Donovan, Richard. 1994. BOSCOSA. In D. Western and R. M. Wright, eds., *Natural Connections.* Washington, D.C.: Island Press, 215–233.

Douglas, Paul H. 1972. *In the Fullness of Time.* New York: Harcourt Brace Jovanovich.

Downs, Anthony. 1957. *An Economic Theory of Bureaucracy.* New York: HarperCollins.

Dunlap, Riley E., George H. Gallup, Jr., and Alec Gallup. 1992. Worldwide Environmental Poll. *Gallup Poll Monthly,* Vol. 320: 42–47.

Durant, Robert F. 1992. *The Administrative Presidency Revisited.* Albany: State University of New York Press.

Dye, Thomas R. 1966. *Politics, Economics, and the Public: Policy Outcomes in the American States.* Chicago: Rand McNally.

Edelman, Murray. 1988. *Constructing the Political Spectacle.* Chicago: University of Chicago Press.

Edelman, Murray. 1977. *Political Language: Words That Succeed and Policies That Fail.* New York: Academic Press.

Edelman, Murray. 1967. *The Symbolic Uses of Politics.* University of Illinois Press.

Edelson, Nathan. 1993. Parks without People. *Wall Street Journal,* 26 May: A18.

Editors of the *Calgary Herald.* 1984. Parks Battle Looms. *Calgary Herald,* 4 May: A4.

Editors of the *Washington Post.* 1987. Parks and Preservation. *Washington Post,* 21 August: A22.

Egan, Timothy. 1989. Land Sought as Buffer Around Parks. *New York Times,* 3 March: A14.

Eidsvik, Harold K., and William D. Henwood. 1990. Canada. In Craig W. Allin, ed., *International Handbook of National Parks and Nature Resources*. New York: Greenwood Press, 61–81.

Eisner, Marc A., and Kenneth J. Meier. 1990. Presidential Control versus Bureaucratic Power. *American Journal of Political Science* 34 (February): 269–287.

Emerson, Scott, and Georgina Windsor. 1997. Review Threatens Land-Share Deal. *The Australian*, 20 May: 1.

Enloe, Cynthia. 1975. *The Politics of Pollution in a Comparative Perspective*. New York: McKay.

Environment Canada. 1990. *Canada's Green Plan: Summary*. Ottawa: Environment Canada.

Environment Canada. 1987. *1986–87 Estimates*. Ottawa: Environment Canada.

Environment Canada. 1992. *1992–93 Estimates*. Ottawa: Environment Canada.

Environment Canada. 1988. *Legislation Governing the National Parks of Canada*. Ottawa: Environment Canada.

Erskine, Hazel. 1972. The Polls: Pollution and Industry. *Public Opinion Quarterly*, Vol. 36, No. 2: 263–280.

ESD Working Groups. 1991. *Final Report-Tourism*. Canberra: Australian Government Publishing Service.

Estes, Carol. 1995. Sea of Grass. *National Parks*, Vol. 69, No. 3: 38–44.

Everhart, William C. 1983. *The National Park Service*. Boulder, Colo.: Westview Press.

Farhling, Bruce. 1986. A Still-Wild Chunk of America Is Vulnerable to Development. *High Country News*, 31 March: 1.

Faulkner, Hugh. 1979. The Opening Address. In J. G. Nelson, ed., *The Canadian National Parks: Today and Tomorrow Conference II*. Waterloo, Ont.: University of Waterloo, 3–10.

Fenge, Terry. 1979. Policy Making for Northern National Parks. *Park News*, Vol. 15, No. 4: 9–14.

Fenno, Richard F., Jr. 1978. *Home Style: House Members in Their Districts*. Boston: Little, Brown and Company.

Ferejohn, John A., and Charles R. Shipan. 1989. Congressional Influence on Administrative Agencies: A Case Study of Telecommunications Policy. In Lawrence C. Dodd and Bruce I. Oppenheimer, eds., *Congress Reconsidered*, 4th ed. Washington, D.C.: CQ Press, 303–410.

Ferguson, Gary. 1996. *The Yellowstone Wolves*. Helena, Mont.: Falcon.

Figgis, Penelope, and Geoff Mosley. 1988. *Australia's Wilderness Heritage*. Willoughby, NSW: Kevin Weldon & Assoc.

Fiorina, Morris P. 1981. *Retrospective Voting*. New Haven: Yale University Press.

Fisher, Louis. 1991. Congress as Micromanager of the Executive Branch. In James P. Pfiffner, ed., *The Managerial Presidency*. Pacific Grove, Calif.: Brooks/Cole, 225–237.

Fleiner-Gerster, Thomas. 1992. Federalism in Australia and in Other Nations. In G. Craven, ed., *Australian Federation*. Melbourne: Melbourne University Press, 14–32.

Fletcher, Christine. 1992. Reform of Intergovernmental Relations in Australia. *Public Administration*, Vol. 70: 591–616.

Fordney, Chris. 1994. Embattled Ground. *National Parks*, Vol. 68, No. 11: 26–31.

Foresta, Ronald A. 1984. *America's National Parks and Their Keepers*. Washington, D.C.: Resources for the Future.

Foresta, Ronald A. 1985. National Parks for Northern Canada. Document prepared for Parks Canada.

Forstenzer, Martin. 1995. National Parks: Heritage in Decay. *Conde Nast Traveler*, May: 35–57.

Fossey, Dian. 1983. *Gorillas in the Mist*. Boston: Houghton Mifflin.

Franke, Joseph. 1993. *Costa Rica's National Parks and Reserves*. Seattle: The Mountaineers.

Franks, C. E. S. 1987. *The Parliament of Canada*. University of Toronto Press.

Freemuth, John. 1997. Ecosystem Management and Its Place in the National Park Service. *Denver University Law Review*, Vol. 74, No. 3: 697–727.

Freemuth, John. 1991. *Islands under Siege: National Parks and the Politics of External Threats*. Lawrence: University of Kansas Press.

Freemuth, John. 1989. The National Parks: Political versus Professional Determinants of Policy. *Public Administration Review*, 49 (3): 278–286.

Frome, Michael. 1992. *Regreening the National Parks*. Tucson: University of Arizona Press.

Frome, Michael. 1971. *The Forest Service*. New York: Praeger.

Frome, Michael, Roland H. Waver, and Paul C. Pritchard. 1990. United States: National Parks. In Craig W. Allin, ed., *International Handbook of National Parks and Nature Reserves*. New York: Greenwood Press, 415–430.

Fuller, W. A. 1970. National Parks and Nature Preservation. In J. G. Nelson, ed., *Canadian Parks in Perspective*. Quebec: Harvest House, 264–283.

Galbraith, Paul. 1989. An Evaluation of the Status of Aquatic Resource Management in Canadian National Parks. In D. C. Harvey, S. J. Woodley, and A. R. Haworth, eds., *Use and Management of Aquatic Resources in Canada's National Parks*. University of Waterloo: Heritage Resources Center, 39–52.

Gale, Fay, and Jame M. Jacobs. 1987. *Tourists and the National Estate*. Canberra: Australian Government Publishing Service.

Galligan, Brian. 1993a. Australian Federalism. In Ian Marsh, ed., *Governing in the 1990s*. Melbourne: Longman Cheshire, 288–312.

Galligan, Brian. 1993b. Federalism and Policy-Making. In A. Hede and S. Prasser, eds., *Policymaking in Volatile Times*. Sydney: Hale & Iremonger, 175–192.

Gallup Opinion Co. 1985–1997. *Gallup Report*.

Game, Kingsley W. 1979. Controlling Air Pollution. *Policy Studies Journal* 7 (Summer): 728–738.

Gardner, J. E., and J. G. Nelson. 1980. Comparing National Park and Related Reserve Policy in Hinterland Areas. *Environmental Conservation*, Vol. 7, No. 1: 43.

Gibbins, Roger. 1982. *Regionalism*. Toronto: Butterworths.

Glick, Daniel, and Andrew Murr. 1997. On the Brink. *Newsweek*, 23 June: 60–61.

Gottlieb, Alan M. 1989. *The Wise Use Agenda*. Bellevue, Wash.: The Free Enterprise Press.

Graves, John. 1974. Redwood National Park. *National Parks* 48 (October): 14–19.

Gray, Charlotte. 1992. Lobby Horse. *Saturday Night*, July/August: 20–25.

Great Barrier Reef Marine Park Authority. 1991. *Annual Report*. Townsville: GBRMPA.

Great Barrier Reef Marine Park Authority. 1993–94. *Annual Report.* Townsville: GBRMPA.

Great Barrier Reef Marine Park Authority. 1994. *Keeping It Great.* Townsville: GBRMPA.

Great Barrier Reef Marine Park Authority. 1981. *Nomination of the Great Barrier Reef.* Townsville: GBRMPA.

Greater Yellowstone Coalition. 1994. *Blueprint for the Future.* Bozeman, Mont.: GYC.

Green, Roger. 1981. *The Battle to Save the Franklin.* Melbourne: Fontana/ACF.

Gregory, R. G. 1991. How Much Are Australia's Economy and Economic Policy Influenced by the World Economy? In F. G. Castles, ed., *Australia Compared.* Sydney: Allen & Unwin, 103–123.

Greve, Frank. 1997. Park Perks Come with the Territory. *Chicago Tribune,* 26 November: A1.

Gruen, Fred, and Michelle Gratton. 1993. *Managing Government: Labor's Achievements and Failures.* Melbourne: Longman Cheshire.

Haigh, David J. 1995. Hinchinbrook—In Defence of World Heritage. Paper delivered at Defending the Environment Conference in Adelaide, 20 May.

Hall, Colin Michael. 1992. *Wasteland to World Heritage.* Melbourne: Melbourne University Press.

Hall, Colin M. 1989. The Worthless Lands Hypothesis. In K. J. Frawley and N. M. Semple, eds., *Australia's Ever Changing Forests.* Canberra: Australian Defence Force Academy.

Hall, Peter A. 1986. *Governing the Economy.* New York: Oxford University Press.

Halperin, Morton H. 1974. *Bureaucratic Politics and Foreign Policy.* Washington, D.C.: The Brookings Institution.

Hanson, Roger A. 1978. Toward an Understanding of Politics through Public Goods Theory. In W. Loehr and T. Sandler, eds., *Public Goods and Public Policy.* Beverly Hills: Sage, 67–95.

Harf, J. E., and B. T. Trout. 1986. *The Politics of Global Resources.* Durham: Duke University Press.

Harris, John F. 1991. In Shenandoah Park, an Outspoken Shepherd. *Washington Post,* 16 November: A1.

Harrison, J., K. Miller, and J. McNeely. 1984. The World Coverage of Protected Areas. In McNeely and Miller, eds., *National Parks, Conservation and Development.* Washington, D.C.: Smithsonian, 24–33.

Harrison, Kathryn, and George Hoberg. 1994. *Risk, Science, and Politics.* Montreal: McGill-Queen's University Press.

Harrison, Kathryn, and George Hoberg. 1991. Setting the Environmental Agenda in Canada and the United States: The Cases of Dioxin and Radon. *Canadian Journal of Political Science,* Vol. 24, No. 1: 3–27.

Harroy, Jean-Paul. 1974. A Century in the Growth of the National Park Concept throughout the World. In Hugh Elliott, ed., *Second World Conference on National Parks.* Switzerland: IUCN, 24–32.

Hartzog, George B., Jr. 1988. *Battling for the National Parks.* Mt. Kisco: Moyer Bell Limited.

Haslen, Benjamin. 1995. Greenie Wooing by Goss Irks Cattlemen. *Weekend Australian,* 15 July: P6.

Hawke, R. J. L. 1989. *Our Country, Our Future*. Canberra: Australian Government Publishing Service.

Hawkes, Suzanne, and Peter Williams. 1993. *The Greening of Tourism*. Simon Fraser University.

Hay, P. R. 1994. The Politics of Tasmania's World Heritage Area: Contesting the Democratic Subject. *Environmental Politics*, Vol. 3, No. 1: 1–21.

Head, Brian. 1986. Economic Development in State and Federal Politics. In Head, ed., *The Politics of Development in Australia*. Sydney: Allen & Unwin, 3–55.

Heclo, Hugh. 1977. *A Government of Strangers*. Washington, D.C.: The Brookings Institution.

Hefley, Joel. 1995. Do We Need All These Parks? *Washington Post*, 24 January: A17.

Heidenheimer, A. J., H. Heclo, and C. T. Adams. 1990. *Comparative Public Policy*, 3rd ed. New York: St. Martin's Press.

Heinz, J. P., E. O Laumann, R. L. Nelson, and R. H. Salisbury. 1993. *The Hollow Core*. Cambridge: Harvard University Press.

Herman, Dennis J. 1992. Loving Them to Death: Legal Controls on the Type and Scale of Development in the National Parks. *Stanford Environmental Law Journal*, Vol. 11: 3–67.

Heston, Alan, and Robert Summers. 1997. Penn World Tables. Unpublished data.

Hildebrandt, Walter. 1995. An Historical Analysis of Parks Canada and Banff National Park, 1968–1995. Unpublished manuscript for Banff-Bow Valley Study.

Hill, M. A., and A. J. Press. 1994. Kakadu National Park. In D. Western and R. M. Wright, eds., *Natural Connections*. Washington, D.C.: Island Press, 135–157.

Hill, Rosemary, and Mike Graham. 1984. Greater Daintree National Park. In J. G. Mosley, ed., *Fighting for Wilderness*. Melbourne: Australian Conservation Foundation, 7–22.

Hinds, Michael deCourcy. 1992. Much Steaming over 'Steamtown. *New York Times*, 8 February: 12.

Hoberg, George. 1993. Comparing Canadian Performance in Environmental Policy. In David Thomas, ed., *Canada and the United States: Differences That Count*. Ontario: Broadview, 101–126.

Hoberg, George. 1992. Governing the Commons: Environmental Policy in Canada and the United States. In Richard Simeon and Keith Banting, eds., *Canada and the United States in a Changing World*. Forthcoming.

Hodgins, Doug. 1996. Governance and Land Management. Banff, AB. Prepared for the Banff-Bow Valley Study.

Honchin, Darin. 1994. Providing for Reasonable Use. Unpublished manuscript.

Hopkins, Jack W. 1995. *Policymaking for Conservation in Latin America*. Westport, Conn.: Praeger.

Howlett, Michael. 1994. The Judicialization of Canadian Environmental Policy 1980–1990. *Canadian Journal of Political Science*, Vol. 27, No. 1: 99–127.

Howse, John. 1989. An Identity Crisis. *MacLean's*, 27 February: 48.

Huff, Don. 1985. Good News Comes out of Parks Conference. *Seasons*, Vol. 25, No. 4: 8.

Hughes, Robert. 1986. *The Fatal Shore*. New York: Vintage Books.

Hummel, Monte. 1985. Environmental and Conservation Movements. In James H. Marsh, ed., *The Canadian Encyclopedia*. Edmonton: Hurtig Publishers, 585–586.

Immergut, Ellen. 1992. *Health Politics*. New York: Cambridge University Press.

International Union for the Conservation of Nature. 1993. *Parks and Progress*. Switzerland: IUCN.

International Union for the Conservation of Nature. 1992. *Protected Areas of the World*. Switzerland: IUCN.

International Union for the Conservation of Nature. 1994. *United Nations List of National Parks*. Switzerland: IUCN.

International Union for the Conservation of Nature. 1971. *United Nations List of National Parks and Equivalent Reserves*. Brussels: Hayez.

Israelson, David. 1989. National Parks to Grow Four-Fold, Minister Vows. *Toronto Star*, 14 December: A2.

Israelson, David. 1987. New National Parks 2 Steps on Long Road. *Toronto Star*, 10 July: A22.

Ise, John. 1961. *Our National Parks Policy*. Baltimore: Johns Hopkins University Press.

Jagger, David. 1994. Shadowing the Minister. *Habitat*, Vol. 22, No. 4: 22–23.

Janda, Kenneth. 1980. *Political Parties: A Cross-National Survey*. New York: The Free Press.

Janzen, Daniel H. 1983. Searchers on That Rich Coast. In Janzen, ed., *Costa Rican Natural History*. University of Chicago, 1–11.

Johansson, T. B., H. Kelly, A. K. N. Reddy, and R. H. Williams. 1993. Renewable Fuels and Electricity for a Growing World Economy. In Johansson et al., eds., *Renewable Energy*. Washington, D.C.: Island Press, 1–71.

Johnson, Dick. 1972. *Lake Pedder: Why a National Park Must Be Saved*. Adelaide: The Griffin Press.

Johnstone, D. A. 1984. Future Directions for the Australian Realm. In J. A. McNeely and K. R. Miller, eds., *National Parks, Conservation, and Development*. Washington, D.C.: Smithsonian, 301–308.

Kanamine, Linda. 1995. Pet Projects Make the Cut. *USA Today*, 15 August: A3.

Katznelson, Ira. 1981. *City Trenches*. New York: Pantheon Books.

Keen, M., D. Mercer, and J. Woodfull. 1994. Approaches to Environmental Management at the Australian Local Government Level. *Environmental Politics*, Vol. 3, No. 1: 43–67.

Keiter, Robert B. 1988. Ecosystem Management. In R. G. Wright, ed., *National Parks and Protected Areas*. Cambridge: Blackwell, 63–88.

Keiter, Robert B. 1991. An Introduction to the Ecosystem Management Debate. In Keiter and Mark S. Boyce, eds., *The Greater Yellowstone Ecosystem*. New Haven: Yale University Press, 3–18.

Keiter, Robert B. 1988. National Park Protection: Putting the Organic Act to Work. In David J. Simon, ed., *Our Common Lands*. Washington, D.C.: National Parks and Conservation Association, 75–83.

Keiter, Robert B. 1997. Preserving Nature in the National Parks: Law, Policy, and Science in a Dynamic Environment. *Denver University Law Review*, Vol. 74, No. 3: 649–695.

Keiter, Robert B., and Mark S. Boyce. 1991. Greater Yellowstone's Future. In Keiter and Boyce, eds., *The Greater Yellowstone Ecosystem*. New Haven: Yale University Press, 379–413.

Kelleher, Graeme. 1987. Management of the Great Barrier Reef Marine Park. *Australian Parks and Recreation*, Vol. 23, No. 5: 27–33.

Kelleher, Graeme, and Richard Kenchington. 1984. Australia's Great Barrier Reef Marine Park. In J. McNeely and K. Miller, eds., *National Parks, Conservation and Development*. Washington, D.C.: Smithsonian, 267–273.

Kellow, Aynsley, and Jeremy Moon. 1993. Governing the Environment. In Ian Marsh, ed., *Governing in the 1990s*. Melbourne: Longman Cheshire, 226–255.

Kelly, Paul. 1992. *The End of Certainty*. St. Leonards, NSW: Allen & Unwin.

Kelly, Paul. 1983. Government to Reconsider Dam. *Sydney Morning Herald*, 1 October: 1.

Kelman, Steven. 1987. *Making Public Policy*. New York: Basic Books.

Kendell, Jeni, and Eddie Buivids. 1987. *Earth First*. Sydney: Australian Broadcasting Corporation.

Keohane, R. O., P. M. Haas, and M. A. Levy. 1993. The Effectiveness of International Environmental Institutions. In Haas, Keohane, and Levy, eds., *Institutions for the Earth*. Cambridge: MIT Press, 3–24.

Key, V. O. 1966. *The Responsible Electorate*. New York: Vantage.

Khademian, Anne. 1996. *Checking on Banks*. Washington, D.C.: The Brookings Institution.

Kihss, Peter. 1972. Mayor Accompanies McGovern in Queens. *New York Times*, 25 September: 42.

Kilgour, David. 1991. Ending Regional Favoritism. *Policy Options*, Vol. 12, No. 9: 3–7.

King, Thomas F. 1988. Park Planning, Historic Resources, and the National Historic Preservation Act. In David J. Simon, ed., *Our Common Lands*. Washington, D.C.: National Parks and Conservation Association, 275–291.

Kingdon, John W. 1984. *Agendas, Alternatives, and Public Policies*. New York: HarperCollins.

Kitschelt, Herbert P. 1986. Political Opportunity Structures and Political Protest. *British Journal of Political Science* 16: 57–85.

Kraft, Michael E., and Norman J. Vig. 1990. Environmental Policy from the Seventies to the Nineties: Continuity and Change. In Vig and Kraft, eds., *Environmental Policy in the 1990s*. Washington, D.C.: CQ Press, 3–31.

Krayna, Philip. 1995. Theme Park: Siloland. *Mother Jones*, Vol. 20, No. 2: 20.

Kriz, Margaret. 1995. Land Wars. *National Journal*, No. 35, 2 September: 2146–2151.

Kutay, Kurt. 1991. Cahuita National Park. In P. C. West and S. R. Brechin, eds., *Resident Peoples and National Parks*. Tucson: University of Arizona Press, 114–129.

Lake Pedder Committee of Enquiry. 1974. *The Flooding of Lake Pedder*. Canberra: Australian Government Publishing Service.

Lancaster, John. 1990a. Parks, Perks and Pork. *Washington Post*, 1 December: A1, A8.

Lancaster, John. 1990b. Payback Time for Parks' Poke at Perks. *Washington Post*, 20 November: A21.

LaSelva, Samuel V. 1993. Federalism as a Way of Life. *Canadian Journal of Political Science*, Vol. 26, No. 2: 219–234.

Lash, Jonathan. 1984. *A Season of Spoils*. New York: Pantheon Books.

Laurie, Nate. 1991. Sharing Canada's Power. *Toronto Star*, 22 September: B1.

Laycock, David. 1994. Reforming Canadian Democracy? *Canadian Journal of Political Science*, Vol. 27, No. 2: 213–247.

Layden, Paul, and Michael Manfredo. 1994. National Park Conditions. Washington, D.C.: NPCA.

Lea, John P. 1992. Tourism Impacts in a National Park. Paper delivered to Royal Australian Institute of Parks and Recreation Conference, Melbourne, 1991.

Leal, Donald. 1990. Saving an Ecosystem. In J. A. Baden and D. Leal, eds., *The Yellowstone Primer*. San Francisco: Pacific Research Institute, 25–45.

Leighton, Douglas. 1985. Banff Today: Struggling to Cope with Success. *Canadian Geographic*, Vol. 105, No. 1: 16–21.

Leithner, Christian. 1997. Of Time and Partisan Stability Revisited. *American Journal of Political Science*, Vol. 41, No. 4: 1104–1127.

Leman, Christopher K. 1987a. The Concepts of Public and Private and Their Applicability to North American Lands. In E. J. Feldman and M. A. Goldberg, eds., *Land Rites and Wrongs*. Cambridge, Mass.: Lincoln Institute of Land Policy, 23–37.

Leman, Christopher K. 1987b. A Forest of Institutions: Patterns of Choice on North American Timberlands. In E. J. Feldman and M. A. Goldberg, eds., *Land Rites and Wrongs*. Cambridge, Mass.: Lincoln Institute of Land Policy, 149–200.

Leopold, A. S. 1963. Wildlife Management in the National Parks. Report to Secretary of the Interior Udall, 4 March.

Lertzman, K., J. Rayner, and J. Wilson. 1996. Learning and Change in the British Columbia Forest Policy Sector. *Canadian Journal of Political Science*, Vol. 29, No. 1: 111–133.

Lewis, J. E. 1979. Federal-Provincial Relations. In J. G. Nelson, ed., *The Canadian National Parks: Today and Tomorrow Conference II*. Waterloo, Ont.: University of Waterloo, 69–72.

Lincoln Institute of Land Policy. 1995. Managing Land as Ecosystem and Economy. Lincoln Institute.

Lindblom, Charles E. 1959. The Science of Muddling Through. *Public Administration Review*, 19: 79–88.

Linn, Amy. 1995. Treaty in the Tallgrass. *Audubon*, Vol. 97, No. 2: 118–123.

Lipset, Seymour Martin. 1989. *Continental Divide*. Washington: Canadian-American Committee of C. D. Howe Institute and National Planning Association.

Loehr, William, and Todd Sandler. 1978. On the Public Character of Goods. In Loehr and Sandler, eds., *Public Goods and Public Policy*. Beverly Hills: Sage, 11–37.

Long, Michael. 1997. The Grand Managed Canyon. *National Geographic*, Vol. 192, No. 1: 116–135.

Lothian, W. F. 1987. *A Brief History of Canada's National Parks*. Ottawa, Ont.: Environment Canada.

Lovejoy, Thomas E. 1997. Lesson from a Small Country. *Washington Post*, 22 April: A19.

Lowey, Mark. 1987. 75m Urged for New National Parks. *Calgary Herald*, 1 June: A1, A2.

Lowey, Mark. 1985. National Park 'Jewels' Are Losing Their Shine. *Calgary Herald*, 13 July: A5.

Lowi, Theodore J. 1979. *The End of Liberalism*. 2nd ed. New York: Norton.

Lowry, William R. 1994. *The Capacity for Wonder*. Washington, D.C.: The Brookings Institution.

Lowry, William R. 1992. *The Dimensions of Federalism*. Durham, N.C.: Duke University Press.

Lowry, William R. 1997. Providing Intergenerational Goods. A paper delivered to the Midwest Political Science Meetings in Chicago, April.

Lowry, William R. 1996. State Parks Found to Be Sources of Innovation. *Public Administration Times*, (October). Vol. 19, No. 10: 1, 12–13.

Lubin, Martin. 1986. Public Policy, Canada and the U.S. *Policy Studies Journal*, Vol. 14, No. 4: 555–565.

Lucas, P. H. C. 1992. The State of World Parks. *National Parks*, Vol. 66, No. 1: 22–23.

Lumb, R. D. 1984. The Franklin Dam Decision and the External Affairs Power. *Queensland Law Journal*, Vol. 13, No. 2: 138–142.

Lundquist, Lennart. 1980. *The Hare and the Tortoise*. Ann Arbor: University of Michigan Press.

Lunney, Daniel, and Harry F. Recher. 1979. National Parks. In Recher, Lunney, and Dunn, eds., *A Natural Legacy: Ecology in Australia*. Rushcutter's Bay, NSW: Pergamon, 184–199.

Machlis, Gary E., and David L. Tichnell. 1985. *The State of the World's Parks*. Boulder, Colo.: Westview Press.

MacIvor, Heather. 1996. Do Canadian Political Parties Form a Cartel? *Canadian Journal of Political Science*, Vol. 29, No. 2: 317–333.

Mackintosh, Barry. 1984. *The National Parks: Shaping the System*. Washington, D.C.: Dept. of the Interior.

Madison, James. 1787. (1901). Vices of the Political System of the United States. In G. Hunt, ed., *The Writings of James Madison*. Vol. 2. New York: G. P. Putnam's Sons, 361–362.

Magraw, Daniel Barstow. 1988. International Law and Park Protection: A Global Responsibility. In David J. Simon, ed., *Our Common Lands*. Washington, D.C.: National Parks and Conservation Association: 143–173.

Mapes, Glynn. 1966. Severe Overcrowding Brings Ills of the City to Scenic Yosemite. *Wall Street Journal*, 24 June: 1.

Marchak, M. Patricia. 1995. *Logging the Globe*. Montreal: McGill University Press.

Marsh, John S. 1970. Maintaining the Wilderness Experience in Canada's National Parks. In J. G. Nelson, ed., *Canadian Parks in Perspective*. Quebec: Harvest House, 123–136.

Marsh, J. S. 1985. Parks, Provincial. *The Canadian Encyclopedia*. Edmonton: Hurtig Publishers, 1362–1363.

Masterman, Bruce. 1985. National Parks Wary of New Liquor Laws. *Calgary Herald,* 14 May: D1.

Martin, Glenn. 1994. High Hopes for Marin Ranch Deal. *San Francisco Chronicle,* 17 March: A19, A26.

Mathai, C. V. 1995. The Grand Canyon Visibility Transport Commission. *Environmental Manager,* Vol. 1: 20–31.

Matthews, Trevor. 1991. Interest Group Politics. In F. G. Castles, ed., *Australia Compared.* Sydney: Allen & Unwin, 191–218.

Mayhew, David R. 1974. *Congress: The Electoral Connection.* New Haven: Yale University Press.

Mazmanian, D. A., and J. Nienaber. 1979. *Can Organizations Change?* Washington, D.C.: Brookings Institution.

McAllister, Ian. 1994. Dimensions of Environmentalism. *Environmental Politics,* Vol. 3, No. 1: 22–42.

McCanahay, Mary Jo. 1993. Sweet Waist of America. *Sierra,* Vol. 78, No. 1: 42–49.

McCay, Bonnie J., and J. M. Acheson. 1987. Human Ecology of the Commons. In McCay and Acheson, eds., *The Question of the Commons.* Tucson: University of Arizona Press, 1–34.

McGillivray, Fiona. 1997. Party Discipline as a Determinant of the Endogenous Formation of Tariffs. *American Journal of Political Science,* Vol. 41, No. 2: 584–607.

McLaren, Christie. 1986. Creation of More National Parks Urged. *Globe and Mail,* 2 June: A10.

McManus, Reed. 1998. What Money Can Buy. *Sierra,* Vol. 83, No. 1: 35.

McMichael, D. F., and N. C. Gore. 1984. Keynote Address. In J. McNeely and K. Miller, eds., *National Parks, Conservation and Development.* Washington, D.C.: Smithsonian, 258–266.

McNamee, Kevin. 1992. Out of Bounds. *Nature Canada,* Vol. 21, No. 1: 34–41.

McPhee, John. 1971. Profiles: Ranger. *New Yorker,* 11 September: 45–89.

Meier, Kenneth J. 1985. *Regulation: Politics, Bureaucracy, and Economics.* New York: St. Martin's Press.

Mercer, David, and Jim Peterson. 1986. The Revocation of National Parks and Equivalent Reserves in Tasmania. *Search,* Vol. 17, No. 5: 134–140.

Miles, John C. 1995. *Guardians of the Parks.* Washington, D.C.: Taylor and Francis.

Milik, Michael. 1989. The Fine Print. *Far Eastern Economic Review,* Vol. 145: 32–33.

Minister of the Environment's Task Force on Park Establishment. 1987. *Our Parks—Vision for the 21st Century.* Ottawa: Environment Canada.

Mintzmayer, Lorraine. 1992. Disservice to the Parks. *National Parks,* Vol. 66, No. 11: 24–25.

Mitchell, Robert C. 1984. Public Opinion and Environmental Politics. In N. J. Vig and M. E. Kraft, eds. *Environmental Policy in the 1980s.* Washington, D.C.: CQ Press, 51–74.

Moe, Terry M. 1985. The Politicized Presidency. In John Chubb and Paul E. Peterson, eds., *The New Direction in American Politics.* Washington, D.C.: The Brookings Institution, 235–271.

Moe, Terry M. 1989. The Politics of Bureaucratic Structure. In John E. Chubb and Paul E. Peterson, eds., *Can the Government Govern?* Washington, D.C.: The Brookings Institution, 267–329.

Mondor, Claude. 1981. The National Park System: Filling in the Gaps. *Nature Canada*, Vol. 10, No. 2: 14–15.

Montgomery, Bruce. 1995. Voices in the Wilderness Finally Get Their Say on Pedder. *The Australian*, 22 February: 13.

Moore, David W. 1995. Public Sense of Urgency about Environment Wanes. *Gallup Poll Monthly*, October, 17–20.

Morris, John D. 1972. Nixon Approves Plan to Assure Product Safety. *New York Times*, 29 October: 1.

Mosley, J. G. 1990. Australia. In C. W. Allin, ed., *International Handbook of National Parks and Nature Preserves*. New York: Greenwood Press, 36–59.

Mosley, J. G. 1984a. Introduction. In Mosley, ed., *Fighting for Wilderness*. Melbourne: Australian Conservation Foundation, 1–3.

Mosley, J. G. 1984b. Protected Areas and Environmental Planning in Australia. In J. A. McNeely and K. R. Miller, eds., *National Parks, Conservation, and Development*. Washington, D.C.: Smithsonian, 274–282.

Munro, Margaret. 1987a. New National Park a Costly Triumph of Idealism. *Montreal Gazette*, 8 July: A1-A2.

Munro, Margaret. 1987b. National Parks: Greed Triumphs over Pride. *Montreal Gazette*, 22 June: A7.

Nash, Roderick. 1982. *Wilderness and the American Mind*. 3rd ed. New Haven: Yale University Press.

Nathan, Richard P. 1983. *The Administrative Presidency*. New York: Wiley.

National Academy of Sciences. 1963. *A Report by the Advisory Committee*. Washingon, D.C.: NAS.

National Parks and Conservation Association. 1995. Congress Takes Aim at National Parks. *National Parks*, Vol. 69, No. 5: 10–11.

National Parks and Conservation Association. 1995. Congress Weighs Parks, Contract, and LWCF. *National Parks*, Vol. 69, No. 3: 12–13.

National Parks and Conservation Association. 1995. *National Parks*, Vol. 69, No. 1: 47.

National Parks and Conservation Association. 1988. *Investing in Park Futures*. Washington, D.C.: NPCA.

National Parks and Conservation Association. 1979. NPCA Adjacent Lands Survey. *National Parks*, Vol. 53, No. 5: 4–9.

National Parks and Conservation Association. 1979. NPCA Interviews Philip Burton. *National Parks*, Vol. 53, No. 5: 22–26.

National Parks and Conservation Association. 1992. New Evidence Out in Yellowstone Probe. *National Parks*, Vol. 66, No. 9: 8–9.

National Parks and Conservation Association. 1994. 1995 Park Service Budget Approved. *National Parks*, Vol. 68, No. 11: 12.

National Parks and Conservation Association. 1991. NPCA News. *National Parks*, Vol. 65, No. 11: 8–16.

National Parks and Conservation Association. 1991. NPCA Opposes Land Swap at Santa Monica. *National Parks*, Vol. 65, No. 5: 13.

National Parks and Conservation Association. 1995. NPS Works to Protect Gettysburg Battlefield. *National Parks*, Vol. 69, No. 3: 14–15.

National Parks and Conservation Association. 1991. Relief in Sight for Grand Canyon. *National Parks*, Vol. 65, No. 11: 8–9.

National Parks and Conservation Association. 1995. Tallgrass Prairie Bill Introduced in Congress. *National Parks*, Vol. 69, No. 5: 11.

National Parks and Conservation Association. 1996. Transit Experts Come to Yosemite. *National Parks*, Vol. 70, No. 5: 23–24.

National Research Council. 1993. Protecting Visibility in National Parks Wilderness Areas. Washington, D.C.: NAS.

Nature Canada. 1981. Beginnings. *Nature Canada*, Vol. 10: 10–13.

Nelson, Barry, and Bruce Patterson. 1979. Park Responsibility Shifted. *Calgary Herald*, 7 June: A1.

Nelson, J. G. 1970a. Introduction. In Nelson, ed., *Canadian Parks in Perspective*. Quebec: Harvest House, 9–15.

Nelson, J. G. 1970b. Man and Landscape Change in Banff National Park: A National Park Problem in Perspective. In Nelson, ed., *Canadian Parks in Perspective*. Quebec: Harvest House, 63–96.

Nelson, J. G. 1979. Introduction. In Nelson, ed., *The Canadian National Parks: Today and Tomorrow Conference II*. Waterloo, Ont.: University of Waterloo, 15–21.

Nelson, Robert H. 1982. The Public Lands. In Paul R. Portney, ed., *Current Issues in Natural Resource Policy*. Washington, D.C.: Resources for the Future, 14–73.

Nemetz, Peter N., W. T. Stanbury, and Fred Thompson. 1986. Social Regulation in Canada: An Overview and Comparison with the American Model. *Policy Studies Journal*, Vol. 14, No. 4: 580–603.

Netting, Robert McC. 1997. Unequal Commoners and Ucommon Equity. *The Ecologist*, Vol. 27, No. 1: 28–33.

Neustadt, Richard. 1980. *Presidential Power*. New York: Wiley.

New South Wales National Parks and Wildlife Service. 1994. *Annual Report 1993–94*. Hurstville: NPWS.

Nicholson, E. Max. 1974. What Is Wrong with the National Park Movement? In Hugh Elliott, ed., *Second World Conference on National Parks*. Switzerland: IUCN, 32–37.

Nicol, J. I. 1970. The National Parks Movement in Canada. In J. G. Nelson, ed., *Canadian Parks in Perspective*. Quebec: Harvest House, 19–34.

Nikiforuk, Andrew. 1990. Islands of Extinction. *Equinox*, No. 52: 30–43.

Niskanen, William. 1971. *Bureaucracy and Representative Government*. Chicago: Aldine Atherton.

Nolte, Carl. 1995. Management Firm Sought for Presidio. *San Francisco Chronicle*, 12 February: A3.

Nolte, Carl. 1994. New Presidio Invites the Public to Sneak Preview. *San Francisco Chronicle*, 24 March: A17.

Nolte, Carl. 1990. Yosemite is 100 and Ailing. *San Francisco Chronicle*, 28 September: A1.

Norris, Ruth. 1992. Can Ecotourism Save Natural Areas? *National Parks*, Vol. 66, No. 1: 30–34.

North, Douglas C., and Barry R. Weingast. 1989. Constitutions and Commitment. *Journal of Economic History*, Vol. 49, No. 4: 803–832.

Noss, Reed F. 1996. Protected Areas: How Much Is Enough? In R. G. Wright, ed., *National Parks and Protected Areas*. Cambridge, Mass.: Blackwell, 91–120.

Oliphant, Mark. 1978. Opening Remarks. In G. Mosley, ed., *Australia's Wilderness*. Sydney: Australian Conservation Foundation, 11–13.

Olson, Mancur. 1965. *The Logic of Collective Action*. Cambridge: Harvard University Press.

O'Neill, Karen M. 1996. The International Politics of National Parks. *Human Ecology*, 24 (December): 521–539.

Ostrom, Elinor. 1990. *Governing the Commons*. Cambridge University Press.

Ostrom, Elinor, and Edella Schlager. 1996. The Formation of Property Rights. In S. Hanna, C. Folke, and K. Maler, eds., *Rights to Nature*. Washington, D.C.: Island Press, 127–156.

Ostrom, Elinor, Roy Gardner, and James Walker. 1994. *Rules, Games, and Common-Pool Resources*. Ann Arbor: University of Michigan Press.

Ostrom, Vincent, and Elinor Ostrom. 1977. Public Good and Public Choices. In G. S. Savas, ed., *Alternatives to Delivering Public Services*. Boulder, Colo.: Westview Press, 7–49.

Ovenden, Norm. 1992. Hornet's Nest Forces Parks Service to Change Its Plans. *Calgary Herald*, 12 February: A8.

Ovington, J. D. 1984. Ecological Processes and National Park Management. In J. McNeely and K. Miller, eds., *National Parks, Conservation and Development*. Washington, D.C.: Smithsonian, 60–64.

Ovington, J. D. 1969. Management Problems of National Parks. In L. J. Webb, D. Whitelock, and J. Le Gay Brereton, eds., *The Last of Lands*. Milton, Queensland: Jacaranda, 36–42.

Ovington, J. D. 1980. A National Perspective. In J. Messer and G. Mosley, eds., *The Value of National Parks to the Community*. Sydney: Australian Conservation Foundation, 45–56.

Papadikis, Elim. 1991. Does the New Politics Have a Future? In J. G. Mosley, ed., *Australia Compared*. Sydney: Allen & Unwin, 239–257.

Papadikis, Elim. 1990. Environmental Policy. In C. Jennett and R. G. Stewart, eds., *Hawke and Australian Public Policy*. Melbourne: Macmillan, 339–355.

Papadikis, Elim. 1994. Environmental Policy. In A. Parkin, J. Summers, and D. Woodward, eds., *Government, Politics, Power and Policy in Australia*. 5th ed. Melbourne: Longman Cheshire, 385–397.

Papadikis, Elim. 1993. *Politics and the Environment: The Australian Experience*. Sydney: Allen & Unwin.

Parent, C. R., and F. E. Robeson. 1976. An Economic Analysis of the River-Running Industry. Washington, D.C.: NPS.

Parkin, A., J. Summers. 1994. The Constitutional Framework. In Parkin, Summers, and D. Woodward, eds., *Government, Politics, Power and Policy in Australia*. 5th ed. Melbourne: Longman Cheshire, 5–25.

Parks Canada. 1996. *Banff-Bow Valley: At the Crossroads Executive Summary*. Ottawa: Parks Canada.

Parks Canada. 1996. *Banff-Bow Valley: At the Crossroads Technical Summary*. Ottawa: Parks Canada.

Parks Canada. 1985. *Parks*. Ottawa: Environment Canada.

Parks Canada. 1979. *Parks Canada Policy*. Ottawa: PC.

Parks Canada. 1995. *Prince Albert National Park Management Plan*. Ottawa: PC.

Parson, Edward A. 1993. Protecting the Ozone Layer. In P. M. Hass, R. O. Keohane, and M. A. Levy, eds., *Institutions for the Earth*. MIT Press, 27–73.

Patterson, Bruce. 1979. Rents in National Parks May Soar. *Calgary Herald*, 27 June: A1.

Peters, B. Guy. 1988. *Comparing Public Bureaucracies*. Tuscaloosa: University of Alabama Press.

Pfiffner, James P. 1987. Political Appointees and Career Executives: The Democracy-Bureaucracy Nexus. *Public Administration Review*, Vol. 47, No. 1: 57–65.

Pfiffner, James P. 1990. Presidential Control of the Bureaucracy. In Frederick S. Lane, ed., *Current Issues in Public Administration*. New York: St. Martin's Press, 84–105.

Philip, Tom. 1991. The Sky's the Limit. *San Jose Mercury News*, 11 November: 1A.

Pigou, Arthur C. 1920. *The Economics of Welfare*. 4th ed., 1962. London: Macmillan.

Postel, Sandra. 1993. Facing Water Scarcity. In L. R. Brown, ed., *State of the World 1993*. New York: Norton, 22–41.

Power, Thomas Michael. 1997. Ideology, Wishful Thinking, and Pragmatic Reform. In J. A. Baden and D. Snow, eds., *The Next West*. Washington, D.C.: Island Press, 233–254.

Praxis, Inc. 1996. Banff Householder Survey. Report submitted to Planning and Building Dept., Town of Banff.

Pressman, J. L., and A. Wildavsky. 1984. *Implementation*. 3rd ed. Berkeley: University of California Press.

Price, Clive. 1978. Role of National Parks and Wildlife Authorities in Queensland. In J. G. Mosley, ed., *Australia's Wilderness*. Melbourne: ACF, 234–243.

Princen, Thomas. 1994. The Ivory Trade Ban. In Princen and M. Finger, *Environmental NGOs in World Politics*. New York: Routledge, 121–159.

Princen, Thomas, and Matthias Finger. 1994. Introduction. In Princen and Finger, *Environmental NGOs in World Politics*. New York: Routledge, 1–25.

Pritchard, Paul. 1995. 260. *National Parks*, Vol. 69, No. 3: 4.

Pross, Paul. 1985. Parliamentary Influence and the Diffusion of Power. *Canadian Journal of Political Science*, Vol. 18, No. 2: 235–266.

Purser, Richard. 1982. Proposal to Close National Parks Highway Is Dropped. *Calgary Herald*, 12 October: D7.

Queensland Department of Environment and Heritage. 1990. *Annual Report 1989–90*. Brisbane: DOE.

Queensland Department of Environment and Heritage. 1993. *Annual Report 1992–93*. Brisbane: DOE.

Queensland Department of Environment and Heritage. 1994. *Annual Report 1993–94*. Brisbane: DOE.

Queensland National Parks and Wilderness Society. 1994. *Great Sandy Region Management Plan*. Brisbane: NPWS.

Rabe, Barry G. 1994. *Beyond NIMBY*. Washington, D.C.: The Brookings Institution.

Rachowiecki, Rob. 1991. *Costa Rica*. Berkeley, Calif.: Lonely Planet.

Rainforest Conservation Society of Queensland. 1986. *Tropical Rainforests of North Queensland*. Canberra: Australian Government Publishing Service.

Rauber, Paul. 1992. The August Coup. *Sierra*, Vol. 77, No. 1: 26–28.

Reagan, Ronald. 1982. The State of the Union. In L. J. O'Toole, Jr., ed. *American Intergovernmental Relations*. 2nd ed. Washington, D.C.: CQ Press, 343–345.

Rees, Jacqueline. 1991. Saving a Wasteful System. *Far Eastern Economic Review*, Vol. 154: 12–13.

Reid, R. A. 1979. The Role of National Parks in Nature Preservation. In J. G. Nelson, ed., *The Canadian National Parks: Today and Tomorrow Conference II*. Waterloo, Ont.: University of Waterloo, 105–113.

Reid, T. R. 1987. Great Basin Park a First for Reagan. *Washington Post*, 15 August: A1, A11.

Reid, T. R. 1989. Passive Policy on Natural Forest Fires Reaffirmed. *Washington Post*, 2 June: A3.

Rettie, Dwight. 1995. Parks Compromised. *National Parks*, Vol. 69, No. 3: 56–57.

Reuters News Service. 1966. 1972 Olympics Go to Munich and Winter Games to Sapporo in Japan. *New York Times*, 27 April: 54.

Ridenour, James. 1994. *The National Parks Compromised*. Merrillville, Ind.: ICS Books.

Ringquist, Evan J. 1995. Political Control and Policy Impact in EPA's Office of Water Quality. *American Journal of Political Science* 39 (May): 336–363.

Ripley, R. B., and G. A. Franklin. 1976. *Congress, the Bureaucracy, and Public Policy*. Homewood, Ill.: Dorsey Press.

Risser, Paul G., and Kathy D. Cornelison. 1979. *Man and the Biosphere*. Norman: University of Oklahoma Press.

Roddewig, Richard J. 1978. *Green Bans*. Sydney: Hale & Iremonger.

Rogoff, Kenneth. 1985. The Optimal Degree of Commitment to an Intermediate Monetary Target. *Quarterly Journal of Economics*, 100 (November): 1169–1190.

Rolbein, Seth. 1989. *Nobel Costa Rica*. New York: St. Martin's Press.

Roosevelt, Theodore. 1908. Publicizing Conservation at the White House. In R. F. Nash, ed., *American Environmentalism*. 3rd ed. 1990. New York: McGraw-Hill, 84–89.

Rosenbaum, Walter A. 1995. *Environmental Politics and Policy*. 3rd ed. Washington, D.C.: CQ Press.

Rothenberg, Lawrence. 1988. Organizational Maintenance and the Retention Decision in Groups. *American Political Science Review*, 82: 1129–1152.

Rourke, Francis E. 1984. *Bureaucracy, Politics, and Public Policy*. 3rd ed. Boston: Little, Brown and Company.

Rourke, Francis. 1991. Presidentializing the Bureaucracy: From Kennedy to Reagan. In James P. Pfiffner, ed., *The Managerial Presidency*. Pacific Grove, Calif.: Brooks/Cole, 123–134.

Rovinski, Yanina. 1991. Private Reserves, Parks, and Ecotourism in Costa Rica. In T. Whelan, ed., *Nature Tourism*. Washington, D.C.: Island Press, 39–57.

Runte, Alfred. 1979. *National Parks: The American Experience*. Lincoln, Nebr.: University of Nebraska Press.

Runte, Alfred. 1987. *National Parks: The American Experience*. 2nd ed. Lincoln, Nebr.: University of Nebraska Press.

Runte, Alfred. 1990. *Yosemite: The Embattled Wilderness*. Lincoln, Nebr.: University of Nebraska Press.

Russakoff, Dale, and Felicity Barringer. 1982. Budget Office Proposes National Parks Closings. *Chicago Sun-Times,* 9 December: 64.

Russell, Rupert. 1985. *Daintree.* McMahan's Point, NSW: Weldon.

Ruys, P. H. M. 1974. *Public Goods and Decentralization.* Netherlands: Tilburg University Press.

Ryan, Patricia. 1981. Environmental Court System. *University of New South Wales Law Journal,* Vol. 4: 11–28.

Sabatier, Paul, and Hank Jenkins-Smith, eds. 1993. *Policy Change and Learning: An Advocacy Coalition Approach.* Boulder, Colo.: Westview.

Sabatier, Paul, John Loomis, and Catherine McCarthy. 1995. Heirarchical Controls, Professional Norms, Local Constituencies, and Budget Maximization. *American Journal of Political Science,* 39 (February): 204–242.

Sagoff, Mark. 1997. Saving the Marketplace from the Market. In J. A. Baden and D. Snow, eds., *The Next West.* Washington, D.C.: Island Press, 131–149.

Samuelson, Paul. 1954. The Pure Theory of Public Expenditure. *Review of Economics and Statistics,* 36: 387–389.

Saunders, Cheryl. 1985. Australia's Federal System and the Division of Power. In P. Drysdale and H. Shibata, eds., *Federalism and Resource Development.* Sydney: Allen & Unwin, 25–32.

Saunders, Rob. 1992. Voices in the Wilderness. *Australian Parks & Recreation,* Vol. 28, No. 1: 16–19.

Sax, Joseph L. 1980. *Mountains without Handrails: Reflections on the National Parks.* Ann Arbor: University of Michigan Press.

Sax, Joseph L., and Robert B. Keiter. 1988. Glacier National Park and Its Neighbors: A Study of Federal Inter-Agency Cooperation. In David J. Simon, ed., *Our Common Lands.* Washington, D.C.: National Parks and Conservation Association, 175–241.

Scace, R. C. 1968. *Banff: A Cultural Historical Study of Land Use and Management in a National Park Community to 1945.* University of Calgary: Studies in Land Use History.

Schattschneider, E. E. 1960. *The Semisovereign People.* New York: Holt, Rinehart and Winston.

Schlesinger, A. M. 1965. *A Thousand Days.* Boston: Houghton Mifflin.

Schmanske, Stephen. 1991. *Public Goods, Mixed Goods, and Monopolistic Competition.* College Station: Texas A&M Press.

Schneider, Howard. 1997. Economy, Ecology Lock Horns. *Washington Post,* 27 October: A1.

Schwartz, Mildred A. 1986. Comparing United States and Canadian Public Policy: A Review of Strategies. *Policy Studies Journal,* Vol. 14, No. 4: 566–579.

Seale, Ronald G. 1979. It's Time to Realize National Parks Can't Be All Things to All People. *Calgary Herald,* 3 July: A7.

Sears, Val. 1992. Interest Groups the New Power in Ottawa. *Toronto Star,* 28 April: A17.

Sellars, Richard West. 1997. *Preserving Nature in the National Parks: A History.* New Haven: Yale University Press.

Sewell, W. R. D., P. Dearden, and J. Dumbrell. 1989. Wilderness Decisionmaking and the Role of Environmental Interest Groups. *Natural Resources Journal,* Vol. 19, No. 1: 147–169.

Shands, William E. 1979. *Federal Resource Lands and Their Neighbors*. Washington, D.C.: The Conservation Foundation.

Shankland, Robert. 1970. *Steve Mather of the National Parks*. 3rd ed. New York: Alfred A. Knopf.

Shanks, Bernard. 1984. *This Land Is Your Land*. San Francisco: Sierra Club Books.

Shelby, Bo, and Joyce M. Nielsen. 1976. Motors and Oars in the Grand Canyon. Washington, D.C.: NPS.

Sigurdson, Richard. 1994. Preston Manning and the Politics of Postmodernism in Canada. *Canadian Journal of Political Science*, Vol. 27, No. 2: 249–276.

Sinclair, John. 1994. *Fighting for Fraser Island*. Sydney: Kerr.

Sinclair, John. 1990. *Fraser Island and Coloola*. Sydney: Weldon.

Slatyer, R. O. 1989. The World Heritage Convention. *Heritage Australia*, Vol. 8, No. 1: 3–7.

Smith, Adam. 1776. *The Wealth of Nations, Vol. 2*. 1960 edition. London: Dent.

Smith, B. C. 1985. *Decentralization*. London: Allen & Unwin.

Smith, Claire. 1993. Writing Happy Ending for Four Storied Parks. *New York Times*, 18 July: 8.

Smith, James N. 1972. The Gateways: Parks for Whom? In *National Parks for the Future*. Washington, D.C.: The Conservation Foundation: 213–236.

Smith, Steven S. 1985. New Patterns of Decisionmaking in Congress. In J. Chubb and P. Peterson, eds. *The New Direction in American Politics*. Washington, D.C.: The Brookings Institution, 203–234.

Sobel, Andrew. 1994. *Domestic Choices, International Markets*. Ann Arbor: University of Michigan Press.

Solomon, David. 1994. The High Court. In A. Parkin, J. Summers, and D. Woodward, eds., *Government, Politics, Power and Policy in Australia*. 5th ed. Melbourne: Longman Cheshire, 105–118.

Solow, Robert M. 1993. Sustainability: An Economist's Perspective. In Robert and Nancy Dorfman, eds., *Economics of the Environment*. 3rd ed. New York: Norton, 179–187.

Spolar, Christine. 1993. Designs of Park Service, Pentagon Differ on Converting the Presidio. *Washington Post*, 28 December: A3.

Sproull, Richard. 1997. Native Title Allows ALCAN Bauxite Project. *The Australian*, 6 August: 1.

Stankey, G. H. 1980. Some Observations on the Future of Wilderness. In R. W. Robertson et al., eds., *Wilderness Management in Australia*. Canberra: Canberra College.

Stephenson, Marylee. 1983. *Canada's National Parks*. Englewood Cliffs, N.J.: Prentice-Hall, Inc.

Stevens, William K. 1997. A Dam Open, Grand Canyon Roars Again. *New York Times*, 25 February: B7.

Stimson, J. A., M. B. MacKuen, and R. S. Erikson. 1995. Dynamic Representation. *American Political Science Review*, 89: 543–565.

Strider. 1984. Kakadu in Context. In J. G. Mosley, ed., *Fighting for Wilderness*. Melbourne: Australian Conservation Foundation, 96–106.

Stroup, Richard L. 1990. Rescuing Yellowstone from Politics: Expanding Parks while Reducing Conflict. In John A. Baden and Donald Leal, eds., *The Yellowstone Primer*. San Francisco: Pacific Research Institute: 169–184.

Sullivan, J. L., J. E. Piereson, and G. E. Marcus. 1978. Ideological Constraint in the Mass Public. *American Journal of Political Science*, 22 (May): 233–249.

Summers, John. 1994. Federalism and Commonwealth-State Relations. In A. Parkin, J. Summers, and D. Woodward, eds., *Government, Politics, Power and Policy in Australia*. 5th ed. Melbourne: Longman Cheshire, 80–104.

Sundquist, James L. 1981. *The Decline and Resurgence of Congress*. Washington, D.C.: The Brookings Institution.

Suter, K. D. 1991. The UNESCO World Heritage Convention. *Environmental and Planning Law Journal*, Vol. 8, No. 1: 4–15.

Sutherland, Sharon L., and G. Bruce Doern. 1985. *Bureaucracy in Canada: Control and Reform*. Toronto: University of Toronto Press.

Swem, Theodore R. 1970. Planning of National Parks in the United States. In J. G. Nelson, ed., *Canadian Parks in Perspective*. Quebec: Harvest House, 249–263.

Tartter, Jean R. 1983. Government and Politics. In Harold D. Nelson, ed., *Costa Rica*. Washington, D.C.: American University, 183–239.

Taylor, C. J. 1990. *Negotiating the Past*. Montreal: McGill-Queen's University Press.

Taylor, Leslie A. 1996. Development Decisions in Banff National Park. Paper for Banff-Bow Valley Study.

Tellier, Paul M. 1990. Public Service 2000: The Renewal of the Public Service. *Canadian Public Administration*, Vol. 33, No. 2: 123–132.

Theberge, J. B. 1979. The Role of Ecology in National Parks. In J. G. Nelson, ed., *The Canadian National Parks: Today and Tomorrow Conference II*. Waterloo, Ont.: University of Waterloo, 673–684.

Theberge, John B. 1976. Ecological Planning in National Parks. In G. R. McBoyle and E. Sommerville, eds., *Canada's Natural Environment*. Toronto: Methuen Publications, 194–216.

Thompson, D. N., A. J. Rogers, and F. Y. Borden. 1974. Sound-Level Evaluations of Motor Noise. Washington, D.C.: NPS.

Thompson, Peter. 1984. *Bob Brown of the Franklin River*. Sydney: Allen & Unwin.

Thoreau, Henry David. 1851. The Value of Wildness. In R. F. Nash, ed., *American Environmentalism*. 1990. 3rd ed. New York: McGraw-Hill, 36–39.

Thrup, Lori Ann. 1990. Costa Rica's Resource Challenges. *Hemisphere* 2: 20.

Toyne, Philip. 1994. *The Reluctant Nation*. Sydney: Australian Broadcasting Corporation.

Trinder, Colin, and Stephen Sparkes. 1995. Port Hinchinbrook and Beyond. Paper delivered at the Defending the Environment Conference, Adelaide, 21 May.

Tyson, Ann Scott. 1994. Prairie Preservation Moves Ahead. *Christian Science Monitor*, 4 November: 1.

Uhr, John. 1994. Parliament. In A. Parkin, J. Summers, and D. Woodward, eds., *Government, Politics, Power and Policy in Australia*. Melbourne: Longman Cheshire, 26–43.

Ulph, A. M., and I. K. Reynolds. 1981. *An Economic Evaluation of National Parks*. Canberra: Australian National University.

United Nations Educational Scientific and Cultural Organization. 1982. *A Legacy for All*. Paris: UNESCO.

U.S. Congress, Conference Report on Appropriations. 1986. 99th Congress, 2nd Session. *Making Appropriations for the Department of the Interior and Related Agencies*. Washington, D.C.: GPO.

U.S. Congress, House Committee on Appropriations. 1983, 1984, 1985, 1986, 1987, 1988. *Department of the Interior and Related Agencies Appropriations Bill*. Washington, D.C.: GPO.

U.S. Congress, House Committee on Interior and Insular Affairs. 1985. *Greater Yellowstone Ecosystem*. 99th Congress, 1st Session. Washington, D.C.: GPO.

U.S. Congress, House Committee on Interior and Insular Affairs. 1988. *Establishing a National Park System Review Board, and For Other Purposes*. 100th Congress, 2nd Session. Washington, D.C.: GPO.

U.S. Congress, House Subcommittee on National Parks, Forests, and Lands Hearings. 1995. *National Park System Reform Act*. Washington, D.C.: GPO.

U.S. Congress, Senate Subcommittee on National Parks, 1971, *Hearings on S. 27, A Bill to Establish Glen Canyon National Recreation Area*, 92nd Congress, 2nd Session. Washington, D.C.

U.S. Congress, Senate Subcommittee on Public Lands, National Parks, and Forests Hearings. 1990. *Concessions Policy of the National Park Service*. 101st Congress, 2nd Session. Washington, D.C.: GPO.

U.S. Department of the Interior. 1983. *Land and Water Conservation Fund Grants Manual*. Washington, D.C.: DOI.

U.S. General Accounting Office. 1994. *Activities Outside Park Borders Have Caused Damage to Resources and Will Likely Cause More*. Washington, D.C.: GAO.

U.S. General Accounting Office. 1996. *An Assessment of the Environmental Impact Statement on the Operations of the Glen Canyon Dam*. Washington, D.C.: GAO.

U.S. General Accounting Office. 1995. *Information on the Condition of Civil War Momuments at Selected Sites*. Washington, D.C.: GAO.

U.S. General Accounting Office. 1987. *Limited Progress Made in Documenting and Mitigating Threats to the Parks*. Washington, D.C.: GAO.

U.S. General Accounting Office. 1992. *Many Issues Unresolved in Yellowstone Bison-Cattle Brucellosis Conflict*. Washington, D.C.: GAO.

U.S. General Accounting Office. 1991. *Recreation Concessionaires Operating on Federal Lands*. Washington, D.C.: GAO.

U.S. General Accounting Office. 1993. *Scope and Cost of America's Industrial Heritage Project Need to Be Defined*. Washington, D.C.: GAO.

U.S. General Accounting Office. 1997. *Similarities and Differences in the Management of Selected State and Federal Land Units*. Washington, D.C.: GAO.

U.S. General Accounting Office. 1991. *Status of Development at the Steamtown National Historic Site*. Washington, D.C.: GAO.

U.S. General Accounting Office. 1993. *Transfer of the Presidio from the Army to the NPS*. Washington, D.C.: GAO.

U.S. National Park Service. 1979. *Colorado River Management Plan*. Washington, D.C.: DOI.

U.S. National Park Service. 1989. *Colorado River Management Plan*. Washington, D.C.: DOI.

U.S. National Park Servcie. 1991. *Criteria for Parklands*. Washington, D.C.: NPS.

U.S. National Park Service. 1979. *Final Environmental Statement of Proposed Colorado River Management Plan*. Washington, D.C.: DOI.

U.S. National Park Service. 1977. *Grand Canyon Addendum to Natural Resources Management Plan*. Washington, D.C.: DOI.

U.S. National Park Service. 1988. *Grand Canyon Backcountry Management Plan*. Washington, D.C.: DOI.

U.S. National Park Service. 1976. *Grand Canyon Final Master Plan*. Washington, D.C.: DOI.

U.S. National Park Service. 1995. *Grand Canyon General Management Plan*. Washington, D.C.: DOI.

U.S. National Park Service. 1977. *Grand Canyon Natural Resources Management Plan and Environmental Assessment*. Washington, D.C.: DOI.

U.S. National Park Service. 1976. *Guadalupe Mountains National Park Master Plan*. Washington, D.C.: NPS.

U.S. National Park Service. 1972. *National Park System Plan*. Washington, D.C.: NPS.

U.S. National Park Service. 1992. *National Parks for the 21st Century*. Washington, D.C.: NPS.

U.S. National Park Service. 1994. Report on Effects of Aircraft Overflights on the National Park System. Report prepared pursuant to P.L 100–91.

U.S. National Park Service. 1994. *Restructuring Plan for the NPS*. Washington, D.C.: NPS.

U.S. National Park Service. 1991. Scoping Brochure for Relocation of Fishing Bridge Campsites. Washington, D.C.: NPS.

U.S. National Park Service. 1980. *State of the Parks 1980*. Washington, D.C.: NPS.

U.S. National Park Service. Various years. *Statistical Abstract*. Washington, D.C.: NPS.

U.S. National Park Service. 1996. *Strategic Plan: Final Draft*. Washington, D.C.: NPS.

U.S. National Park Service. 1988. *Yellowstone Fishing Bridge Environmental Impact Statement*. Washington, D.C.: DOI.

U.S. National Park Service. 1974. *Yellowstone Master Plan*. Washington, D.C.: DOI.

U.S. National Park Service. 1991. *Yellowstone Statement of Management*. Washington, D.C.: DOI.

U.S. National Park Service. 1992. *Yellowstone Wildland Fire Management Plan*. Washington, D.C.: DOI.

U.S. National Park Service. 1994. *Yosemite Alternative Transportation Modes*. Washington, D.C.: DOI.

U.S. National Park Service. 1980. *Yosemite General Management Plan*. Washington, D.C.: DOI.

U.S. National Park Service. 1996. *Yosemite Guide* (summer). Washington, D.C.: NPS.

U.S. National Park Service. 1987. *Yosemite Valley/El Portal Comprehensive Design*. Washington, D.C.: DOI.

Val, Erik. 1987. Socioeconomic Impact Assessment, Regional Integration, Public Participation, and New National Park Planning in Canada. In M. L. Miller,

R. P. Gale, and P. J. Brown, eds., *Social Science in Natural Resource Management Systems*. Boulder, Colo.: Westview Press, 129–148.

Vaske, Jerry, and Glenn Haas. 1996. American Views on National Park Issues. Washington, D.C.: NPCA.

Vaughan, Christopher, and Carlos Manuel Rodriguez. 1997. Managing beyond the Borders: The Costa Rican National System of Conservation Areas (SINAC). Unpublished paper.

Victoria Department of Conservation. 1994. *Annual Report on the National Parks Act*. Melbourne: DOC.

Victoria Department of Conservation. 1994. *Annual Report 1993–94*. Melbourne: DOC.

Victoria Land Conservation Council. 1994. *Annual Report 1993–94*. Melbourne: LCC.

Vig, Norman J. 1990. Presidential Leadership: From the Reagan to the Bush Administration. In Vig and Michael E. Kraft, eds., *Environmental Policy in the 1990s*. Washington, D.C.: CQ Press, 33–58.

Vogel, David. 1990. Environmental Policy in Europe and Japan. In N. J. Vig and M. E. Kraft, eds., *Environmental Policy in the 1990s*. Washington, D.C.: CQ Press, 257–278.

Vogel, David. 1986. *National Styles of Regulation*. Ithaca: Cornell.

Vogel, David. 1993. Representing Diffuse Interests in Environmental Policymaking. In R. Kent Weaver and Bert A. Rockman, eds., *Do Institutions Matter?* Washington, D.C.: The Brookings Institution, 237–271.

Vogel, David with Veronica Kun. 1987. The Comparative Study of Environmental Policy. In Dierkes, Weiler, and Antal, eds., *Comparative Policy Research*. New York: St. Martin's Press, 99–170.

Volgy, T. J., and J. E. Schwarz. 1996. In Search of Economic Well-Being. *American Journal of Political Science*, Vol. 40, No. 4: 1233–1252.

Walker, Jack L. 1969. The Diffusion of Innovation among the American States. *American Political Science Review*, Vol. 63, No. 3: 880–899.

Walker, Jack. 1983. The Origins and Maintenance of Interest Groups in America. *American Political Science Review*, Vol. 77, No. 2: 390–406.

Walker, William. 1992. Feds Falling Behind on National Parks Program. *Vancouver Sun*, 18 January: A13.

Walker, William. 1991. National Park Plan in Peril, Groups Say. *Toronto Star*, 9 October: A4.

Wallace, David R. 1992. *The Quetzal & The Macaw: The Story of Costa Rica's National Parks*. San Francisco: The Sierra Club.

Wanna, John. 1994. Public Sector Management. In A. Parkin, J. Summers, and D. Woodward, eds., *Government, Politics, Power and Policy in Australia*. 5th ed. Melbourne: Longman Cheshire, 61–79.

Warhurst, John. 1994. The Australian Conservation Foundation. *Environmental Politics*, Vol. 3, No. 1: 68–90.

Warwick, Donald P. 1975. *A Theory of Public Bureaucracy*. Cambridge: Harvard University Press.

Watts, Ronald L. 1991. Canadian Federalism in the 1990s—Once More in Question. *Publius*, Vol. 21, No. 3: 169–190.

Wearing, Stephen, and Michael Brock. 1991. Management of Parks for Tourism. *Australian Parks & Recreation*, Vol. 27, No. 1: 31–34.

Weaver, R. Kent. 1992. Political Institutions and Canada's Constitutional Crisis. In Weaver, ed., *The Collapse of Canada?* Washington, D.C.: The Brookings Institution, 7–75.

West, Patrick C., and Steven R. Brechin. 1993. *Resident Peoples and National Parks*. Tucson: University of Arizona Press.

Wet Tropics Management Authority. 1995. Backgrounder. Cairns: WTMA.

Wet Tropics Management Authority. 1992. *Wet Tropics Plan: Strategic Directions*. Cairns: WTMA.

Whitaker, Donald P. 1983. The Economy. In Harold D. Nelson, ed., *Costa Rica*. Washington, D.C.: American University, 131–181.

Whitaker, John C. 1976. *Striking a Balance*. Washington, D.C.: American Enterprise Institute.

Wilkinson, Todd. 1997. Yellowstone's Bison War. *National Parks*, Vol. 71, No. 11 (November): 30–33.

Wilson, Bruce M. 1997. The Political Consequences of Institutional Rules. Unpublished manuscript.

Wilson, Bruce M. 1994. When Social Democrats Choose Neoliberal Economic Policies. *Comparative Politics*, Vol. 26, No. 2: 149–168.

Wilson, Bruce M., and Fabrice E. Lehoucq. 1997. Politics and Government in Costa Rica. Unpublished manuscript.

Wilson, James Q. 1989. *Bureaucracy*. New York: Basic Books.

Winks, Robin W. 1995. Debating Significance. *National Parks*, Vol. 69, No. 3: 24–25.

Wirth, Conrad L. 1980. *Parks, Politics, and the People*. Norman, Okla.: University of Oklahoma Press.

Wise, Charles R., and Kirk Emerson. 1994. Regulatory Takings. *Administration & Society*, Vol. 26, No. 3: 305–336.

Wlezien, Christopher. 1995. The Public as Thermostat. *American Journal of Political Science*, 39 (November): 981–1000.

Wood, B. Dan, and Richard W. Waterman. 1991. The Dynamics of Political Control of the Bureaucracy. *American Political Science Review*, Vol. 85, No. 3: 801–828.

World Almanac. 1992. *World Almanac 1992*. New York: Scripps Howard.

World Resources Institute. 1993. *Environmental Almanac*. Boston: Houghton Mifflin.

World Resources Institute. 1992. *World Resources 1992–93*. Oxford: Oxford University Press.

World Wide Fund for Nature. 1995. The Application of the Interim Biogeographic Regionalisation for Australia. Unpublished paper.

World Wildlife Fund. 1995. *Endangered Spaces Progress Report*. Toronto: WWF Canada.

Wright, George M., Joseph Dixon, and Ben Thompson. 1933. *Fauna of the National Parks of the United States*. Washington, D.C.: GPO.

Wright, Judith. 1977. *The Coral Battleground*. Melbourne: Thomas Nelson Limited.

Wright, R. G., and D. J. Mattson. 1996. The Origin and Purpose of National Parks and Protected Areas. In R. G. Wright, ed., *National Parks and Protected Areas*. Cambridge, Mass.: Blackwell, 3–14.

Wright, R. G., and J. M. Scott. 1996. Evaluating the Ecological Suitability of Lands. In R. G. Wright, ed., *National Parks and Protected Areas*. Cambridge, Mass.: Blackwell, 121–132.

Zaller, John, and Stanley Feldman. 1992. A Simple Theory of the Survey Response. *American Journal of Political Science*, 36 (August): 579–616.

Zarafonitis, Bess. 1991. The War to End All Wars. *National Parks*, Vol. 65, No. 11: 37–39.

Zielenziger, Michael. 1988. Nation's Parks Stagnate Under Reagan. *San Jose Mercury-News*, 19 September: 1A.

Zifcak, Spencer. 1994. *New Managerialism*. Buckingham: Open University Press.

Index

Aborigines and Australian lands, 119, 129, 131–135, 143

Advocacy Coalition Framework (ACF), 28–31, 42

Agriculture, 31, 42, 103–104, 121, 139, 190, 198

Air pollution, 78–80, 92

Alaska lands issue, 64, 67–68

Alberta provincial government, 149, 171–174, 179, 182–183, 185–186

Albinski, Henry, 115

Albright, Horace, 46, 49, 57, 58, 83

Allin, Craig, 15

Alternative use coalition, 31, 37–43

American Indians, 70

Ameringer, Charles, 197

Andrew, George, 174

Anthropological studies of inter-generational processes, 11

Antietam Battlefield, 81

Antiquities Act of 1906, 57

Arctic National Wildlife Refuge (U.S.), 68

Arias, Costa Rican President Oscar, 193, 201, 207

Arnberger, Rob, 90, 93

Atwood, Margaret, 168

Australian Academy of Science, 114, 122

Australian Association for the Advancement of Science, 121, 143

Australian Conservation Foundation, 103–106, 114

Australian Heritage Commission (AHC), 113, 124

Australian High Court, 110, 112, 116, 119, 129, 132–133, 136–137, 140

Australian National Parks and Wildlife Service (ANPWS), 113, 124, 133

Australian Nature Conservation Agency (ANCA), 113, 126, 130, 221

Australian Parliament
background, 112
relations with agencies, 118–119, 124, 137

Australian preservation efforts
compared to other nations, 17–18
in enhancement of individual units, 133–146
summarized, 219–220
in system expansion, 120–132

Austria, 32

Availability of land for preservation
defined, 33–34
impact on variation in preservation, 37–43

Babbitt, Bruce, 74
Balanced budgets, 2, 4, 215, 225–226
Banff Centre for Management, 222
Banff National Park (Canada)
  background, 148, 149, 169–176
  Banff-Bow Valley Study, 179,
    181–187
  established, 22, 158–159
  incorporation of town, 179–181
  planning, 1, 172–179, 214, 220,
    221
Beaman, Jay, 163
Biodiversity, 14, 189
Bjelke-Petersen, Queensland Premier
  Joh, 139, 144–145
Blais-Grenier, Suzanne, 165–166, 223
Blue Ridge Parkway (U.S.), 55
Bob Marshall Ecosystem (U.S.), 81
Boza, Mario, 190, 191, 194, 196, 197,
  199–200, 201, 202, 205, 212, 222
Braulio Carillo National Park
  (Costa Rica), 199, 201–202, 210
British Columbia provincial
  government, 167–168, 185, 187,
  229
Brundtland, Norwegian Prime
  Minister Gro Harlem, 24–25
Bryce, Lord James, 22, 95, 97
Buchanan, James, 4
Bureaucracy
  as advocate for intergenerational
    goods, 10–11, 32
  as affected by politics, 12–13
  impact on variation in
    preservation, 37–43
  measurement, 32–33
  See also civil servants; political
    control of the bureaucracy

Burnett, John, 213
Burton, Representative Phil, 65, 72
Bush, President George, 54, 70
Byrd, Senator Robert, 55, 71

Cabo Blanco Biological Reserve
  (Costa Rica), 190, 200
Canadian Conferences on National
  Parks, 150, 161
Canadian Environmental Advisory
  Council, 166
Canadian Pacific Railroad, 170–171
Canadian Parks and Wilderness
  Society (CPWS), 150, 180, 182
Canadian Parks Service, 22, 33, 153,
  165, 221, *See also* Parks Canada
Canadian Parliament
  background, 149, 161
  relations with agencies, 154, 156,
    174, 186, 223
Canadian preservation efforts
  compared to other nations, 17–18
  in enhancement of individual
    units, 169–187
  summarized, 220
  in system expansion, 158–169
Canadian Wildlife Federation, 149
Canadian World Wildlife Fund, 158,
  165
Canyonlands National Park (U.S.),
  60
Cape Cod National Seashore, 60
Cape Tribulation, 1, 101, 139, 214,
  220
Cape York (Australia) 1, 129, 141,
  214, 220
Capture theory, 230–231

Carlos, Juan, 192, 209, 211
Carlton, Joseph, 81
Carruthers, John, 164
Carson, Rachel, 23
Carter, President Jimmy, 67–68, 229
Case selection, 16–18
Charest, Jean, 167
Chretien, Prime Minister Jean, 151, 152, 164
Church, Ian, 174, 180
Churchill (Canada), 169
Civil rights, 23
Civil servants
  as compared to elected officials, 10, 32
  motivation of, 10–11, 17
  See also bureaucracy
Civil War, U.S., 58, 70, *See also* specific battlefields like Antietam
Clapper, Charlie, 65, 78
Clinton, President Bill, 54, 70, 87, 202, 226
Cochran, Senator Thad, 55
Cohen, Barry, 132
Colorado River, 44, 90–94, *See also* Grand Canyon
Colorado State University, 45, 48
Committee of Inquiry into the National Estate, 101, 102, 114
Common-pool resources, 5–6, 9–11, 215, 227–228
Comparative public policy literature, 8–10, 14–15
Conservation Foundation, 66, 78–80
Convention on International Trade in Endangered Species, 226–227
Coopers & Lybrand consulting firm, 179

Corcovado National Park (Costa Rica), 202
Costa Rican Department of National Parks, 193–194
Costa Rican Legislative Assembly
  background, 192
  policies, 193, 195
  relations with agencies, 197–199
Costa Rican Ministry of Natural Resources, Energy, and Mines, 192, 194, 209, 211
Costa Rican National Parks Service, 194, 200–201
Costa Rican preservation efforts
  compared to other nations, 17–18, 31–32, 33
  in enhancement of individual units, 204–213
  established, 41
  summarized, 220, 222–224
  in system expansion, 199–204
Council on Environmental Quality, 23
Crespi, Carlos, 213

Daly, Herman, 34
Davidson, A.T., 166
Day, Dave, 180, 182
Demographics of populations, 9
Denali National Park (U.S.), 68
Dinosaur National Monument (U.S.), 47
Domestic environmental coalition
  defined, 30–31
  impact on variation in preservation, 37–43
Douglas, Senator Paul, 54

Dunphy, Myles, 121
Dupuy, Michel, 181, 183

Ecological Sustainable Development
    Working Groups, 108
Economic analyses
    of intergenerational processes,
    12–13
Eco-tourism, 32, 108, 192, 196, 209,
    224
Ehrlich, Paul, 23
Eidsvik, Harold, 21
Ekey, Bob, 82
Elected officials and theoretical
    relation with intergenerational
    goods, 8, 219, 228
Ellsmere Island (Canada), 168
Endangered species, 91, 102, 163,
    188, 203, 226–227
Environmental Assessment and
    Review Process in Canada
    (EARP), 154, 176
Environmental Impact Statement of
    Australia, 116–117
Esau, Nicky, 120
Evans, Gareth, 132
Everglades National Park (U.S.), 57,
    80
Everhart, Ron, 67
Executive federalism in Canada,
    156–157

Faulkner, Hugh, 158
Federalism
    in Australia, 114–117, 120,
    126–147, 222
    in Canada, 156–158, 164–169

in Costa Rica, 195–197, 207,
    209–213
    summarized, 217–218, 228–229
    as theoretically important, 12, 16
    in United States, 52–53, 93
Figueres, Costa Rican President Jose,
    191, 193, 194, 202, 219
Finley, Mike, 82, 87, 89–90
Fire policy in Yellowstone, 84
Fishing Bridge issue in Yellowstone,
    83, 88
Fishing interests, 135–136, 145, 160,
    228
Foresta, Ron, 63, 71
Fortin, Gaby, 172, 178–179
Fossey, Dian, 227
Francis, Jeff, 112, 119, 126, 127, 128
Franke, Joseph, 213
Franklin Dam controversy, 106,
    109–110
Fraser Island
    background, 141–144
    Defense Organisation (FIDO),
    103, 144
    planning, 144–145
    restoration efforts, 144–145
Fraser, Prime Minister Malcolm, 112,
    116, 131
Freedom House categories, 31, 38–39
Freemuth, John, 60

Galligan, Brian, 115, 117
Galvin, Denis, 44, 56, 70, 72, 75, 77,
    82
Gap Analysis Programs, 14, 25
Garcia, Randall, 211
Garvin, Ian, 140–141

Gates of the Arctic National Park (U.S.), 68

Gateway National Recreation Area (U.S.), 66, 69

General Accounting Office, U.S., 78, 82

General Agreement on Tariffs and Trade (GATT), 31

Geographic Information Systems, 14, 179, 221

Germany, 32

Gettysburg Battlefield (U.S.), 81

Glen Canyon National Recreation Area (U.S.), 60

Global warming, 30

Golden Gate National Recreation Area (U.S.), 66, 72

Goldwater, Senator Barry, 80

Gore, Vice President Al, 71

Goss, Queensland Premier Wayne, 129, 136, 141

Gough, Mark, 128–129, 141, 144–145

Gowans, Rod, 117, 129–130

Grand Canyon National Park (U.S.)
background, 44, 47, 80, 191, 231
flooding of, 93–94
planning, 1, 90–94, 214, 219, 221
restoration efforts, 90–94

Grand Teton National Park (U.S.), 57, 80–81, 84

Grasslands National Park (Canada), 1, 148–149, 167, 214, 220

Gravel, Senator Mike, 68

Gray, Robin, 109

Grazing interests, 49, 70, 125, 126, 129, 171

Great Barrier Reef Marine Park (Australia)
background, 110, 135–136

operating funds, 137
planning, 135–138, 220
restoration efforts, 135–138

Great Basin National Park (U.S.), 69

Great Smoky Mountains National Park (U.S.), 57, 191

Greece, 5, 21

Green bans, 103–104

Greenpeace, 106, 150

Green Plan of Canada, 152, 163

Greens political party, 103, 106, 109

Grizzly bears, 83, 85

Gross Domestic Product (GDP)
in Australia, 105
in Costa Rica, 195
defined, 31, 34
impact on variation in preservation, 37–43

Gross National Product (GNP), 34

Guadalupe Mountains National Park (U.S.), 64

Guanacaste Conservation Area (Costa Rica)
background, 192
planning, 1, 205–209, 214, 220
restoration efforts, 205–209

Haigh, David, 138

Hall, Colin, 102, 103–104, 122, 125, 126, 127, 147

Hammond, Governor Jay, 68

Hansen, Representative James, 74

Hartzog, George, 41, 48, 59, 60, 76

Hatch, Senator Orrin, 92

Hawke, Prime Minister Robert, 110, 111, 112, 116, 117, 139

Hefley, Representative Joel, 74

Heston and Summers' Penn World
    Tables, 34
Hildebrandt, Walter, 174, 187
Hinchinbrook Channel, 137–138
Historic Sites Act, 58
Hodel, Donald, 92
Holdridge, L.R., 200, 201
Honchin, Darin, 111, 136, 138
Hopkins, Jack, 198
Howard, Prime Minister John, 112,
    129

Impure public goods, 2–4, 6
Indiana Dunes National Lakeshore
    (U.S.), 54
Interest groups in general
    in Australia, 104, 105, 109
    in Canada, 150, 154, 155
    in Costa Rica, 198
    as related to advocacy coalitions,
        29
    and their theoretical impact on
        intergenerational goods, 7–8
    in United States, 47, 52, 54, 74
    See also specific groups like the
        Sierra Club
Intergenerational goods
    defined, 3–5, 215
    difficulty of provision, 4–13, 216,
        224, 230–231
    examples of, 2, 215
    measurement of, 26
Intergovernmental relations
    impact on intergenerational
        goods, 12
    See also federalism

Interim Biogeographic
    Regionalisation for Australia
    (IBRA), 126, 130, 222
International Biosphere Reserves, 24
International demands in general
    as an advocacy coalition, 30–31
    impact on variation in
        preservation, 37–43
    on intergenerational goods, 8
International Union for the
    Conservation of Nature (IUCN)
    Commission on National Parks,
        21, 22
    established, 22
    official mandates, 5, 25, 31, 125
    statistics, 15, 19, 26–27, 42
Irazu Volcano (Costa Rica), 193, 210
Ireland, 32

Jackson, Senator Henry, 59
Jacobson, Perry, 174, 180
Janzen, Dan, 188, 190, 192, 196, 197,
    204–213, 222
Jasper National Park (Canada), 170,
    171, 172, 174–175, 176, 178
Jazz Historical Park (U.S.), 72
Jenkins, Chip, 96
John Day Fossil Beds National
    Monument (U.S.), 64
Johnson, President Lyndon B., 50, 54
Johnston, Senator J. Bennett, 72

Kaeding, Beth, 89
Kakadu National Park (Australia)
    background, 108, 131–132, 135

Kakadu National Park, *continued*
  planning, 132–135
  restoration efforts, 132–135
Keating, Prime Minister Paul, 112, 116, 136
Kennedy, President John F., 50
Keynes, John Maynard, 4
Kootenay National Park (Canada), 170, 171, 172, 176
Kopps, Sheila, 183, 186

Lake Louise (Canada), 169, 170
Lake Pedder (Australia), 102, 103, 105, 106, 113, 116
Land and Water Conservation Fund (LWCF), 50–51, 54, 65, 69, 73, 74
Land Conservation Council (LCC) of Victoria, 129–130
Las Baulas Marine National Park (Costa Rica), 196, 212
Laxalt, Senator Paul, 70
Leopold Report on National Parks, 46, 83
Lincoln Institute for Land Policy, 216, 218, 222
Locke, Harvey, 180, 182
Lott, Senator Trent, 55
Lowry, William R., 15
Lucas, P.H.C., 1
Lunney, Daniel, 125–126

Mabo, Eddie, 119
Machlis, Gary, 15
Madison, James, 217
Mammoth Cave National Park, 58

Man and the Biosphere Program, 24, 35, 109
Manassas Battlefield (U.S.), 81
Manuel Antonio National Park (Costa Rica), 202–203
Manzanar, 70
Markets
  as sources of intergenerational goods, 2, 4, 215
  as sources of private goods, 3
Marshall, Graeme, 108, 118, 130
Mather, Stephen, 57
McComb, Murray, 148, 158
McDade, Representative Joe, 71
McGovern, Senator George, 66
McMillan, Tom, 166, 173–174
Meech Lake Accord, 157
Mendez, Luis, 194
Mining
  background, 31, 68
  in Australia, 103–105, 121, 125, 126, 127, 131–135, 135–136, 139, 143–145
  in Canada, 150, 160, 171
  in Costa Rica, 202
  in United States, 66–67, 85–87
Mintzmayer, Lorraine, 85
Mission 66, 47–48, 50
Misty Fjords National Monument (U.S.), 68
Mitchell, Jerry, 95, 99
Montreal Protocol, 30
Moresby Island (Canada), 167–168
Morrow, Duncan, 44
Mosley, J.G., 117, 125, 126
Moss, Senator Frank, 60
Mountain Parks Planning Program, 173

Muir, John, 22
Mulroney, Prime Minister Brian,
    151, 157, 165
Murtha, Representative John, 71

Natchez Trace Parkway (U.S.), 55
National Academy of Sciences, 46
National and Provincial Parks Asso-
    ciation, 173
National Biodiversity Institute, 201
National Biological Service, 74–75
National Business Plan of Canada,
    153, 155–156
National Historic Landmarks, 58
National parks in general
    criteria for, 22–23
    first established, 22
National Parks and Conservation
    Association (NPCA), 57, 70,
    78–80
National Parks and Recreation Act
    of 1978, 65
National Parks Association, 57
National Parks Foundation, 201, 212
National Park System Plan (U.S.),
    56, 61–64, 75–76
National Park Trust, 73
National System of Conservation
    Areas (SINAC) in Costa Rica,
    206–207, 210, 211, 213
National Trails System, 60
National Wilderness Inventory of
    Australia, 126
Nature Conservancy, 8, 196
Neotropical Foundation, 201
New Area Studies Office, 64, 69
New Deal in United States, 52, 58
New Resource Economics, 215

New River Gorge National River
    (U.S.), 55
New South Wales state government
    National Parks and Wildlife
        Service, 122, 127
    system expansion, 123, 127, 128
New Zealand, 147, 221
Nicaragua, 206
Nicholson, E.M., 23
Nicol, John, 152
Nixon, President Richard M., 26, 53,
    54, 66
Nongovernmental organizations
    (NGOs), 30, 201, 212
Noranda mining, 85–87
Nuclear weapons, 24

Oduber, Costa Rican President
    Daniel, 193, 202
Official commitments to
    preservation
    in Australia, 113–114
    in Canada, 152–153
    in Costa Rica, 193–194
    summarized, 217, 225–228
    as theoretically important, 10–11,
        30–31, 230–231
    in United States, 49–51
Oliphant, Sir Mark, 114
Olson, Mancur, 4
Olympic National Park (U.S.), 59
Ordinary Least Squares (OLS), 36
Organization for Tropical Studies,
    189–190
Osa Peninsula (Costa Rica), 1, 211,
    212
Otton, Judy, 155, 176–179, 180–185

Ovington, J.D., 114
Ozark National Scenic Riverways, 60

Page, Robert, 182, 186
Panama, 33
Park Barrel legislation, 65
Park closure legislation, 74
Parks Canada
    background, 22, 33, 152–153, 155
    policy, 153, 160, 163–181
Pearson, Prime Minister Lester, 156
Pelosi, Representative Nancy, 72
Phantom Ranch, 44
Phillips, David, 118, 125
Pictured Rocks National Lakeshore,
    60
Pigou, Arthur, 215
Plato, 21
Poas Volcano (Costa Rica), 193, 198,
    200, 210
Point Reyes National Seashore, 81
Political control of the bureaucracy
    in Australia, 117–120
    in Canada, 153–156, 223
    in Costa Rica, 197–199, 223
    summarized, 218–219, 229–230
    as theoretically important, 12–13,
        16, 230–231
    in United States, 53–100, 222
Political parties in general
    as an ineffective source of long-
        term demands, 7
    in Australia, 106, 115–116
    in Canada, 151–152, 154
    in Costa Rica, 192–193, 198
    in the United States, 49, 51, 52
    See also specific parties like the
        Greens

Political stability
    in Australia, 112–113
    in Canada, 151–152
    in Costa Rica, 192–193
    summarized, 217, 227–228
    as theoretically important, 9–10,
        30–31
    in United States, 48–49
Preservation
    defined, 5
    See also systematic preservation
Presidio (U.S.), 66, 72
Prince Albert National Park
    (Canada), 186
Princen, Thomas, 226
Pristine areas
    defined, 28
    as a variable, 37–43
    in world, 35, 41
Privatization, 74, 223–224
Property rights, 14, 53, 82, 215, 218
Protected areas
    defined, 27–28
    as a variable, 37–43
    in world, 35–36, 41
Provincial parks in Canada, 150,
    160–161
Public opinion
    on intergenerational goods, 7, 9,
        30, 226
    regarding Australian parks,
        106–108, 109–110, 112
    regarding Canadian parks, 113,
        149–151, 163, 181
    regarding Costa Rican parks,
        191–192
    regarding U.S. parks, 45, 48, 54
Public support for preservation
    in Australia, 102–112

Public support, *continued*
  in Canada, 149–151
  in Costa Rica, 189–192
  summarized, 217, 225–228
  as theoretically important, 9–11,
    30–31, 230
  in United States, 45–48
Pure private goods, 3–4, 6
Pure public goods, 3–4, 6

Quebec, 157, 166, 168, 223
Queensland state government
  reaction to World Heritage, 128
  system expansion, 121, 123, 125,
    128–129

Reagan, President Ronald, 50, 52, 54,
  69–70, 226, 229–230
Redwoods National Park (U.S.), 57,
  59–60, 67
Regional Conservation Units (URCs)
  in Costa Rica, 207–213
Renewable energy sources, 228, 229,
  230
Representation of diverse ecosystems
  in Australia, 120–130
  in Canada, 158–169
  in Costa Rica, 199–204
  as a goal, 13–14, 23–26, 216–217
  in United States, 56–77
Restoration of ecosystems
  in Australia, 130–146
  in Canada, 169–187
  in Costa Rica, 204–213
  as a goal, 13–14, 23–26, 216–217
  in United States, 77–99

Rettie, Dwight, 76–77
Ridenour, James, 69, 76, 96
Rockefeller, John Jr., 57
Rodriguez, Carlos Manuel, 194
Roosevelt, President Franklin D., 58
Roosevelt, President Theodore, 7, 90,
  231
Royal National Park (Australia), 22,
  121
Rwanda, 227

Santa Rosa National Park (Costa
  Rica), 188, 193, 200, 206
Saratoga National Monument (U.S.),
  55
Saxon, Earl, 111, 119, 140–141
Shenandoah National Park (U.S.),
  57, 81
Shepherd, Alison, 117, 125
Sierra Club, 47, 59, 182
Sinclair, John, 144
Skinner, Milton, 83
Smith, Adam, 4, 5, 215
Smith, Mallory, 91, 94
Snyder, Hank, 96
Solomon, Representative Gerald, 55
Solow, Robert, 4, 214
South Africa, 33
State park systems (U.S.), 53, 57, 59,
  64, 93
Steamtown National Historic Site
  (U.S.), 56, 71
Stevens, Senator Ted, 68
Strategic Defense Initiative, 226
Summers, John, 117
Sustainability (sust. development),
  6, 9, 10, 25, 108, 180, 181, 194,
  205, 211, 214, 227–228

Sweden, 207

Switzerland, 33

Symington, Governor Fife, 93

Systematic preservation
  defined, 13–14, 23–26, 216–217
  stability as a goal, 224–225
  variance determined by factors,
    17–18, 26–43, 216–217

Tallgrass Prairie National Preserve
  (U.S.), 56, 72–73, 81

Taylor, Representative Charles, 55

Theberge, John, 164

Thoreau, David, 7

Tichnell, David, 15

Timber (or logging) interests
  in Australia, 121, 125, 127, 139,
    141, 143–144
  in Canada, 150, 160, 167, 187, 229
  in Costa Rica, 190, 199, 201–202
  in United States, 47, 59, 60, 67,
    68, 80, 85, 225

Toll goods, 6

Tourism
  in Australia, 108, 126, 135–136,
    139, 145
  in Canada, 159, 171–172, 173–175,
    180, 181
  in Costa Rica, 196, 210
  defined, 31–32
  impact on variation in
    preservation, 37–43
  in United States, 45–46, 59, 75
  See also eco-tourism

Toyne, Philip, 127, 132

Trudeau, Prime Minister Pierre, 151,
  152, 157

Udall, Representative Morris, 67

Udall, Secretary of Interior Stuart, 59

Ugalde, Alvaro, 190, 191, 194, 197,
  200, 201, 202, 205

Uluru (Australia), 147

Umana, Alvaro, 194, 212

United Nations, 23, 24, 35

United States Army Corps of
  Engineers, 54

United States Bureau of Land
  Management, 33, 84

United States Bureau of
  Reclamation, 47

United States Congress
  background, 49, 53, 222
  and establishment of
    Yellowstone, 21
  impact on ecosystem restoration,
    77–100
  impact on park system
    expansion, 56–77
  and short-term incentives, 8, 54
  theoretical impact on
    preservation, 45, 53–55

United States Department of
  Interior, 44–45, 49, 64, 85

United States Forest Service, 49, 84,
  87, 93

United States Geological Survey, 225

United States National Park Service
  (NPS)
  appropriations to, 78–79
  established, 22, 33, 49–50
  role in systematic preservation,
    56–100, 219, 221, 222

United States National Public Radio,
  213

United States preservation efforts
  compared to other nations, 17, 22

U.S. preservation efforts, *continued*
in enhancement of individual
units, 77–99
summarized, 219
in system expansion, 56–77
Universidad de Costa Rica, 189, 200,
201
Urban parks in the United States,
65–67

Vail Symposium, 55, 76, 222–223
Vento, Representative Bruce, 54, 219
Vietnam War, 23–24
Vogel, David, 15
Voting on intergenerational goods,
7, 48, 87

Walker, William, 193, 206
Wallace, David, 200, 201, 212
Wallop, Senator Malcolm, 84
Wall Street Journal, 48
Wanna, John, 118
Warrumbungle National Park
(Australia), 108
Water scarcity, 227
Watt, James, 50, 69, 73, 223
Wayburn, Edgar, 67
Wessberg, Olof, 190, 202
Westminster system of government,
112, 151
Wet Tropics World Heritage Area
(Australia)
background, 138–140
Management Authority, 111,
140–141
planning, 140–141
restoration efforts, 140–141

Whitlam, Prime Minister Gough,
112, 116, 131
Wild and Scenic Rivers, 60
Wildavsky, Aaron, 218
Wilderness Act, 50, 54
Wilson, Mel, 185
Winks, Robin, 71
Winter Olympics of 1972, 149, 173
Wirth, Conrad, 50, 59
Wootton, Michael, 73
World Conferences on national
parks, 5, 22–23, 31, 35
World Heritage Convention
in general 19, 24, 26, 35
impact in Australia, 31, 108–112,
113, 128, 131–134, 138–139, 145
impact in Canada, 170
as a variable, 31
World Resources Institute, 26
World Wide Fund for Nature, 130
World Wildlife Fund, 106, 150, 207,
211
Worthless lands thesis, 15, 128–129
Wright, George, 1, 45–46, 77, 83

Yard, Sterling, 57
Yellowstone National Park (U.S.)
background, 82–84, 200
Centennial celebration, 23
established, 21, 49
planning, 82–90
reintroduction of wolves, 25,
89–90
restoration efforts, 82–90, 224
Yoho National Park (Canada), 169,
170, 171–172, 175, 176
Yosemite National Park (U.S.)
background, 48

Yosemite National Park, *continued*
   planning, 1, 94–99, 214, 219, 221
   restoration efforts, 94–99
   Valley Implementation Plan,
     97–99

Young, Senator Don, 68

Zaire, 227
Zurhellen, Barbara, 73